in Its Social and Organizational Context

Anthony Hopwood Selected Papers

置于社会与组织环境中的会计研究

安东尼·霍普伍德论文精选

汤谷良 〔日〕冈野浩 李苹莉 主编

北京大学出版社
PEKING UNIVERSITY PRESS

图书在版编目(CIP)数据

置于社会与组织环境中的会计研究:安东尼·霍普伍德论文精选:英汉对照/汤谷良等主编. —北京:北京大学出版社,2013.6
ISBN 978-7-301-22558-5

Ⅰ.①置… Ⅱ.①汤… Ⅲ.①会计-文集-英、汉 Ⅳ.①F23-53

中国版本图书馆 CIP 数据核字(2013)第 109687 号

书　　　名：置于社会与组织环境中的会计研究——安东尼·霍普伍德论文精选
著作责任者：汤谷良　〔日〕冈野浩　李苹莉　主编
责 任 编 辑：李　娟
标 准 书 号：ISBN 978-7-301-22558-5/F·3625
出 版 发 行：北京大学出版社
地　　　址：北京市海淀区成府路 205 号　100871
网　　　址：http://www.pup.cn
电 子 信 箱：em@pup.cn　　　QQ:552063295
新 浪 微 博：@北京大学出版社经管图书
电　　　话：邮购部 62752015　发行部 62750672　编辑部 62752926
　　　　　　出版部 62754962
印 刷 者：北京大学印刷厂
经 销 者：新华书店
　　　　　　730 毫米×1020 毫米　16 开本　20.25 印张　268 千字
　　　　　　2013 年 6 月第 1 版　2013 年 6 月第 1 次印刷
定　　　价：49.00 元

未经许可,不得以任何方式复制或抄袭本书之部分或全部内容。
版权所有,侵权必究
举报电话：010-62752024　电子信箱：fd@pup.pku.edu.cn

论会计研究(代序)

安东尼·霍普伍德的研究使会计的学术基础得以拓宽和加强。他所具有的对会计的综合属性以及会计研究的多重途径的卓越预知和洞察力,在他的早期学术生涯中就已经开始显露。他对会计研究的无穷尽的兴趣和探索以及其清晰而严谨的思维能力,确立了他在这一领域的永久地位。他的研究对牢固确立会计所具有的远超出简单技术性实务的地位做出了贡献。这本精湛的翻译为中文的论文集除了其所收集的论文本身的重要性外,更重要的是,它给对会计的社会和组织属性感兴趣的读者提供了一个跳板,使我们能通过这些论文涉足由此延伸的大量作品。

在开始阅读这本论文集前有一个必须讨论的特定议题,那就是要对会计学术研究形式的多样性抱有愿意了解的心态。我们固然可以从"科学"领域的研究方法的选择和应用中学到很多,但必须记住会计不是和万有引力一样的自然现象。会计模式既不是自然的,也不是必然的,而是在特定的环境中及其环境变化之间持续地选择和抉择的结果。对会计稳定的内在规律的探索需要对这些规律的支持框架所具有的潜在流动性有高度的敏感;同样,对会计特定时期特性的研究也常常得益于临时性的安排和协议具有的异乎寻常的耐久力和影响。对这一事实的重要性在 Young, J. J. (2006)的论文中得到了特别的强调。这篇论文发表在由霍普伍德教授创办的杂志《会计、组织和社会》2006 年的第 6 期,并获美国会计学会 2011 年度的会计研究突出贡献奖。

然而,这两大类方法是同等重要的。它们之间不是互相排斥,而是互相补充的。如果没有对另一种方法至少一定程度上的了解,这两种方法中的任何一种都会因此不完善。正因为如此,这本论文集对于发展迅速并日益自信(这是值得肯定的)的中国会计学术界具有重要意义。会计界团体和个人都已经在追求会计的"科学"研究、采用统计分析的方法和讲究研究的客观性等方面付出了努力,然而,将会计研究仅仅局限于此无疑是忽略了学术研究的一个重要而浓厚的传统,那就是努力深入地了解那些会计发展和实践的直接参与者的看法和观点。对于在这一方面付出努力的学者来说,这本书所收集的论文提供了一套生动且互相补充的文集,将有助于对会计所具有的潜力、影响和局限性的全方位的理解。

克里斯托夫·查普曼教授
英国帝国理工大学
《会计、组织和社会》主编
2013年5月
(李苹莉　译)

On Studying Accounting

The intellectual foundations of the discipline of accounting have been uniquely broadened and strengthened through the writings Anthony Hopwood. Since early on in his academic career he showed himself to be possessed of a remarkable vision and insight into the complex nature of accounting, and of the diversity of ways in which it might be studied. His insatiable curiosity, and capacity for clear and rigorous thinking, have permanently left their mark on the discipline. His work has helped to firmly establish that accounting is so much more than a simple technical practice. This collection of his writings, that has been so ably translated by the editors of this volume, remain vital and interesting in their own right. More than that, however, they offer the reader interested in the social and organisational aspects of accounting a springboard into the substantial body of work that has grown up from the intellectual seeds contained in this collection of writings.

A particular issue that must be taken on board before embarking on the journey of reading this collection is to remain ready to appreciate the diversity of forms that accounting scholarship may take. Whilst much may be learned from the adoption and tailoring of methods of research undertaken in the "scientific" world, it is important to remember that accounting is not a natural phenomenon akin to gravity. The form that accounting takes is neither natural nor inevitable, rather it is the result of ongoing choices and decisions made within and between shifting sets of actors. The search for stable causal "laws" of accounting is better undertaken with a keen sensitivity to the potentially fluid nature of the supporting structures of such laws. Equally, the power of studies of the ephemeral nature of accounting often draw strength from the remarkable durability and force that temporary arrangements and agreements may take on. A particularly salient reminder of the importance of this fact comes in the awarding in 2011 of the American Accounting Association award for Noteable Contribution to the Accounting Literature to an article appearing in the journal that founded by Anthony Hopwood:

Young, J. J. (2006). Making up users. *Accounting, Organizations and Society*, 31(6), pp. 579—600.

These two broad approaches to research are two sides of the same coin, however. The one does not preclude the other, rather they should enrich each other. Each becomes the poorer absent at least some appreciation of the other. In the context of a fast moving and increasingly (and rightly) self-assured community of Chinese Scholars of Accounting, this volume plays a vital role therefore. Much institutional and individual effort has been made in pursuing the "scientific" study of accounting, adopting statistical analysis and the precepts of arms length distance and objectivity. However to reduce our study of accounting to only that which falls within such confines is to ignore a vital and strong tradition of scholarly work that seeks to engage directly and deeply with the viewpoints, understandings of those participating in the development and practice of accounting in every day action. In relation to this latter scholarly effort, the works contained in this volume offer an engaging and complementary set of writings that begin to open out the possibilities for a rounded understanding of the potential, power, and limitations of accounting.

Christopher Chapman
Imperial College London
Accounting, *Organizations and Society*, Editor-in-Chief

编者的话

安东尼·霍普伍德（Anthony G. Hopwood）教授是会计界享有盛誉的杰出学者和领导者。他历任伦敦经济学院（London School of Economics，LSE）教授（1985—1995）、牛津大学赛德商学院（University of Oxford，Said Business School）院长（1999—2006）。他创立了国际顶级学术刊物——《会计、组织和社会》（*Accounting, Organizations and Society*，AOS），并担任第一任主编长达30多年（1976—2009）。他在1977年创立了欧洲会计学会，其后创办了该学会的机关杂志《欧洲会计评论》（*European Accounting Review*，EAR）。霍普伍德教授是行为会计研究的先驱。他的研究着眼于会计的组织和社会属性，将会计贯穿于社会与人文科学中，对牢固确立会计所具有的远超出简单技术性实务的地位做出了卓越的贡献。霍普伍德教授于1998年获得英国会计学会杰出学术奖（Distinguished Academic Award），并且于2008年入选于1950年在俄亥俄州立大学设立、旨在向为会计的发展做出重大贡献的学者表达敬意的《会计名人堂》（*Accounting Hall of Fame*）。

霍普伍德教授于2010年5月8日不幸病逝，但他的研究确立了他在会计研究领域的永久地位。编者们有幸得以在他生前和他讨论本书的编译工作，并在论文的选择和版权获取上得到他的认可及帮助。

本书的翻译出版历时数年，我们要特别感谢国内外同仁的支持和帮助。《会计、组织和社会》的现任主编、英国帝国理工大学的著名管理会计教授克里斯托夫·查普曼（Christopher Chapman）亲自为本书作序，与读者分享他对会计研究方法的思考。查普曼教授将亲临北京主持新书发布会，以表达他对霍普伍德教授的敬意和对本书出版的支持。

会计学界知名教授们亲自参与翻译工作，为论文翻译的精准提供了保障，这实在是编者和读者之幸！我们特别感谢以下译者的支持：卜志强（日本大阪市立大学（Osaka City University）副教授），赵晓东（清华大学博士），于增彪（清华大学教授),王斌(北京工商大学教授),李落落(日本大阪市立大学(Osaka City University)博士)。

  我们也对北京大学出版社的支持表示由衷的感谢,特别感谢责任编辑李娟女士在译文的校对和编辑过程中付出的时间和辛劳。

汤谷良 冈野浩 李苹莉

2013 年 5 月

编者导读

导言

本书是从安东尼·霍普伍德教授的论文集《从外部看会计》(Accounting from the Outside: The Collected Papers of Anthony G. Hopwood) (Garland, 1988) 中选译了部分文章汇集而成的。

进入21世纪,我们经历了安然公司的财务舞弊等事件,目前正面临着金融危机和由此引发的经济危机。整个社会正处于一种十分紧迫的状况之中,对于企业、政府和金融当局来说,需要解决的难题堆积如山。

在这种情况之下,会计就显得尤为重要,而霍普伍德教授的会计研究方法更具有重大的意义。原论文集中收录的33篇论文,可以说每篇都是佳作。尤其是本书中选译的6篇论文更是精品,可称之为国际会计界的共同财富。[①] 通过中文译本,为中国的会计学者(特别是年轻会计学者)提供接触和了解霍普伍德教授的会计理论的机会,是我们多年的愿望。

下面我们在解说上述6篇论文的同时,参照 Hopwood and Miller (1994)[②]以及 Chapman, Hopwood and Shields (2008)[③],简述这种会计理论的最新进展,以期为会计学者和实务工作者理解这一理论提供方便。

[①] 2005年春,在牛津大学赛德商学院的院长办公室里,霍普伍德教授当场同意我提出的关于出中文版的建议。

[②] Hopwood, A. G. and P. Miller, *Accounting as a Social & Institutional Practice* (Cambridge University Press, 1994).

[③] Chapman, C., A. Hopwood and M. Shields, *Handbook of Management Accounting Research* (Elsevier, 2008).

置于社会与组织环境中的会计研究

对收录论文的解说

1. 领略会计的灵性

本文是霍普伍德教授的《从外部看会计》论文集的第一篇。通过回顾其学术生涯,本文系统阐述了霍普伍德教授的学术思想。从伦敦政治经济学院的大学时代到留学美国在芝加哥大学攻读博士,从关注组织论、社会学及社会心理学到创立欧洲会计学会,从创办国际杂志《会计、组织和社会》(AOS)到创立欧洲高级管理学院以及对于社会问题的关注等,所有这些活动都展现了立志创建"作为社会科学的会计学"的霍普伍德教授的学术生涯。① 当时,芝加哥大学的组织论、社会学以及行为科学领域的教育水平在全美国居于领先地位,培养出众多的优秀学者。由此可以推测,对于原本就有英国社会科学理论素养的霍普伍德来说,在芝加哥大学所受到的教育具有非常重要的意义。

2. 会计与信息系统研究的组织视角

在这篇论文里,作者不但强调会计与信息系统在组织机能方面起着重要作用,而且强调研究会计、组织、社会之间的相互关系的重要性。这样的会计研究或许被理解为仅仅是在引用诸如人文学、社会学、组织论、历史学等相邻学科的方法,可是作者强调这种研究是从会计研究者的"内部"涌现出来的(Hopwood and Miller,1994)。在这里,我们可以看出霍普伍德和他的同事们试图通过与以往不同的方法对社会实践进行分析,以确立和发展作为社会科学的会计学的坚定信念,同时我们还可以窥视到霍普伍德教授所制定的宏大的"学术战略"。

3. 论在会计运作环境中研究会计

一般认为,会计是一种与作为其产生根源的社会利益冲突(或者斗争与革新)相分离的现象,而作者认为不能将社会因素与组织因素完全割裂开来。也就是说,一方面社会因素表现在组织之中,另一方面组织因素又是构成社会的重要部分。作者试图从组织中找出政治因素来,这里所谓的政治与通常意义上的政治有所不同。会计能够创造出"具有局部影响力的模式"并赋予其可视性。

---

① 霍普伍德教授将自己的学术研究分为以下七个方面:(1)关于会计的使用情况;(2)组织背景下的会计;(3)会计与公共部门的变迁;(4)合理性的多样化与会计变化的动态;(5)社会会计与会计的社会意义;(6)对学术历程的回顾;(7)AOS 杂志的编后记。

按照与通行会计不同的"替代会计"的思想,会计不仅可以通过"它不是什么"来评价,更进一步地,还可以作为"不断变化的现象"来理解。在这篇论文发表后的第二年,即1984年,作者在威斯康星大学举行的学会上阐述了上述思想。在1987年发表的论文(即本书第六篇文章)中作者扩展了这一思想,提出会计可以从"它不曾是什么"的角度来研究。

4. 会计在组织和社会中的作用

这篇论文明确地提出了会计、组织和社会的相互关系,被认为是阐明了《会计、组织和社会》(AOS)杂志宗旨的经典论文。①

"不能把会计看成是纯粹的组织现象",并且"促使会计出现的社会和组织方面的压力大量存在,而且其中有些压力是相反的"。以上述观点为前提,作者认为会计既适应组织与社会,又使组织与社会的形成成为可能。因此,必须考察社会因素和组织因素相互交织于会计之中的方式,而且由于会计的"社会与政治的性质"已经明显地显现出来,因此,必须考察会计在具有组织生活和社会生活特征的政治过程中所扮演的角色。

5. 社会环境中的会计学——价值增值会计在英国的历史

这篇论文在扩展组织会计研究范围的同时,聚焦于社会背景下的会计,以价值增值会计为案例探讨了社会会计的扩展。

在这里所使用的一个分析概念是"舞台"。作者在分析价值增值的社会意义时,首先将价值增值的应用领域分成"会计准则"、"宏观经济政策"和"劳资关系与信息公开"三个舞台,然后用"会计星座"这一概念来说明三个舞台之间的相互关系以及嵌入组织与社会之中的会计实践。作者认为迄今为止我们还没有发现有关会计变化的一般理论,现有的会计变化模型在许多方面仍然停留在权变模型的范围。因此,必须从批判的观点,阐明由会计的"环境适应能力"与"环境形成能力"所构成的"会计变化过程的二元特征"。作者还认为除了组织边界的确定、组织空间的内部划分之外,会计还与组织内部功能的可视化相关。

为了使会计研究和会计研究者从对现行制度的"服从"状态下"解放"出来,作者以"会计能与会计对抗"为口号,提出替代会计和替代会计制度的思想,并提出了对会计的替代形态与可能的会计进行研究的必要性。

---

① Mackintosh, N. B. and T. Hopper, *Accounting the Social & the Political*: *Classics, Contemporary & Beyond* (Elsevier, 2005)

6. 会计体系考古学

会计体系在不断地变化。在这篇论文中,作者首先指出我们对于影响会计变化过程及其组织结果的前提因素知道得不多,然后通过三个会计变化的事例,即 Wedgwood 陶瓷厂、M 企业及 Q 企业,从会计的"反映性"和"建构性"两个侧面,讨论影响会计变化的种种因素。

作者对 M. Foucault 的历史方法论进行了考察,试图用"考古学"和"系谱学"的方法,从社会与制度实践的角度把握会计。传统的研究往往从其产生的社会经济背景来解释会计体系。作者的上述研究方法则强调从我们生活的世界和社会现实中,找出可供企业和个人采纳的新选择方案与发现将多样的活动和过程重新组织、治理的方法的重要性。①

作为组织与社会实践的会计

按照霍普伍德的观点,会计的形态因企业所处环境的变化而变化。而随着会计形态的变化企业的活动也在变化。在记述这种会计与企业活动之间的"相互渗透"现象时,霍普伍德所采用的是历史方法。但是,我们应该注意这种历史方法并非罗列迄今为止的连续的历史事实,而是把焦点放在组织与社会的"变化"或非连续上。也就是说,为了理解特定的会计方法是怎样产生的,为什么具有重要意义,必须超越组织的界限,把会计作为社会、制度实践来探讨。因为新的会计模式产生于在现象发生之后才被称为"会计"的不同技术的组合。对于形成过程的这种分析叫做"计算系谱学"。可以说,之所以称之为"变化"而不是"历史",就是为了强调这一点。可以通过对于会计实践的产生、普及和发展的地区及其程度的调查,根据各个国家所处的状况以及时期的不同,弄清其社会关系的类型。②

为了明确上述会计与企业活动之间的"相互渗透"关系,我们不能仅仅把会计看成记录和报告经济活动事实的某种中立性装置,而应该将其理解为在我们生活的世界和社会现实中,找出可供企业和个人采纳的选择方案的方法,管理

---

① 冈野浩(1995,2002)『日本的管理会计的展开:「原価企画」への歴史的視座』(初版)(第 2 版)中央经济社。

② Scott 也就今后制度化方法的研究方向,提出了以下三点:(1) 从制度形成到消灭的整个过程(出现—持续—劣化);(2) 制度化过程与组织化过程之间的关系;(3) 各种不同类型的制度的比较研究。具体参见 Scott, W. R., *Institutions and Organizations* (Sage, 1995)。

与组织各种活动与过程的方法,以及对于治理他人和我们自身的方法产生影响的一系列"实践"。

为了叙述"实践的历史",必须采纳社会史及文化史的多种多样的方法。尤其文化乃是由个人或者集团所创造并享受的东西,从创造者、文化财富以及享受文化财富者三者之间的关系,可以跟踪文化的发展。然而,如果将文化与其产生的社会状态割裂开来,文化就无从谈起。在这里,"创造"主体与"享受"主体之间的交流是至关重要的。

霍普伍德教授尤其重视的是 Chris Argyris 基于行为科学理论的预算管理研究。这一点也可以在他为 Hopwood and Miller(1994)的日译本所写的序言中得到印证。

> 当初,人们主要关注的是"会计的行为方面"。Chris Argyris 的开创性研究《预算对人的影响》或许是早期研究中最有影响的。它既为当时的人际关系理论提出了全新的课题,又显示了现场研究的巨大潜力。他采用的是跨学科的研究方法,其著作反映了跨学科研究首先在美国继而在欧洲商学院中兴起的状况。

与工程师、法律专家、经济学家、管理者等专家集团所属的领域相同,会计被视为一个独立的专业领域(Hopwood and Miller,1994)。会计用多种多样的计算技术得出一个最终数字,即利润。而且,会计以利润为依据而引发行动。在这唯一的数字中,包含着会计应有的中立性和客观性。通过这个装置,会计与政治以及策略领域相分离,试图在竞争中获得基于某个要求的"正统性"。是把会计视为集中埋置在会计功能之中,还是将其视为分散埋置在多个相关组织之中,将会产生决定性的差异。因此,必须突破仅仅从会计与技术两个方面认识理解问题的现有思维模式,从文化的差异和多样性的角度探究这些问题。

结束语

以上,我们考察了霍普伍德教授从"外面"观察到的、在现实世界里正在实行的会计实践理论。在这里,让我们再次引用霍普伍德教授为 Hopwood and Miller(1994)的日译本所写序言的片段。

> 在安然事件发生之后的今天,会计开始具有比以往更大的意义。这是因为有关组织与社会的会计研究给解决类似的问题带来了一线曙光。会计研究不应是研究者们为自己建造起来的象牙塔,而应该具有使会计实践的状态曝光的能力。对会计的这样一种期待,在更为广泛的社会中日益高

置于社会与组织环境中的会计研究

涨。因此,毫不奇怪,人们比以往更加关注会计学中基于组织、制度以及社会研究传统方法所取得的研究成果。虽然这样的研究还有很长的路要走,但是我们可以说,对于认识并解决现在发生的问题,会计研究从组织与制度的角度提供了某种可能性,而且这种潜在可能性将越来越为人们所认识。

霍普伍德教授进一步论述道,"对于面临着许多共同难题的会计研究者来说,全球性对话的必要性及其潜在能力从来没有像今天这样大"。这一论述非常重要,因为迄今为止对于不同国民文化与传统的国际比较会计研究一直被忽视。我们衷心希望本书的出版能够有助于进一步促进社会、组织因素与管理会计的相互渗透,推动对各国管理会计变化等方面的研究。

冈野浩
2013 年 5 月
(卜志强　译)

目 录

论会计研究（代序）	I
On Studying Accounting	III
编者的话	V
编者导读	VII
领略会计的灵性	1
会计与信息系统研究的组织视角	12
论在会计运作环境中研究会计	22
会计在组织和社会中的作用	39
社会环境中的会计学 ——价值增值会计在英国的历史	64
会计体系考古学	90
Observing the Accounting Craft	119
Towards an Organizational Perspective for the Study of Accounting and Information Systems	136
On Trying to Study Accounting in the Contexts in Which It Operates	153
The Roles of Accounting in Organizations and Society	181
Accounting in Its Social Context: Towards a History of Value Added in the United Kingdom	218
The Archaeology of Accounting Systems	268

领略会计的灵性

序言

我一直为会计而着魔！少年时代，我曾有机会接触会计实务，有两次差点儿因此而辍学。还好，我没辍学，而是到伦敦政治经济学院学习会计。当时，作为少数没有参加职业培训的毕业生之一，我拒绝有可能从事产业经济学或金融学研究的诱惑，决定到芝加哥大学继续深造会计。从此会计成为一种不懈地观察、好奇和探索的神奇现象。

为何会计令我着魔？其原因很难解释，且是多方面的，而且这些原因可将我遥远的过去和眼下的状况之间用一条主线紧密地连接起来。我对会计的兴趣产生于英国会计飞速发展的时期。当时，会计在工业和金融重建中的广泛应用使会计成为媒体讨论的焦点，并吸引着广大公众的目光，也开始了我的会计启蒙。特别是，那些颇具现代和理性形式的知识与技能很容易影响年轻的学生，而因为有家庭成员从事会计工作，这种影响就更大。我记得当时的讨论相当生动，题目包括：新式美国方法的传闻、会计对公司重组的参与、英国财务总监初期发展以及英格兰北部相对落后地区的生产和工作中应用会计的意义。

正是这种模模糊糊的认识把我引导到会计领域。早期加入会计实务界的企图使我更加着魔般地领悟到那些由精英猎头公司所使用的社会招聘标准。因为家庭成员的参与，我有机会目睹会计师及其他相关管理团队为实现经济上的合理化而引发的个人和组织性的紧张、焦虑及矛盾。不仅地方经济中的某些部分被看成更加宽泛的经济驱动因素，而且在更加宽泛的组织情境中，与会计相关的管理实务也为人们提供了洞察这些实务如何改变影响力和判断力的模式。当时，人们已经开始将会计当作一种具有多面性的现象，也就是说，会计不可能游离于人类行为和社会生活之外——尽管就程序而言，会计是技术性的。我记得当时我已经意识到会计工作具有相互矛盾的特征。尽管职业中立性的原则和服务公众的理念作为会计师的操守而被广泛倡导，但会计师还是被广泛地视为只求遵守法律的字面意义而非精神的那些人的应声虫，尤其是税务领域。只要最终结果具有选择性的特征，那些与会计实务沾边的东西就会使人们对会计师的技能具有模棱两可的印象。与纯粹算账相比，会计学显然包含更多内容。

我在伦敦政治经济学院上大学期间更是加深了这种印象。在 Will Baxter、Harold Edey 和 Basil Yamey 的高度关注下,会计逐渐演变成一门充满问题的学问。尽管会计作为庞大社会科学体系的组成部分在当时还不发达,但以经济学为导向的会计研究作为伦敦政治经济学院(Dev,1980)学术传统的重要部分,为会计实务技术层面的分析提供了一个包容性更强的框架。成本和利润被描述为一种具有多面性、复杂性和概念性的现象,而解释这种现象则要求从更广泛的但依然是经济学的视角去理解这种现象赖以存在和产生效果的环境。政治问题和社会问题与经济计算方法相互交织并改变经济计算方法。对我来说,理解这个观点的基础——尽管并未执意探索——在伦敦政治经济学院学习时就已经建立起来,尤其是关于社会成本—收益分析方法应用环境的讨论,裨益最大。

就这样,我对会计的兴趣逐渐浓厚起来。我的会计好奇心日益强烈,这促使我继续研修会计,而不仅仅是做一名职业的会计教书匠。然而,在 20 世纪 60 年代中期的英国,会计以及其他大多数管理学科的教育几乎不可能提供足够的研究训练。当时,大多数商学院都在筹建阶段,研究的基础设施非常薄弱。得知这些情况,我决定申请美国的博士项目。这样,在接下来的 5 年里,芝加哥大学就成了我的学术研究园地。

芝加哥大学与现实会计之探索

芝加哥大学确实是一片学术沃土,大大拓展了我对现实会计的研究兴趣。尽管这些兴趣的重点在后来发生了很大变化,但是探究会计如何实际运行的想法已经萌芽并在芝加哥大学富有创造性的学术环境中茁壮成长。对商业现象进行持续且严谨的研究是当时芝加哥大学工商管理研究生院学术生活的重要组成部分,并引导出一股令人兴奋、令人奋进和快速蔓延的学术思潮,实验方法也因此而问世。

在芝加哥大学研修会计的确是一段令人兴奋的时光。那时,经验主义研究刚刚兴起,其大部分为 David Green 所倡导,并经过他的博士生研讨会以及《会计研究杂志》(JAR)的出版发行,得以广泛传播。会计学与经济学、数量方法甚至行为科学之间开始相互融合,并使用哲学术语进行研讨,芝加哥大学工商管理研究生院逐渐创建了现代金融理论及其经验性基础。当时的学生们也都出类拔萃并极具创新精神,例如,Bill Beaver、Philip Brown、Joel Demski 和 Mel Greenball 是比我年级高的博士生,Ray Ball 和 Ross Watts 在我之后不久也加入进来。

在这样的环境中,学术研究很自然地受到特别关注并被置于优先地位。刚从英国来的人非常明显地感受到,学术研究是一项职业性活动而非绅士般的爱好。我以为,无论教师还是博士生都意识到知识本身正处于变化之中。新知识挑战旧知识,而对新知识产生的动因也都进行坦率的探讨和辩论。

我对会计的行为和组织层面的研究兴趣非常偶然地被一个研究机构激发,而该研究机构致力于经济理性这个相当特殊概念的推广。后来,为满足博士生培养计划的课程要求,我不得不研修组织理论这门课。授课老师是Paul Goodman(现就职于卡耐基—梅隆大学),其课程不仅讲授得机敏和风趣,而且为如何研究会计提供了新的视角。我的兴趣如此之强烈,遇到的挑战如此之大,以至于我必须重新安排博士生学习计划:置原本的金融研究方向而不顾,一心钻研会计系统的行为层面。当然,当时有人认为这是不明智的,但也有人给我许多有益的建议,特别是时任博士项目主任的George Sorter、刚从密歇根大学调入的社会心理学家Dick Hoffman,他们的建议极大地缓解了我对学术转向的疑虑,也激发我去探究会计与会计赖以运行的组织环境之间的关系。

管理会计系统的功能紊乱后果曾一度是我特别感兴趣的研究课题。受Chris Argyris的开拓性研究论文《预算对人的影响》(1952)的启发,带着早期接触会计的模糊功能所留下的疑惑,当然也受芝加哥大学大量行为科学研究中社会心理学研究方向的影响,以及对当时的组织理论中新兴权变理论的迷恋,我开始探索影响会计系统的行为后果和组织后果——功能紊乱或者其他——的因素。

坚持实地研究的信念也在早期形成,其原因现在已很难追溯。或许这正是我早期对会计实际运行的兴趣发挥了作用。我依然记得我提出的观点,即会计是一种组织现象,应该在组织环境中进行研究。由此可以看到,我真正的兴趣在于发展基于行动或者在更加富于人文主义的基础上理解管理当局对于会计的种种反应,从而能更充分地理解会计作为一种重大的组织和社会的实务如何发挥其功能。那时,实验室试验研究刚刚引入到会计研究中,我也很担心它的有效性。一项尝试性的试验研究使我更加怀疑试验研究方法的可信度,特别是用来理解会计作为一种组织实务如何运作。我非常熟悉也很担心心理学实验中社会心理学的研究,因为其研究成果往往被实验研究文献因贪图便利而忽略。就我而言,实验室并不是研究现实会计的首选场所,必须开展实地研究。尽管我清楚地意识到实地研究的难度大,尤其对一个刚到芝加哥的英国人,但我坚信这才是我应该做的事情——尽管这在芝加哥大学会计研究史上尚无先例,并且在一开始就饱受质疑。

置于社会与组织环境中的会计研究

找一个合适的组织作为研究的依托很不容易,为此我整整9个月备受煎熬。芝加哥大学商学院是一家研究型的商学院,那时与工商企业几乎没有合作关系。尽管有家保险公司允许我对其进行研究,但因其过于传统,我放弃了。最初抱着侥幸心理到佛罗里达州和智利进行实地研究,后来发现完全不切合实际,甚至未来的国务卿为我奔走,都没有找到适合做研究的组织。最后,我获准到印第安纳州加里市的一家大型钢铁企业进行实地研究——其环境问题令人焦虑,于是,此后数年,这里成了我的第二故乡。

"你不必以一名行为科学家的身份来了解这些,而应该是一名有血有肉的人类学家,"一名资深的车间工友向我建议,"你现在已经进入丛林了",他接着补充道,钢铁企业里边几乎每个部门都有自身的种族和文化特征,就像中西地区的移民史一样。新员工似乎总是从车间里粗重、危险的工作开始,缓慢地提升,经过一段时间就会从事相对干净且安全的工作。那时我的周围是英国人的后裔,沿着生产线相继是德国人和斯堪的纳维亚人(即北欧人,主要指丹麦、挪威、瑞典、芬兰和冰岛),黑人领班则被安排在熔炉附近。

出于某些不同的原因,我勉强算得上是一名人类学家。带着最基础的研究目的和假说,且无任何研究先例可供参考,我开始了实地研究工作。大量时间被用于理解一个异常复杂且相当精密的会计系统如何运作,它怎样融入更广泛的组织流程,以及如何产生实际后果。最初的研究尚处于探索和观察的阶段。我值夜班,在生产工艺的最前端——熔炉附近工作时,我的衣服被烧破了。我花费大量的时间用于观察、倾听和交流,后来我将这种实践称为了解企业语言文化的窗口。一段时间之后,我逐步了解到同一会计系统在组织流程中应用的不同模式,以及反映和塑造这些不同模式的语言间的微妙差异。这些不同模式的差别后来成为研究的重点,语言间的差异也成为通过问卷调查进行后续研究的基础。而后者却为许多研究者所忽视,在类似工厂的研究中表现更甚。

博士论文的形式不仅受到研究问题的影响,还受到研究场地的限制。由于实地研究是一种全新的会计学研究方法,尤其是在芝加哥,最终的研究设计需要依托于一种更加系统化的方法,因此,问卷设计、发放、分析以及复杂的非参数统计分析成为必需的研究程序。实际上,早期实地探索研究刚刚起步并且很少为主流的会计研究者所接纳,而且会计研究本身对研究内容尚缺乏自信,其结果就是重要的探索性研究成果从最终论文中被剔除,这样论文在形式上就显得结构完整、可以预测、可信,更像是科学研究。

最终的研究成果于1973年出版,全名为《会计系统和管理行为》(Hopwood, 1973),它提供了认识管理流程的新视角,会计数据也因此赋予了组织含义和重要性。通过关注不同管理者使用相同会计系统的不同方法,研究结果提供了一些有关组织因素如何调节和影响会计系统运行后果的途径,即提供了一种可以评价多类影响的方法,不仅仅限于那些不可避免的、可预期的或其他的影响。该研究成果还为评价一些因素如预算过程的参与性和其他组织环境等,如何影响和改变工作流程提供了基础,进而为未来的研究提出了许多新问题。用当代的话来说,这项研究对于研究组织文化和管理哲学如何影响会计系统的重要性及其运行后果同样也具有指导意义。

对我来说更有意义的是,这项在芝加哥完成的研究表明探索会计的现实运作极有可能而且也很有价值。尽管我从未拓展那项分析的缜密形式,但是观察和探讨实务会计的更广泛基础已经建立起来。我并没有仅关注于技术分析并将会计与其组织背景分离开来进行研究,而是开创了一条新的探索方式,即关注于对会计的观察而非传播,关注于对会计的组织性和社会性基础的探讨而非单纯的技术性分析,关注于尝试评价其实际运行后果而非毫无怀疑地接受其基本原理。

组织兴趣的发展

1970年回到英国时我感受到了来自知识方面和社会方面的文化冲击。由于在美国已经建立起对组织问题的研究兴趣,理所当然地我认为社会心理学方法是会计研究的主流研究方法,并直接导致个人的倾向(Kassem,1976)。因此,我与英国观点的差别并不明显,尤其是与曼彻斯特商学院活跃的组织研究团体极为相似,这个团体引入了人类学、社会学甚至制度经济学等重要学科的研究思想。因此,我需要开始重新将自己融入组织研究之中,然而幸运的是,当时的环境非常具有活力、注重创新,研究内容同时关注学术和实务以及两者的结合。

《会计与人类行为》(Hopwood,1974)让我想清楚在更宽泛的组织背景下进行会计研究的潜在风险,同时也提供了探究新文献、深化现有认识,并引发一系列与组织会计相关问题的背景。尽管这篇文章现在看来略显陈旧(虽然仍在使用),我仍惊讶于其中一些见解的新颖性,以及对那时出现的理解会计灵性新方法的反映程度,有时我甚至琢磨在那时自己怎么能够有那些想法。

多种思潮开始反映到我的研究作品中,不仅多学科融合十分明显,而且会计实务的内容也逐渐增多。面向具有工作经验管理人员的授课经历,以及曼彻斯特商学院提供的与成熟、雄心勃勃而又非常聪明的研究生一道工作的机会发挥了重要作用。此外,我还受到学院管理控制研究课题组研究计划的鼓舞。该课题组由Morris McInnes和Tony Lowe资助创立,制订了一项极具野心的研究计划,旨在调查英国企业中运行的各式各样的管理控制系统并给予分类总结。要知道,当时几乎没有任何先期的研究成果可供参考,已有的概念框架和分类糟糕透顶,根本不足以反映实务中管理控制系统的多样性,而且用于描述这种多样性的方法还存在问题。毫不奇怪,伴随着大量的观察和数据记录以及极少量的公开研究成果,课题组的努力引发了许多争论。尽管如此,该项研究却让我们看到了实务中管理会计的复杂性,强有力地说明了许多已有理解的不完整性。研究发现使人们能够正确地评价会计,特别是关于会计与其他组织活动的相互融合以及会计系统在组织结构中发挥作用的方式,而不仅仅是反映组织活动。

这些经历使我意识到应该以组织为背景来理解会计。会计的技术层面逐渐与会计赖以发挥作用的组织和更为广阔的背景联系起来。一些研究领域开始得以拓展,如会计和组织结构的内在联系、企业的技术和竞争环境方面与反映组织生命特征的动态管理流程等。虽然这时我意识到源于组织理论的权变理念并深受其影响,但我也发现这些理论框架尽管很有用却并不全面,至少其表述是不充分的。它们的确提供了用来描述会计系统的组织依赖特性的方法,但是这种表述过于死板,仅提供了一种非常狭窄的视角来研究极端复杂的内在依赖性特征(我越来越清楚地认识到这些特征会影响组织中会计功用的发挥),而且忽视了一些更为微妙的路径,即会计信息在组织范围内传递和扰乱相关影响力、权力、价值和重要性的方式。

意识到上述这种方法的局限性,我开始着手展开一项更加开放的个人研究计划,旨在探究会计的组织功用和重要性。为获取这个领域的教学方法,我抱着极大的兴趣着手建立一个更具一般性和有用性的框架,该框架将有助于我们理解会计的组织性结构、功能和后果。作为对比但并不矛盾的是,我还有志于创建用于评价特定组织会计系统特定功用的两种研究方法,以及可能导致更为普遍的采用组织视角来洞察会计的研究战略。研究兴趣也由早期的会计"使用"开始扩展到会计系统对组织决策和组织流程产生影响的不同方式。同时,我也对会计的微观政治产生兴趣,对会计变革如何影响管理术语以及组织目标、问题和可能性越来越敏感。特别感兴趣的是会计如何卷入到更大范围的组织变革中,于是我开始探讨在何种程度上会计系统的精巧设计就是对组织危机的反应。在飞速变化和恶劣的环境中信息流的管理也引起了我的好奇,关于会计可能受组织重组影响的复杂路径开始列入我的研究计划中。

遗憾的是,这些研究设想的大部分并没有形成特定的研究项目,但其中关于会计灵性的技术性评价和当时形成的所谓行为视角却让会计研究者深感不安。前者的偏执和隐含在讨论中的关于组织理性的限制性观点引起了很多不满,正如会计学术团体中行为研究对个人主义的强调。后者因不能解决许多组织实务中的会计难题从而不利于学术研究的发展。另外,我还特别关注基于行为学观点设计的实用会计系统存在的局限性。也许来自当时商学院的教学要求产生了一定影响,尽管我从没有关注学术和实务之间的冲突,但我开始对这两股思潮创造的会计知识产生兴趣。

显而易见,关于会计变革动态性的研究兴趣在这时就已经出现了。实地研究的发展在前文已述,推动会计发展的许多原理也开始凸显重要性,并诱导了持续的经验性和理论性探索。虽然当时对此的评价可能并不完整,但学术界和实务界在创造会计知识中扮演的角色却越来越明显了。总之,未来的研究计划、独特的理论框架以及知识所扮演的角色都已经成形,并会对未来的研究方向和思路产生深远的影响。

研究机构的参与

对于我个人广泛参与会计研究机构的兴趣从何而来已难以清晰表述,出于巧合而非刻意安排,我有幸成为英国当时会计研究机构发展过程中三个重大事项的活跃分子。它们分别是:由社会科学研究协会——研究人类和社会科学的政府基金会——发起的会计研究项目;由在布鲁塞尔新近成立的欧洲高级管理研究中心创办的欧洲会计研讨会,其活动直接催生了欧洲会计协会;创立强调会计的行为学、组织学、社会学分析的国际性研究杂志《会计、组织和社会》。所有的这些事务耗费了我大量的时间,有些现在依然如此。尽管它们在一定程度上对我个人的研究和写作造成影响,但并没有阻止这些努力,而且若干年后还产生了巨大的影响。

欧洲会计研究者网络的建立使我能接触到不同的会计研究传统、评价会计的理论方式和从事会计研究的策略,很难评价和摆脱这些方面对个人研究工作的影响,尽管它们很少留下特别的东西,但是我很清楚这种积累效应,尤其是关于丰富的洞察力和纯粹的实地组织性探索,而后者正是斯堪的纳维亚特别是瑞典在会计和信息系统以及其他管理学领域的研究传统。我和斯堪的纳维亚研究学者的私下接触和友情使我受到直接的理论影响,他们也促使我对组织研究兴趣进行重新定位,远远不同于北美学术圈的研究模式,而是朝着欧洲大陆完全不同的智慧传统方向发展。参照美国的模式和我个人早期的探索,尽管很难精确地描述,我开始沿着欧洲学术的传统方向发展。

欧洲式研究传统的全面发展应该由年轻学者来促成,而不是我们这些人,尽管我们很荣幸曾经参与建立跨国的会计研究者网络。这些网络的建立过程给我带来了很多快乐,而且我也期待着有一天它能带来完全不同的理解和

置于社会与组织环境中的会计研究

洞见。

不容置疑,不同的制度形式能改变探索的模式,产生不同的认识和知识形态。正是基于这种想法,我才试图去创办一本新杂志,专门关注会计的组织、行为和社会分析。尽管远未完善,但是我认为《会计、组织和社会》杂志已经开始发挥作用,包括开辟新的研究领域,合理融合各种不同的学术传统,并建立一个更加国际化和开放的研究团体,为那些有志于探究具有人文社科属性的会计理论和实务的研究者们提供便利。

创办《会计、组织和社会》的最初想法来自课堂。和曼彻斯特商学院的其他同事一道,我根据帕加马出版公司(Pergamon Press)的实际情况设计出一个角色扮演的案例,该公司在当代英国会计史中发挥了不小作用。为了让学生有机会向当事人提问,而不是仅仅依赖媒体报道和官方资料,我邀请了主要的当事人参与案例教学。Robert Maxwell是帕加马出版公司的创建者和企业家,也是受邀嘉宾,他借机询问我是否有创办新研究杂志的想法!

正如后来所发生的那样,我的确有这样的想法。那时我越来越清楚地认识到鸿沟的存在,即对于从组织和社会视角理解会计的潜在需求与当时已有的会计研究杂志的内容和编辑政策之间的缺口。这个缺口直接产生了创办新杂志的提议,经过反复的周密盘算和商议后,《会计、组织和社会》杂志在1976年开始发行。

回想杂志创办初期的简单想法和杂志建立的现实条件之间存在的巨大差异还是挺有意思的。就杂志名称达成一致也是当时的难题,很多人强烈建议杂志名称为"行为和社会会计杂志"。但由于非常厌烦这个名称会限制研究内容,我需要更加具有建设性的名称,以鼓励在组织和社会背景下研究会计的功能。20世纪70年代关注的焦点是行为和社会会计,但是我预想的杂志应该能鼓励与组织和社会背景下经济性预测有关的更广泛问题的研究。于是,"会计、组织和社会"这一名称诞生了,满载希望地创造而非仅仅反映其创办的背景。

现在并不是回顾《会计、组织和社会》杂志创办历史的时刻。尽管我非常清楚还有许多领域有待研究,但我认为它已经收获颇多。它的确耗费了我大量的时间和精力,而且现在依然如此。当我尝试着去驾驭和影响它时,《会计、组织和社会》杂志对我也产生了重要的影响。我从中知晓什么已经发表,从研究计划中获益良多,而且通过杂志联系起来的研究者网络使我变得更加睿智。就全世界范围而言,有志于会计的组织和社会分析的研究团体已经建立起一种开放、友好、互利的传统,并以一种互惠的方式带来友谊和求知欲。

社会兴趣的兴起

当《会计、组织和社会》杂志尚处于发展初期时,我加入了牛津大学管理研究中心(即现在的牛津大学谭普顿学院)帮助建立会计研究项目。尽管我待在牛津大学的时间不长,但却正是我的多产期和重要时期。这段活跃且成功的基金筹备期使我得以设计更加专注的研究项目,并招募了一批天赋极高的研究人员,包括 Stuart Burchell、Colin Clubb、John Hughes 和 Janie Nahapiet。远离许多教学和行政事务的压力,新成立的研究小组很快就建立起适宜且富于创造性的运行机制。

研究小组的计划是明确的。我们都有志于推进对于会计的组织性和社会性分析中最关键要素的理解。当我和其他人指出会计的组织性和社会性基础以及会计实务的后果时,这种呼吁仅仅指明了一种探索会计功能新方式的可能性。对此,研究小组太清楚不过了,早期的讨论集中于三点,其一是该观点所言及的"什么是最重要的";其二是采用哪些方式描述会计的特征能够增加组织和社会范围内对会计的理解;其三是推进这一观点的理论和方法上的先决条件是什么。研究小组一致认为研究的重点应该是会计的变革,即并不是直接探索会计是什么,通过探索会计的现状形成、变革以及新状态形成过程,可能会对会计了解得更加深入。据此,我们能更深刻地理解推动会计变革的动因以及会计扰动所产生的组织性和社会性后果。尽管我们意识到变革是一个相对事实,其结果是我们关注于会计的描述而不是更细微的变化,然而,我们确信这种分析可能会提供实证证据,进而激发、驱使和影响我们对于会计在新状态进程中的理论探索。

研究小组特定的经验研究兴趣同时受到实用性和知识性方面的综合考量,并且总是这样。其中一个项目是关于在国家健康服务组织的某地区引入预算系统,另一个项目旨在探索某些欧洲国家对社会会计日益增长的兴趣,尽管初始状态存在着多样性,但是该项目着重去理解产生社会会计的社会动态性特征和相应社会重要性的本质。还有一个项目是关于会计系统变革的组织性研究。这些项目提供了大量的经验研究素材,但截至目前只有一部分已经发表和出版。经验研究结论的广度和深度极大地激发了理论上的探索,提出若干帮助理解决定因素运作机理的问题以及在复杂的组织和社会条件下的会计变革方式。

调查产生了大量有价值的文献,全部收录在这本论文集里。早期探索、质疑以及使我们远离按传统方式理解会计等内容都反映在《会计在组织和社会中的作用》一文中。当意识到存在着传播会计的不同方式时,关于研究兴趣和计划的一些最初表述出现在《国际视野下的会计发展:过去的焦点和新问题》(现

置于社会与组织环境中的会计研究

在读起来依然是很基础性的文章),以及《"来自火星的信息"和对过去的其他回忆》(该文的经验研究发现是更一般性理论的催化剂)中。更为成熟的研究论述出现在《社会环境中的会计学——价值增值会计在英国的历史》中,后来发表在《会计体系考古学》中。

另外一些文章描述会计的组织性和社会性分析方法。一部分关于会计组织性理解的概要出现在《管理会计和组织行为:序言》和《会计和组织行为》中。关于社会本质问题的讨论在简短的"经济和计划机制"中得以说明,该文反映了我对于计划实践简单发展的担心,不论这些实践是基于经济学原理还是基于社会学原理。此外,《幕后委员会的故事:会计与社会共舞的不一致》和《会计研究和会计实践:两者的不明确关系》也讨论了社会本质问题。考虑到会计在英国公共部门的潜在发展(以阐述会计的组织性和社会性分析的更多问题),许多论文采用试探性的方式进行研究,典型的例子是《会计和效率追求》以及《会计和公共领域:近期发展一瞥》。尽管建立在与公共部门的相当广泛接触的基础上,这些分析还是非常初步的,特别是因为我自己对经济计划在组织变革(这些变革试图探寻社会的特殊概念)中角色的模糊认识。

这些文章的研究视角并非偶然出现的。它们不仅以实例描述了利益攸关的重要问题和潜在影响,部分还试图概述出关于会计实务的社会性理解的若干启示。虽然相当初步,但是论文建立的这些主题有望形成一条主线,尤其是与其他组织和经济视角对比时。

我们强调会计的思考和构成方面。认识到会计不是自动的计算操作,我们将注意力集中于增进对会计的理解上,不仅包括会计的外部因素如何影响和改变会计,而且包括这种混合作用如何发生以及会计如何干预和反映其他的组织和社会环境。同样,我们也强调会计的能动性和创造性。在探索认识会计如何创造特殊和局部可见形式的同时,分析也开始提供基础,以理解会计怎样不时扰乱其他组织和社会环境。抓住会计实践中经济分类和语言差异的特殊性,可以为评价会计计划实践渗入和塑造组织焦点的方式,以及相关概念的理解等提供坚实的基础。

这些分析越来越强调会计以何种方式牵涉在经济优先权和关系的传播中。更多的关注给予了与会计实践相联系的计划合理性的组织和社会后果,关于与会计有关联的不着边际的理论概念也得到越来越多的关注。认识到技术实践并非独立于其功能和基本原理,尽管它们之间的关系既不直接又不统一,部分论文反映了这些能够得到推进和传播的知识及认识。

在所有的情况下,对会计变革动态性的理解总是很复杂的,关于功能的简单想法受到质疑。会计并不只是反映毫无疑问的本质和规则。详细地理解会计变革产生的特定环境,能够证实影响会计及其后果的多种因素的存在性,与会计相关的相当复杂的环境、问题和实务,以及同样重要的,会计变革的无意识和无法预测的后果所扮演的角色。

很明显,上述理解反映了理论和经验兴趣的结合,它们产生于对实地调研和描述会计实务特性的关注。与此观点相同,我一如既往地投入大量的时间观察会计,总是保持对会计新生事物和会计变革的兴趣,试图清晰地用新兴的或者拓展的基本原理去解释会计实务。研究任务的实质就是只有很少部分的素材最终能够公开发表,尽管许多其他的素材会影响我的研究计划。同样,我对会计的理解反映了这样一个观点,即这些评价并非隐含在观察到的环境中,而是反映了可解释理论的运用。不容置疑的是,多年以来我一直试图使自己更具有理论意识,同样也投入了大量时间去了解人类和社会科学的理论发展。我也更加关注于理论化的准则,认识到这种理论化是人类努力的结果,我更加意识到我探寻的特殊理解应该与知识和理论本身的普遍含义相一致。我经常说理论家应该捍卫自己的理论!尽管我知道许多关于会计的经济、组织和社会本质的理论,不可避免地会遭遇到反面意见的回馈,但是我还是很高兴地说,当遇到反面意见时,我会捍卫自己的观点!

结束语

尝试着将许多研究成果贯穿起来并不容易。同样,对于尚无定论和新生的事物进行详细描述也是相当困难的。

所列的文章一如既往地反映了对会计的钻研,观察和探索会计的功能,建立描述会计功用的框架,以及正如我时常所说的,描述会计本身。不是被动地接受会计,也不是不假思索地去探索以增进会计的功能并提升其理性,而是一如既往地理解会计,识别会计是什么、做什么、如何做。因此,我研究会计的角度总是充满争议的,总是从外部而不是从内部认识会计。这种做法将得以延续,因此《从外部看会计》非常适合作为这本论文集的名字。

参考文献[①]

(赵晓东 译)

---

① 参见本文英文参考文献。

会计与信息系统研究的组织视角

许多人可能认为所谓论文集的导言应该是为读者解除疑惑,展示每一篇论文是如何启发他人,以及对整个知识体系累积的贡献程度,由此确保这些多样贡献的统一性与一贯性。但是,在这里,对于这一尚处于概念发展阶段的课题来说,我相信依照这一思路尝试写篇导言并不现实。当然,作为一个例外的情况,本论文集的文章是由 1976 年年底会议的两个研讨会集中起来的①,所有的文章都关注同一个主题,即组织与会计信息系统的关系问题。但是确定的筛选文章的标准试图审慎地提供理论和实证视角的多重性。因此,从一开始我们就需要指出,这一多样性将不会被隐瞒,而是将被公开地表达出来。至少在我看来,它所代表的不是一种病态条件下对会计信息系统的调查研究,而是恰好相反。概念性与研究战略的多样化反映了学术的动态变化。人类对任何一个领域的探索,其调查研究都建立在不同的概念体系、推理、分析与方法论的争论的过程中,无论其清晰与否。至少,本论文集旨在分析说明这种争论对会计(与信息系统)的思想与实践的潜力。

传统研究重点

早期关于组织内会计系统的运作(或可能运作)方式的许多研究关注的重点是获取一种相对静态的,基于更多心理学和社会心理学角度考虑的理解。比如,不同的会计方法、数据的布局及其报告模式对经理人的决策行为与决策结果的影响,就是众多研究的焦点之一。现在,这种研究传统已经为有关人们处理、解释和使用会计信息的研究重点提供了原理,且这一研究重点日益具有影响力并相对严密。尽管如此,现在人们意识到,此类及相关的研究已经倾向于将组织环境排除在外,而组织却恰是会计系统作用存在的原因。

人们很少认为个人对会计信息的反应与其所处组织的其他动态作用方面

---

① Bariff and Galbraith、den Hertog 和 Hedbery and Jönsson 三篇论文的最初版本是在 1976 年 11 月 10—12 日举行于洛杉矶的"美国 Decision Science 研究所"会议上,由 Anthony Hopwood 教授组织的主题为"在变化的环境中为组织设计管理会计系统"的研讨会上首次提出的。Waterhouse and Tiessen 的论文是修改后的版本,其最初提出于同一会议上由 Vijay Sathe 组织并主持的主题为"基于会计系统设计的现代组织理论的相关性"的研讨会。对第二个研讨会内容的简要报告将在本文后面讨论。

间的关系存在着明确的问题。因此,大量对会计信息处理的研究,必然不得不采用相对不完整的组织决策流程和信息角色的观点。因此,人们不得不将重点放在特定的个人对特定的信息表现的反应上,却忽视了更为具体的作用,这一作用可能是持续的管理学习及随之而来关注重点的转换所导致的,同时人们也忽略了一些研究的更为宽泛的结论,这些研究试图寻找管理者在组织中进行决策的方法及规范的信息系统,在此过程中可能或不可能起到的作用,例如会计系统(March and Olsen,1976;Mintzberg,1973,1975;Pettigrew,1972,1973,1977)。尽管由此所形成的相对简单的组织观点不同于个人行为,但其重点在于应对信息分散表现的先动、目标导向的行为上(Atkin,1978)。该观点表达得很隐讳,但事实确实如此。

尽管会计已经在其所处的组织环境中被予以研究,但是研究的重点仍然更多地放在如何获取一个对更多个人或组织中的绝大部分,即流程的方方面面的相对静态的理解上。所以举例来说,经理个人或员工对不同程度的预算松紧的反应曾一度被细致地研究过。但是,这些研究并没有将众所周知的社会或个人因素对此类反应的影响考虑进去,同样没有考虑进去的还包括个人与组织的学习、不同预算标准与格式之间可能存在的关系所带来的影响,还有,比方说,组织权力和影响力的分配与管理,以及应对不确定性风险的战略的影响,尽管人们已经认识到管理层对预算的反馈可能依赖于组织而非公开的技术方式。

本领域中的其他文章对预算过程参与问题所进行的研究,也都倾向于集中在参与度与一些事项的静态关系上,这些事项诸如预算系统中的管理导向、业绩的内在与外在驱动因素、个人满意程度,以及避免采取如"拼凑"预算或"乱做账"等的保护性战略,而是尝试获取目标完成的组织流程的正确评价,或预算与其他组织控制框架和战略关系的正确评价。的确,会计学者们不仅自己没有研究过此类流程的动态方面,而且他们只是象征性地很少甚至没有利用过其他社会学学者针对这种问题的开创性的研究成果(Argyris,1952;Bower,1970;Pettigrew,1973;Roy,1969;Whyte,1955;Wildavsky,1964)。当诸如管理风格和管理者与其下级关系的特点成为研究重点时,相关静态的自由主义的研究同样也明显地存在于关注会计信息的实际使用方式的研究中。

经过艰苦的研究辨别,我们发现已有的大量试图理解会计系统运作方式的研究成果都存在一定的片面性,可以说,对于一个新兴的研究领域,我们不能期望此类研究能为我们提供一种对其问题范围的系统的全面的观点,更不要说对其进行正确的评判了。我们不仅不得不做出选择,并接受由此带来的片面性和不完善,而且如果要想让这些调整更加彻底和日益增多的话,这类选择就必须要做出。然而,在尊重这个新生领域专门化的必然性的同时,我们仍然需要追

置于社会与组织环境中的会计研究

溯确认已经做出的选择是否合适,特别是当研究的备选方法和领域都存在明显压力的时候,而且,我们更有必要仔细思考一下可能影响将来发展方向的因素。

特定学术影响

首先,可以说对会计学行为方面静态的和自由主义的研究导向反映了社会学研究发展的普遍影响。基本上此领域中的所有前沿研究以及由此得出的大部分研究成果都出自美国,或者至少主要是受美国研究方法和关注焦点的影响。因此,会计学领域中所使用的具有行为学特色的概念和方法均与美国社会学领域的主流研究重点相关联,这一点是毋庸置疑的。事实可能正如上所述。尽管对于影响社会学知识发展的复杂的社会、政治、制度、哲学方面因素的充分理解尚待获取,大批的评论家(Hage,1978;Karpik,1978;Kassem,1976;Lammers,1976;Wilson,1977)都曾指出,美国和欧洲在社会学的研究传统和关注方面存在着差异有时甚至是分歧,而英国,至少出于此目的,相对兼顾了这两种学术风格。

这些评论者,特别是 Kassem(1976)在他关于组织行为研究观点比较的讨论中,已经尝试着将美国的微观导向与欧洲的宏观导向进行比较,美国的微观导向倾向于组织哲学的研究,而欧洲的宏观导向更倾向于组织社会学问题的研究方法。此类比较强调了美国学者研究重点的中心思想,即重视个人对组织的贡献问题,正像人类关系的演变与激进的心理学个人主义所反映的那样(Whitley,1974),由此所形成的对组织机制的研究将个人的表现和回报与组织的行为、目标实现联系起来,无论这种机制被看作是提升组织理性的方法,还是被看作用来管理责任、动机以及所带来业绩的社会的、程序化的方法。比起美国这种实用主义的特点,欧洲的兴趣点更多地在于对组织流程和行为的结构化、更为宽泛的环境影响上,这很可能是由于欧洲对问题定义的广度,更多的是针对提供概念性、解释性甚至是批判性的评论,这种评论对组织行为具有历史性和特殊性的影响(Hage,1978;Sandberg,1976,pp.29—32)。

对于这种类型我们很难做出宽泛的归纳概括,因为有太多例外的情况,其中还包括很多颇具影响的情况。在美国已经进行了很多重要的社会学研究,其中比较有影响力的包括芝加哥社会学院的早期研究,Merton、Gouldner、Blau、Etzioni、Hage、Perrow 的研究,以及其他一些近期的权变研究成果。在欧洲,这种例外情况也不少。但是从整体来看,相反的情况仍然存在,特别是在会计处理的具体环境中当进一步考虑学术系统本身固有的筛选过程的时候。大体来说,在美国许多主要的商学院中,更为微观的心理学和社会心理学视角要比社会科学圈更占优势。

或许与上述宽泛的学术研究相关,亦或许在某种程度上,独立地建立在其上的是另一种因素,而这一因素是在分析对会计系统运作影响因素的研究发展状况时所必须考虑的。这就是宽泛的研究目的所持的观点。

研究可以用于解释说明,并可以在解释学传统(Taylor,1971)中为在组织和社会机制下提供阐释和理解会计系统及会计人员所扮演角色的基础,并且还可以有更加务实的考虑,效果可能立竿见影。研究以提高会计系统功能为导向,即为我们所知的旨在提高目前系统的有效性,或旨在为会计系统的设计提供基础,使会计更接近于Simon(1976)所说的"人造科学"。并且,除非我们忘记了,否则就目前的研究现状而言,学术调查同样可以对当前会计模式所起的作用加以批判性的评价,并在这一过程中质疑会计模式在深化组织行为所带来的经济利润的影响中所起的作用,以及质疑其可能在此基础上迈向其他可能选择的会计方式的设计中所起的作用。

不同的研究导向对知识的需求有所区别。不论是阐释性的还是批判性的视角,都要求对会计系统的社会和组织环境有比较宽泛的了解,尽管很显然批判性研究方法还要求对会计和社会兴趣以及组织理论的关系有一个透彻的认识,无论其批判与否,这对于任何尝试建立起以设计为导向的观点都是十分重要的。只有当研究像接受它自身很少谋求在当前系统有效性方面有所提高一样接受目前的会计理论时,对理论知识的需求才会减少。因为在这种研究导向下,对会计的组织基础的评价才可能没有对像报告的模式和格式这样的设计以及调解任何既定系统效果的心理学和社会心理学流程的更为具体的各个方面所起作用的理解那样重要。

大量的会计研究可能(某种程度上可能是很公正的)受限于对目前的会计功能的认可,这一观点受到了其他一些学者(如Jensen,1976)的支持,这些学者注意到了研究导向与对理论知识的需求以及对会计学术调查方向之间的关系。的确,随着其他会计研究领域从有限的研究视野中分离出来,在此过程中逐步摆脱既定会计方式的传统限制,其目的是为理解会计在组织、经济和社会中所扮演的角色进行铺垫,我们可以观察到这些变化的过程。这对于资本市场上会计信息作用的调查、信息与控制系统设计的经济学原理以及最近对会计准则的社会政治基础的研究同样适用。

我们上面所讨论的范围宽广的传统研究很可能会通过所研究的机构组织环境具体而即时的方面将其影响施加给研究团体。比如说,我们已经提到了在商学院的某些文章中对自由主义夸大的可能性。研究者们将其出发点定位于实用性及易理解性,并减少对现有方法的质疑,这将有易于为人们所接受,正如

置于社会与组织环境中的会计研究

产业心理学案例(Baritz,1960)中所阐释的那样。之后,Kassem(1976)指出,社会研究的微观组织导向在方法论上更为可靠,它不仅在不同的原则与功能方面与传统的学术研究相一致,而且与研究成果的加速产出相协调。在学术团体内部的回报机制下,这两方面的因素都非常重要,它们对个人的进步与交流渠道构建的可接纳因素都将产生影响。

关注点的转变

所谓"常规科学"(Kuhn,1970)的方法承载着其自身的进步与最终的延续性。因此,尽管我们可以部分地解释以往的研究为何集中在对其他方面的损害上,但是对于以往的研究重点能否持续下去,此类评估就无法为其提供必然的评价了。的确,其相反的情况更可能出现。因为当研究观点的制度落实为一种限制影响时,诸如奖励机制,历史经验就为我们提供了克服大部分(如果不是全部的话)此类限制因素的基础,其过程可能有时会比较困难并会延迟,但通常都是以惊人的质量和速度完成的。

如今,一些信号说明至少有一些压力来自为行为会计研究领域的变化,其中一些压力源自目前知识的更新变化,其他压力则来自社会科学研究更广泛、持续的变化。在另外来自宽泛定义的委托人方面的压力中,一些是来自在公司管理中现有委托人的利益变化,还有一些来自在会计知识与研究中对其他社会团体利益的合法性的逐步确认。

当然,心理学与社会心理学对于会计系统在组织设置中运行方式的理解的日益积累,本身已经提供了将更为结构化和组织化的事件确认为疑难问题的基础。例如,Hofstede(1967)在预算的社会心理学纬度的研究中指出,部门和组织成本结构中所反映出的技术和组织因素的作用,可能会发挥于调节预算流程的有效性方面。Swieringa and Moncur(1975)所进行的对预算流程中参与度的比较分析的研究,为其提供了更为直接的证据。即使是对单个组织机制下的社会心理学研究,在个体研究的不同结果被排列出来时,也将不具有建设性。因此,举例来说,Hopwood(1973)和Otley(1978)的研究结论中对差异和共性的比较解释了组织层级的差异所起的作用,特别是当与此相差的结果偏离相对假设及Baumler(1971)的研究结果的时候。

更多的信号将被作为实证研究进程被发现,并且人们应当记住这仅是宝贵的一点而已,这一推测被受到更多组织而非个人或团队观点影响的研究结果支持。早期由Simon和他的同事(1954)进行的关于组织的会计功能的研究,已经被许多教材作者在对会计信息可选择模式的分析中引用,但其大量的结论常常被忽略,这一研究提供了一个对这一评价相关性的清晰的信号。接下来的Khandwalla(1972)、Bruns and Waterhouse(1975)、Watson(1975)、Watson and Baumler(1975)和Hayes(1977)的研究,更直接地受到了组织行为领域中前沿知识的影响,并证明了不仅方法具有丰富性、相关性和潜在性,而且会计行为学研究的演进发展方式正逐步认识到理解组织问题的重要性。

这种对组织行为研究的认识本身就十分重要,毫无疑问我们可以期待更多对这类问题的阐述。当然,与这种及其他报刊相一致的新兴方式,无论其成功与否,都可以支持这一结论。同样相关的是进行组织研究的学者们对会计与信息系统相关问题的兴趣日益浓厚。尽管这不算是一种新的现象,正如先驱的且颇具影响力的Agyris(1952)和Simon(1954)的一系列研究所证明的,同样受到关注的还有Roy(1969)、Dalton(1959)、Whyte(1955)、Blau(1966)和Wildavsky(1964),包括其他一些文章在内的研究都认为组织中会计与信息系统所扮演的重要角色正被组织行为学的学者们普遍研究着(Pfeffer,1977;Pettigrew,1973;Pondy,1970;Heydebrand,1977;Connolly,1977;等等)。如果事实确实如此的话,那么它只会加深我们对这一领域的理解,并很可能在这一过程中推动会计学者对相似研究视角及方法的接纳程度。

变化所带来的压力也并非只来源于研究团体的内部。因为在企业和公共团体中,我认为对于组织环境的理解会有一个渐增式的评价,这里我们只能在个人经验和印象的基础上以一种尝试性的方式来探讨这个问题。在某种程度上,它不可避免地反映了对现有实用主义观点和方法的种种限制(Earl,1978)。更为重要的,它反映了对会计及信息系统创新需求及新知识在此过程中所起作用的日益认可程度。

在此之前,会计与信息系统的发展一直是一个非常注重实效的事情,并且毫无疑问是由对现行方法的不足与可供选择的方法的相关性的认识所引起的。尽管变化经常是真实的并且是主要的(Chandler,1962,1977),但是我们却只能假设它是由实际的经验和偶尔的忽略所引起的,并且由经验的规律以及试验和失误的教训而塑造。显然在这方面只有很少的研究甚至根本没有任何系统性可言,更不要说在学术领域中的研究了。

这一过程的结果构成了现在我们所知的管理会计的大部分(Gardner,1954;Parker,1969;Pollard,1965)。某些学者对此持批判态度,至少这些批判中的一部分可以通过评估一些创新部分以及由企业界的前辈们所创造的看似边缘化且常被遗忘的发展成就来调和,尽管如此,这仍为今天更为技术化的研究提供了基础,就其主题而言,可以包括业绩的分部衡量、成本方式以及资本投资估价等。

然而,变化速度的加快以及组织规模和复杂性的增长对会计及信息系统的

置于社会与组织环境中的会计研究

发展提出了更快、更精细熟练的要求。尤其是组织复杂性的增长,提高了更清晰理解信息(和会计)系统及组织设计之间关系的相关性和需求(Galbraith,1973)。因此,商业和公共组织转向外部顾问和研究者寻求帮助,有时,它们也创建自己的专家发展团队。信息系统技术的日益成熟为这一现象提供了许多例子,正如重大、长期项目的成本和控制方面,以及生命周期日趋缩短的产品的生产以及商业政策的决策方面不断增加的困难一样。相类似地,同样甚至更有意义地,包括会计系统在内的信息控制系统的设计的复杂性也由于大规模的现代空间和防御组织而引起众多大学教师以及诸如 RAND Co. 这样的专业机构的密切关注(Chandler and Sayles,1971)。特别在这一领域,对组织以及信息结构和程序的联合设计的需求早已存在且被广泛认可。

很少有会计学者(本身)已经卷入这一革新中,而这一事实既没有降低其实用性,也没有降低会计信息系统知识发展的学术重要性,尽管这可能表明主流会计原本并未关注组织事件。但是考虑到正如其他信息控制系统那样,会计系统的功能和设计与组织设计更广的方面是交互相连的,而组织设计也正像日前逐步增强的矩阵式(Knight,1977)、网络式及松散关联(Weick,1976)的组织形式相关性所证实的那样,从来没有并且也不可能是静止不变的,过去自身的孤立不可能消除对会计系统设计的组织基础的新理解的持续压力。

更广泛的社会压力同样会加重这些压力。最近的一些研究(Braverman,1974;Hales,1974;Heydebrand,1977;Marglin,1974;Whitley,1974)已经阐述了这一现象,即组织的管理实践与结构,包括现行的会计信息系统(Munford and Sackman,1975),是对更广泛的社会结构、机制和意识形态的反映。尽管我们社会这些方面的变化并不迅速,但有迹象表明已经出现了对这一问题的兴趣,以及可选方法的现实性,正如新的社会团体获得一定的实力以及对于管理观念相关性的理解(Sandberg,1976)。例如,欧洲的研究已经开始对参与度更强的会计信息和控制系统的方式(Magnusson,1974;Stymme,1977)以及更加注重人力而非资本的系统方式(Briefs,1975;Nygaard and Bergo,1975)进行研究。并且,欧美两方都将注意力集中到了信息和会计系统的设计上,而这将便于对工作组织新形式的管理和评估。

前景和相关问题

毫无疑问,尽管大型组织对会计信息系统运行方式的评价所带来的压力是各不相同的,但确实是真实存在的。从那些始于普及科学的发展范畴(这是由现有利益集团需求的变化所引起的),到源于更多问题甚至是批判的观点,所有这些都渐渐地引起了研究的尝试以及崭新的认识。但是,在此阶段,方法、关注点和相关成果的多样性,正是对以往工作的整体评估,并且这种评估并非仅局限于这篇介绍性文章所涉及的范围。这些新发展已经显示出了一种日渐兴起的潜在性,同时,与之重要性相当的,还有一些在将来的研究中可能遇到的问题。

首要的并最为明显的优势就是组织观点为我们提供了一种建立在已有进展的研究发展之上的方式。正如我们所讨论的,有些学者已经在受会计和其他信息系统影响的组织化进程、组织成员的意识和行为、组织因素甚至更为宽泛的环境因素所影响、塑造和限制的会计及信息系统所采取的模式,以及它们所发挥的功能方面打下了基础。目前研究中 Waterhouse and Tiessen 和 Wildavsky 的论文以及 Sathe 的报告都突出了这些新发展及其潜在性。并且,如今在与心理学和社会心理学导向的研究成果进行比较中,其差异是比较明显的,而现有研究工作的暗指,以及在将来关注中更为明确的观点,也可能为更好地理解这一点奠定基础。关于这一点的例子已在上文中提到过了。

这些发展是相当重要的,其理由很多,不仅是因为它为理解会计在补充其实务中的复杂性方面的功能提供了潜在可能性这一点。除了达到在理解整个组织的会计功能概述方面的满意度之外,组织研究者们可能要在认识上逐步与异质、不断变化并且反过来塑造了这一模式的状况,以及特定组织或部门中会计的重要性和影响力相关联。为了更好地表达和证实这一认识,我们应考虑到会计和信息的功能,这一功能已超越了目前技术、程序和现有科技组合的特性。虽然这已组成了整体的一个重要并且最为显眼的部分,但当考虑到会计技术在发挥其作用时的组织结构和流程时,这一特性的片面性就会显现出来。正如 Simon 和他的同事所阐述的那样,组织的会计功能本身以及那些与组织的其他部分相关联的组织联结与方法和流程一样重要,并通常还更加难以解决和管理。然而,我们对于组织模式以及会计功能核心的认识是很少的,只有会计研究开始利用组织社会学家和理论学家的视角及成果时,用于评价和分析会计系统异质性的基础才能取得进步和发展。

与社会学领域中广阔的发展具有如此密切的关系,这一潜力已经在会计研究的其他领域进行了阐述,这将能够使对这些重要话题的思考显示出重要性,但迄今为止,还没有进行系统的调查研究。

其他的一些社会学者曾试图探求组织决策的制定与会计行为之间的动态关系(Bonini,1963;Bower,1970;Crecine,1971;Pettigrew,1973;Whyte,1955;Wildavsky,1964)。而会计研究学者们目前所得出的基于行为学的理解是立足于以上研究成果的生硬比较之上的。日渐兴起的在某些方面的新认识正为理解会计行为提供有趣且重要的导向,这些方面包括诸如回馈流程(Annett,1969;

Rosenthal and Weiss,1966)、伴随并塑造预期决策制定的回顾性阐述(March and Olsen,1976;Weick,1969)、资源配置中的议价和商谈的作用(Bower,1970;Pondy,1970;Wildavsky,1964)、承诺在形成和影响生产及信息使用中的方式(Bower,1970;Staw and Ross,1978),以及以下两者之间的关系:一方面是信息和会计系统的设计,另一方面是在组织环境下,组织权力的所有者试图对其方式与重要性的分布进行管理的方式(Jönsson and Lundin,1977;March and Olsen,1976;Pettigrew,1977)。正如 Bariff 和 Galbraith 在此项研究中所提出的,社会学对组织中权力与矛盾研究的再现(Burn and Buckley,1976;Pfeffer,1977;Zald,1970)与社会学科存在着明显的关联,而这一学科在组织控制、影响和限制中的作用已被广为认可。

新兴的组织评价的一个重要方面(这也是基于立竿见影的实用主义的关注考虑),是其为一个更为明确的会计导向设计所提供的随之而来的可能性。虽然会计系统是组织的"人工制品"(Simon,1969),是有意识进行设计和改变的,但对其的研究更多地倾向于概括性的特定事项,而对设计程序的本质、设计选择受到限制的方式,以及系统随组织环境调整的方式的关注较少。如果说会计系统设计的理论基础确实存在,那么目前只存在于会计实践者和咨询师的经验性的理解中。

但是,新会计和信息系统理论所面临的许多实用性的压力要求对影响和限制系统设计的因素有一个更为明确的评价(Bjφrn-Andersen and Hedberg,1977)。在这一变化较为适度的时期,可能更多的是一些固有的观念。然而,当组织结构随规律性的增长而变化时,正如 den Hertog,Hedberg and Jönsson 对目前这一问题的讨论,存在着对过去设计的限制性影响的日益实现,以及当更多的社会利益方尝试影响设计的选择和进程时,一种更为系统化的表述清晰的理解就变得尤为重要了。

尽管会计功能的组织评价的潜在性是真实的,但是其结果也并非没有问题存在。因为进步的取得不仅依靠会计研究者对新的方法论和理论观点的掌握,至少其中的一些起初会与在这些研究发生的机制中所体现和看重的方法论及理论观点存在冲突,而且还依靠于与组织的思想和研究的发展本质保持一致的研究。对于所有交叉学科的研究来说,将重点放在某些邻近学科上是相当具有吸引力的,这些邻近学科通常是已经牢固建立起来的,而非那些仍在建立过程中或已遭淘汰的领域。然而,不管在理论中或常规(更不要说革命性的)科学进步的环境下存在多么优异的趋势(Kuhn,1970),随之而来的引用的延迟将不仅没有限制研究的发展,同时也没有阻碍这种发展关注接下来提出的视角和结论,如果值得信任的话。因此,会计研究在其实证基础及现有理论受到质疑的时候开始转向对权变理论相关性的研究(Penning and Tripathi,1978;Aldrich and

Mindlin,1978;Weick,1977)。

会计的组织性研究所面临的进一步的困难与我们对会计功能的理解的变化是相关联的。会计与组织中权力和矛盾的治理关系方面的研究将面临挑战。会计系统设计流程的权变本质的证据将扰乱技术的普遍主义者(的思维方式)。同时,对那些为新的价值观服务的会计具体方面的研究,将被视为对现有利益集团的威胁。

然而,在不得不解决后一个问题,以及源于研究本身真正的本质问题时,会计研究才会处理那些在大多数科学进步中常见的难题。

结论

会计和信息系统在组织的功能中起着至关重要的作用。因此,它们已经并且仍然正在对组织和环境的变化做出回应。对于这一点,没有理由认为将来会有什么不同。我们对新知识和观念的需求是不间断的。尽管在过去,研究或许没有起到主要的作用,但是它至少有影响未来的可能性。

从这个方面讲,基于对会计和信息系统的设计及运作的组织基础理解的研究是尤为重要的。尽管先前已有大量工作为此做了铺垫,尤其是信息系统本身,即使在无法很好地表述这些方法和流程或其专业具体性的情况下,调查研究已经做得相当完备,但是对某些因素我们仍然知之甚少,这些因素要么形成信息系统的设计,要么塑造信息系统的进程,从而影响组织参与者的意识和行为。换句话说,对会计行为的理解所带来的挑战仍然是确实存在的,尽管这种转变的压力是相当明显的,这在前面业已讨论过。

或许,抛开这样一种背景,在《会计、组织和社会》这一期中发表的各篇文章之间的差异可能会比其相似之处来得更加明显。当然不同知识的、社会的和注重实效的基础是显而易见的。无论运用何种方法,它们共同阐述了会计和信息系统是怎样设计的,并且其功能正对基于组织视角的理解、压力以及更宽泛的环境变化的挑战做出回应。

参考文献[①]

(于增彪 译)

---

① 参见本文英文参考文献。

论在会计运作环境中研究会计

会计已经日渐被认为在组织功能中起关键作用。通过评定组织活动的成本与效益、制定财务标准和规范、评价与报告组织业绩,以及财务规划与控制,会计已被用来赋予现代组织功能的所有重要方面以经济含义。通过对组织活动的特定经济表述及其对内部成员和外部利益相关者的意义,会计已经介入特定组织秩序和组织目标的构建。在维持一定形式的组织层级、结构和控制,以及促进组织活动的经济理性的同时,会计与观察及试图改变组织程序和活动的特定方式相联系(Batstone,1979)。的确,在许多情况下,决策程序、组织活动的构架甚至组织边界的确定,都不能离开会计表述而独立存在。会计已经不仅仅是重要而有价值的管理实践,而且其存在和结果已很难与组织功能相分离。换句话说,会计已经成为现代组织的核心组成部分。

在会计如此交融于组织功能的同时,不可思议的是我们对会计活动的组织属性几乎一无所知。尽管早期的会计实务研究着重于理解会计在组织中扮演的角色及其重要地位,许多最近的研究则将会计从组织设置中剥离,更多地倾向于在个体层面而不是组织层面来研究会计的意义。① 尽管必须承认,这样的研究在会计信息的解读和如何有助于决策制定方面提出了有趣和有用的看法,但却没有明确提出一个组织的会计活动可能产生的影响,而正是后者为会计业提供了足够的理性。个体层次的研究既不能说明会计与其他的组织活动、决策制定过程以及权力结构相互影响的方式,也不能说明引起会计现象产生及变化的因素。②

将相关的论文收集在此*,旨在提供一些在组织框架内对会计的认识。这

---

① 关于这一倾向的原因已在其他地方讨论(Hopwood,1976,1978)。Gowler and Legge (1981)也对这一问题进行了有趣的讨论。在最近有关会计的行为和组织特征的研究中,后者引用了 Platt(1976,p.42)特别有意思的一段:"……人们为很强的制度因素所驱动而倾向于学科归属明确的研究方法。那些还没有在某一特定领域建立稳固基础或地位的年轻人对这种学科归属的压力感尤其强烈……"我认为可以明确地说这种状态已在会计的行为研究中盛行。如果将管理会计与财务会计相比较,结果会更令人瞩目,主流观点认为在财务会计领域,制度(如市场)层面而非个体层面的研究才是正统。

② 关于这一点的讨论及类似的观点,请参看 Connolly、March and Shapira、Cummings, Pondy and Weick in Ungson and Braunstein (1982) 的论文。

* 这里是指发表于《会计、组织和社会》(Accounting, Organizations and Society)1983 年第 8 期的相关论文。——译者注

些论文在较早期的研究成果基础上（例如，*Accounting, Organizations and Society*, Vol.3, No.1 (1976)），显示了组织层面会计研究的潜在前景及可行的研究方法。然而，在试图总结这些论文的主要观点及因此而引发的讨论之前，有必要描述组织层面会计研究的特征及其重要性的原因。

从组织层面关注会计的原因

个体层面的会计总是视会计现象为理所当然。如此，会计的一切都是确定的。会计研究的主要关注点是如何理解以及如何更好地解释会计信息。这些研究常常被看作协调的基础，而不是更多地从根本上来改革会计实践和技术。此外，绝大多数的这一类研究中，这一着重点使得会计脱离了组织设置和其他的组织实践。会计被看作独立的艺术，其任务和结果主要由会计信息的认知特性而不是会计被置于其中的组织设置来决定。的确，在许多场合，对会计认知特性的极度关注证明了其研究设置转向大学教室和实验室的合理性。

组织层面的研究不会否认这种认知特性的重要性，会计影响个体行为的方式也是其中心部分。然而，胜于将会计独立于组织设置，组织层面的研究者致力于理解在特定组织设置中会计被赋予的意义，其着重点不是会计所提供的信息，而是作为组织设置一部分的特定会计系统在组织设置构建过程中所起的更为积极的影响、协助，甚至直接参与的作用。在这些学者看来，会计不能独立于导致其存在或使其存在具有意义的过程，这些过程有的是在特定设置或会计起作用的机构中，有的则没有这些组织层面。

对认知理论学者来说，会计主要是一个自变量。尽管在观察对它的反应所获得的理解基础上，学者们也可能试图改变、改善被作为独立组织本体来看待的会计陈述。而对组织学者来说，会计既可以是自变量，也可以是因变量。一些研究会计的组织学者试图强调会计的权变性，致力于研究会计如何内生于组织和社会设置。然而，这样的研究并没有必要为会计的特定表现形式提供解释。也有其他一些组织学者将研究重点放在会计如何影响，同时也受制于组织设置的方式上。总括来说，这些组织学者试图探索会计影响组织存在的意义和行为的社会过程。

然而，这样的区别仅仅对组织层面的会计研究提供了一个相对肤浅的看法。考虑到对比，特别是联系当今的研究进行比较的重要性，有必要更具体地探讨现有文献中从组织角度对会计现象的不同看法。这些文献包括收集于此的，以及其他公开发表的。

置于社会与组织环境中的会计研究

会计不断地推陈出新

会计既不是静止的,也不是单一的现象。在时间的长河中,会计的所有形式都发生了变化,不断地推陈出新。而且会计也不是一种单一的技艺。在一种民族文化内部,管理会计和财务会计都具有多元性特征,而在交叉文化氛围中,这种多元化更明显(Horovitz,1980)。显然,会计是一种能超越它的界限和历史的现象。

遗憾的是,我们对影响会计改变或者有助于形成不同会计模式的因素几乎完全没有了解。尽管有大量关于会计历史的研究,但是许多都侧重于技术层面,着重于已有的发展,而不是探求改变后面的理性(Hopwood et al.,1980);即使是对潜在动因提出问题,也都轻易地采取功能主义,甚至改革主义的立场。的确,一直到最近,会计现象的历史研究和比较分析都采取极端的非理论研究的立场,极少将其研究扩展到公司形式及其相应的社会、经济制度的发展,以及会计在新兴组织形式、组织与其他组织和利益群体的关系中所起的作用。

然而,这些问题已受到会计和其他领域学者的关注。Johnson(1983)、Flamholtz(1983)、Meyer(1983)和 Tiessen and Waterhouse(1983)的论文及评论对此做出了说明。

在历史研究方面,会计发展的研究开始采用更多的理论分析,包括对新兴公司形式及其内部控制和外部合法性的研究。有趣的是,其他社会科学领域的学者也开始对会计重要性的日益增加以及会计在现代组织形式的兴起中所扮演的角色感兴趣。研究领域涵盖了在促进有助于特定组织利益的组织可视性中会计所扮演的角色,在作为新兴组织特征的冲突管理中,会计和其他管理活动发挥作用的方式,以及在推动由法律虚构的无私管理理念和秩序的清晰与普及过程中会计的贡献。

从组织角度对会计多元性的研究已经融合了权变理论的观点,尽管还不是很确定,但很有益处(Otley,1980)。研究包括组织环境、技术和管理结构对会计实务的潜在影响。尽管尚处于启蒙阶段,但对于超越静态研究和机能主义假设的限制的必要性已日益取得共识。目前,主要的研究兴趣在于试图了解会计变革的组织过程。虽然进展缓慢,但有迹象表明研究开始关注其他管理活动和外部环境与会计相互作用来推动改变的方式,以及在理解代表组织特色的多种事件对于会计的影响方面所遇到的困难。另一个逐渐引起关注的问题是会计如何在组织和社会冲突情况下改变以创造不同于以往但仍然令人信服的组织目标和成就。更为重要的是,因会计知识的专业化和会计积极的调整对促使其改变的现象的理解,会计在其自身变革中所扮演的角色也开始得到认同。

有意思的是,与新兴组织形式及相应的控制问题相关的课题也吸引了经济学家的目光。不再满足于将组织看作一个毫无疑义的黑箱,经济学家们开始探索主流的组织形式可能固有的理性,议题涉及市场竞争优势、层级结构及其他组织形式,以及组织能借以调整、促进经济利益与责任模式的途径。正如Johnson(1983)、Tiessen and Waterhouse(1983)和其他学者(Baiman,1982;Spicer and Bellew,1983)所指出的,这些研究强调监督和控制程序所起的重要作用,从而有助于认识会计功能的起源。然而,大多数的这一类研究至今都只强调了技术和经济利益的作用。与历史学和组织学的研究相反,迄今为止经济学家很少或根本没有考虑经济与社会、政治的交互作用,或者更独特的有关会计本身如何以不同的名义规范经济利益的问题。

目前所有这些关于会计的潜在理性的研究尚处于发展的初级阶段。历史学、经济学和组织学的研究在很大程度上还是相互独立的,各自都倾向于对组织会计的出现及其促使其变革的因素做出独立的解释,很少有针对某一特定会计模式的出现和发展的研究。然而这些试图理解会计变化的过程的研究仍然具有重要意义,相当重要的原因是它们有可能就如何理解会计的影响提供非常不同的、很有可能是系列化的观点。

传统的会计观视会计为相对没有疑问的一种技术,假设会计是用来协助组织和社会活动的(关于这一观点的进一步讨论,请参见 Burchell et al., 1980)。可以被检测的(如果有的话),也仅仅是协助的种类和结果。尽管成本、利润和其他的财务业绩指标可能不能说是毫无疑问的,但根据传统观点,问题也只是来自操作性的有关组织及社会的实际状况和成就的预期方面。按此构想,会计基本上只是披露,其目的只是反映,而不是更积极地构建对组织实际状况和成就的综览。试图说明和呈现一种反映组织业绩的毫无疑问的工具,虽然常常很困难,但会计被看作这样一种从导致其产生的社会冲突和发明中分离出来的现象。

对于那些致力于清楚表达和传播传统会计观的人来说,他们不会满足于这些太过明显的关于会计的观点,但对那些愿意接受的人来说,它们至少提供了一种理解会计及其问题的可能途径,这些问题和导致会计产生的历史条件及其发展与使会计日益重要的现今组织都是协调一致的。

会计和组织活动

通过帮助塑造和监督组织程序及活动,现代会计获取了越来越重要的地位。然而,尽管会计课本、声明、建议都不断地强调会计在组织效率、管理者和员工激励、业绩以及有效分配资源方面的贡献,对于会计是否及如何实现这些

置于社会与组织环境中的会计研究

目标却知之甚少。相对于对会计技术的研究程度,对于会计试图去激活的组织程序的研究极少,而技术只有通过组织程序才能发挥其潜能。

在组织参与者对于组织的愿景和目标的构建过程中,会计到底扮演什么样的角色?会计是否涉及组织特定时代概念的创造?如果是,起到什么样的作用?组织业绩的报告什么时候及如何对行为产生激励?会计如何有助于组织目标的清晰表达?通过什么样的方式会计所带来的组织透明度可以有助于组织内部控制?这种控制是否可以以社会或技术的术语来表达?会计所强调的定期信息报告制度如何与组织中无处不在的大量的非正式决策相关?换句话说,会计如何取得和保持在组织中的重要地位?

这样的问题还可以列出很多。尽管因会计在组织中所扮演的角色和所可能产生的结果,我们已经在提高和精炼会计技术基础方面投入很多,但对如何实现这些所声称的会计的潜能仍然知之甚少。这对于一直强调其技术在组织中的实际应用的行业来说,在一定程度上是荒谬的。

会计的组织观可以从很多方面说明会计所需要进一步研究的问题。例如,它可以有助于我们理解会计在特定模式的组织结构的形成以及所产生的后果中所扮演的角色,这在所提供的横向的信息与会计一贯所重视的纵向的信息流不一致的情况下尤其重要。同样,它也使我们对组织业绩评价的作用有更深刻的认识,包括业绩评价为组织环境和组织内部过程提供映像,从而有助于在变革时期和经营中断期设计更有效的信息系统。许多人也会发现会计的组织观有助于理解不同的且常常是相互矛盾的组织业绩评价方法在决策制定和稀有资源分配中的作用:无论是已实现业绩还是期望业绩。究竟会计对于经济效益的重视是如何与寻求技术、人本和更广泛的环境目标的组织业绩相联系的?会计对于新环境进行独立分析的责任又如何服务于形成对实际业绩的实现至关重要的责任的需要?对这些特征的进一步认识至少可以将会计的技术基础植根于组织活动,从而有望使所宣称的会计潜能得以实现。然而,目前这样的认识仍然停留在经验阶段,很少抽象上升为理论,大都概括于会计实务的技术性手册中。

会计与会计目标的实现

惯常讨论对于会计能实现其所被赋予的使命确定无疑。我们被告知,会计有助于提高组织效率和业绩(但未提及会计在其所致力于提高的终极目标中所扮演的角色),会计能在管理者和员工激励中起积极作用,会计所提供的信息有助于管理决策,特别是在非确定的环境中。

然而,这些高度概括的声明越来越多地被用来与来自研究和实务的更有歧义的结论相比较。

寻求会计潜在的和显明的功能性及非功能性结果的学术研究已有很长时间。最近有研究指出会计的作用在组织危机中激增,而在较少有疑问的增长和成功期降低。也有进一步的研究甚至认为在这样的状况中随之而来的增强控制的要求会降低而不是增加管理决策的弹性。

如此对于会计实际的而不是声称的作用的关注已经得到一些会计实务界人士的回应。面对经济约束和日益增加的竞争压力,这些实务界人士开始关注会计所提供常规信息的局限性。

通过审视现今的会计信息如何反映过去的危机,这些实务界人士开始意识到有必要重新认识会计系统是如何在实践中运作的,以及它能够为管理决策提供什么。尽管这样的忧虑,不管其原因,还需要系统的论证,但这并不妨碍人们表达对于组织程序中刚性的常规控制,以及渗透于传统会计的固定时间范围的不满。许多人也担心会计对于经济和财务因素的高度强调所导致的问题,也常常听到非常传统的实务工作者明确表达他们对于因重复的年度预算回顾和授权而被合法化的无效率的忧虑。在更一般的层次上,一些组织开始关注整个会计和其他的控制技术,认为这些控制程序脱离了被控制的实践本身。

显然,这些忧虑在实务工作者中并不具有普遍性。常常只是在大的组织中,一个时期的严峻的经济约束会导致一些会计工作者和管理人员探查他们对会计的投入中已实现的和未实现的。尽管仅仅局限于他们所服务的组织的现有系统,这样的质疑已经导致人们对于会计技术与人类、社会之间的相互依存关系的新的认知,而且对这样的认知的表达比会计学者的方式更敏锐,会计学者往往将行为和组织的研究看作仅仅为愿意锦上添花的少数学者提供基础。

遗憾的是,会计的组织学研究状况还不能完全解决实务工作者的忧虑。目前的研究着重于会计的特定方面,常常是寻求如何实现传统定义中的会计目标,而不能对会计的作用提出更多的质疑。只有很少的关于会计的行为和组织方面的研究探查会计与其他组织活动之间更广泛的联系,为目前来自实务界的质疑提供了研究的基础。

如此,组织层面的研究可能为理解实务界的忧虑提供基础。例如,与传统的、独立于其他组织活动的会计理念相反,组织层面的研究更多地关注组织活动之间的交互影响(Ashiton,1976)。从后者的视角,一种活动干涉的后果取决于被清晰表达和动员的组织活动的主观意图和手段以外的因素。对会计来说,实际的效果取决于会计程序通过与其他组织活动及组织成员的目的和活动之间的交互影响,反映、分析从而影响现代组织各个层面的实际能力,其中不可避免地存在由推动一系列组织活动所引发的阻力。如此看问题的话,就至少有可能容纳组织生活中任何特定的干涉,可以是会计或其他形式的组织活动,部分甚至完全不能实现预期目标(甚至导致完全超出预期的结果),因为最终结果受最初的考虑理由之外的因素影响(Merton,1936;Boudon,1982)。正如 Hindess (1982,p.498)所述:

> 结果……可能与预期目标一致或不一致。导致这些结果的活动在一定的条件下发生,也面临一定的障碍,其中包括其他活动的影响。①

在这样的观点影响下,毫不奇怪地,人们开始关注会计实现或未能实现其所宣称目的的不同环境。充斥于会计教科书和专著的、与组织分离的学术观点被用来与会计和其他组织活动相关的方式,以及其他的组织控制方法的基本原理相比较。会计被与组织设计有关的问题相联系,考虑到它如何与生产、人事和财务管理等相互关联的活动一起发挥作用。最后,会计所面临的障碍也开始被调查,并被看作是决定会计实际应用的行为过程,这一过程发生于会计也被盘绕其中的组织内。但也必须看到,会计的组织观在实际应用中才刚刚起步。我们还非常需要进一步地反省和质询我们是否理解会计实现其结果的过程,这一结果应该是会计试图要实现也的确实现了的。

组织研究回顾

毫无疑问,对于会计的组织特性的兴趣还可以有许多其他的理性解释。更多的关注可以放在会计参与组织权力流行概念的构建和促进组织利益的方式;或者会计试图维护的组织秩序的特性以及会计如何在企业内部创造特定方式的经济和财务透明度;同样可以是对有助于决策的组织导向的会计的需要及如何构建能明确揭示组织功能不同方面的新组织会计系统。这些考虑至少有一部分被间接提及,更重要的是,会计的组织特性的讨论已经试图为会计的不同视角提供基础。尽管可能还是局部的,但它仍然勾画出了一个对会计感兴趣的各方来说都很重要的、需要进一步研究和探索的领域。而这也是本次会议的宗旨所在。

会议宣读的论文从不同的组织视角讨论了一系列的不同主题。与试图提供某一种组织观的努力不同,会议有意识地将目标确定为提供一个机会来提出

---

① Hindess(1982)进一步争论,"可靠的结果总是很难达到的,这是因为存在至少以下两方面的特定情形:其一,代理人的活动所采用的方法依赖于代理人所不能控制的条件;其二,这些方法的应用总是面临障碍,其中包括其他人的对抗性活动。一般来说,很难保障成功地克服这些障碍"(p.501)。他在结论中提出需要认真考虑"这些活动和冲突所发生及其结果所生成的特定环境"(p.509)。

和讨论如何分析及理解会计植根于其中的组织世界。

由 Johnson(1983)和 Flamholtz(1983)作为评论人,Tiessen and Waterhouse(1983)提出了理解会计发展过程的几点不同看法。在综合组织的社会观和经济观的基础上,他们为理解会计如何参与现代商业组织的构建提供了基础。通过这种参与,会计提供了一种使组织与更广泛的经济和社会利益,包括 D. Flaholtz 所注释的国家利益,相联系的方法。然而,尽管目的可能是相关的,但是 Johnson 和 Tiessen and Waterhouse 所采用的方法却极不相同。Johnson 为理解会计对现代商业企业出现的贡献提供了一种历史观。至少部分地,这样的历史观使我们能观察会计为企业组织形式所影响,以及反过来塑造企业组织形式的双重方面。与此相反,Tiessen and Waterhouse 采用了管理会计的权变观,试图理解会计如何被用来构建一个组织管理和组织外的利益寻求者之间的核算界面。通过采用组织合理性的经济概念,他们解释了会计如何通过将经济秩序的特定方面可视化而发挥作用。而另一方面,Johnson 提出最终的秩序既为会计所揭露,也为会计所创造。从这样一种观点出发,企业可以看作是导致内部可控领域产生的历史冲突及将管理活动如会计用于其维护和发展的产物。

Birnberg et al.(1983)、Flamholtz(1983)(和其评论者 Kerr,1983)、Boland and Pondy(1983)、Markus and Pfeffer(1983)及 Hayes(1983)着眼于会计是如何参与组织的运作过程的。这一组论文没有集中于某一固定的视角或主题,在一定程度上,因其多样性而值得重视。的确,Hayes 明确提出从不同方面理解会计现象的组织意义。然而,在多样化的表象下,一系列的主题凸现了。

从非常不同的角度,Flamholtz 和 Markus and Pfeffer 讨论了会计和组织权力基础的关系。在两者的论文中,不仅关系存在的事实,而且目前表达模式的合法性都是可以接受的。但在 Flamholtz 的论文中,会计对于调动强大的、以权力为基础的组织的贡献是被含蓄地接受的,这似乎也不称其为会计任务的问题。真正的挑战是如何形成充分的组织连接,使会计的潜能得以发挥。Markus and Pfeffer 似乎同意会计(与其他信息和控制系统)助长组织权力观念的方式,尽管没有评价,但明确讨论了权力层次的多重性、会计与权力行使的关联方式,以及设计和实施新的会计信息和控制系统的策略。所以尽管组织在一定程度上被看作"争论的岩层"(Edwards,1979),但表面上仍然存在这样的策略去促进会计对特定强大利益的实现的贡献。这样两篇论文都认为会计不能单纯从技术层面去理解,也都对组织如何才能凭技术来运作提出了建议。

会计目标的技术基础和组织基础之争也遍及其他论文。Birnberg 等将规定的会计目标和组织成就的一些方面进行了比较。Hayes 试图研究会计中的符号学、语言学和法学。Boland and Pondy 从理性和自然的角度进行了更直接的讨论,前者与传统讨论中的技术观相关,后者着重于会计如何起因于社会交互影响过程,两者都反映和创造了赋予组织意义和重要性的符号结构。Boland and Pondy 勾画出了两种非常不同的会计如何牵连于组织运行的看法,并试图论证这两种观点的有效性。他们有意识地要说明理性如何为自然性提供了框架,而自然性能为理性的出现和详细说明提供基础。如此,他们十分明确地聚焦于将两者并列所产生的争论,而争论会创造会计发展的基础并赋予其含义。

反思这样的讨论,Meyer(1983)和 Cooper(1983)提出了一些相关的更广泛的议题。Meyer 着眼于会计所创造的符号领地,这一领地对形成合法的、形式上一致的、为现代世界机构所需要的实体非常重要。尽管承认如此构架的理性领地只是松散地与组织的发展相联系,Meyer 仍然强调渗透于会计的抽象的虚拟对组织的决策制定和行为有极为真实的影响。这不仅仅是因为符号定义了真实,而且因为如此产生的真实能够且常常因符号而被改变。因为最初以松散形式出现的连接极有可能变成非常紧密的联系,Meyer 因而呼吁要更好地理解这一变化的过程,并重视这一过程所涉及的更广泛的社会和意识形态的因素。Cooper 也强调后一点。他也认为技术和理性可能以自然的形态出现,换句话说,一种表面看来是自然秩序的新形态可能是凭技术创造的。然而,Cooper 及越来越多的其他学者认识到这样的新组织秩序既不是毫无疑义的,也不是凭技术就能完全理解的。与 Meyer 一样,Cooper 强调认识技术更广泛的社会特性及其所参与创造的组织世界对会计研究是非常重要的。他要求我们比以往更有意识和更系统地分析过去特定的技术和理性的概念形成过程中所涉及的社会、制度和意识形态因素,以及它们对组织和社会运行的作用。

尽管大会的最后一组论文和上述讨论只有间接的联系,Mirvis and Lawler(1983)和 Mitroff and Mason(1983)的兴趣至少部分地是由于对结合于会计理论的理性观点和当今会计的组织后果不满。Mitroff and Mason 强调在日益复杂和不稳定的社会中信息及会计系统的设计者所面临的两难局面。不满于构架当今反映组织活动和业绩的会计系统的单一逻辑,他们呼吁在系统设计中更有意识地勘查作为组织特征的矛盾、压力和两难选择。但和 Mirvis and Lawler 一样,他们也承认新组织秩序会面临阻力。在 Mitroff and Mason 看来,这样的阻力来自文化、心理和社会方面,是对他们试图逐渐输入的不同理念的无理性反应。另一方面,Mirvis and Lawler 开始调查存在于旧组织秩序的弹性中的组织力量,而该旧组织秩序是最初的改革对象。Meyer and Cooper 也以此为基础提出了更广泛的质疑。

超乎想象地,提交"会计与组织"研讨会的论文对从组织角度分析会计现象进行了非常丰富的讨论。在以上的评注中,我仅仅以个人的判断强调了一些相同和相左的观点,以及其应用和趋势,势必挂一漏万。进行详细评估的任务只能留给读者自己。

出现的一些课题

研讨会的价值不仅仅在于正式准备并提交的论文,而且也在于因此引发的非正式讨论。本次会议也不例外。对会议讨论中提出的议题、忧虑、关注点及前景进行简要总结应该是有价值的。

变化中的会计

我们对会计是如何演变的以及可以用来改变会计的策略进行了大量讨论。毫无疑问,在Johnson(1983)和Flamholtz(1983)的历史观以及Tiessen and Waterhouse(1983)的社会—经济学方法的激发下,大会的讨论着重于会计的变化特性,涉及影响因素和实现方法两个方面。对于会计推陈出新的事实也有从未有过的共识。然而,我们也意识到对这一变化过程、变化所产生的影响及后果知之甚少。这不仅仅是因为我们已认识到的不恰当的会计基本原理,而且也因为在会计现象日益普遍深入的时候,我们总是强调按前因后果目前无法面对这些至关重要的问题。

传统的会计历史分析因为没有能力提出这样的问题而令人不满。就我们所知而言,它只是记录变化中的会计现象和所使用的技术,而不能了解引起变化的根本的社会、制度、经济和政治因素。的确,我们不得不承认,大量的会计历史的研究有意无意地采用了一种非理论的思维方式,忽视了在试图提供对会计的恰当的社会理解时所遇到的问题。会计的作用被视为相对确定的,且常常是现代的。会计发明在组织、市场(包括劳动力市场和资本市场)与政府关系中的并置没有受到重视。会计历史学家将他们自己与企业社会理论学家、企业状态和更近代的历史学中的理论发展割裂开来。

同样,对导致会计变化的主要因素的研究也不尽如人意。尽管权变理论对会计多样性提出了一定的解释,其相对静态和实用主义的假设同样被质疑。这一理论在面临组织和会计改变的动态性时显得束手无策。由于采用较窄的组织视角,权变理论在差异和变化的根本原因研究中限制了可能因素的范围。在研究会计如何从政治过程中产生进而推及组织而不是出于更理性的经济秩序的支配时,其采用的较单一的组织目的和业绩的概念预先排除了很多的可能性。

在批评过去的研究时,应该说,现今研究也不例外。在试图对会计变化的过程提供更恰当和更有说服力的解释时,与会代表也意识到概念上的和经验主义的困难。很明显,所涉及的问题属于社会科学的前沿课题。尽管意识到会计研究并不落后于其他社会科学学科,但如果会计学者能更多地了解组织的和社会的学术观点以及可以借鉴的其他理论,会计理论研究应该可以有更大的突破。研究视角的调整至少可以促进对会计系统和实务的产生及发展的更持续性的研究。这也许可以为会计改变的因素和过程的研究提供更丰富的实证基础。

会计多样性

会计的多样性也吸引了同样的注意,特别是就管理会计实践方面。不仅仅有大量应用中的技术(一位与会代表总结为"只要你叫得出名字,就一定有人在用它"),而且对将会计与其他信息和控制系统植根于组织运作过程的组织连接的多样性颇有研究。会计和控制部门的设置各不相同,不同组织层次的计划、预算和业绩控制程序取决于不同程度的参与,有不同的目标及其修订方法,甚至可以考虑不同时间周期。会计也有助于建立不同方式的组织分割和对不同方式的组织内互相依赖关系的管理。从这里及其他的研究可以看出,会计呈现的多样性似乎与充斥于会计教科书和指导会计改变及改革的手册的普遍印象不符。

再一次地,引起关注的是我们理解的不充分,不仅仅是对于这一多样性的根本原因,而且是这可能有也应该有的对于会计实践评价和改革的影响。

在这样的背景下,权变理论变得更为重要。在讨论会计的多样性时,至少会计行业的权变特征得以确认。不同的技术、环境、管理结构、企业文化和其他因素都被提及。但也认为不仅仅是从这个角度的研究没有取得其应有的进展,而且对于已经讨论过的权变方法所有的困难也没有给予足够的重视。一般认为,多重可能性引起的问题是重要的;现有权变理论的确定性特征引起关注;注意力集中在如何理解管理决策和任何被认为由组织环境所强加的约束之间的相互影响;也有呼声要求更直接地讨论会计的交互性影响特性,确认会计如何为所处的环境所影响,以及这一环境的某些方面如何反过来被会计自身影响。

更一般地,我们承认对会计多样性和会计改变的研究确实有潜能解决会计实务中的很多关键问题。关于会计与其所在环境之间的关系就是会计实务工作者和咨询人员非常关注的问题之一。通过剖析特定会计系统形成、运行和改变的过程,我们可以具体了解实务工作者必须应付的会计环境。

组织中存在的相匹敌的账目记录

虽然不是很明确,但是试图描述组织及其成果特征的多种多样的会计报告仍然引起注意。在个体层次上,每一个参与者都会对组织状态有自己的蓝图,描绘自己所了解的组织的意义、存在的问题和机遇,也会按自己的方式确认重要的组织边界、他们所认为的权力和影响的中心,以及那些应该也确实影响决策和行为的基本理念。即使在合乎经济原则的信息和管理系统领域,形形色色的账目记录也充满整个组织。工程和生产管理人员提供实物和技术记录;这一系统提供实物的数量、流量、质量、存量和业绩差异等信息,借此塑造和影响实际物流。人事、市场、财务和销售部门都以自己的记录影响组织。作为组织的参与者,会计人员也投注复杂的程序描述其试图管理和改变的组织世界、记录组织属性以及影响其他组织参与者的认识和社会行为。因此,会计账目仅仅是试图使组织的特定方面及应用于其上的约束可视和凸显的方式之一。不是作为一种孤立存在,会计处于一种与其他多种形式的账目共存的平衡状态,试图以特定的观点、秩序和使命影响以大量相匹敌的账目存在为特征的领域。

当如此看待会计时,将某一种特定的账目明文昭示为会计就会引起疑问。被质疑的问题包括多种账目之间的相互影响,可能会影响相对权力、结果及其关系的因素,而随着时间的推移,这种账目运用之间的关系也会影响组织决策和行为的方式。

迄今为止,会计研究方法都太过狭隘。会计职业人员所提供的经济和财务报告被赋予特别重要的意义。结果,一种特定的账目被接受为会计账目,当有理由使其他的利益特定化时(这在一个以日益增加的系统多元化和技术复杂化为特征的世界并不为怪),毫无疑问,接受的优先权和不合理的组织秩序相结合,不仅仅已经限制了对会计实务组织特征及会计本身所面临的问题的探索,而且,也许更为重要地,还阻碍了人们寻求被赋予如此重要意义的一种账目背后的组织和更广泛的社会因素——在现实世界和理论界都一样。一般认为对于这一系列问题的研究将有助于说明会计环境的某些关键方面、会计被期望扮演的角色及其执行和使用所形成的平衡。

组织秩序和无秩序之间的平衡

这样一种相匹敌的账目记录的观点使注意力集中于会计试图创造的组织秩序的不稳定特征。会计的详细描述和改变很少会是毫无问题的。更常见的是,组织参与者对于什么是重要的、什么是理想的已经有了自己的看法,并且受其他试图按照自己的意愿和目的改变组织的参与者的影响,这种看法常常被调整。因此,会计处于竞争之中,其结果要通过挑战占统治地位的、预先存在的组织秩序和目的来实现。因此,会计的特征不仅表现为被赋予的目的,而且表现为其所酿成的阻力。正是这样的阻力激发了行为研究并引起会计从业人员的关注和忧虑,会计从业人员已经对没有实现预定结果以及偏离最初设想而实现了的预定结果进行思考。

会计所处的组织世界存在着它寻求实现的秩序和因其运行而要面对的、一部分也是其引起的无秩序。这一观点的两个方面可以被简单地描述为组织行为的纵向和横向纬度。纵向地,会计要加强组织权力的概念。会计要创造一种局部的但有影响的可视性来帮助分权制度下的层级管理,自上而下地分解组织目标并监督实际业绩。如此,会计就是掌握于权力之手的工具。横向来看,会计是财务和经济意义上的行为指南,寻求可以以技术、市场和社会语言表达的组织愿景的可替换概念,或者作为将目标转换为经济语言的工具,这种转换一直处于修订过程中。会计的这两个纬度都旨在创造组织秩序的特定概念,而这一概念的两个方面总是相互竞争和挑战,虽然有效程度不同。

只是强调会计所寻求的秩序而不是其所处的环境会带来当前的危机,即行为会计学者只是揭露目前会计机制的缺点而走向改革,对会计所处的多样和竞争的组织政体认识不够。

也许听起来有点荒谬,但往往是那些会计已经成功地施加了其特定秩序影响的环境引起注意。然而,在为这种成就喝彩外,至少也有一些与会代表注意到可能导致的组织结果,这可能是更一般意义上的组织效率和会计来帮助加强的特定的权力政体。

另一引起关注的潜在问题来自在单一视角基础上试图引导和管理一个复杂而多样化的组织。这种忧虑部分反映了对官僚政治的僵硬化危险的注意,这种官僚政治可能来自导致特定组织可视性的、与会计相联系的常规化程序。此外,对会计所处的组织环境的讨论已经导致了对具有多样性的会计描述非常不同但又同样重要的内部和外部环境的需要的确认。近似于单一的信息系统被认为太狭隘,限制了可供组织成员选择的信息、选项,进而行动。因而需要一种更植根于组织的会计观,即会计应该是与其补充职能相称的而不是反应过度强烈的信息控制系统,从而可以满足于组织的有秩序和无秩序状态。

从会计的潜在能力角度,会计的单一组织秩序的观点也受到质疑。会计处于构建关于组织目标和成就的观念的中心。会计涉及组织愿景的详细说明和清晰表达,而不仅仅是站在中立立场反映影响到组织的约束和责任。既然如此,它就不能被看作是无私的。会计至少与特定的利益的表达有关,尽管这种关系因会计的自治特性、其所处环境的复杂的制度结构和影响其运作和程序的代理者的多样化而有所缓和。依据这一观点,对会计的质疑使利益审查成为必要,同时也必须考虑会计目标实现的效力,以及在其他的利益主体质疑或利用会计时应对的策略。

诉诸成为会计基础的对于组织成就和政治体制的看法,秩序和无秩序的概念不再被看作无疑义的。尽管它们可能有区别,但已确认两者对会计查询都没有什么影响。

会计的反映和创建功能

迄今为止,会计的组织研究都强调会计系统反映其所处环境的其他方面的方式。如已经讨论的,主要的关注点包括技术和市场对会计的影响、组织结构和会计系统设计及使用的关系,最初的兴趣见于关于文化对会计和其他控制系统的影响的研究。如此,会计已经明显是作为一种权变现象,根据组织环境的其他重要特征而设计和使用。

尽管目前处理权变关系的理论和实证研究技巧的适当性引起关注,但是对于彼此依赖的会计的一般观点并没有争论。然而在大会上,这一观点被认为有失偏颇,因为尽管会计在描述组织的管理、作业和外部环境方面起重要作用,但是它也有能力主动塑造和影响组织。

组织环境可以用会计术语表达,如"有利可图"或"损失惨重","现金牛"或"上升的明星"。相类似地,影响会计的组织结构也不会完全独立于会计反映。分权管理的组织模式按成本中心、利润中心和投资中心来定义;组织单位同样有会计和管理边界;监督下属单位业绩的会计机制使反映在组织结构图中的权力潜能得以发挥。同样,会计不仅反映组织运行,而且表达并影响有组织的活动的预定目标。利润的有效定义是一种强有力的观念,然而,其他概念的潜能也必须给予重视,如现金、营运资本、资产、成本。这些说明了会计在那些方面对经济事项提供了实用而有效的、抽象的概念。

通过上述各种方式,会计对组织概念的形成起到了积极的作用。除了反映组织的限定因素,会计在包括自身在内的组织构架中,以及形成对有组织的活动的限定因素和其为之努力的目标起到了更为积极的作用。换句话说,会计的反映和创建职能之间有着复杂的、相互影响的关系[①],前者形成会计对自己置身其中的组织的依赖,而后者凭会计的可能性和潜在性形成对组织的约束。

---

① 有关会计的反映和创建职能的进一步讨论,参见 Burchell *et al.* 即将发表的文章。

置于社会与组织环境中的会计研究

内部会计的外部起源

这次会议着重于会计的组织特性,其目标是为了解会计是如何与组织运行的其他方面紧密地联系在一起的提供基础。

然而,在会议早期,这只是目标之一。正像会计不可能离开组织,组织也不可能离开其置身其中的社会环境而独立存在。因此,会计越来越被认为是取决于特定组织及组织运行其中的社会环境的影响的一种现象。

组织对会计的影响大多被看作是社会影响、压力和张力的表现形式。例如,政府为有助于其目标的实现,就要不断地为企业的详细核算提供基础。其控制价格和工资的策略会导致定义、审查、限制和计划这些在国家层次上有宏观意义的事项的会计程序的加强。凭借经济危机和增长的名义,政府试图在组织和选民中增强其政治体制的经济意识,如劳动力流动就被认为与此有关。考虑到经济的效率和效力概念(最近被称为"value for money"),政府不断地努力改革其自身的行政管理体制和那些在国民经济中起重要作用的组织的管理。

更广泛的社会机构,包括政府机构、媒体和会计职业组织,都可以在建立会计的现行技术状态和合法的、有序的管理惯例中起更重要的作用。关于什么是当前的、什么是现代的、什么是理想的和什么是可实现的,因来自特定组织的历史和特殊需要的一定程度上的自治,可能有不同的理解。职业化的会计,可能实现且的确已经实现了一定程度上的独立。答案可能反过来寻求问题,会计本身也可能影响组织。同样重要地,试图对来自环境的压力做出反应的组织也可能凭借被赋予的外部合法性,而不是依据预定的内部结果,来利用特别的会计和管理活动。因着社会的和组织的原因,一个理性的管理体制可能会将内部程序和活动与外部导向的活动区分开来。所以尽管为社会所影响,但组织仍然处于与社会的融合状态。

组织内部的张力和冲突也不可能与社会运动分离开来。特定组织的管理人性化很少独立于为其提供语言基础和目的的社会运动而存在。强调会计的社会特征是试图按不同条件构建组织的一种表现。同样,会计寻求在组织内推动特定的层级管理的方式也不能脱离不同社会团体的冲突来理解。这样,会计既反映了其所处的环境,也使其能按固有的方式运行。只有某些东西可以说是昂贵的。特别被强调的是时间概念。已经被包括在会计考虑中的效益不能离开与其相联系的社会—经济构架而实现。换句话说,会计在社会和组织的融合中起到了重要的作用,因而不能被作为纯粹的组织活动看待。

在一个致力于探索会计的组织特性的研讨会中得出这样的结论是荒谬的。然而,这反映了我们这个社会的高度相互依赖的特性,以及会计融入日常生活的复杂方式。社会不是也不能独立于组织。事实上,社会至少部分地在组织中得以表现,而反过来,组织又成为社会的重要组成部分。将组织和社会看作两个交集也许会有帮助,更广泛和更局部化的考虑需要会计来形成一个具有多重性但有限定范围的真实的概念。

会计研究的方法

会议认为实证研究的缺乏是一个主要的约束。我们不断提到必须承认对会计了解之少。

组织学的同事认为会计研究者应该是应用社会科学家,致力于探索实践中会计的复杂性。他们认为行为学和组织学的研究应该已经导致了对会计与组织的联系方式的清楚的认识。的确,会计与组织、战略和社会的关系已经得以说明。但这种期望并不能成为现实。简单的事实是会计研究倾向于将其本身与实践中的会计,如果不是会计实践的话,分离开来。绝大多数的研究致力于加强会计技术,而不是探索会计与组织紧密联系及其占有现在的重要地位的方式。

很明显,如果会计研究者要能促进我们对会计的了解的话,不同的研究方法是必需的。对会计系统设计和应用的有理论深度的研究是迫切需要的,更需要对会计反映、加强或约束特定组织的战略态度的方式的研究,以及会计与保证目标一致、垂直负责的组织之间的联系方式的研究。会计改变的研究也可以在很大程度上有助于了解影响会计的内外部的多元化力量。这样的研究也可能帮助我们认识到会计中随处可见的多重性在沟通不同但不是相互冲突的迫使会计改变的压力中所起的积极作用。

所有这些问题的研究要求一种承诺——承诺与会计所处的环境相联系去研究、分析和解释会计,这是目前的会计研究中所缺乏的。这方面做得很少的事实说明改变的不易。对组织的实证研究的约束是实实在在存在的。目前,会计研究者缺乏接近的途径和缺乏经验是主要的因素。但更重要的因素也许是鼓励研究速度和数量的学术奖励机制、给予实证研究的非常低的甚至是荒谬的正统性,以及许多会计学术研究人员对研究的低投入。遗憾的是,这些约束因素仍然非常真实地存在,因而改变不会在即日出现。示范是必经之路。我们只能希望慢慢地,但肯定地,有愿意冒险的研究者作为先例来探索当今会计环境背后的真实。

结论

组织研究是会计研究的新领域。尽管会计拥有组织合理性,但是我们对其运作环境中影响会计系统的因素仍然知之甚少。

回顾迄今为止的对会计的组织研究,很明显它受研究范围的限制,是不连贯的,基本上是非理论的。最初的关注总是值得肯定的,但仍然限于揭露会计的过失和寻求改革现行实践的基础。尽管这样的研究也许是有益的,但危险的是,如果在性质上太不连贯,就可能使关于会计的组织基础的谜团长久存在,甚至激励其存在。这里需要的是能有助于理解和解释会计活动的大量的调研。然而这样的研究至今仍被忽略。

不过,这里收集的研究成果显示了对会计的组织特征的研究兴趣的出现。最早的起源是多元的、有跨度的经济学、组织理论和社会学。常常是非会计人员起领导作用。例如,经济学家开始探索会计在现代组织形式形成中的作用及其和外部代理人的关系。组织理论学家最近开始对信息和控制问题感兴趣,正在探索不仅仅是会计被假定所具有的职能而且包括与会计交互影响的组织的象征意义和政治因素。社会学家也认识到会计所提供的研究潜能,开始探讨会计如何在现代社会中提供精细的核算,其为有助于企业组织控制的新的可视性提供强大的核算工具的方式,以及会计职能的合法化。

这些讨论大多被收集于此。这是一个方兴未艾的研究领域。这些论文(和相关的评论)对当前的研究提供了有用的见解,提出的未来的研究领域对进一步的研究也是非常有益的。

参考文献①

(李苹莉　译)

---

① 参见本文英文参考文献。

会计在组织和社会中的作用[*]

摘要：本文依据实务中的会计功能，试图对比分析人们所声称的各种会计作用。首先讨论分析了与会计实务相关联的各种基础理论的背景，以及有关会计作用的各种代表说法的理由是否充分。之后，讨论了会计是如何与组织和社会实践相互交融的。最后，本文总结了会计研究的延伸含义。

在服务于现代工业社会的进程中，会计所占据的地位越来越重要。会计发端于财产、交易及公司萌芽期时的各种管理实践（Chatfield，1977），如今已成为现代组织和社会管理的重要组成部分。无论是在私有性质还是在公众性质的组织中，会计都已不再只是单纯地局限于财务资源管理，它还与特定的组织模式的形成（Becker and Neuheuser，1975）、组织的具体构架和管理结构设置（Chandler and Daems，1979），以及组织内生成或强化某些权力及影响力的特定方式（Bariff and Galbraith，1978；Heydebrand，1977），有着千丝万缕的关系。随着各种主流经济论调对会计作用以及组织功能在会计框架中内置的首肯，会计的重要性已经在组织成员中达成共识。从整个社会的层面来看，会计的作用并不局限于过去各式不同甚至变化着的组织领域，而且对整个现代化国家的兴起也至关重要。那些由组织中的会计系统所提供的经济数据信息，不仅被作为政府征税的依据，还被作为更广泛的国家经济管理政策的重要手段（Hopwood, et al. ,1979；Kendrick,1970；Studentski,1958）。如今，会计信息被政府用于制定和实施各项政策，如经济稳定政策、价格和工资调控、产业和贸易领域的特定规则，以及在不同时期（战争或和平、繁荣或萧条）整个国家的经济资源规划与管理。事实上，在推动经济发展、提高社会效率的同时（Bowe，1977；Haber，1964；Hays,1959；Searle,1971），政府也在作为一个积极的推动者，推动着会计系统在工商业的持续发展（Hopwood et al. ,1979），并将会计系统引入社会的其他领域中（Gandhi,1976）。

会计向其他领域的延伸对会计理论和实务的发展有着重要的意义。正如

---

[*] 本文的写作得到了 Anglo-German 基金会（为推动工业社会的研究而设立）以及 Management Education 基金会的大力支持，在此向它们表达我们最诚挚的谢意。

置于社会与组织环境中的会计研究

许多管理学家所言(Anthony,1965),会计已不再只是为了评估单个经济体而进行数据搜集的工具。尽管成本和利润在会计程序中的分量仍然很重,但现代企业的增长,使企业所涵盖的组织形式多种多样,包括职能式的协调与集权型组织(Litterer,1961,1963)、事业部式的组织(Johnson,1978)以及现时的矩阵式和项目式的组织(Ansari,1979;Chapman,1973;Sayles and Chandler,1971)。与此同时,资本市场、政府机构以及会计职业组织对财务信息需求的不断提高,要求财务报告和信息披露更加全面和准确(Benston,1976;Hawkins,1963)。因此,需要解决的会计问题变得更为具体、简明且相互关联,人们不仅需要解决当前实务所带来的新问题,而且要求阐释那些一直以来都含糊不清的老问题。

正是由于会计的不断发展,会计在当今组织和社会中赢得了其重大的影响力。会计不再仅仅是一堆枯燥数字的集合,还作为一套有机结合的作用机制,为经济和社会管理服务。但会计为何有如此重要的作用?会计为何变得如此复杂且极具影响力?会计在发展过程中面临着怎样的压力?会计在组织和社会中究竟扮演着怎样的角色?为什么?上述所有问题都需要我们去探索和思考。尽管我们在会计技术、技能等的研究和描述上,已经投入了大量的时间和精力,但我们对会计自身存在和发展方面的基础理论的研究,还远远不够。但愿如人所愿,本文试图对这些未知的领域进行初步探讨。鉴于之前关于这方面的研究太少,我们的研究结论最多也只是一个初步的。不过我们相信,开始着手对这些过去不曾讨论的,甚至在以前可能是一些想当然的问题展开讨论,至少是非常重要的。

本文首先讨论我们现已知晓的会计发展中的两大趋势:会计行业的日益制度化(institutionalization)和会计知识的不断抽象化或客观化(abstraction or objectification)。在此基础上,为了详细表述会计在组织和社会中的作用这一基础理论,我们将进一步考察会计发展所面临的这样或那样的压力,以及这些压力是如何促使人们加强对这一基础理论问题的研究的。在讨论一些至少已达成共识的会计作用之后,我们试图透过我们的观察和利用已有的学术成果,来分析这些会计作用的提出理由是否充分,并说明这些研究的目的是如何内化于行动之中,而不是作为会计行业本身的基础的。为强化这些观点,我们还分析并考虑了会计在组织和社会中所扮演多种角色的多种特定因素,本文最后讨论我们的观点在未来会计研究的延伸含义。

制度化、抽象化以及对基础理论的探讨

会计行业可能有多种发展趋势。它可能是指会计在某些知识和实务新领

域的最新发展,也可能是指会计影响力的某些变革。或者是,人们也可能强调会计在组织与社会层面已取得的最新进展,以及会计自身组织的变革。基于本文的讨论,我们指出会计发展的两大趋势,即会计行业的制度化和会计知识的抽象化。① 这两大趋势对于更好地理解会计现状和会计作用(它所产生的作用及人们对其作用的诉求),都具有重要意义。不仅如此,这些趋势还引发了人们对会计的思考与争议,引发了着手进行会计变革,并引入了组织内会计职位的设置方式的讨论,这些组织内的会计职位为会计从业者们提供了就业机会,拓展了组织对会计领域的需求,并推动了会计理论与实务的向前发展。

无论是从组织层面来说还是从整个社会的角度来看,都要求会计行业的制度化。在商业组织和政府部门内,随着会计渗入各种组织实践,簿记(bookkeeping)转化成了会计这一新形式,并发挥着极为重要的影响力(Garner,1954;Pollard,1965)。组织内的多项活动,包括预算管理和标准成本核算、部门细分和管理控制、计划与资源分配体系等,使得会计人员作为管理团队中的一员,日益受到尊重。在这种情形下,产生了独立的会计部门,录用了专家型会计人员,会计系统也走向了规范化、标准化和制度化,会计与其他管理实践间的联系也相应建立起来。不仅如此,随着对外财务报告与对内信息报告的逐步分离,以及与公司流动性管理和财务结构管理的分离,会计自身也处于持续不断的改进之中。

会计的发展推动了组织的发展,而组织的发展又加速了会计行业的职业化。会计职业组织自诞生之日起,就充当了政府机构和企业间相互交汇的桥梁。在欧洲大陆,会计师就高度介入了早期商法的制定与管理(ten Have, 1976),而在英格兰和威尔士,会计职业组织最初形成的理由主要来自会计自身职能的延伸,这些延伸职能是由一些成功公司实践和破产法规等所带来的,政府所颁布的这些破产规则条例主要针对诸如铁路、建筑业和市政公共事业等行业部门(Brown,1905;Chatfield,1977;Edey and Panitpakdi,1956;Littleton,1933)。美国的情形是,会计职业在其早期并没有受到政府的管制,不过之后随着政府

---

① Popper,Kuhn and Foucault 对制度化、客观化和抽象化之间的区别做了一些描述。Popper(1972)将客观知识(如那些保存在图书馆或电脑里的期刊、杂志及著作中所记录的各方面知识)描述为"第三层级",将自主意识、观念描述为"第二层级",将自然世界描述为"第一层级"。Hacking(1975)也有过类似的描述。Kuhn(1970)将它们区分为"类型一"和"类型二"。前者主要包括那些逻辑性的、概念化的以及其他各方面的科学知识,而后者主要指这些知识存在的社会和制度条件。Foucault(1977)将它们分为"知识"和"权力"两个方面,他将权力定义为"社会关系的复杂性—社会制度",并认为知识存在于权力之中。

干预的加深,会计职业得以繁荣起来(Chatfield,1977)。事实上,无论是在美国还是在英国,随着会计职业团体的建立,很多会计领域的制度创新应运而生,这些制度创新都是在会计与政府管制机构间的相互交融中产生的。因此,至少在早期,美国证券交易委员会(SEC)对会计领域的管制相当少,从而使得会计职业界投入大量精力致力于对财务会计实践的阐释、标准化和规则化,而所有这些都是通过职业机构的制度演变而得来的,从最初的会计原则委员会(APB)到后来的财务会计准则委员会(FASB)。随后不久英国也出现了类似的情况,会计准则指导委员会(ASSC)在政府压力和专业机构要求保持其制定会计规则权力的呼声中诞生了,它推动了会计行业的发展。然而在其他地方,会计的制度化则是国家行为的一种直接结果。例如,在战前的德国,为了服务于战时的国民经济,政府采取法律强制和制度规范方式来使企业会计实现标准化(Singer, 1943);而在法国,这些创新则始于战后,政府机构需要利用会计所提供的信息进行微观经济计划。

会计职业制度化发展的模式对会计本身来讲是很重要的。为使会计能更好地发挥作用,以及使人们能更好地理解会计的角色,我们更感兴趣的是这一制度化发展模式的延伸含义。首先,会计的出现以及它在组织中极富影响的专业性,使得会计实践在组织中享有了一定的自主权。随着会计部门的出现及各地会计专业精英(Gouldner,1957)的录用,在组织中,会计系统的发展与管理、会计职能的扩展相互交融在一起。至少从存在的事实上,会计在其发展中还被当作组织中的"垃圾罐"(garbage can)角色(Cohen et al., 1972)。会计师们应当在组织内寻找拓展其领域的机会,而不仅仅只是为了满足先验式的组织需要。随着会计师们阐释会计系统的潜能,并建立起会计与组织内其他部门间,特别是与生产管理间的紧密联系,当下的会计担纲了更多的角色。其次,职业机构和职业团体的出现,推动了会计实务的标准化和规则化,它为会计业界的各种问题争议提供了讨论平台,从而引发会计实务的变革。财务会计的发展已不再是企业与资本市场机构,甚至企业与国家间直接相互作用的一种必然结果,会计改革的压力还可能来自会计职业机构、与会计实务规则制定相关的专业团体、大型合伙制会计师事务所、政府的利益相关部门以及其他的商业组织与团体。由于会计改革的压力可能更多地来自各个不同的机构或组织,而不是会计自身职能所涉及的新的实务问题,因此,在这种情形下,为会计实务中的会计进行角色定位就变得更加困难。再次,变革中的制度结构为会计知识的独立积累创造了新的空间。① 在这些职业团体的帮助下,会计程序以图示或手册指南的方式被规则化,同时伴随着在培训、资格考试及制定规则等方面的兴趣,这些职业团体还进一步为会计研究与讨论提供了刺激和动力,从而有可能将会计研究从会计实务技能中分离出来。此外,政府对企业会计的关注也越来越多,这也导致了会计信息披露制度方面的规范化,并着手于会计标准化。Chatfield (1977,p.121)认为:

> 为核实由实业公司和所有权缺失而出现的资本、利润和资产中的会计问题,审计师们不得不对现有的各种实务进行经验推断,并最终将他们对会计实务的恰当处理方法理念化为会计准则。透过对财务报表的详细审计,最终有利于簿记技术自身的逻辑化,这些详细审计不仅需要通过内部控制程序,而且更需要直接通过对交易事项的提炼分析、科目的分类及财务报表披露的规则来进行。英国的社会环境催生了审计服务业,并培育出了一批比过去素质更高的会计师。通过对会计实务中的习惯做法的分析,审计师们给会计理论带来了一些早期实务运用的阐释。此外,为了推进会计实务的标准化,英国议会还将会计理论中的一部分以规则的方式写进了公司法中。

通过这些方式,会计成了组织和社会实践中的一种可辨认的作用形式(identifiable form),它可以被阐释并规则化,可以被争论并接受挑战,并最终进行变革。会计讨论的热点可能会受到来自实务中所遇到的各种不同冲击的影响,而那些与会计行业并不存在必然联系的其他思想体系,也可能会影响会计思想的发展,通常它们远离会计实务。比如,会计思想可能与经济学(Baxter,1978)、生产工程学(Wells,1978)和科学管理运动(Epstein,1973)等产生相互作用。这种发散式的思想交融过程,为会计变革奠定了坚实的基础,这一过程既可以透过实践的直接应用来实现,也可以通过下述各方对会计所施加的影响来达成,即政府、与会计行业标准化有关的职业组织与团体、独立评论家和分析师们。

---

① 会计制度化与会计知识发展之间的关系相当复杂,尤其是当人们认为制度已不再像知识那样零零碎碎的时候。比如,一个职业,必然牵涉到大量的管制、部门分类、程序、行业标准以及法律法规等。因此,对于上述两者间的区别和关系的分析,需要认真深入并格外小心。Popper(1972)和 Foucault(1977)曾用不同的方式对两者间的关系进行过描述。他们通过对"抽象化"(abstractions)、"类型 1"或依据"制度"(institutions)所得到的"知识"、"类型 2"或"权力"之间关系的描述,来说明制度化与知识间的关系。我们不是争论制度导致抽象化,或者相反,而是更倾向于去发现两者间的结合点。比如,正规化会计知识(formalized accounting knowledge)可被看作是会计职业化成为可能的前提条件,而会计的职业化又因此而推动了会计知识的发展与完善。

会计制度化和抽象化还为人们寻求正式定义会计的角色提供了基础。正如人们在其他领域所努力寻求的一样（Hacking, 1975; Popper, 1972），一种抽象和客观的思想的存在,激发起人们对该思想本质和理论基础的探究。① 就像到底什么是会计以及会计所起的作用是什么等问题,都已开始进入人们的研究范畴。随着会计行业变得越来越重要,以及在制度化进程中各种问题的日益复杂化,这些问题都可能与会计实务、会计管制及发展等诸多相关因素有着某种特殊的关联。

如果会计变革的根源不是来自新的会计实务冲击,那我们就没有理由指望那些业已存在的合理的会计基础理论,能够为它在会计实务中的公开应用提供有益的指导。从社会的角度看,任何公众行为要么需要通过强有力的政治手段来推行（Moonitz, 1974）,要么需要通过更广泛的社会影响力和法制化来引导（Posner, 1974）。对于后一种情况而言,公众行为需要被视为由一些可期待的、可接受的社会目标来引导的行为。换句话说,公众行为需要一个表述清楚的公共原则（Watts and Zimmerman, 1979）——一种对所体现的目标和意图的正式表述。

当然,政府是在经管责任（accountability）和提高组织与社会效率的名义下,对会计采取行动的（Searle, 1971）。会计职业团体及那些关注会计规则的其他机构,也采取了类似的态度,不过这些团体与机构更强调会计在为股东投资决策提供有用信息上的重要角色。而且这些组织内的会计实务,更趋于关注会计是否与提高组织效率、维持组织控制等管理事务相关。

这些作用不仅仅是对会计实务的解释,会计角色的产生可能远离会计实务,它们通常受各种不同制度背景和不同思想体系的左右,进而为会计实务变革提供基础。在会计的天然职能方面,会计作用与会计实务间的关系只能是间接的。

会计的天然职能

我们都非常熟悉会计所声称的作用,它们大多散见于会计教科书、职业声明以及与会计行业监管的发展相关的各种条文陈述中。就像古老格言开场白中所诉求的天使般的道义和权威一样（Yamey, 1974）,会计所声称的这些作用,试图为会计的使命（accounting mission）提供一种更为世俗化的解释基础。在这样的背景下,人们认为会计有一个本质（essence）,即存在一个功能式、内在天然

---

① 在某些方面,对会计理论和实务的详细表述就是对会计所扮演角色的解释。

的核心。① 这一本质即表述为下述一系列内容:"为决策提供相关信息"、实现"资源的合理配置"、保持制度的"经管责任"和"受托责任"(stewardship)等,而且我们大家都被说服而相信了这样的表述。会计的这些功能属性被认为是会计努力尽责(accounting endeavor)的基础,在证实会计行业存在的合理性方面,这些论调为会计的继续发展提供了理论依据。

在会计的职责定位上,另一些学者提出了完全不同的观点,他们认为会计系统是社会和组织的影像(mirrors)。在社会层面上,会计被认为是对组织所处的社会关系的根本反映。封建社会有封建社会的会计制度,资本主义社会有资本主义的会计模式(Ross,1977),后工业化时代需要新的会计框架(Gandhi,1976)。而将这种想法移植到组织层面,则是近期的事,它深受近代组织行为中权变学派思想的影响(Bruns and Waterhouse,1975;Hopwood,1974;Sathe,1975;Waterhouse and Tiessen,1978;Watson,1975)。此外,也有人认为会计系统是下述一系列综合特征的产物,如:组织的复杂性、组织环境的不健全和不确定性等(Galbraith,1973;Khandwalla,1972),企业的技术进步因素(Daft and Macintosh,1978),公司管理的战略(Chandler,1962)等。尽管支持这些会计规范理论的证据并不存在或并不可靠(Hopwood,1978),但却难以阻止这些理论的日趋普及和影响力的扩大。然而,他们大多在这一点,即能否在会计与想象中组织和社会决定因素之间建立起某种基础性机制关系这一点上保持沉默,而保持沉默这一事实是因为他们从来就不认为这是一个问题,特别是对那些希望会计发生必要的变革,同时也期待着对会计进行精心设计的人而言。此外,许多组织理论的有效性都是建立在一系列假设基础之上的,即假设那些权变性设计会进一步促成组织取得更高的管理秩序,进而促进明确的、前后一贯的、高度认同的组织,实现其目标,而这一目标部分地由各种不同的会计系统来完成,就像其所声称和解释的那样(Pfeffer,1978)。

然而,我们选择将重点放在它们的某些特征上,而不是试图将重点放在对会计的特定解释,或者更一般意义上的规范性阐释上。

设定中的会计职能是要为会计思想提供一个规范性框架。通过对会计使命的表述,它们为诸如会计是什么、会计应该做什么等问题提供了一种说法。而且正是基于这一点,它们也促进了对会计实务的评价。以会计正在发挥的作

---

① 在对会计作用这一基础理论进行探索的进程中,取得进展的是 Littleton(1953,p.18)。他认为:必定存在一些基本概念,通过这些概念能使会计有别于所有其他的数量分析方法;必定存在某些核心观点,这些观点在表达会计的特征上比其他概念如目标(objective)、效果(effects)、结果(results)、目的(ends)、宗旨(aims)等要更贴切,即所谓的"内核"(centre of gravity)。

用为名,人们对会计提出了很多挑战,并促使其产生变革。为提升"公司经管责任"并有助于"理性决策",人们试图扩展会计的领域。也有人指出,社会的变化必然使会计实务受到挑战(Gilling,1976)。然而,一旦承认会计的天然职责和会计实务之间确实存在着模棱两可的关系,那么,会计的天然职责就被当作鉴别与会计实务间差异的一种工具,在此基础上,会计的天然职责还被用来纠正我们所看到的会计实务中出现的各种偏差。

事实上,很多有关会计职责所声称的观点正在偏离会计实务。这些观点由职业团体、会计行业规则的制定机构、政府机构以及有重要影响的学术界提出,学术界经常对相关机构施压,并表达了对会计进行立法的要求,进而指导会计实务的愿望。在特定制度的需求和组织行为下,会计天然职责的观点试图为会计使命提供更为具体的解释。尤其是将会计定位于公共作用(public roles)的学术界,它们通常要反映其他团体组织的管理思想和管理实务对会计的影响,并将会计定位于与其他管理思想相互交织的自主知识体(an autonomous body of knowledge)。在这方面,惯用的经济学论调和管理学理论对会计的影响尤为重要。

事实上,人们应当记住,依据会计能够促进经济效率和增强决策理性等,人们并不能导出会计存在的本源逻辑。这不仅因为这些基础理论从概念上难以定义(Winston and Hall,1959),而且因为这些基础理论其实就是会计实践的结果,是这些会计实践自身为预先设定经济目的提供对实务的理解,尽管这些会计实践被假定是服务于这些经济目的的。① 在这里,会计理论和经济学理论之间存在何种关系,其实来自那些会计学、管理学以及经济学理论家们的讨论,他们致力于分析和指导会计工作,并没有从这两种学科的知识与实务体系中所预先设定的基本属性上去探究问题的本质。

最后值得注意的是,尽管人们普遍认为会计职能可被用于鉴别会计实务所出现的偏差和错误,但是当人们面对会计实务中所出现的各种歧义时,却很少有人对这些所声称的会计职能提出质疑。这些源自不同社会背景的会计职能,已经变得过于绝对化。作为世俗化的会计使命的捍卫者,这些会计职能似乎已对各种质疑漠然视之,而且很少直面会计实务的冲击。

因此,我们可以暂且得出结论:会计的职能应能告诉我们人们是如何看待会计的,会计理论的影响因素是什么,以及人们寻求影响会计的基础是什么。会计职能改变着会计实务,而且毫无疑问的是,会计职能也受到会计实务的影

---

① 后者正是 20 世纪之初,企业界在大行效率和科学管理运动之风时所倡导的特定情形(Haber,1964;Hayes,1959;Searle,1971)。

响。但这并不是说,会计职能就是对会计实务的描述。正如 Argyris and Schon (1974) 所指出的那样,信奉某种理论与运用某种理论,其实是两回事。我们至多可以说,会计职能和会计实务之间可能存在某种相当模糊的关系。

会计实务的复杂性

然而,在最近我们已经看到了这样一种苗头,即人们对会计使命的各种提法已开始进行再评价和反思了。来自学术界调查和实务界质疑的双重压力,促使观察家们开始认识到会计在具体操作中的复杂性,并在此基础上,开始对过去从不被认为是问题的问题提出质疑,对以前认为理所当然的观点进行反思。基于不同原因和不同基础,这一趋势在财务会计和管理会计领域都表现得十分明显。

会计研究中一个持久并极具影响力的分支,是研究会计数据对资本市场的影响(Dyckman,Downes and Magee,1975)。这类研究为我们重新审视会计的实际功能提供了一个新的基础。研究发现,投资者并不必然将会计数据当作他们股票的面值,在公司年报正式披露前,公司年报中很多的信息含量和账户数据都已经反映在股票价格中了(Ball and Brown,1968),这一发现突出说明了确实存在着一个有关公司业绩的高度竞争的信息市场,而在这一信息市场中,会计报告仅仅是其中的一部分。投资者会评价、质疑、证实信息,他们并不单纯是被动的信息接受者,他们为进行决策而判别信息的重要程度,并使用他们各自的相关性标准。现在,人们还着手进行会计信息的多元化利益(multiplicity of interests)方面的研究,它并不仅限于投资者这一团体,还包括其他更多的领域。沿袭并基于信息经济学的研究概念,将决策相关性概念真正用起来,并将其真正用于实际决策情形之前的信息筛选,这即使不是不可能,也是非常有难度的(Demski,1973)。正如有关投资者行为的实证研究所说明的,信息相关性更多地取决于其所使用时的具体状态,而并不是如我们所预见的那样,受人为决定的信息格式的影响。

在何种情况下,究竟什么因素会影响所提供(如果不是使用)会计信息的性质呢?遗憾的是,在单一企业层面上,对这一方面的认识少得可怜。当人们在考虑信息披露方式是如何卷入代理关系的形成和运行中时,这一论点还有待实证研究来检验。一系列观察为我们提供了制度层面而非企业层面的影响力的片面评价,而这些观察是基于会计政策管制的,在这一点上,Moonitz(1974)和 Horngren(1973)都已经为我们提供了他们的真知灼见,他们特别强调这一过程的政治因素。会计规则的技术成分被置于一个复杂的制度性和其他影响因素的模型中讨论,作为一种补充,通过寻求制度性和政治性支持来探寻会计技术性问题的解决之道。肇始于这些研究,人们现在已经对了解这些问题的基础逐渐达成共识,即在处理会计涉及的各方利益时决定、相互关联的基础是什么(Watts and Zimmerman,1978,1979)。例如,现在已经在讨论这样一个问题,即源于公司过去经营情况的会计系统所形成的会计利益是如何影响公司未来的(Zeff,1978)。随着资本市场不再被认为是唯一最重要的会计数据使用者,更多的研究重点被放在政府机构所扮演的角色上。

财务会计与报告越来越被认为是各种未被认知的复杂制度演变的产物(Burchell et al.,待发表)。目前,更多的观点认为,会计职责是各种压力作用的结果,是这些压力而不是会计使命的本质,促进了会计的创新和变革。

会计行业出现的另一个类似问题也慢慢呈现出来,这一问题源于组织及行为层面的有关管理会计系统的作用。一些学者已经质疑会计信息在组织中的利用程度(Mintzberg,1973,1975),其他学者则指出会计信息的作用更多是象征性的,而不是技术意义上的(Gambling,1977;Meyer and Roman,1978),另外一些学者则强调在特定组织环境中会计系统的作用方式(Cammann,1976;Hopwood,1973;Otley,1978;Rahman and McCosh,1976)。与其说会计系统的作用后果仅仅是由它们的存在所决定的,还不如说这些作用源于组织过程,这些组织过程赋予会计作用更独特的含义和更重要的影响力(Pettigrew,1973,1975)。相关研究已经涉及管理风格和管理哲学(Argyris,1977;Hedberg and Mumford,1975;Hopwood,1973)、组织的规范化环境(Otley,1978)、权力和影响力结构(Argyris,1971;Pettigrew,1973,1977)、信息传播的组织机制(Shortell and Brown,1976)、外部压力和各种限制(Meyer and Rowan,1978;Olofsson and Svalander,1975)等各种因素对会计作用的影响。其他的一些研究者更多关注会计系统是如何来自又是如何服务于我们已知的组织构造中的各种微观政治程序的(micropolitical processes)(Pfeffer,1978)。例如,Wildavsky(1965,1978)生动地呈现了在会计实务中,各种微观政治程序是如何影响和作用于复杂的预算系统的。同样详尽的描述还有 Pfeffer and Salancik(1974)和 Dalton(1959)等学者的论述,他们认为,组织的资源配置是预算和计划系统与政治程序体系相互交融的产物,在资本预算程序中 Bower(1970)也得出了类似的结论。

组织研究已开始对会计系统和有效组织业绩之间存在着相关关系(随意性很强的正相关关系)这一自然推论(automatic presumptions)提出强烈的质疑,这一推论式的假定或暗或明地使会计教材增色不少,并且美化了会计从业人员和咨询师们。虽然我们已渐渐地对这一争论有所淡忘,其实早在十年前 Ackoff(1967)就提出了这一想法。同时,正如我们所知道的那样,组织设计及其功能作用掺揉了大量的会计系统因素,会计系统甚至能使组织采用分部管理(Braverman,1974;Johnson,1978),一些尝试性的研究(Child,1973,1974,1975;Rosner,1968;Turcotte,1974)至少表明,组织在财务上取得的成功,将可能大幅避免复杂的会计、信息和控制系统等在其应用上的僵化。相似地,会计系统还在非正式的计划与评估实务(Child,1974)、多样复杂的信息流(Baumler,1971;Grinyer and Norburn,1975)、组织参与者间持续性协调与谈判(Georgiou,1973)中,发挥重要的作用。事实上,如果组织出于配置稀缺资源,或者与外部代理人进行一项新的协商谈判等目的,而投入大量资源用于增加额外的内部管理控制机制的话,将势必造成组织出现"新的贫困"(newly poor)(Olofsson and Svalander,1975),或者说,组织将受到来自组织之外因素的威胁(Khandwalla,1978;Meyer and Rowan,1978)。

尽管我们对会计系统的实务运作知之甚少,但已有研究成果还是能让我们对许多基于财务和管理会计系统的会计系统的职责描述的准确程度提出质疑。这些职责可能是根据特定的社会和组织效率概念、理性及相关性等的名义照抄照搬过来的。但在实践中,会计系统所发挥的功能是各式各样的,它们与制度性政治程序、组织和计算实践的其他运作方式相互交织在一起。会计系统可能被赋予了"有意而为之"的属性,它的目的性不是与生俱来的。研究表明,人们在阐述会计的目的性时,已经毫无争议地引用了太多的有关人类学、组织与社会理性,以及会计、决策和组织行动三者关系等领域的观点。尽管我们对于会计系统与组织、社会效率间关系的有关推定,可能有助于证明会计使命的合理性,可能为会计实践提供各种运行方式,还可能有助于简化会计系统的设计及其实施,但是联系到现实中的组织与社会生活,其间的关系还是值得怀疑并有待求证的。

遗憾的是,由于我们对会计实践的知识知之甚少,由此而回避了对会计实务中会计系统作用方式的全面分析与讨论。在这篇文章中,我们能做的也仅仅是对会计系统所扮演的角色提出一些建设性看法。为此,我们首先考察会计系统是如何与组织实践相关联的,尤其关注会计系统是如何深度介入组织决策过程的;然后,区别于会计在组织中的功能,我们在社会这一层面上尝试讨论会计系统问题。

会计系统与组织实践

会计与组织决策之间的关系研究,为分析、发展和传播会计的规范性作用及"解决方案",提供了极其重要的基础。因此,许多学者已经指出,会计系统在决策信息的提供、决策过程理性的提高,以及维持组织运行即所谓的控制中,能够而且应当发挥作用。然而,这些观点的一个突出问题是,会计信息与决策做出之间到底是什么关系,人们却很少有严格的分析与讨论。换句话说,它们间的关系只是在理论上被假定的,而不是被实证描述的。例如,我们假定会计系统的规范、设计和应用是既有的,且先于决策做出;针对不同决策环境,会计系统在决策中所起的作用可能是一成不变的;会计信息的作用是促进(facilitate)或中止(ease)决策过程,而不是积极地影响(influence)或校正(shape)决策过程。尽管这些假设式推定可能触及了会计使命的潜在影响力,但是,在会计系统发挥作用的实务过程中,它们之间的关系却要复杂得多。

鉴于目前的知识,我们一时还难以对会计与组织决策程序间的相互作用关系进行全面或权威性的说明与描述。因此,我们根据 Thompson and Tuden (1959)所提出的组织决策模型,来进行我们的分析。他们的模型其实很简练,就是将各种不确定状态进行特征化描述,从而在决策过程中生成一系列可能集,并将其加入传统分析框架中。这样至少为我们讨论各种不同方式下的组织决策程序提供了基础,正是这些不同方式涉及了会计的利益问题。

如表 1 所示,Thompson and Tuden 区分组织行为目标的不确定性(或是不一致性,因为在组织层面上这两者的效果是一样的)和决定行为结果的因果关系的不确定性。当目标清晰且无争议,而且行动的后果是可预知的时,Thompson and Tuden 就认为它可以通过计算来进行决策。在这种情况下,无论所考虑的各种因素的行动结果(一个或一组结果)是否满足事先确定的目标,我们都可能通过计算而求得。然而,随着因果关系变得越来越不确定,这种通过计算而求得结果的计算能力就逐渐消失了。Thompson and Tuden 随后考察了依判断进行决策的情形,在这一情形下,组织参与者会基于相对确定的目标,依据个人的主观评价得出一组可能的决策结果。正如在行为结果中引入不确定性概念会产生不同的决策方法一样,这样做也就等于承认了人们对目标本身存在着各种争论和不确定性分歧。在因果关系确定的条件下,Thompson and Tuden 认为,行为目标的分歧或不确定性,将可能会导致决策过程中具有政治性而非计算性倾向。在这种情形下,各种行动的利益关系被连接在一起,其结果是,决策过程的特征更趋于妥协和讨价还价。而当因果关系不确定时,Thompson and Tuden 认为,决策过程更倾向于一种依灵感而决策的本性。人们对决策行为所依据的先期逻辑知之甚少,以至于人们以为这些逻辑是在决策进程中产生的。

表 1　决策制定与组织中的不确定性

		目标的不确定性	
		低	高
因果关系的不确定性	低	依计算进行决策	依妥协进行决策
	高	依判断进行决策	依灵感进行决策

基于对组织中的不确定性及利益冲突的了解，由 Thompson and Tuden 所提出的这套决策制定方法，为我们试图理解会计和其他信息系统在组织中所发挥的作用提供了可能。而且更重要的是，尽管这套方法体系很简单，但他们的分析框架确实触及了一些核心观点，即信息加工机制是减少不确定的机制（Galbraith，1973），信息价值的大小在于它所降低的不确定性程度的高低。然而，与其假定信息与不确定性之间的这种关系，倒不如让我们来分别考察会计系统在不同决策环境下可能扮演的角色，换句话说，即会计系统是如何与计算决策、判断决策、政治妥协决策和灵感决策相关联的。

让我们用并不十分恰当的"机器"（machines）一词来类比，表 2 列示了这样一套会计系统在组织中的作用，它有助于我们评价会计系统在实务中的作用方式（Earl and Hopwood，1979；Hopwood，待发表）。在行为后果及行为目标的不确定性都较低的情况下，我们借鉴管理科学中有关不确定性的定义，在这一定义下，运算法则、公式和规则都能通过计算而得到。或者说，这种情况可能与 Simon（1960）所说的结构性决策相类似，在这类决策中，知识、设计和选择都是可规划的（programmable）。在这一情形下，会计系统可承担"问题回答机器"的角色，即提供简单的投资决策评价方法、库存控制系统和日常信用控制流程，这些简单方法在大量的管理会计教材中都有体现。

表 2　不确定性、决策制定与会计实务的作用

		目标的不确定性	
		低	高
因果关系的不确定性	低	问题回答机器	弹药机器
	高	问题回答机器 / 学习机器	理性机器

在目标明确但因果关系不确定的情况下，情况略显复杂。在这种状况下，人们会希望看到这样的情况，即组织参与者需要发现问题、提出难点、说明假设、分析问题并最终做出决策判断。这种情形下，会计系统与其说是在提供答案，倒不如说是在提供决策帮助，正如 Gorry and Scott-Morton（1971）所说的决策支持系统（decision support systems），或者如 Churchman（1971）所说的咨询系统

(inquiry systems)。事实上,我们确实发现会计功能的"学习机器"效用:接受背景资料、进行本质分析、代入"如果—将"模型(what-if models)、进行敏感性分析。不过,这样一些决策领域,无非是传统决策方法在实际利用时进行了大量延伸拓展而已。对于不确定性情形,人们认为它确有难度但又不可避免,因此需要投入更高级的计算系统来掩饰和搪塞(如果不能减少不确定性的话)。相应地,与管理学家们一起,会计师们又创造出了另外一些系统模型并加以应用,如最优化模型、概率模型、风险分析等,试图劝导人们普遍接受决策环境的相对确定性,因此,拓展到会计领域的"问题回答机器"功能,要么假定,要么强迫人们接受经济理性和科学理性这一概念,然而,经济理性与组织决策过程中的决策理性在概念上并不是一回事,它们间的关系至多是模棱两可的。

让我们来考虑这样的情形,决策目标存在不确定性或不一致性,但是因果关系、价值(values)、原则(principles)、观点(perspectives)和利益冲突(interests)等相对确定,为指导组织工作所用的各种评价标准则疑问颇多。在这种情况下,政治程序在决策制定过程中的意义就得到凸显,会计模型只是起到"弹药机器"的作用,组织内各利益团体都试图利用会计系统这一弹药机器,来展开纷争并提升各自的特殊地位。为表示出对组织使命中某些特定概念的接受愿望(Batstone,1978),并有选择地引导信息分配(Pettigrew,1973),组织行为中的各利益团体都接受并引进新东西,如为组织控制而设计的各种新机制、信息流管理等。

类似地,我们猜想:在依灵感而决策的情形中,决策中固有的不确定性也需要会计系统,这一系统所充当的是组织"合理化机器"的作用。既然在行动上是名正言顺的,那么在这情形下,立足于过去的会计系统就将具有更特殊的组织意义和价值。

诚然,简单地说,我们有关会计作用的研究框架也仅仅只是建议性的。通过指出会计系统在组织清晰度(organizational clarity)管理中的各种不同方式,我们懂得了会计系统在组织中的各种不同作用。我们不敢说我们对所有这些问题都展开了讨论,但至少我们可以假定,与会计作为"回答问题机器"和"学习机器"作用相关的现有文献,都已经全部提到了。因此,我们紧接着要讨论那些计算性实务(computational practice)的扩展问题,这些计算性实务看起来拓展了"问题回答机器"方法的范围,产生并应用了组织的"弹药机器"功能,同时强化了会计系统可能在组织"理性机器"模型中的作用。

计算性实务的扩展

计算性实务向决策判断拓展,其背后的原因仍不明了。然而,我们至少能指出两点。第一点来自管理知识不断成型化和客观化,第二点则来自日趋变化的管理内容,即随着新的、更为复杂的分部式组织与管理的发展,会计实务也随之发展并日益复杂化。

在过去的几十年中,组织管理成了人们高度关注的重点领域。借助于经济学,特别是数学和统计学的观点和方法,很多管理问题都有了一些正式的答案和说法。许多实务工作者、咨询师和学者们试图利用数学化、公式化和标准化原则,重构组织决策中的核心部分,并使决策过程程序化和高度专业化(Galbraith,1967;Simon,1960)。在内容扩展上,计算性实务作为对人为判断的一种补充(假如不是替代的话),得到了长足的发展。

在管理实践中,会计系统也全面介入到这些变化的设计与实施过程中去。投资评估和规划程序的不断格式化,提高了财务计算的范围和程度。在很多情况下,一些对管理决策和判断来讲非常重要的因素,如各种财务风险和不确定性等,现如今都已被数字化了,它使得决策过程越来越多地采用计算方式。会计实务的发展,使得组织效率和组织业绩等都有了可操作的依据,也使得行动目标变得更加具体而不再模糊。借助于计算手段,预算和计划系统的应用为组织活动的协调与合作提供了有效方法。例如,生产管理和营销管理能够用一种更为特有的方式被整合在一起;存货政策也将随着组织环境的变化而得以评估与修正;对某些特殊的组织资源,如现金等,其资源计划的结果也能得以计算和评估。类似地,随着生产和存货控制程序的引入,人们对更详细的财务信息及其他信息的需求也越来越多,而这些都是计算性实务所扩展到的领域。

计算性实务的拓展还与组织管理的其他方法高度融合。例如,组织的分部化管理要求拓展会计的技术技能。显然,从会计角度对新的组织架构进行描述,根据总部管理目标对组织的下属经营单位进行业绩评价,用信息和财务报告的术语来处理组织间更为复杂的相互依存关系(这种关系都基于各分部的经营战略)等,这些能力都极大地促进了分部组织(Chandler,1962;Johnson,1978)、项目导向组织(Sayles and Chandler,1971)等现代组织形式的创建。利用组织设计并将组织的技术核心(technical core)从组织的环境波动(environmental fluctuations)中分离出来,也使得人们能够并且也需要开发出一套计算技术,以帮助组织进行技术控制与组织管理,如存货管理技术。与此相类似,为了评估和衡量组织业绩而产生的会计程序,与组织参与者个人的薪酬体系与业绩评估交织在一起,而这一业绩评价与薪酬体系,使得会计将关注重点放在组织经营的效率(efficiency)与生产率(productivity)这一角度。以这种组织理论为基础所确定的会计,其实大量地来自在管理中会计与其他管理方法的有效联结(conjunction)。会计不再作为一个独立和基础的功能发挥作用,会计系统的功能已经与组织实践的很多其他管理形式紧紧联系在一起。

置于社会与组织环境中的会计研究

当我们从更宽泛的组织层面讨论它是如何促进会计计算实务的拓展时,我们已经意识到,这一讨论超出了本文所讨论的范围,更不用说从社会的层面来展开这一讨论了。① 但是,促进会计计算实务发展的一些内在动力至少还是应当提及的。比如,会计计算领域的扩展导致了会计专家的雇用,这些专家们不仅能够挖掘会计的组织作用,而且还能够对会计的组织作用做出积极反应。然而,更重要的是,会计计算发展自身能够为会计实务和组织实践的后续变革(subsequent changes)提供条件,这些后续变革与初始变革(initial changes)引入的逻辑关系十分缜密。例如,在引入一种新的组织形式时,会计计算实务通常能够明显改变组织参与者对问题及可能性的看法。为此,新的会计计算体系可能得以产生,以对旧的计算体系的不足进行补充(Jones and Lakin, 1978, pp.89—96);甚至新的计算体系可能会改变其他管理实务赖以存在和发挥作用的条件及环境。例如,对效率的计量评价,为组织管理的新目标和组织激励的新基础提供了可能。同样,分部会计的实施能够为企业内部的组织重构提供基础,进而可能改变组织权力与影响配置。在这种情况下,会计计算实务的发展要考虑很多其他复杂多变的环境因素,新会计实务的发展自身也为管理实践的进一步发展提供了可能,这些新管理实践的产生及其作用发挥,其变革的动力与旧体系下完全不同。

组织的"弹药机器"

在目标不确定或目标有争议的情况下,会计系统不仅创建了一个对话或交流的平台,而且是经常用于沟通和增进特定利益立场的平台。因为组织亘古不变的特征是,为实现特定目标,组织内既有基本立场的冲突,又存在组织手段的冲突。组织不是作为理性行为的聚合机制而存在的,而是一个利益的联合体(Cyert and March,1963),是各种不同利益团体参与其间的平台,凸显组织生命特征的是组织内的政治过程。在任何单一利益的名义下,组织的变革和控制都会饱受质疑。

人们开始认识到,组织控制的各种机制来源于组织生命的政治、利益冲突等特性,正如 Pfeffer(1978)所说的:

> 组织结构似乎不仅仅是一种管理程序的结果,该程序是为确保高额利润而进行的组织设计。组织结构更像是组织自身利益冲突得到妥协的过

---

① 很明显,会计上的技术可能性并不是组织实施与有效运用的充分条件。关于组织与社会因素是如何渗透到会计变革进程中的讨论,可参见有关效率管理运动的文献(Haber,1964;Hayes,1959;Searle,1971),以及我们关于英国出现的价值增值会计的论述(Burchell et al. ,待发表)。

程的产物,当人们讨论组织各利益方的满足标准是什么时,产生了各式各样的决策。组织结构可被当作组织内部的控制权和影响力争夺的结果,组织结构安排如组织资源配置决策一样,极可能是政治过程的结果。

信息和会计系统的设计,与组织政治过程的管理紧密交织和关联。

在各种组织行为及其后果中,会计系统能够对其中那些相对可观察的行为,尤其是高级经理们的行为,产生影响(Becker and Neuheuser,1975)。而这些已建立起的行为的可视性(visibility)经常是不对称的。借助于会计系统,高层容易监督低层,但反过来不是这样,正如一个特定的监控模型所建立的那样。正因为如此,对各种活动的集中协调机制能够建立起来。然而,同样,各种需求、要求、压力和影响力等可以很便捷地在组织内传递下去,尤其在财务和经济方面,因为会计数字的特性是可以分解的(Hopwood,1973)。预算、计划和报告等管理实务能够提供一个综合框架,在该框架内,能产生一个可评价、可观测的授权体系。人们可以建立预期模式,同时,会计实务所增强的管理活动的可视性,能为组织的激励提供奖惩基础。甚至通过作用于组织内部的各种协商和争议机制,会计系统有助于指出组织内问题之所在、可行的解决方法,也许更重要的是,在组织决策选择中所用到的决策标准到底是什么等。也就是说,会计系统不仅为决策制定提供信息,而且通过对其他信息的筛选、汇集、评估来影响决策标准的确定。

然而,会计系统的后果,不能视为形成会计系统的各种利益关系的简单反应。新的会计系统的产生一定是出自各种特定的利益考虑。所设计的新的会计系统,应有助于增强某些特定管理活动的可视性,有助于贯彻组织的某一特定使命和团队意识,有助于建立组织内部的一套特定的命令体系(a particular chains of command)。事实上,会计师们用自身的语言来描述这些结果,尽管其暗含的发挥作用的基本原理可能与系统设计、应用的基本原理有所不同。因为一旦在发挥作用层面上讨论,会计系统就是一种组织现象。会计系统有其自身的做法,它们会对组织作用的发挥限定一些条件,对利益的有效定义施加影响,而不是对事先设定的利益进行简单描述。因此,尽管会计系统可能受到特定参与者的影响,但会计系统不太可能是某一单一利益体所专属的,相反,它们演变成了一种共同机制,在这种机制下,各方利益得以协调,不同利益诉求得以表达,政治程序得以进行。它们可能会影响利益各方争论所使用的语言、种类、形式,甚至时间等问题,但它们却很少能左右谈判的结果。

会计和行动理性

会计使命只关注决策前的会计作用。着眼于过去的会计也被赋予了未来的含义。然而在组织中,业已制定的决策也需要进行验证,并使程序规范化和决策合理化。通常情况下,很少有人(如果有)能全面理解如此复杂的组织过程(Weick,1979);或者在依灵感而决策的情形中,组织目标和因果关系这两方面都是动态变化的(Thompson and Tuden,1959),它需要人们对各种行动进行回顾,需要精确描述组织的理性,或者至少从表面看,对组织理性的描述应当与正式表述的组织目标相一致。而且,在外在利益主导决策制定的情况下,就更应当是这样的(Myers and Rowan,1978)。

会计可能而且经常是与组织过程交织在一起的。正如 Bower(1970)和其他人所看到的那样,资本预算程序的广泛应用,使人们能够充分利用项目决策,从而为组织行动提供一种校正。类似地,各种预算和计划也将围绕着"它们应当是什么"来构建,从 Meyer and Rowan(1978)的更广泛讨论中,可以得知:

> 在现代组织中许多非理性活动的出现,是因为组织本身必须维持一个理性的法人角色:我们发现计划者和经济专家们,将大量时间浪费在使计划程序化、证实和说明价格合理性,以及想方设法为逃避冲突而处理人际关系等方面。现代组织中的生活就是这样一种持续的、由两种活动相互作用的过程,一方是我们需要执行计划的活动,而另一方则是我们需要给出组织计划的活动。

当然,根据我们自己及他人的调查,对组织决策结果合理性的证实(justify)和程序合规化(legitimize)的需要,推动着复杂会计的发展。例如 Pringle(1978)描述了在19世纪中叶的印度,英国政府官员在采用"成本效益分析"这一领先工具时,是如何以证实决策合理性为导向,而不是以决定应当干什么为导向的。

> 正如现在一样,那时的成本效益分析,其主要目的是证实项目的可行性,而不是将其当作投资计划的工具……主要诱因好像来自确定在印度的英国公务员的需要量,从而确定政府投资。如果要给政府部门的管理者提供有关经济作用的建议,那么发展一套有关项目评估的方法论是必需的。它需要展示并考虑政府投资所取得的各种收益。因而,在19世纪印度的例子中,成本效益分析就起到了这样的作用,它使得政府确信其所从事的各项基本建设项目中,无论是对投资者还是对社会都有收益。

在这样的环境中,会计的出现是为了调和不同利益群体的冲突,是为了证实特定状态的合理性,且更为重要的,是为了创造一种象征性结构,即在这一结构下,人们能进行沟通,行动能付诸实施。

我们对会计的组织功能的讨论是有失公正的。透过一个特定的参考框架和极其有限的组织描述,我们竭力说明会计是如何卷入组织行为之中的,但是我们忽略了一些可能同样重要的其他因素。我们还关注了会计在日常经营中的组织作用问题,并对会计的组织作用按其序列而非整体进行了讨论,然而有一点是可信的或者是可能的,即在组织联盟内,对会计发展和变革的支持,来自各式各样的组织理性(Banbury and Nahapiet,1979),且会计职能一旦得以执行,同样的会计系统就能服务于不同的组织目的,就如同被不同的人以不同的方式应用一样(Hopwood,1973)。另外,我们的讨论受制于会计在组织运营方面的研究空白:我们不知道的东西太多了。

然而让人希冀的是,我们已经成功地展示了会计功能与具体实践这两方面的作用差异。会计可能并且事实上是依据其基本的内生职责而运作的,它是在构成组织的各种复杂的政治过程中发挥作用的。我们至少指出了各种管理活动的压力是如何来自组织功能,会计又是如何竭力塑造组织现实的概念,从而会计和会计系统又是如何反映并作用于管理活动的各种压力的。会计作用不是作为会计使命的基础而存在,而是在面对组织管理活动的各种压力下产生、成型并变革着的。会计作用发生于行动之中,而不是在行动之前。

会计及其社会实践

不管从哪种意义上,会计都不能仅仅被单纯地看作一种组织现象。会计来源于组织与制度的压力,它是我们社会生活的一种普遍特性,只适用于特定组织的特有会计系统几乎不存在。事实上,在众多组织体中,许多重要的会计变革几乎都在大体相近的时期内发生(Burchell *et al*.,待发表)。这些会计变革似乎都满足了人们对会计计算实践进行拓展的需要,这些计算实践体现在社会生活的各个方面,组织活动只是社会生活的一个组成部分。自然,会计自身的发展是与其他众多的有关信息加工、社会及经济计算等学科的发展并驾齐驱的,这些学科包括统计学(有关社会及经济管理的信息的编辑加工),以及有关社会和经济类别的其他学科工具,如医学、精神病学、教育学、法学、商业及经济生活(Baritz,1960;Cullen,1975;Kamin,1974;Kendrick,1970;Sutherland,1977)。进一步说,会计变革来自会计与其他一系列彰显社会意义的学科的相互作用。监管部门、专业机构、社会利益代表及促成会计规范的政府代理机构等,面对完全不同的社会、政治及经济压力,它们所发挥的作用通常比直接作用于商业企业的其他因素更宽泛。

会计与社会及组织实践相伴而生。但遗憾的是,无论对于会计思想与实践的社会属性,还是社会与组织的交互作用,我们都知之甚少。一些学者给出了

置于社会与组织环境中的会计研究

一些一般性见解,他们指出了社会起源以及会计工具的重要性,尽管这些见解后来要么不攻自破,要么被后来的质疑颠覆。其他一些有关社会、经济发展的史学研究中也提出了一些真知灼见(Kula,1976),但那些阐述几乎很少与会计直接相关。因此,抱着对这些不确定性结论所持有的谨慎态度,我们不想试图去冒险探究我们所未知的领域。我们对于会计的社会性评价很简要,首先关注会计工具的社会意义,然后关注其延伸内涵。

会计的社会意义

会计有很多不同的社会意义。如马克思所阐述的,会计作为一种意识形态而存在,作为一种虚伪的意识形式,会计为人们提供了一种蒙蔽世人的方法,它没有揭示出存在于产品生产中的社会关系的实质。① 其他学者则用一种显得不那么教条化的态度,指出了会计玄妙的、符号性的以及形式主义的角色(Coppock,1977;Douglas,1977;Gambling,1977;Meyer,1979;Wildavsky,1976)。在这样的背景下,会计被看作已卷入经济运行和社会特征,一种介于竞争着的社会代理机构与正在形成并发展着的社会规则间所构建的符号性创造。会计通过某种形式传递着经济和社会的意义,它至少部分地被视作为构建某种符号性秩序(a symbolic order)而建立的,在所构建的这些符号性秩序之中,社会代理机构能够相互作用。

Weber(1969)强调了会计在发生和维护社会经济理性的特定秩序中的贡献,他认为(Vol.1,p.86):

> 从纯技术观点来看,货币是最"完美"的经济计量工具。也就是,它是主导经济活动的最常见的理性工具。

事实上,Weber是根据计算性方法(the calculative means)来确定经济理性的,他将"经济活动的正规理性"(formal rationality)定义为"不仅在技术上可行而且在实际中能应用的各种数量计算或会计"(1969,Vol.1,p.85)。同时,在区分正规理性和内含于活动中的"真实理性"(substantive rationality)时,Weber认为前者提供了足够的方式以达到后者。最近的一位评论者是这样阐述的

---

① 马克思将会计看作部分资本主义者进行理性决策时使用的一种完美妥帖的工具。他的思考角度被 Most(1963)和 Bailey(1978)吸纳,Most 甚至痛心于马克思没有抛弃他的意识锦囊,而专注于管理会计。但是,需要重点关注的是马克思呼吁揭露会计中蕴含的社会理论,这些在有关社会关系本质之谜的文章中被提到。《资本论》第三卷中的第一部分,即第45页,马克思写道:"剩余价值借助利润率转化为利润的方式,只是在生产过程中已经发生的主体与客体的颠倒的进一步发展。我们可以在生产过程中看到,劳动的全部主观生产力怎样表现为资本的生产力。一方面,价值,即支配着活劳动的过去劳动,人格化为资本家;另一方面,工人反而仅仅表现为物质劳动力,也就是商品。从这种颠倒的关系出发,甚至在简单的生产关系内,也必然会产生出相应的颠倒的观念……"

（Hirst，1976，pp.98—99）：

> 依据效率（efficiency）概念，只有正规理性能够对为达到各种目的而采用的手段进行调整，因为正规理性提供了一种效率的定量计算方法（quantitative measure），资源使用效率的质量评价方法（qualitative measure）在逻辑上是不可行的。因此，所有经济活动都需要正规理性概念，并基于正规理性来建立模型。离开数量计算，资源不可能做到理性配置以实现其经济目的。经济行为都是基于正规理性来定义的。正规理性与真实理性并不是可以相互替代的，它们也不是两种相同的理性计算方法。经济环境下的目的理性行为（end-rational action）需要正规理性计算（formal calculation）（正如最初所强调的）。

然而，在阐释经济理性可能作用于会计的理论和实务时，其内涵便更加不确定。对Weber而言，它极可能是利益好处的某种实现（an achievement for the good）①，而对于Schumpeter（1950）而言，它可能包含了我们所知晓的商业文明衰败的胚胎（germs）。这种理性的计算性思维在其诞生之时曾对资本主义发展起到了重要的作用，但它却受到权贵阶层的非理性特权的强烈反对，这一现象表明"财产权这一托词正如那些贵族一样虚无"（the pretensions of property to be as empty as those of the nobility）（Heilbroner，1977）。他这样讲道（1950，pp.123—124）：

> 这些理性习惯一旦蜂拥而至，便在有利的教育体系的影响下四处传播……至其他环境，并且总会有人关注着这些令人惊讶的事情，事实上……资本主义实践将货币单位转化为成本收益的理性计量工具，标志性事件即是复式记账法的产生，从根本上说它是经济理性演变的产物，成本收益的微积分分析回应了这样的经济理性。会计通过具体化和数字化，极大地推动了企业经营的逻辑化。这样，通过为经济部门所做的定义及量化，这种逻辑、态度或方法开始出现在管理者的职业生涯中，理性征服了人类的一切，包括人类的工具和哲学、医学实践、世界观、生活状态以及任何现实的东西，包含了人们对于美和正义的理解以及精神追求。

---

① 需要注意的是，Weber确实考虑到了通过减少贫瘠、无根无据的机械性计算领域这种状态，正规理性计算实际会颠覆真实理性的可能性。在《基督徒教义与资本主义精神》中（1958，p.182），他谈道："美国在其发展最快的时期，人们对于财富的追求，对于宗教和道义的利用，都趋于与纯粹的世俗激情相关，这些激情实际上常带有运动（sport）的特质。没有人知道谁将在未来生存于此，或者在历经巨大变革之后全新的先知者是否真的会出现，或者陈旧古老的思想或理论是否将会得以重生，或者如果以上都不是，人们以焦躁不安式的自命不凡为掩饰。在这种文化发展的最后阶段，人们可能会真实感叹道：'精英失去了灵魂，凡夫俗子失去了心智；其文明程度上的可悲景象前所未有。'"

置于社会与组织环境中的会计研究

其他评论者则从更微观的层次来讨论会计的社会角色及意义,他们通常强调会计工具的作用功能。尽管一些人强调了会计在决策分权时的作用,但是另外一些人指出决策集权时会计面临的截然不同的内部压力,无论在单一企业(Chandler,1962)还是国家(Bettleheim,1976)掌控权力的情形。人们考虑了很多会计的微观作用方式,在这些方式的作用下,会计通过在重构企业组织时所引入的管理方法,强化和促进了特定效率的概念,并将观念和任务控制从其实际执行中分离了出来(Braverman,1974)。

在这一领域,一些无可辩驳的会计思想,构建起了一系列有关会计作用复杂性和潜在影响力的研究议题,尽管其中这些研究议题的有效性还有待检验。用超越会计的眼光来看待会计工具的内涵,人们(通常是以非会计人员的视角)从更广泛的社会影响力角度来探求会计的社会意义。人们发现会计是一种代理机构,是为深化理性活动的特定概念的一种代理机构。正如我们现在所了解的那样,会计反映并促进了社会的构建,通过各种制度形式和社会行动方式间的相互作用,促进了社会的发展。

会计及会计规范机构

通过在会计规则(accounting regulation)方面所日益达成的共识,我们已经弄清了会计作用于社会的很多不同的侧面。在以前,人们专注于会计的技术性阐释和标准化,而现在,人们的注意力已转移到规则的制度性和政治性因素上来了。会计在这样一个由各类机构所交织的网络中运作,这些机构包括会计职业机构、代表社会利益的集中组织、会计职业界中的主导合伙人以及政府的有关利益团体。所有这些组织和机构,都有权制定会计规则并实施会计标准化,但是它们都会受到来自各方的压力,而这些压力则来自受会计规则冲击最强烈、最深的各类组织。在会计规则的范围和形式饱受争议和变革的同时,会计标准化所涉及的技术因素,正变得与人们的意愿混杂在一起,人们希望会计规则能获得制度上的合法化和支持。人们的关注点不得不转移到会计发展过程中不同利益层面的初衷上来,并且随之而来的是,会计变革所体现的社会作用,被看作未曾有过的政治压力的产物,这些政治压力和会计变革同生同长。

例如在英国,我们看到会计规则的制度机制是如何在下述两方面的交互作用中产生的,一方面是主流媒体及国家的相关机构,另一方面则是职业机构,且职业机构关注的重点是如何维持其自身的规则制定权和控制力(Zeff,1972)。尽管会计准则通常被认为是以信息使用者利益为导向的,但会计准则的内容则持续反映了变化着的制度内容,会计准则是制度演变的一种衍生结果。

物价变动会计便是这一作用的一个特别有趣的例子。通货膨胀经济的事实无疑促使了会计变革（Mumford,1979）。但是，单单这一事实本身却不足以让人理解：问题是如何产生的，争议的进程是什么，或者过渡性结论是什么。所有这些争议都源于人们对政府导向的会计规则的质疑，源于会计职业界、政府机构和行业组织等之间的利益关系。因此，在通货膨胀情况下所进行的财务会计调整，受到了一系列问题及各方利益的影响，这些利益影响或者推动了行业的会计变革，或者要求对这些特殊情形和会计调整建议进行合法化。在这些不同利益体中，政府利益变得尤为重要。物价变动会计首先涉及的是政府管理机构的利益，这些政府机构关注企业纳税收入，关注为宏观经济管理而进行的政策制定。在那样的情形下，这些会计变革所扮演的角色尤为特殊，对其评价有好有坏。但是，从那之后，政府的其他机构也开始对通货膨胀会计给予充分的关注，这些政府机构关注通货膨胀会计对为产业复兴和经济增长而制定的各种微观经济政策及其实施和深化可能产生的社会影响。在这一经济剧变期，其他利益团体也不甘落伍，但它们关注的是，在应对经济危机和社会权力结构裂变所带来的共同威胁中，通货膨胀会计可能扮演的角色是什么。在这种情形下，物价变动会计的有关争议反映了来自社会和组织层面的各种压力。一些争议问题从根本上可能与会计技术没有关系，而另一些争议问题并非来自组织的会计实践活动，而是源于会计规则的压力。在这样的方式之下，曾一度争议颇多的会计的潜在作用，其制度影响力无论是在作用范围还是作用水平上都发生了改变。事实上，只有从总体上而非单一的基础上，方可赢得人们对争议的肯定，并且那些会计技术变化才可能（或不可能）出现。

其他国家的会计变革路径与此大体相同。例如，在一些欧洲国家，通过改进会计信息披露从而使有组织的劳工运动能从中得到好处，不仅强化了政府对会计政策制定权的集中，而且也使这一制定权的集中变为可能。同时，我们也指出了，在战争期间和进行国民经济管理时期，会计及会计变革由于被赋予各种不同的角色而承受着各种压力（Hopwood *et al.*,1979）。

在监管环境中，着手会计变革所需要的条件确实非常复杂。会计技术和概念框架方面的发展是必不可少的，为使这些技术和概念框架更具影响力，它们必须根植于各种激烈的讨论之中，从而构成会计的生成情境。在那样的争论中，会计实践、会计作用及其功能都将随着所出现的新问题、与会计间所确立的新连接关系等而改变，对会计实践标准化的新需求也由此而生。面对来自各类组织——要求彰显会计的广泛社会作用的组织——的众多压力，这些与会计变革相关的社会作用，与那些交织于实务操作及运用层面的会计角色，在意义上可能是完全不同的。

> 置于社会与组织环境中的会计研究

结论及会计研究的延伸含义

我们有关会计的组织作用和社会作用的讨论,试图说明会计问题不但很多,而且大部分未知并且过于复杂。尽管会计的发展产生了会计的作用属性,并将其用于评价会计功能和改变会计技术,但是,我们的分析则试图说明会计实践是如何与人类、社会的各种不同目标的促进相关联的。在组织层面上,我们已经强调:在其他形式管理实务不断发展的背景下,会计是如何进行角色创新的;作为组织控制模式,会计系统是如何与组织内部的政治程序相互作用、与组织外部机构相互交融的;会计是如何参与决策而不是仅仅在决策之前发挥其作用。在社会层面上,我们的讨论更多地属于尝试性的。但是,我们至少已经认同了这样的观点,即会计具有相当大的社会意义。作为非常早期的探索,我们还探讨了会计变化在法规环境中所能起的作用。

因此,我们特别强调下述两者的区别,即会计被赋予的功能以及会计在组织和社会环境中所发挥的作用这两者间的区别。前者具有天然的目的性,经常被用以引导会计变革,但我们更为强调的是:组织和社会活动的参与者是如何赋予会计目的性的。因此,当看到会计已经与其所作用的环境相互交融时,我们仍要指出,会计甚至只是单一的会计系统也具有各种不同的功能。会计作为一种存在,其面对的压力巨大,且各方压力相互冲突,难解其情理。会计作用一旦转化为现实,会计就成了一种组织和社会现象,会计产生的各类结果就会被组织内的众多参与者利用。

遗憾的是,我们的想法只是初步的,我们对会计的实际功能知之甚少。的确,对会计系统的组织运行这一课题的经验研究也非常少,对会计领域内监管机构的实际运作,以及会计发展和变革的社会背景等的研究就更少了。直到最近,有志于研究的会计学家们似乎也乐意接受这个结果,并将其研究精力集中于会计技术的完善上。我们无须批评这样一种研究导向,但是我们认为,视会计为社会和组织的一种现象,并在这样的环境下所进行的会计研究,可以为在会计环境内所进行的各种流行的分析方法提供有益的补充。

当然,并不是这样的研究不存在问题。我们已逐渐意识到,一个过去不曾被质疑的研究议题可能难以让人产生研究兴趣。像其他研究一样,它的研究潜力巨大,但需要改变会计界的观念。

但是,假如有人愿意去研究会计的作用功能,那么哪类研究可能是必需的呢?我们认为,如今真正需要的是关于会计发展史方面的研究。比如,会计是如何演变出这些现在已知的功能的?在会计的产生和发展过程中,有哪些社会问题和组织机构介入其中了？会计是如何与社会生活的其他领域融合在一起的？我们所看到的会计的社会后果是什么？我们应该记住,到目前为止,有关会计变革及其新会计产生的社会分析的研究几乎没有。学者们似乎更多的是研究会计变化的结果以及变化的相关因素,而不是研究变化的机理。而且在本质上,他们更多地把精力放在了会计技术发展的编年史式的序时说明上,而不是放在会计发展产生和发挥作用的机制进程上。当然,组织层面也有类似的情况。实际上,当看到存在下述事实时人们会惊诧万分:有关会计的组织功效方面的研究非常之少,尤其是已有的这方面研究,其所用的时间跨度是如此之短；研究的关注点在于应用中的会计系统是如何构成的,而不去研究会计系统存在的条件背景是什么。我们所疑惑的是,会计到底是如何演变成与现代大规模、科层组织在功能作用上的相互交融的？特定的会计系统是如何从组织程序和管理活动中产生的？组织中有哪些活动介入了会计系统的设计、执行与运作？会计系统创新、变革和扩张的机理是什么？

对上述问题的研究,要求人们在理论和方法论上进行创新。例如,关于会计行为(the behavioral in accounting)的研究者,将不得不超越社会心理学观点,尽管迄今为止这些观点仍占主流地位。如果要探寻会计的组织和社会意义,而不是去研究人们是如何应用会计技能的话,人们将不得不面对各种不确定因素,即人们对组织行为和社会活动的知识仍然是不确定的。必须考虑信息和会计在政治过程中的作用,这些政治过程构成了组织和社会生活的特征；同时,还必须考虑我们所知的构成组织的各种势力,以及在这些势力下,会计在组织和社会中相互交错的方式是什么。不同的参考框架和知识体系应当有不同的研究要求。并且,我们应该意识到,至少在可预见的未来,现有且可信的各种观点将会产生各种不同的观点见解(insights)、问题(problems)和未来研究线索(leads)。

最初这样的研究又会给会计研究带来各种不确定性。如果只是基于这个理由,一些人可能就不会沿着这条路线去冒险。不过我们相信,如果学术研究是去揭示会计理论,且这些会计理论又能帮助人们去理解会计在社会和组织中的影响力——这种影响力已经存在而且能够做到——那么这种研究导向上的改变还是必要的。

参考文献[①]

（王　斌译）

---

① 参见本文英文参考文献。

社会环境中的会计学

——价值增值会计在英国的历史

摘要: 尽管会计和社会之间的关系经常被人们在原则上确认,但是很少有人就此做过系统研究。这篇论文回顾了现有的关于会计的社会本质的相关理论,并借此明确一些重要的概念问题。论文对英国20世纪70年代出现的有关价值增值会计的案例进行社会学上的分析,并试图对由此产生的理论和问题进行阐述。论文最后讨论这些理论在会计的社会学分析中的应用。

会计作为一种社会现象而不仅仅是技术现象的认识获得了越来越多的认同。会计学的社会环境在得到越来越多的认同的同时,也带来了越来越多的问题。但逐渐地,人们对会计与其运作的环境之间的相互影响的方式开始有所认识。与此同时,会计也越来越积极和明确地被当作社会管理和变化的工具。会计改革也在朝着发挥其社会潜能的方向努力。也有将会计作为社会学和经济学范畴的研究,通过具体化和定量化来提供对组织的社会功能的认识。这方面的研究包括社会会计、社会报告、社会审计、社会经济报表、社会成本效益分析以及人力资源会计。

然而,尽管有这些对于会计与社会的交互关系的明确确认,对会计的社会功能我们仍然知之甚少(Hopwood,1985)。会计似乎仍然停留在技术范畴。尽管现在已经认识到社会能影响会计技术实践,并且这种影响反过来动员并改变社会环境,但对这种交叉影响的过程却鲜有研究。也仍然缺乏对会计的社会功能和潜能的研究。社会开始与会计相联系,但没有对两者的融合的研究。结果我们就对会计的技术实践如何受制于社会环境、更广的社会因素如何冲击和改变会计,以及会计如何在社会环境中发挥作用、对其施加影响等都知之甚少。到目前为止,对会计与社会的关系还仅仅是被声明和假定,而没有被描述和分析。①

在确认当前认识上的重要缺陷的基础上,本文致力于说明和讨论会计与社会交互作用的特定案例,即价值增值会计于20世纪70年代在英国的兴起。我们描述了这一事件的轮廓,并分析了这一会计形式发挥作用的场所。在这一分析基础上,我们试图以价值增值会计作为特定案例来阐述如何理解更广意义上会计的社会功能的产生。我们将首先讨论对会计与社会的关系的现有认识,以此提供一个对会计问题的社会研究的可能性和困难的认识基础。

会计与社会变化

从对社会责任运动的较一般的关注中(Ackerman and Bauer,1976; Vogel, 1978),70年代出现了一些或多或少和社会变化对会计的影响直接相关的研究(如 Bedford,1970;Estes,1973;Gambling,1974;Gordon,1978;Livingstone and Gunn, 1974;Vangermeersch,1972)。然而,尽管确认了社会对会计的挑战,这一组文献的大部分接受社会改变及其对会计的相关性事实,其主要目标是以社会环境的名义改变和改革会计。除了对不同会计模式的建议和可能性的研究,对会计与社会环境的交互影响的过程的特征几乎没有阐述和描述。一旦变化的必要性得以确认,技术改革就优先于社会理解。

Gilling(1976)是上述倾向的一个例外。尽管他也注意到并支持环境(包括社会的和技术的)变化影响下会计变化的必要性,但他也对其中潜在的社会因素和制度因素给予了关注。他的关注点是他所观察到的应用过程的滞后。他认为会计变化滞后于环境的变化是因为会计界缺乏能力对所需要的合适的会计技术的改革做出决策或达成一致。相应地,这种会计变化主体的不作为来源于对会计的占主导地位的认识的缺乏,Gilling 称其为会计思想体系②的缺乏。这样,会计实践适应环境的变化而作出调整的过程滞后不仅仅是由于会计理论一定程度上的不恰当,也是因为它们代表不同的会计理论而带来的利益冲突。这其中任何一个理论"都可能独立地为会计界的努力提供秩序和方向"

---

① 一个值得提及的例外是 Tinker 的研究,参见 Tinker(1980)、Tinker et al. (1982)、Tinker(1984)和 Neimark and Tinker(待发表)。尽管他的研究和我们的有很大差异,但我们仍然承认他和他的同事在会计实践的社会起源和功能方面的研究贡献。也可参见 Cooper(1981)。

② Gilling(1976,p.69)这样解释思想体系:任何一种职业都有一种定义的思想体系,用以建立起职业界的思维方式及观察世界的方式。这一思维方式规范这一职业的活动、问题以及解决问题的合适方式。职业界对环境的行为反映其对环境的察觉力。一旦对环境的认识建立了,行为就为这一认识及由此产生的参照系所决定。只要其认识和察觉对于现实世界来说是合适的,对现实世界的行为就是合适的。一旦察觉力与现实世界不吻合,行为就不合适和不相关了。

(p.70),然而都没有提供协调和包容其他理论的可能。Gilling 认为这一僵局的后果就是会计职业的自治权和专业性受到了挑战——这带来了危机"由于不能对新的环境做出反应,会计职业面临公众信任和身份危机"(Gilling,1976,p.64)。

这样,在 Gilling 的框架中,会计被从环境中划分出来,随着时间的推移,后者要求前者改变。会计因而被认为是而且应该是一种反映性的现象。环境的发展和进化要求会计来满足其不同的需要。会计变化的过程通过会计界且依靠他们的觉察力来决定需要什么样的会计调整。相应地,这些觉察力是由以会计的主体、目的和功能的假设为特征的会计理论体系构成的。①

这样一种对会计变化的权变观在大多数讨论中普遍存在(例如,Bedford,1970;Chambers,1966;Flint,1971)。然而,其在细节上有着很大的差异,尤其在对会计需要回应的环境变化的描述上。② Gilling 自己也没有提供准确的详述。他认为过去 40 年最主要的环境变化在于"对会计信息的公共特征的确认"(Gilling,1976,p.65)。这是由于公众对于商业企业活动的关注,他写作时代关于公司社会责任的辩论为此提供了例证。接下来会计界对于如何改进会计报告的准确和一致性的探索导致了会计标准及准则制度的产生,而这构成了会计环境的一个极其重要的新的组成部分。③ 其他研究确认了日益增加的劳动者的权力(Barratt Brown,1978;Carlsson et al.,1978;Gold et al.,1979;Hird,1975),对消费者权益的确认(Medawar,1978;Vogel,1978),对企业道德行为重要性的认识(Estes,1976;Frankel,1978;Ramanathan,1976),以及演变中的会计责任概念。Gandhi(1976,1978)进一步研究了非市场经济崛起中的环境发展。对他来说,这一发展的重要性在于会计单一的货币计量特征使其成为一种不恰当的工具。

---

① Gilling(1976,p.69)进一步阐述了他对不同且冲突的会计思想体系的看法:会计中有一些潜在的冲突,如是现时的还是永久的假设,会计准则和实务的发展是采用案例法还是建立一个充分一致的理论基础等。即使在理论基础上达成一致,也会在现金等同物、所有者权益估价、重置成本等方面存在分歧。更进一步地使这一问题复杂化的分歧是会计应该被看成技术还是决策制定。

② 即使在环境变化的描述上有一些共识,其含义也往往存在差异。例如,Churchill(1973)在评价对社会责任会计的探索及随之而来的过多的计量指标和方法时,并没有论及威胁或危机,相反,是当作会计领域扩展的机会。

③ 其他的评论员和学者也同意 Gilling 的观点,即确认这样一种会计法规制度的出现对其后的会计实践的发展是至关重要的。然而,不同的分析对这些团体的功能给出了完全不同的看法。例如,Watts and Zimmerman(1978,1979)认为会计法规完全不适应,是一种浪费。寻求一套有共识并能作为会计法规的基础的会计准则是注定要失败的,因为 Gilling 所讨论的不同的会计思想体系背后隐藏了大量的植根于商业环境中的个体的不同地位中的利益冲突。更进一步地,会计准则实际上降低了社会福利,因为官僚主义不会有助于公众利益因而导致值得关注的政治交易成本的存在。也可参阅 Benston(1969,1976,1983)。霍普伍德对这些团体的出现和功能,以及这些对会计的意义提出了不同的看法,请参阅 Hopwood(1984)。

他倡导"业绩评价不应只限于财务指标"（Gandhi,1978）。

暗含于上述会计改变的权变理论中的环境成为一个广为传播但只是部分地得以清晰表达的概念。作为或愿意成为一种反映性现象的会计的重要性,对于会计改变的理解带来了很大程度上的不确定性。改变的必要性得以确认的同时①,其解释和影响的方式还不够精确,研究也相对不够。

Wells（1976）对会计改变提出了不同的诠释。他在一定程度上颠覆了权变模式,认为目前的会计危机不是会计缺乏对变化中的环境的应对问题,而更多的是会计理论中自治发展的结果。以 Kuhn（1970）的研究为基础,Wells 主张一个清楚可辨认的会计学科体系是在 20 世纪 40 年代首次形成的。这一体系为常规科学的研究提供了一个框架,并随之受到学者、商人及法律界的批判的影响,给会计理论带入了一系列的非常规概念。正是这些非常规引起了危机。在 60 年代和 70 年代,随着讨论的深入,为应对非常规和批评采取了一系列的特别措施。这至少在一定程度上引起了对会计理论基础的更广泛的关注,并使 60 年代成为"会计演绎研究历史上的黄金时代"（Nelson,1973,p.4）。然而,问题远没有解决,这些理论反而只是"显示了学科体系的缺陷和放松了传统的束缚"。其结果是出现一些不同原则起点因而不可比的理论学派。② 从原则上来说,这些学派的每一个都可以成为新的学科体系产生的基础,然而 Wells 希望看到会计理论的发展能进入一个新的阶段,即如 Kuhn 所描述的,"改变对仅仅某一个理论学派的热衷"（Wells,1976,p.480）。

Wells 的研究论证了会计的本构能力,除了反映其所处的环境,还有能力影响其环境。会计学科发展中的困难和争论能带来会计的发展以及会计领域内部和外部对危机的认知。会计发展能改变其所经营的环境也得到进一步的认同。会计环境至少部分地会随会计的变化而改变。实际上 Gilling（1976）和 Wells（1976）都承认会计变化的二元性。尽管 Wells 强调会计的本构能力而 Gilling 着重于会计的反映能力,但两者都对会计（Wells 使用会计理论）术语及其环境的辩证关系提供了最初的研究。最初部分地被会计创造的环境呼唤会计的变革。

> Kuhn 认为变化只在一系列的故障出现后才会发生,即"现有的实践适时停止以解决由环境所带来的问题"（Wells,1976,p.472）。

会计和环境的相互依赖导致由相互适应所带来的变化。环境需要带

---

① 关于会计必要性的讨论,请参阅 Burchell et al.（1980）。
② 差别的一个重要方面是这些不同流派的学者对作为他们各自学科的研究对象的现象有不同看法。特别地,不同会计理论流派中企业的概念也是不同的。

来会计实践的变化,而会计的变化又导致环境需要和期望的改变(Gilling, 1976,p.61)。

看来无论如何表述,环境—会计的权变模式都不可避免地需要解决其所倡导的会计变化过程的尚不明确的二元特征。①

我们对价值增值会计的研究旨在加深对会计与社会的相互依赖关系的认识,但我们更着眼于会计和社会的渗透。在随后的讨论中,我们不是将"会计"和"社会"作为互相排斥、清楚区别的两个范畴。相反,我们着重于"价值增值会计"出现和发挥功能的特定实践及制度,以及其被提及和讨论的相关背景和方式。我们将看到社会或环境贯穿于会计;反之,会计也解构、拓展和改变社会。

价值增值会计的起源

本论文特别关注 20 世纪 70 年代后期发生于英国的一场突如其来的"价值增值会计热"现象(Cameron, 1977b)。② 这场热潮本身基本上可以说是没有什么争议的,所以我们将以这一共识为前提展开讨论。"价值增值"这个概念,显示了由各种不同组织(比如私有企业、报社、政府机关、工会、雇佣者协会、职业会计人员等团体)的活动所创造的价值。这个概念还意味着很多实践活动:编写财务报告,构建工资体系,利润分配制度,进行经济分析,向员工及工会披露信息等。在此之前,价值增值概念基本没有出现过,或者至多仅仅存在于一些很有限的领域里。

会计专业人员间广泛开展有关价值增值的讨论,是从其出现在《企业报告》(*The Corporate Report*)上开始的。这是一份由会计准则起草委员会(Accounting Standards Steering Committee, ASSC,后来更名为会计准则委员会(Accounting Standards Committee))在 1975 年 8 月根据该委员会中进行的各种讨论整理出版的资料集。至少对于会计人来讲,这是对价值增值概念的首次正式接触。

《企业报告》特别指出,"应鼓励编制价值增值计算报告,以显示利润作为企业努力的成果是如何在员工、股东和国家之间分配的"(ASSC, 1975, p.48)。继《企业报告》之后,英国贸易署(Department of Trade)于 1976 年 6 月

---

① Hopwood (1985)进一步讨论了会计变化的概念及构成。也可参阅 Roberts and Scapens (1985)。
② 本论文主要讨论增值会计在英国的情况。不过,在同一时期,欧洲其他国家也都对此问题产生了很大的兴趣。请参照 McLeay(1983);关于该现象在德国的情况请参见 Dierkes(1979)、Reichmann and Lange(1981)、Schreuder(1979) 和 Ullmann(1979);关于在荷兰的情况请参见 Dijksma and Vander Wal (1984);在法国,表现在对剩余会计(surplus accounting)的关注之中(参见 Maitre, 1978; Rey, 1978, pp.132—134)。

9日发表了题为"企业报告的目的和范围"(Aims and Scope of Company Reports)的最初草案。作为一份解说性文件,这份草案对《企业报告》的内容做了如下解释:

> 在《企业报告》中指出的有关以新法律法规为基础的信息披露问题里,根据其未来的必要性,可以做出以下的排序:
> (a) 价值增值;
> (b) 员工报告(Employee Report);
> (c) 未来预测(Future Prospects);
> (d) 企业目标(Corporate Objectives)。
> (*The Accountant*, 1, July, 1976, p. 13)

当政府绿皮书《企业报告的未来》(*The Future of Company Reports*)于1977年7月最终出版发行时,其中包含的具有立法性质的提案之一,就是有关价值增值计算报告的(英国贸易署,1977b,pp. 7—8)。

在会计规范领域中进行这样的讨论,是与众多企业开始在年度报告中增加价值增值计算报告或对员工进行该方面的报告的动向同步的。根据英格兰和威尔士皇家特许会计师协会发表的《对公开会计报告进行的调查》(*Survey of Published Accounts*),在调查的300家企业中,有14家企业在1975—1976年度的年度报告中附加了价值增值计算报告(ICAEW,1978)。这个统计数字在1977—1978年度增至67家,1978—1979年度增至84家,1979—1980年度增至90家。之后,1980—1981年度减少到88家,1981—1982年度减少到77家,1982—1983年度减少到64家(ICAEW,1980;Skerratt and Tonkin,1982;Tonkin and Skerratt,1983)。而其他调查结果显示,在20世纪70年代后期,英国大型企业中五分之一以上编制了价值增值计算报告(Gray and Maunders,1980)。

尽管也有人提到在对员工的报告中也披露了价值增值信息,但详细情况并不清楚(如Fanning,1978)。不过下面这些使用价值增值概念的事例却是极令人感兴趣的。比如,在各个公司竞相编制员工报告的"会计时代"中,价值增值(这一概念)曾被广泛利用;技术性业主联盟(Engineering Employer's Federation,EEF,1977)曾鼓励使用价值增值作为对员工进行企业业绩报告的手段;而英国工会(TUC)在对员工进行信息披露问题进行讨论时,曾提到利用价值增值作为业绩评价指标(TUC,1974)。

技术性业主联盟对披露价值增值信息进行的推奖,是从该联盟初期文件中显示的立场上发展起来的。这份资料,即《经营业绩和劳资关系:作为经营管理工具的价值增值》(*Business Performance & Industrial Relations: Added Value as an*

置于社会与组织环境中的会计研究

Instrument of Management Discipline)于1972年由该联盟出版。正如其标题所示,文中不是仅仅将价值增值作为企业财务报告或对员工的报告中财务信息披露的形式加以认识,而是将其作为"经营管理的实践性工具"来加以讨论的。在这里,"实践性工具"的作用是将价值增值运用到有关劳动利用与劳动支付的决策之中。

> 本联盟的目的是鼓励使用价值增值,所有的经营者不论是否有会计实务经验,都应使用该概念对财务状况进行评价,并在此基础之上进行有关人力资源的相关决策(EEF,1972)。

1977年下半年,EEF的宣传手册中关于价值增值应用的讨论有了新的进展。从讨论利用其作为决定工资的指标有什么样的好处,发展到了讨论如何(以价值增值概念为基础)构建价值增值薪酬制度(VAIPS)。在当时,VAIPS本身受到了广泛的关注。据估计,1978年大约有200—300家企业计划或实施了价值增值导入计划(Woodmansay,1978)。

这样,价值增值先是作为信息披露的手段出现,继而又发展成为决定企业工资制度的准则,最终进入了有关英国产业业绩预测的议论之中(Jones,1976,1978;New,1978)。另外,价值增值概念还作为企业的利润分配计划的改革手段被加以讨论(Cameron,1977a),并作为企业的财务业绩分析手段出现在股票中介商的报告书之中(Vick da Costa,1979)。

我们所称的价值增值现象已经推动了一些研究和分析性的反思。英国的四大会计师职业团体,包括英格兰与威尔士会计师协会、苏格兰会计师协会、成本与管理会计师协会和注册会计师协会,都发布了以价值增值为主题的研究报告(Renshall et al.,1979;Morley,1978;Cox,1979;Gray and Maunders,1980)。然而,我们的关注点与这些报告不同。这些报告都将"对价值增值的兴趣激增"视为理所当然,讨论的重点是其可能的用途、计量原则和报告的格式。作为对价值增值现象的反思,我们的探讨可以看作是这一现象的一部分或延续。目前我们试图揭示的是这一现象发生的原因,以及它的发生对社会变化的贡献:

> 会计提供利润报告已延续了几百年,为什么我们现在需要提供价值增值报告?一个答案就是它反映了社会变化:股东的权力弱化,而政府和工会的力量增强(Morley,1978,p.3)。

在价值增值案例中,上述的观点并不是孤立的(参见Pakenham-Walsh,1964;Wilsher,1974;Robertson,1974)。会计变化与社会变化之间的关系正是我们的兴趣所在,也是我们研究价值增值现象的动机。

价值增值会计和社会

表面上看,价值增值现象的基本轮廓已经很清晰了。但如果要对其进行更为详细的考察,则会发现价值增值其实更为复杂且有点神秘。首先"什么是价值增值?"Rutherford(1977)引用了 Ruggles and Ruggles(1965,p.50)的定义回答这个问题。

> 对于企业来讲,价值增值是由企业以及企业成员所进行的活动而创造的价值,是由该企业生产出来的商品的市场价值减去从其他生产者购进的商品或原材料的成本所产生的差额来计算的。在计算价值增值时,要从企业生产的总价值中,剔除由其他生产者所做出的贡献。所以,这个尺度实质上等于仅由该企业创造出来的市场价值。价值增值测量尺度显示了经济的整体生产价值中每个企业的纯贡献程度。把这些纯贡献的数额加总就可以得到经济整体的价值增值总额。

但是,Rutherford 同时又指出这个定义其实并没有对价值增值的计算进行明确的说明。他和其他一些人指出了价值增值的计算实务实际上是多种多样的(Rutherford,1978;Vickers da Costa,1979;Morley,1978)。比如说,有多种折旧方法(McLeay,1983),税金的计算方法也是多种多样的,等等。这些计算实务上的多样性,带来了价值增值计算报告的多种表现形式(比如表格、柱状图、饼图、图片等)。另外,也导致了名称的不一致性(比如附加的价值、创造的财富、货币的流向等)(Fanning,1978)。现实中确实存在多种多样的价值增值。

在对所声称的价值增值的优点的考察中,另一个奇妙的特征浮现出来。我们已经指出价值增值的多种用途——支付系统、公司报告、对职工和工会的信息披露、经济分析等,然而,很少讨论的是在任何一种应用中,对价值增值的功能的描述或说明都带有二元性的特征。价值增值会计被看成计算和表征系统。

以工资奖金制度为例(参见 Bentley Associates,1975;Smith,1978),价值增值是一个明确定义的财务概念,按确定的计算程序计算劳工收入。然而,除了这样一种计算系统外,价值增值同样被描述为表征系统,虽然后者往往和前者是互相缠绕的。表征系统自身有两个方面。其一,价值增值是财富的表征,准确地说,它代表相应会计主体所创造的财富。更进一步,这一表征属性为更好地计算企业业绩的相关重要指标提供了基础,如效率性和生产性等(如 Ball,1968)。其二,也有人认为价值增值能够揭示(表现)生产的社会特征。这是传统的损益计算表所不能及的部分。增值揭示了生产中创造的财富是一系列代理人共同努力所产生的成果。"价值增值测定的是由股东、债权人、劳动者、政府共同的努力而创造的财富"(Morley,1978,p.3)。所以,价值增值"在由资本家、经营者、员工共同组成的企业中,可以使对共同创造的利润进行合理解释成为可能"(ASSC,1975,p.45)。综上所述,价值增值的这个表征属性,使更为合理的生产统制成为可能,也有助于进行更为协调的共同生产。

现在,这些传神的属性提供了技术和社会合理性,却带来了一个困境。因为要使价值增值能够将一个公司表征为一个合作的团队,这个公司必须首先是这样一个团队。可我们的调研却显示价值增值被当成了实现这一目标的工具。价值增值不只是简单地表征作为合作团队的公司,而且被认为在创造这种和谐合作中起积极作用。将企业作为一个协力性集体来看待时,价值增值对促进这种协力关系的协调性具有积极的作用。以下观点是在价值增值成为多方面关注对象之前提出的:

> 我们所关心的增长,是指国民总生产的增长。国民总生产的增长是由企业生产的扩大来实现的。如果企业的经营者不能自觉地认识到生产是企业的主要目的,这就无法实现;如果职业会计人不能根据这一见解对经营实践的方向进行修正,这一增长也是不能实现的。损益报告,特别是公开发表的报告资料,不仅有害于改善劳资关系,而且阻碍了有望提高的生产性。
>
> 资本家和劳动者之间的对立近年来虽有减少,但只要不改变获取利润是企业的最终目的这一观点,利润最大化和使劳动报酬最大化这一劳资双方关心焦点的根本对立,就会阻碍劳资间隔阂的消除(Pakenham-Walsh,1964,p.268)。

在这样的背景下,价值增值被当成实现理想的手段。会计的变化意味着所观察事物的变化进而行动的变化。这样社会和谐也许没有完全为价值增值所披露。像我们已经指出的,我们处于进退两难的处境,而这是社会—会计权变模式的核心。一方面,价值增值被宣称导致了更广的社会变化和变迁(参见Morley,1978;Robertson,1974;Wilsher,1974),而另一方面,同样的社会变化又似乎不是独立于价值增值的存在的。如此,价值增值至少需要一些自身的先决条件。

用声称的功能去解释会计创新陷入了循环解释的逻辑陷阱(参见 Burchell et al.,1980),而对价值增值会计的功能从一开始就没有一个一致的认识。我们以上描述的功能并不能完全反映这一会计创新的意义。从社会合理性角度,价值增值作为劳动的体现,如 Stolliday and Attwood(1978)中所指出的,并不能解释为什么劳动者没有在利润分配过程中产生促使减少对其他员工的分配的行为。如果这样考虑问题,则对于协力型生产实态,增值的概念所表达的有关生产的"真实"性有可能与迄今为止的认识不同。也可以认为增值概念其实是"对劳动者进行误导",尝试对"利润问题"进行美化(参见 Hird,1980;*Labour Research*,1978)。这时,增值就作为扭曲现实的装置发挥作用。增值被描绘成以企业财务业绩对利害关系进行调整,而实际上,利害斗争在根本上依然存在。从这点来看,可以清楚地看出增值其实是一个暧昧的社会性指标。

关于价值增值的功能,还有另一个问题。我们已经指出,计算上的多样性是我们试图阐明的价值增值现象的重要特征。实际上这一领域的研究者都把这一特征看作是破坏性的:

> 迄今为止公开发表的价值增值报告具有使用暧昧的用语、利用与价值增值格式不相符的项目、计算表内部缺乏一贯性等特征。价值增值计算表的利用者对其抱有的印象极为混乱——价值增值和利润一样,可以根据会计人的意图随意改变(Rutherford,1978,p.52)。

> 至于价值增值的优点,遗憾的是,现在由于(会计)实务的多样性,其有效性受到了怀疑(Morley,1978,p.141)。

> 几乎所有可利用的(价值增值报告),都被设计成显示价值增值中有多少是属于员工的,有多少是归属于政府的,有多少是分配给股东的这一固定形式(Vickers da Costa,1979)。

与其说增值计算表减少了利益相关者之间的冲突,倒不如说增加了混乱和疑问。这种状况意味着,增值的社会合理性和其技术上的合理性都应受到质疑。很明显地,由于价值增值具有多样性,生产性和效率性也会具有多样性。这样,价值增值会计总是或多或少有其不当之处,其出现也不能简单地看作是经济学启蒙运动的开始或特定社会变化的表现。

这场讨论的结论就是,价值增值的功能本身并不能为"对价值增值的兴趣激增"提供解释。到目前为止的讨论可总结如下:如果试图用价值增值的功能来解释其广泛应用,我们就陷入了逻辑混乱;还有,对这些功能的精确表述是存在争议的;最后,价值增值会计不是毫无缺陷的。我们建议将其功能作为要考察的现象的一部分,牢记这一点才有可能更详细地提出我们研究的目的及要解决的问题。

在20世纪70年代对价值增值形成的关注热潮中,价值增值概念并不是作为唯一的明确概念突然生成的。关于价值增值的议论以及相关的实践广泛普及的结果,在某一个方向上出现了多种多样的"价值增值"。本文中谈到的价值增值,无论是在其生成上,还是在其功能上都是暧昧的。尽管对其功能没有统一的认识,但有两点是占优势地位的:其一,价值增值常常被论及是计量财富、生产力和效率的较好工具;其二,将生产视为团队合作的过程,价值增值是利润的较好计量。最后,正是对其功能认识的这种暧昧,才使其得以在广泛的、各种不同的政治利害问题中发挥作用,在政治领域里崭露头角。换句话说,这一概念上的暧昧可能隐含于其出现和功能中。将循环推理作为切入点,价值增值可以被看成社会变化过程的决定因素、社会变化的预告或社会变化的结果。Morley(1978,pp.5—6)如此表述:

当提出价值增值报告反映社会变化时,我们并不需要证明它。其实,这一表述至少有三种不同的含义:

(1) 价值增值报告可以用来加快变化,促进权力从资本所有者向劳工和政府转移;

(2) 提供价值增值报告来警示这种变化,希望变化可以因此被逆转;

(3) 希望价值增值报告可以有助于上司的决策制定。

这三种态度也许可以解释为什么政治界的两极都对增值会计充满热情。左翼和右翼都支持价值增值报告,尽管他们对其持有极为不同的期望。

这一高度分化的、价值增值会计在其中出现的社会空间正是我们的研究对象。我们能找到其什么样的生成前提条件——是什么原因促使价值增值会计受到关注的呢?关于这方面的记述和分析工作,将在下一节中由对三个舞台进行详细描述来付诸实践,并通过展示各种问题的复杂性、各种制度、各种知识团体,以及与价值增值会计现象一起发生的各种实践和行为来展开论述。然而,本文的目的不是提供一个关于价值增值起源和发展的完整描述,这样的研究无疑会将我们带回到工业革命之前,而这会远远超出本文的范围(参见 Crum,1982)。我们的目标更适度:仅仅是对会计变化过程提供一点描述和分析。

三个舞台

以下论述的三个舞台,每一个都是价值增值被活用的领域。这三个舞台分别是企业的财务报告准则、国家的经济政策和劳资关系体系。每一个舞台中诸如政府、工会、职业会计等发挥着重要作用的各种机关,其相互间存在的各种关系形态的变化都将得到刻画。所以这些机关中对价值增值的运用方法以及关心的对象领域所发生的变化,比如说生产性、罢工、会计准则的变化等都有可能成为描述的对象。在每一个舞台中,重点都放在经济核算以及总报告,尤其是价值增值报告上。

对于在每个舞台中发展起来的东西、每个舞台中发生的"各种问题"及其"对策",最初都将被相对独立地描述,看起来好像和其他舞台所发生的事件没有什么关联。这确实有些过度的单纯化。比如说,与工资体系相关的宏观经济政策,明显地影响到劳资关系。相反,对劳资关系进行的改革,又与国家的经济表现相关联。同样,会计准则的制定进程,既与宏观经济问题(特别是这一时期的通货膨胀)相关,又与劳资关系的管理问题(在开展工会运动的时代)密切相关。但是,我们用的研究方法,是首先将各个舞台作为独立的实体进行分析,而后再从各个舞台之间相互依存的视点对其进行分析。这样,就建立起了各舞台间的联系了。例如,在试图将经济业绩问题和劳动者地位以及工会之间建立联系时,不是将这种联系作为具有先验性的必然性来看待,而是通过对经验进行调查来展开分析。[1]

围绕经济业绩和劳资关系的辩论与早已存在的关于公司报告的讨论是一脉相承的,后者包括项目分类、报告的原则和形式等。我们将会计作为一个单独的领域来对待,因为我们认为不应将会计仅仅看成事物的还原或反映,而我们以下的讨论采取了一个更积极的态度,即不仅考虑这一领域的构成要素,也考虑其与其他领域的连接。

会计准则

如前所述,价值增值的特征之一是在计算上具有相当程度的多样性。[2] Rutherford通过对公开发表的价值增值计算表进行调查,得出了以下结论,即"系统地分析编制价值增值计算表时产生的多样性是近乎不可能的"(Rutherford,1980)。要想使价值增值成为有益的概念,这种实务中的多样性,对于价值增值应起到的作用、其合理性以及目的性都是不协调的。价值增值的多样性,与其说促进了高效调和的生产活动,不如说损害了价值增值本来应有的作用。特别是计算上的多样性,使管理者为肆意性和偏见备受指责。例如,员工通讯中声称"这些大部分都是被设计用来显示……多少的价值增值是归于员工自己的、多少是政府拿走了的,而股东收到的是如此之少"(*The Accountant*,1978,p.373)。

对这种多样性所产生的问题,一种解决方案是主张将价值增值会计标准化

---

[1] 我们认为效率和民主之间并没有必然的联系。对这种联系的本质也没有多少分析和调查,而这两个概念从各自的经济学和政治学理论中继承了不同的逻辑思维。同样,这也适用于计量、效率和利益之间的关系。

[2] 我们并不认为这是非正常的。大部分的其他会计指标也有类似的定义和多样化的实务之间的不一致。事实上,这一看似为客观现象的特性为会计行业的技术和社会分析提供了一个有趣的视角。

(Fanning,1979;Vickers da Costa,1979)。与这个问题有关的机关是会计准则委员会(Accounting Standards Committee,ASC)。在标准化以及其他的压力下,代表会计准则委员会的四个会计团体开始了对价值增值的研究。不论是英格兰和威尔士皇家特许会计师协会的报告(Renshall et al.,1979),还是苏格兰皇家特许会计师协会(Morley,1978)的报告,都得出了关于价值增值报告重要性的结论。① "价值增值会计实务的标准化应以保持其形式上的标准化为其不可缺少的前提条件"(Reshall et al.,1979,p.38),理由是"为了保持价值增值计算表的可比性,以保护该报告的利用者"(Morley,1978,p.141)。而在由成本管理会计师协会(ICWA)所做的研究报告之中,价值增值仅仅作为链接工资体系与社会之间关系的一种管理工具被提及(Cox,1979)。标准化的问题在这份报告中未被提及。皇家特许会计师协会的研究中,对价值增值报告的潜在利用者的信息要求做了调查,在对这个领域中已有的会计实务进行讨论之后,又对测定以及信息披露的方法进行了讨论(Gray and Maunders,1980)。这里,有关价值增值的两种测定方法被区别开来,尽管提到"从概念上来讲,希望能够自始至终地使用一种或两种方法"(p.28),但也讨论了考虑潜在利用者们的决策要求,为了促进"富有想象的发展",价值增值报告应"置于规定的限制之外"(p.37)。

关于这四份研究报告,有两点值得注意。尽管这些报告都对突然增加的对价值增值的兴趣进行了评论,这种兴趣为它们的讨论提供了借口,但它们都没有调查这一现象的引发因素。它们都对使用价值增值宣称的优势进行了总结,但没有人质疑为什么不早不晚就突然在这个时候意识到。这一点很重要,因为它显示价值增值的出现是深深地植根于处于特定历史转折点的社会—经济过程中的,这样关于价值增值的潜在应用和优点的辩论可能就完全不相关了。第二点是关于与财务会计准则的制定相关的会计政策被相当狭窄地局限于计量和报告形式。一直到最近(Zeff,1978),这些问题的权衡都没有考虑到特定准则的介绍的影响。的确,与美国的经验相关,会计理论所提供的这一领域的讨论的主要方法掩盖了准则制定的政治特征,因而导致了以解决在准则制定上达成一致的问题为目的的无效的程序改革和研究课题(Moonitz,1974;Watts and Zimmerman,1979;Zeff,1978)。在这一点上,具有讽刺意义的是,会计准则委员会在准则制定过程中遇到的完全可能延伸到价值增值标准化过程的困难,恰恰推动了价值增值第一次出现在会计职业中的《企业报告》的出版发行。

围绕企业倒闭以及收购战所进行的大量争论的结果,是在20世纪60年代

---

① 至少有三个会计职业团体发起这个报告,这是回应劳工部要将对价值增值报告的要求立法化的威胁。考虑这是正式会计报告中的新概念,他们正在进行战略性的投资以增进自己对这一概念的理解。

末期,在英国为了对设定会计准则进行公开审议设立了调整机关(Zeff,1972)。可是,制订标准的计划,至少在试图减少会计实务中的多样性这一问题上,立刻陷入了困境(ICAEW,1969)。通货膨胀会计中的议论提示了最富有戏剧性的例子(Whittington,1983),但同样的困难也存在于会计标准化的其他领域。

会计准则起草委员会(ASSC)的活动,尽管最初是利用会计标准化来维持会计专业的支配能力,但同委员会的通货膨胀会计相关的草案一经提出,立刻引发了广泛而激烈的争论。结果是,保守党政府为了对该领域进行专项研究而设立了 Sandilands 委员会(1975)(参见 Hopwood et al.,1980;Hopwood,1984)。该委员会的成立,使职业会计团体感到了自身与政府之间责任的传统划分受到了威胁。于是,通货膨胀会计的内容和形式的相关内容与测定问题一样被写进了《企业报告》之中。职业会计人员的这种危机意识,由于预测到 Sandilands 委员会将在新劳动党政府中遭到批判而变得更为强烈。新劳动党政府的白皮书《社会和企业》(The Community and the Company)(1974)中,提到了为规制企业及其财务制度而需建立一个强大的企业联盟,这威胁到了职业会计团体已有的自我规范制度。

根据对 Sandilands 委员会报告书的预测,会计准则起草委员会(ASSC)为了"从现代的需要和状况出发,对公开财务报告的范围及目的"进行再检查而设立了专门委员会(ASSC,1975)。到此为止,这类问题一直为准则的设定者所忽视。[①]会计准则起草委员会通过出版发行《企业报告》而发表了自己的见解。对现有的报告实务中存在的过分强调利润问题,《企业报告》中进行了以下的评论。

> 对资本家、经营者、员工齐心合力造就的企业而言,利用价值增值计算表(即用销售收入减去原料和费用)是对利益进行解释的最为简单而直接的方法。价值增值是由企业及其员工通过集体努力而创造的财富。价值增值计算表显示了他们对创造财富的贡献程度。该表对利润表提供了有用的详细说明,随着时间的推移逐渐成为记述业绩的适当方法(ASSC,1975,p.49)。

这样,价值增值顺理成章地进入会计决策制定过程之中。[②]

价值增值成为一种业绩评价基准。它使员工成为与其他的利益相关者平

[①] 深入研究已被作为准则制定程序的一个方面被提及,但一直到"企业报告"工作组成立才有具体的行动。关于这个工作组的成立和功能,参阅 Stamp(1985)。

[②] 一位评论者建议"企业报告"工作组进一步调查对价值增值兴趣的起源。我们的调查显示本文的作者之一可能在这方面发挥了作用。如果的确如此,则进一步证实了我们的结论,即会计变化具有非整体和不可预测的特性。

起平坐的集团。这种平等性的主张,由《企业报告》中的利益相关者模型得到了进一步的强化。过去,只有股东被认为是唯一的利益相关者(Sharp,1971),现在更多的利益相关者被认同,并认为每一个利益相关者都应该拥有"知道报告实体相关信息的正当权利"(ASSC,1975,p.17)。员工集团成为利益相关者的一员。《企业报告》中认为,"员工通过工厂或工作现场一级的特别目的报告可以了解到更多更为妥切的信息"(p.22)。同时还指出,《企业报告》不仅可以检测这一类特别目的报告的可信性,而且可以帮助员工来评价经营效率以及企业或个人的未来前景。

不过,价值增值作为评价指标所具有的替代性或补充性优点并没有得到承认。在20世纪70年代后期,价值增值概念和宏观政策之间的关系被确认的同时,该优点也得到了承认。宏观政策中有两个问题,一个是关于所得政策、立法问题以及实践上的主导权问题。另一个是对员工以及工会的信息公开问题。尽管在会计方针决策问题上来讲,价值增值还只是一个新问题,但在这之前,价值增值概念早就在上述两个问题中发挥了作用,建立起了与宏观政策之间的联系。

宏观经济政策

众多学者将所得政策与增值概念联系起来(Beddoe,1978;Cameron,1978;IDS,1977;Lowe,1977)。所有相关的议论,都是通过对价值增值准则工资奖金体系(Value Added Incentive Payment Scheme,VAIPS)的议论而展开的。VAIPS是一种团队奖金计划,一般以工厂为单位来实施。对象包括蓝领工作人员和白领工作人员。可供分配给员工的奖金池和该工厂生产出的价值增值挂钩。比如说数额由经协议而定的工资总额的百分比来决定等。VAIPS是劳动党政府于1974—1979年全面推出的一项政策。从1977年8月政府工资制度改革第三阶段开始,强制执行了以10%为上限的工资安定政策。可是,由于VAIPS可以在生产性协定中利用留用财源而突破了这一界限,因此,VAIPS在20世纪50年代被引入到英国时,受到了很多咨询公司的支持,从而被很多企业采用。这个工资计划,基本上像它的定义那样,使用了自我留用财源,所以在工资政策的第三阶段,这个计划顺利地扎下了根,得到了普遍的使用。

第二次世界大战以后,"国家经济"成为政府政策和审议的对象,但对于关键的经济变数,政府缺乏应对政策。所得政策就是为了应对这一问题的手段之一。不过,引入所得政策并不是出于政府的本意,它是在企图实施物价安定和完全雇佣的财政政策,由金融政策独自完成调和这样一个近代需求政策陷入两难境地的时候,为了冲出困境而不得已引入的。正是在这样一个环境下生产性的增大成为是否增加工资的判断标准。①

生产性在1961年和1962年的所得政策中得到了高度的强调。在物价和所得审议会(National Board for Prices and Incomes,NBPI)的活动期间生产性这一主题被再度提了出来。NBPI是由劳动党政府设立然后于1971年3月解散的。该组织的作用是讨论"价格、工资以及其他货币收入的动向是帮助解释是否与国家利益相关的个案"这一论题(Fels,1972,第三章)。"国家利益"这一概念,曾在1965年4月出版发行的《价格与所得政策》白皮书里被详细解释,继而又在到1970年为止的一系列白皮书里得到了不断的修正。开始时要求"准则"能提供工资津贴的最大涨幅,后来的定义扩展到了将超越这一涨幅的例外情况也包含进来。特别是由于员工对提高生产性做出直接贡献而发生的限额外提升工资现象。在NBPI的活动期间,尽管零准则依然被强调,但上述的这种例外准则为涨工资的理由提供了依据。生产性协定正是在这种制度下得到普及的。NBPI与生产性协定有关的第三号报告中,显示了全部劳动者的25%,主要在1968年和1969年,签订了生产性协定(NBPI,1968)。

但是,这之后的有关生产性协定的调查中,有人对生产性协定的合理性提出了质疑。也就是说,"可以导致生产性提高的原因太多了,所谓的'生产性协定'只不过是将提高工资正当化的一种手段而已"(Turner,1970,p.203)。

从很多生产性协定的经验来看,这些断片的性质正是吸引政府注意力的理由(Elliott,1978)。引起更大的关注的原因恐怕是当时还没有一种体系能将提高生产性和提高单位时间的工资挂钩。不过这个问题在1974—1979年劳动党政府的第二期所得政策结束时发生了变化。当时,政府为了给第三期政策做准备而对构筑生产性挂钩的条件基础极为热心。

在这种背景下,VAIPS作为模型计划被提出来了。VAIPS本身的性质容易被理解,而且将业绩和报酬很好地结合起来。另外,VAIPS含有的测定技术可以解决20世纪60年代NBPI进行生产性协定调查时所遇到的各种难题。

不过值得注意的是,VAIPS之所以被需要,不仅是由于其技术性层面。也就是说,VAIPS的议论中,仅从适用范围、自己财源的性质以及测定技术的角度论及其优点是很少见的。很多时候,为了使这种计划产生效果,会以对组织内各种关系进行改组为前提。结果,这种改组给组织本身也带来了良性效果。对

---

① 在20世纪70年代后半期,价值增值越来越多地用于政界和媒体对于国民经济业绩和政策的讨论(Jones,1976,1978;New,1978)。生产力被看作即使不是价值增值的代名词,也是其密切相关的。从这个角度,讨论着重于收入政策和增加投资的需要,特别是在高价值增值的行业,关于价值增值的研究则致力于行业的研究和发展。以这些方式,价值增值被同时用于描述经济、解释政策问题,以及在VAIPS领域帮助找到解决问题的方案。

组织的变化的讨论通常是通过"信息披露"和"参与"等论点来展开的。在这一领域拥有代表性地位的工商管理咨询顾问指出（Binder, Hamlyn Fry & Co., 1978, p.18）：

> 为了实现价值增值的贡献，必须具有以下条件：
> (a) 对"打开书"之后产生的疑问持欢迎态度的开放式工商管理方式；
> (b) 员工积极地进行参与，独裁式的结果不受欢迎。

其基本理由，可能有以下几个。也就是说，决定奖金的业绩评价单位不单是机械，而是企业或工厂，业绩的改善（由此决定奖金），是以职能部门之间的协力为前提的，另外，各部门内的各种活动以及各团队之间的协力也是前提条件。这种协力，需要为了改善业绩而进行的讨论和协力活动，因此，有必要提供更为广泛和详细的企业信息。Bentley 计划（VAIPS 在英国的一种形态）是"从由员工代表组成的经营管理协议会开始的。这个计划具有员工对广泛的问题进行参与的构造，可以使其对利润、生产性、工资等问题进行讨论并予以改善"（Bentley Associate, 1975, p.12）。工会对 VAIPS 抱有几分戒心。如有工会参加了这样的计划，那么工会就会强烈要求拥有利用该计划所提供的所有关联资料的权利。这一点是很有意思的（Beddoe, 1978）。

关于这种组织上的变革带来的积极的一面，大多是从改善劳资关系的角度进行的评价。创造具有柔软性的劳动条件，激励员工们积极地削减成本，改善生产性，其结果是，围绕劳动条件，劳动者和经营者之间反复发生的直接对立得到了改善（Marchington, 1977; Camerion, 1977b）。在 NBPI 之前，对生产性协定抱有极大的关心也是出于同样的理由。"NBPI 推荐的工资政策会对工资决定的变动提出要求。而且，由于所得政策经常带来团队交涉制度的改革，因此，被当作特洛伊的木马来使用"（Fels, 1972, p.150）。生产性协定是 NBPI 为了替代传统的工资决定方法而构想的，是从实践上对传统的准则施加影响的手段之一。

20 世纪 70 年代，在围绕工资改革而进行的组织改革的议论中，出现了巨大的变化。从经营管理的角度对 NBPI 活动期间的生产性协定全面展开了议论。

> 原来的生产性协定可以带来非常有益的效果。比如说，增强成本意识从而改善管理，获取关于业绩的最新信息以及使用新的业绩评价方法来改善管理，通过注意改变工作方法来改善经营管理。管理上的沟通工作使与工会之间的沟通变得密切，更多的管理者开始意识到劳资关系与技术、财务上的决策密切相关。加班、自由时间制（Flextime）、部门分配等适用该协定，带来了劳动时间和劳动条件管理上的革命。组织、个人、工作训练的规定等发生变化，总经理以及其他的管理层人员能获得比以前更多的信息，

更为容易融入组织之中（Fels,1972,p.133）。

20世纪70年代后期，VAIPS的议论还停留在考虑如何改善经营管理和企业运营的生产性问题上，VAIPS由"参与"以及"工业民主"等词语加以讨论。实际上，与说明的顺序完全相反，工业民主成为VAIPS推行其主张的踏板（如Marchington,1977）。当时，VAIPS的参与特征受到关注并被特别强调，这主要源于劳资关系领域出现的一系列发展。

劳资关系与信息披露

20世纪60年代，英国工会的活动内容发生了明显的变化。政府越来越多地开始介入像"自发性的集体谈判"这种老系统。集体谈判受到了法律上各种关系网络的制约，与劳资关系的调查、规制以及正常运作等相关联的各种新制度一起被重新制定（参见Crouch,1979）。在这些变化之前，发生了两件值得注意的事情。一是1961年第一次对非正式罢工的次数进行统计；二是劳动党政府于1965年设立了以与工会和雇佣方协会有关的委员会——Donovan委员会（Donovan,1968）。因此形成了生产量（production）这一关键统计数据，而这后来被认为是"英国劳资关系上的巨大缺陷"的先兆（Crouch,1979,p.264）。而对这些"缺陷"进行分析并设法对其进行改造的问题，容易进入政府干预计划的概念框架里。

"工业民主"是1974—1979年劳动党政府围绕劳资关系以及政府干预进行讨论时的中心思想（Elliot,1978）。不过，尽管"工业民主"成为这一时期劳资关系的中心思想，但它仍然是一个极为难以定义的概念。实际上，有人甚至认为根本不可能给"产业民主主义"这一词汇下定义（Kahn-Freud,1977）。

工业民主这一概念的暧昧性，至少在价值增值的概念以及实践中，其长处大于弱点。正是因为它的这种暧昧性，才使得价值增值概念广泛渗透到各个社会阶层以及各种社会团体的利害关系中去，使更多的人参与讨论价值增值概念成为可能（Pitkin,1967）。①

Lord Bullock牵头进行的工业民主调查（Department of Trade,1977a）以及1975年《雇佣保护法》的制定，在1974—1979年劳动党政府进行的劳资关系改革过程中起了非常大的作用。不论如何判断工业民主中有关民主的内容，这项

---

① "工业民主"以两种方式发挥其功能。其一，它是附着于工业民主的一个特定政体的名词。例如，以工业民主的名义，工会代表大会推动了在经济、行业、公司和工厂层面开展工会活动的一系列完整的计划（TUC,1974）。要成为民主化，需要一系列的制度和程序安排。其二，它是为评价给定制度和程序的民主内容提供标准，即这些制度代表所有相关人员的程度。

置于社会与组织环境中的会计研究

工程都暗示了民间企业中信息流向的变化。特别是在工业民主中,有必要收集信息、组织过渡性的新机关和团体以及建立对现有团体信息的新收集权。另外,还有必要建立能够监督新规定导入后效果的公立机关。Bullock 报告书的内容虽然没有被立法,但由于它是在年金计划、健康以及安全计划领域中与该领域的发展同时发展起来的,因此,在使劳动者参与经营决策的问题上起到了引导作用(Lucas,1979)。

管理人员面对工会会员时在收集信息以及制定决策等问题上遇到很多困难,正是在这种情形下管理人员对员工报告书产生了兴趣。面向所有者的企业年度报告也尝试着让员工理解(Hussey,1978,1979;Holmes,1977)。围绕着企业发起的这些尝试,人事管理协会(Institute of Personnel Management, IPM)、ICAEW 以及 CBI 等团体也出版了有关个人管理方面的手册或提案式的文献。加上员工报告书的利用,这些文献中,不仅鼓励通过小型会议,而且鼓励通过个人报告或者幻灯、录像等手法对员工传递信息。在试图建立企业和员工间沟通的情况下,价值增值作为适合演讲报告的形式频繁地出现在各种议论中(Hopkins,1975;EEF,1977;Smith,1978;Hilton,1978)。另外,工会议会中有关工业民主政策的报告中,也有应该向员工提供价值增值信息的提案(TUC,1974,p.33)。

工业民主相关议论的终结是利润分配制问题。利润分配制作为"自由劳动派"同盟形成期的政策,由 1978 年的财政法规定并得到了推行(Elliott,1978)。利润分配制度的引入是由 1979 年成为执政党的保守党政府完成的。CBI 认为像利润分配制之类让员工参与企业财务事务的计划,是一种至少可以使"员工拥有企业层面的目的意识"的手段,也是一种可以"对员工参与活动进行有益的贡献"的手段(CBI,1978)。在这里,特别值得注意的是 ICI 公司由于利润分配制而引起的变化。利润分配制于 1953 年开始实施,并覆盖了得到与利润分配相关的年度利润的 100 000 个月付和周付工资的员工,1976 年由于价值增值的导入而对其进行了修正。

从上述几点中可以看出,VAIPS 问世于 20 世纪 50 年代,经历了 60 年代的孵化期,于 70 年代被正式导入,这并不是一件不可思议的事情。当然对员工进行信息披露以及有关经济业绩的问题绝不是一件新鲜的事情(如 BIM,1957;Searle,1971)。不过 VAIPS 作为具有左右经济主体立场性质的用语,被提升到了相当的高度。正是在这样的情况下,利益以及其他相关用语被认为具有不确定性。于是,价值增值概念和实践成为具有合理性及替代性的业绩指标。会计准则的制定、国家经济政策、劳资关系的规制及改革等各种领域中的发展结果交错影响,导致价值增值不仅联结了上述三个舞台,而且成为各个舞台中关注的焦点。

会计星座

我们的焦点在于了解产生价值增值的社会空间前提。如我们前面指出的,这一社会空间的特征是20世纪70年代后期关于效率和生产力的讨论是与那些对员工参与的关注高度关联的。经济业绩所用的语言受到员工参与和民主的高度影响。

这一时期的文献,从效率性和民主性等方面对会计及工资体系等经营实践进行评价,并提出了改善方案。但同时这两个概念又作为两个完全不同的价值观发挥着作用。不知道"效率性"到底如何能与"民主化"相结合,而多数人认为价值增值回答了这个问题。价值增值即使不考虑民主性和效率性,也作为促使员工参与的适当手段被反复提及。被充斥着效率性—民主性的语言的网络中,价值增值作为一个战略性节点,或者说是一个相互作用的交点发挥着作用。

在关于三个舞台的分析之中,我们概括了价值增值概念出现并发展的特定社会空间的三个分支谱系(Foucault,1977)。因此,这一空间被视为构成了增值各种制度、经济及其管理过程、各种知识团体、规范体系与其评价对象以及各种分类技能之间各种关系存在的一个特定领域。我们把这一领域称为"会计星座"。各种实践、过程以及制度相互交错的网络之中孕育了生成价值增值的土壤,而会计星座就存在于这个错综复杂的网络之中。正是这个网络,使计算、管理价值增值成为可能,同时又规定了它作为言说性实践应发挥什么样的功能。

我们论述了三个活动领域各自以及相互间对企业的信息流产生了什么样的影响。政府介入所得政策、国家经济政策、企业和劳动的相关法律、劳资关系的改革、会计规则以及标准化财务报告等问题,同时对企业产生了多种多样的影响。比如说,生产性协定特别是VAIPS使企业的经营管理成为很精巧的东西。而为了通过联结企业各构成部分的活动而确保更高层次的统一,这种精巧性进而得以渗透。生产性协定使员工与企业间拥有更多的关联要素,促使其参与经营决策,生成了工资—劳动的规则(Mckersie and Hunter,1973,pp.21—23),明显地对VAIPS的众多相关言说产生了影响。于是,整体来讲,企业内部反映经济状态的信息量增大,社会关系的各种模式开始在企业内部重新得到了构造。

不过,到此为止还没有解释会计星座的概念,以及它是如何生成、如何变化和如何消失的问题。以下的考察揭示了会计星座的一般性特征。

星座的特征

首先,需要注意的是,这里所讨论的会计星座,是相对于价值增值会计现象的有关问题而言的,并不以规定如何填写、公开、使用所有的会计计算资料时所涉及的各种关系为前提。比如说,折旧、递延税金、通货膨胀会计[①]等问题的相关讨论,也许与价值增值的会计星座一部分重合,但并不是所有的地方都一致。实际上,这个问题只要对这里讨论的价值增值以外的价值增值会计现象进行一下讨论就会明白。比如说,对特定企业里价值增值会计的出现做分析。这是因为,对特定现象的分析,必然是对部分的、特殊的现象的解释。精华的形态既不是特定学问领域的轮廓,也不是事先给定的研究对象的外形。

对利益的追求和预料外的结果

如前所述,本章所论及的会计星座,完全是一个预料外的现象。围绕价值增值所刻画的各种行为,不是出自特定的行为者或机关的计划,所以我们无法对这些行为进行素描。会计星座是由非常多的事情交错出现而产生的结果。有些事情是大家所熟知的,有些事情以书面资料保存,有些事情则根本没有引起任何注意。但另一方面,所有这些事情几乎都是由那些具有明确意图的人干的。比如说,工资交涉、遵纪守法、通货膨胀对策、寻找信息、让劳动者正视经济实态等。尽管这些个人以及政府的行为并不一定能满足社会的需求,但它们确确实实地为本文所讲的会计星座的形成做出了贡献。

会计星座在多种多样的舞台上,由抱有各种目的的行为者根据其自身的需要而产生的各种行动交汇而成。这些行为者在各自的会计行为中通常并不一致,有时甚至会有利害冲突。他们对于这些会计实践所引起的后果以及由其所引起的抵抗力只能认识到其中的一部分(Hindess,1982)。可是这并不意味着事物的结果必然会是主体意图的结果。

缺乏统一性的会计星座

拥有不同目的的人们所做出的各种行为有可能会产生意想不到的结果,这意味着会计星座缺乏统一性。会计星座有可能对如会计或工资体系的采用等

---

① 对于通货膨胀会计的兴起和讨论,参见 Burchell *et al.* (1980)和 Hopwood(1984)。通货膨胀会计和价值增值有一些共同的背景。对两者的会计准则讨论是交叉的,特别在会计法规的政治性方面。通货膨胀会计的讨论也涉及宏观经济管理,尽管是在不同的政策领域。在公积金领域,也涉及劳资关系问题。除了这些交叉的部分,通货膨胀会计有其特定的领域,如税收政策、不同行业的相对业绩、对金融行业的高利润率的质疑。

企业所面临的各种决策思考模式产生影响,并且很有可能会伴随着激烈的争论或巨大的意见分歧。可以想象,尽管员工和企业的经营者双方都同意采用VAIPS系统,但双方都对伴随新的工资体系所发生的手续以及各种组织中的变化产生强烈的抵抗。同样,特定的思考模式和特定的制度环境有可能在会计准则被设定后,引起各种争论(Zeff,1978)。在价值增值的问题上,我们指出了通过三个不同舞台上交错发生的各种事件,产生了一系列什么样的行为。于是可以发现,暧昧性是促使会计星座形成的各种实践的中心所在。像VAIPS这样的系统和价值增值概念本身,作为多种利害关系和目的的媒介发挥其功能。从这一点来看,会计星座与其说是一个由明确的原理、作用、功能所确定的系统或实体,不如说更像是一个垃圾桶(Cohen et al.,1972)。

渗入组织及社会中的会计

我们对会计变迁进行分析的模式有很多地方还停留在条件适合模式上。可是我们所用的手法与会计及环境关系模式有根本上的区别。我们没有从一开始就对会计领域和环境领域进行分离,不是在将会计和环境分离的基础上进行分析的。相反,我们对价值增值计算表、雇用报告书、财务报表等资料中产生的各种社会关系网进行了概述。在这个网络中,会计创造了特定的社会关系,促进了对特定行为者的权利、义务及其行为进行规定,同时还可以看到会计对划分组织的分界线以及组织内部的细分化问题起到了重要的作用。这样看来,会计不仅构筑了各个功能性环境,还渗透其中并起到了促进作用。就如无法将生物体从其栖息地中强行取出一样,也无法将会计从其生存环境中孤立出来。当然,就利益或价值增值概念而言,可以不考虑相关法律法规或主体的权利和义务,只对其进行抽象的议论。但我们所关心的价值增值的特征不是那种孤立的存在。如果想对抽象的价值增值进行调查,则变成了调查一个完全不同的问题。所以,本文中将价值增值的存在方式和功能方式,作为统一在特定社会关系中的一部分加以分析。

会计星座与社会关系和组织实践网络

我们已经将有关价值增值的出现及功能的社会关系视为网络。这一术语的使用与组织理论的展开方法非常相像(Aldrich,1979)。组织论的网络式思维方式,打破了过去组织—环境的两极思维方式,为未来的研究开辟了新的道路。这种研究方法,将焦点从如何适应不断变化的环境这样一个组织内部问题,转移到了组织间关系这样一个更广泛的网络中。

在本文的分析中,将特定的社会关系网作为促使价值增值会计形成的前提条件展开了论述。但该网络的构成要素及其相互间的关联方式,与组织论中的网络完全不同。该网络的主要构成要素不是单个的组织,而是特定的系统和过程,比如工资系统、财务报告系统、信息系统等。我们展示了这些系统是怎样由不同的行为者、机关以及诸系统之间存在的关系网来构成的。同时,我们还通过对三个不同舞台上演绎的发展过程进行分析来对该网络进行说明,并对在这三个舞台上分别进行的各种行为、介入的目的和主体、监视和介入的手段以及各种相关的知识团体进行了描述。我们认为各个舞台中的发展结果是由各种介入的结果,以及特定的行为者、机关和经营管理实践中产生的各种关系交错形成的。而会计星座本身则是由各个舞台中诸过程以及诸实践之间不自觉地相互作用而形成的网络。

在前面的论述中,通过将焦点放在各个舞台中的经营管理系统及其运作上,揭示了在区分组织成员和非组织成员的过程中组织实体是如何形成的。Litterer(1961,1963)使用相关的方法,揭示了"大企业"(Chandler,1962)的组织现象是如何通过作为成体系的管理运动来使用的成本计算,以及生产和在库管理系统来形成的。

同样,我们所显示的各舞台中发展起来的各种东西是由经济、社会和环境等复杂的实体经过变化形成的(参见 Donzelot,1979)。为了介入各种舞台,需要使用多种多样的方法,还要对各种主体及手段进行选择。而在介入组织的过程之中,经营管理实践受社会和经济的影响而渐趋于精巧。由此可见,"组织"可以说是在社会和经济的名义下进行的各种实践发生交错的场所。组织是各种不同的网络交织的节点,而这些网络为了实现介入拥有多种不同的目的和手段。于是,组织又可以是人们划分边界线、进行内部团结、追求某种目的、完成其功能的一种场所。从这点来看,组织、社会和经济实体并不是各自独立的。社会、经济与其说存在于组织之外,正如价值增值会计现象的事例所显示的那样,倒不如说是在其自身形成的过程中就已渗透到组织中的。

价值增值会计的出现和衰退

在讨论了为价值增值的出现提供条件的各种环境的属性、意义和特征后,有意思的是,对价值增值的关心在20世纪80年代初突然衰退了。价值增值活动的三个领域的组织,在1979年诞生的新的保守党政府下突然衰退了。为了实现国家经济政策引入了新的经济政策。有关劳资关系的认识发生了根本性的变化。后来,政府不再介入有关会计准则的相关问题。因此,价值增值的重要性也就不再引人注目了。随着社会环境的变化,价值增值在各种社会关系中的功能接近了技术界限。于是价值增值开始成为历史。

尽管英国的经济从根本上还是由政府控制的,但新政府开始试图用全新的方式来重建其经济。于是金融政策开始收紧,竞争压力得到强调,而工资水平的安定问题未被提到桌面上来,所得政策也没有成为政治的对象。在失业率逐年增高的情况下,市场的压力被认为是控制所得的有效手段。生产性和效率性依然是政府重视的对象。不过,此时多种多样的介入战略被实施。(很多人)认为经营管理的新技术可以提高英国产业的效率性。经济政策中协力和参加的概念退出了历史舞台。竞争压力、扩大职务训练、分散剩余劳动、投资特别是先端技术的投资,以及资本集中等被强调起来。

这样的变化同样出现在劳资关系领域。工业民主、参加、提高劳动者的权利等议论终止了。实际上,(新政府)努力取消由前政府赋予的权力或尽量使其至少不被强化。词汇的用法发生了改变,看不到工业民主与效率性、竞争、自由市场、放松规制、排除独占势力等问题成为新的焦点。比起广泛的社会政治权力,经济上的问题开始得到强调。相比协力和参与,真正的企业家行为成为美德,领导力代替参与成为新时代的秩序。

职业会计界没能及时认识到这一变化。业界虽然普遍预测政府的介入并对此抱有戒心,但实际上政府介入并没有带来像过去那样的威胁。通货膨胀会计中依然残留着过去政府介入的痕迹,但职业会计界特别是会计准则委员会(ASC)开始顺应新的政治形势了。尽管从更广范围的产业界和金融界中选拔代表组成了会计准则委员会(ASC),但国家作为介入者不再站在保护职业会计界的立场上了。作为知识的潜在的正统化手段,一种新的尝试正在开始(Hopwood,1983)。在设定准则的问题上,有关将来必须解决的问题被尽量压缩。特别是有关价值增值的问题,从未来应进行审议的课题中消失了。

价值增值的时代结束了,因为促使价值增值出现、发展并赋予其重要意义的特定的星座消失了。价值增值出现的舞台发生了断裂,价值增值存在所必需的星座消失了。价值增值失去了其生存的社会基础,作为一种具有技术可能性的会计技术,它被置于会计教科书的脚注中。价值增值失去了其广泛存在的重要性条件,这使得价值增值发展的要素也消失了。

价值增值的衰退,并不是一种新的现象。价值增值从 20 世纪 40 年代末期到 50 年代初期,在英国一度成为重要的课题。到了 70 年代中期,涉及和企业员工间沟通、信息披露以及英国经济业绩的问题,对价值增值的关心再次高涨。价值增值被预期成为 70 年代后期的会计实践,而出现在会计报告中(Burchell *et al.*,1981)。在这两个期间之中,有关价值增值的讨论几乎没有出现过。

置于社会与组织环境中的会计研究

对价值增值的原点的讨论,强调了会计概念的功能及其存在方式由复杂的环境所规定。同时,也可以看出适合价值增值的环境条件非常特殊。20世纪50年代初期和80年代初期,对价值增值的关注消失了。这两个时期,与在困难时期采用各种不同的管理方法不同,因为经济的相对繁荣,价值增值赖以生存的环境崩溃了,从而导致了发展的断裂。对价值增值关注的弱化,和其出现与发展一样,证明了本文的理论立场。

结论

我们揭示了价值增值会计现象是如何在各种制度、问题及过程的复杂相互作用中出现的。这一对特定的会计变化的研究使我们不仅能更多地将会计置于其运作的环境中,而且能提出和讨论要试图理解会计的社会功能而不得不面对的重要理论问题。

Zeff(1978)虽然与我们使用的方法不同,但也同样指出了在讨论会计问题时,注意其相关环境的重要性。他在对制定会计准则的讨论中,指出了准则制定会从多方面受到政治因素的影响,而这些因素及其影响是用于讨论会计实务及其采用原因的传统会计模式所无法反映出来的。Zeff认为会计实务的经济以及社会后果在制定会计准则时已不容忽视(Zeff,1978)。因此,为了应对这一问题而构建理论支柱是极为重要的。

最近发展起来的以代理理论((Jensen and Meckling,1976)为基础的会计研究方法可以看作是对Zeff提出问题的直接回应。这一方法已被用于标准制定过程(Watts and Zimmerman,1978)、会计理论的状况和形式(Wattsst Zimmerman,1979)以及特定会计程序(Zimmerman,1979)的分析中。我们认为在本文的结论中值得指出我们的研究方法与代理理论学者的方法的区别,以及这些区别对于会计研究的意义。

一般来说,两种方法的区别是可以清楚表述的。对代理理论学者来说,财务报表是一种经济商品,有需求,也有会产生成本的生产。财务报表的功能就是作为决定财富转移的量的工具,如股利、税收、薪酬和代理成本。会计程序的不同就在于它们对于财富转移的不同影响,因而个体和群体在所使用的会计程序方面来说是没有区别的。这些个体和群体用任何一种给定的会计程序确定他们的财富、做出相应的决策——无论在未受法规约束的还是在有一定约束的市场,都是一样的。我们并不怀疑个体会试图对会计实践变化带来的对财务报表的影响进行分析:作为其会计方法选择的一部分。然而,我们更感兴趣的是特定的利益群体,或对会计感兴趣的群体,其组合的呈现过程。代理理论学者通过区分有法规约束的经济体和无约束的经济体对这种呈现过程的差异进行了一定程度的分析。清楚地表达对经济的干预对会计发展来说是至关重要的(参见 Hopwood et al.,1980),但这并不意味着不可能构建一个比区分有法规约束和无约束更为具体、细微的模型,并对变化的过程进行更具体的研究。我们可以包含那些会计或某一特定的类别和报表在某些特定代理人的利益领域中得以塑形的过程,以及这些代理人与这些特定项目相关的利益的仔细考虑和计量的方式:价值增值会计是如何在劳资关系的领域中显现的?一旦显现,它是如何被评估的?

这样我们的着重点就在于变化的过程,而代理理论学者旨在建立一定类别的活动之间的相互关系,如对所提议的会计准则的态度和持这一态度者的利益的估算。代理理论学者采用利己主义理论模式,而我们关注利己主义,或特定的态度,是如何形成的——包括特定经济计量和会计方法而不是经济演算的一般性在这一过程中所起的作用。代理理论学者得益于来自经济学理论的自我利益计算模式并关注会计报表的某一特定功能,他们的研究预先假设了能指导理性经济行为的元-会计的存在,并寻求对这样一种会计的详尽解释和阐述。我们的分析不采用这一原始会计的假设,我们视计算的功能和模式为特定会计实践的发散的功能组成部分,而不是仅仅作为特定管理或决策制定的参考。

本文利用历史学和谱系学的方法,排除会计具有某种先验性作用和功能的前提进行了考察。我们的工作原则是:"导致事物起源的要因和其最终的完整呈现、它的实际应用及其在有目的的系统中的地位,都是完全不同的。"(Nietzsche,1969,p.77,并被 Minson(1980)引用)这意味着概念形成和由此而产生的哲学难题,最终都要归结到其起源问题上来。如果思想发生了变化,导致这种变化的任何一种原因都会对思想方式产生持续的影响。就好像是概念对时代背景产生了记忆一样(Hacking,1981)。Wells 关于制造费用会计起源的研究就遵循了这样一种思路(Wells,1978)。与此类似,本文指出了价值增值会计现象背后隐含的各种过程决定"价值增值"这一概念及其特性。

参考文献[①]

(李落落 译)

[①] 参见本文英文参考文献。

会计体系考古学

摘要：会计体系随着时间的推移而变化。但是,对于这种变化的前提条件和过程及其对组织的影响,我们知道的却不多。本文回顾和评价了关于会计变化的现有观点,然后讨论了有关会计变化的三个案例。基于这些案例,我们讨论了有关如何理解会计变化过程的若干理论问题。我们讨论的重点:一是隐含在会计变化之中的要素多样化;二是会计的反映性作用和建构性作用;三是会计变化如何改变组织变化的前提条件。

会计不是一种静止不变的现象。随着时间的推移,它已经历了多次变化。许多新技术已经被运用到会计领域中。会计所服务的目的也在不断地增加和变化。对于组织活动及其过程和结果,已经给出了不同的说明。各种会计实践的重点也有所不同。长期以来,会计一直与不同的组织划分类型的创造过程密切相关。组织自治和相关的新的形式——即便这些新的组织形式不是通过会计手段主动地创造出来的——也受到了特别的关注。通过改变对管理职能的会计表述,各种不同的管理职能成为重视的对象。

从上述观点来看,会计一直有着这样一种变化倾向,即它变得与其过去不同。作为一种处于流动和发展中的技艺,其各种技术和与技术相应的观点,都以若干种极不相同的方式,与组织和社会的转变相关联。可是,遗憾的是我们对于会计变化的过程知之甚少。目前,对于以下问题我们的了解是非常有限的:比如,关于诸如会计领域的某个特定概念产生的条件,推动会计发展的动力,会计诠释化及其普及的过程,以及由于会计制度的改变而产生的在个人、组织和社会方面的影响等。

尽管迄今为止已经对会计的历史进行了诸多研究(American Accounting Association,1970;Baladouni,1977;Parker,1977,1981),但是其中大多数研究都采用了一种相当技术型的观点来描述会计的遗留物,而不是主动地探索其基本的过程和作用力。一种古物收集癖在学术界占据着支配地位。人们一直忽视从以广泛的经济和社会为背景的组织的角度来研究会计学的重要意义。对于组织计算在组织的形成中可能起到的作用,它们的外部和内部边界,它们与其他组织和组织集团的关系等,还几乎没有什么研究。对于组织统治和管理的形成过程以何种方式影响进而决定会计的形成的研究,也很少见。因为直到最近(Armstrong,1985,1987;Hoskin and Macve,1986;Loft,1986a;Merion and Neimark,1982;Miller and O'Leary,1987),大多数关于会计现象的历史分析,不是采取一种非推理性的态度,就是满足于将会计变化视为一种技术的精致和改进的过程。

人们常常把会计看成是某种必然变化的结果,而不是将其视为变化过程的多种可能的结果之一。为此,人们提出了一种目的论式的发展轨道理论来解释会计的变化。这种理论用技术或经济的合理性和目的性的概念来解释在会计舞台上各种具体发展变化的出现。① 对于会计的历史遗留物,往往采用理所当然的渐进式的和机能主义的观点进行分析,而不是从影响会计或者被会计影响的诸要素的角度进行探究。

与此相似的观点也一直被用于试图从组织的角度解释会计现象的探讨之中。迄今为止,几乎还没有什么研究能够加深我们对于影响会计实践的各种压力的理解。我们尚不清楚会计实践本身如何产生会计变化和改革的动力,也不太了解会计实践与会计潜能之间所存在的不稳定而且常常是不确定的关系。② 尽管事实表明:会计一直而且仍在不断变化,它包含在组织功能化的广泛的过程之中,而且其变化不一定合乎其本身的经济原则(Burchell et al.,1980),然而从组织的角度对会计的探究往往是以某种将会计与周围环境隔离开来的方式展开的。人们仍然将会计看成是静态的技术现象——这种现象使得组织的功能化成为可能,而不是像现在我们所知的积极地形成组织的功能化。

但是,现在很有必要用一种不同的观点来审视现实中的会计。在另一方面,存在着许多促使会计变化的相当重要的因素。人们提出了这样一些问题,比如会计与不同的组织形式和过程之间有着怎样的关系(den Hertog,1978;

---

① 有关会计(和与其相关的)论述与会计实践的关系的更为详细的讨论参见 Hopwood(1984b)和 Miller and O'Leary(1986,1987)。对于会计论述的实践结果的完整的讨论也应该探究教科书和手册中给出的不同的会计实践的推论的聚合性,探究这些因素所起到的扩散作用,以及将会计论述扩展到组织舞台的会计修辞发展的重要意义,特别是会计技术在管理上的应用的重要意义。会计论述也已经在解释实践的不同性质方面和在从各种各样的例子中分出"好的"和"坏的"方面,起到了富有影响的作用。借助在任何意义上不与会计技艺相关的实践概念,会计论述明确了一个规范的逻辑,这个逻辑是与被看成是会计和组织进步的成就相关的。关于这些论点的进一步的讨论,参见 Hopwood(1986a)。

② 尽管有许多研究试图确定会计功能中的机能障碍,这些障碍通常被看作表明会计潜力的现象,而不是看作由于会计技艺对组织生活的其他方面的不断增加的侵蚀而产生的组织上的紧张和冲突的表现。这样的机能障碍分析往往告诉我们许多有关会计体系运作的理想概念,而实践注定会与这些理想偏离。确实,这样一种对会计潜力而不是会计实际的关注,也反映在试图运用行为理论精确地调整会计的社会技术实践的努力之中。许多行为和组织研究往往被用于动员技术影响力,而不是用于解释会计的组织发生的观念,从而对抗会计的技术实践和相应的目的。

Hedberg and Jönsson,1978；Hopwood,1977,1979)。有越来越多的研究用组织管理的战略概念来探究会计的本质(Goold,1986；Simmonds,1983)。不同的组织都需要会计,特别是那些不属于私营企业的组织(Hopwood,1984a)。各种信息技术正在创造着会计的组织意义持续移动的潜在可能性。尤其重要的是,越来越多的会计研究立足于现有的实际结果而不是一直期望出现的结果(Hopwood,1986；Kaplan,1985)。尽管比较缓慢,但是那些隐含在会计变化中的因素、组织进步以及会计技艺实践的结果已经开始被列入研究的议程表。另一方面,会计研究的视角也开始有了变化。在会计界,不是试图仅仅在会计的技术合理性方面取得进展,而是出现了这样一些迹象,即从更深的和批判的立场进行研究。与此相关,人们开始对会计提出与过去迥然不同的问题。这种研究开始深入探讨会计的组织和社会起源,而不是仅仅接受会计的技术合理性。除此之外,还探讨各种组织的压力和会计内在的基本原理,并考虑随着经济计算(比如会计)形式的发展,利害冲突的各方互相交织在一起的方式。随着会计不再被看作是一种没有利害关系的努力,而被看作是创造一种特别的可见性和具有组织意义的模式,人们更多地关注起组织和社会行动对会计产生的影响。

从这个角度来看,应该研究的课题是非常之多的。过去那种强调技术的、静态的观点与新兴的会计动力学的观点形成了明显的对比。但是,如此众多的课题显然不可能由任何一个单独的研究来解决,因此在本文中我们的讨论有以下几个具体的目的。首先,我们考察了现有的关于会计变化的观点,其目的在于看看这些观点能否帮助我们理解推动会计变化的动力以及会计与组织、社会行动之间相互交织的方式。然后,我们借助几个说明性案例,试图至少是部分地阐明隐含在会计变化之中的压力和过程,这些案例既有历史上的也有现代的。讨论案例的目的在于试图为从另外的角度就会计技艺的另类问题梳理出某些思路,而不是试图对于会计是如何变化的问题做出综合性的分析。基于对这些案例的分析,我们确认并讨论与理解会计变化相关的一些重要问题。分析的总体目的是要更深地提出问题,更好地从组织的角度和动态的角度理解会计。

关于会计变化的某些观点

会计与组织改进

正如前面所说明的,传统研究从组织改革和改进的视角对会计变化进行了探讨。会计之所以变化是为了变得更好。会计技艺一直被看作是逐渐进步的,尽管这种进步可能非常缓慢。分析、调查以及基于经验的学习共同促进会计潜能逐步成为现实。会计的变化被看成是它朝着自身应有的状态迈进的一个过程。

上述会计变化的种种特征都要求会计在提高组织业绩上发挥作用。人们认为,组织的经济性、效率和有效性不仅可以用会计手段来提高,而且是与会计或者其他计算方法相独立而存在的。而且,会计在组织功能化中所起的积极作用,往往是在受其影响的特定的组织实践之前,并且独立于这些特定的组织实践而被确定下来。会计被视为包含在指导、计划、决策、协调、控制和激励管理等过程中。在所有这些领域,特定的会计实践可能而且确实被用来与有关它们的应有状态的那些抽象概念相比较。

以这样一种方式,知识的概念实体在指导我们理解会计技艺方面起着非常大的作用。即便按照传统的观点,会计也不仅仅是一种技术。知识并非处在会计之外。经济的和管理的合理性以及功能性的修辞学构成了我们对于会计的技术性质的评价体系。人们求助于构想、范畴和理论等"概念网络"(Foucault, 1972)来阐释和指导实际的会计工作。因此,会计实践就被看成是上述抽象规则的具体实现或者受挫的表现。从会计实践在特定的组织中与特定功能相关的方式,可以判断会计实践是否充分。因此,人们试图以会计是否符合预期的要求为标准而改进会计。

作为一门学问,会计已经在阐明有关会计应当是什么样的抽象知识体方面,投入了很多的精力。[①] 已经有了许多概念来描述关于什么是好的或者说"最佳的"成本管理,什么是好的计划、报告方式以及评价投资可行性的方法。对于如何梳理关于好的协调与指导的抽象特征,以及它们在会计实践改革上的意义,也做了不少尝试。人们已经将关于决策及其合理性的经济概念和认识概念与会计的具体部分联系起来,从而建立起了一些思想体系,这些体系拥有与会计实践不相关的变化实体和动力学。通过运用来自诸如经济学、政治学、公共管理和心理学的独立论述,或者战略管理的最新概念等构成的知识体,从会计实践和会计功能化中提取有用的东西,我们就可以从另一个角度来评价会计。特定的实践可以按照其符合一般管理和可管理概念的程度来评价。一个抽象的外部知识体既可以用来检验会计实践是否充分,还可以用来改革会计实践使

---

① 这样的理解不仅仅是面向未来的。对于过去非常特别的评价也向我们提供了关于会计的现在和未来的信息。正像已经讨论的那样,人们已经为会计的发展划定了特定的轨道,它把会计的过去和未来强有力地联系起来。关于对过去的理解的更加一般的讨论,参见 Hobsbawm and Ranger(1983)、Lowenthal(1985)和 Wright(1985)。

之变为其真正应有的形态。凭借其真正潜能的抽象的形象,可以动员和改变会计。①

毫无疑问,很多会计变化产生于这种会计潜能的概念。但是,作为理解这种变化的过程或者变化结果的依据,传统观点有很大的局限性。因为这些传统观点不是提供会计产生的原本的历史,而是提供一个不完全的、无知的和过时的历史汇编(当会计不是它应有的形态时),加上少许富于启发性的材料(当会计朝着实现其潜能的方向移动时)。假定会计的功能是独立于其实践存在的(这种实践面向与会计相独立的特定目标),而且实践要解决的问题是改革组织程序,使之实现其内在的目标,那么会计变化就可以用会计之外的知识体来描述和评价。因此,虽然会计潜能的实现或许是有问题的,但是潜能本身却很少被看成是有问题的。会计被赋予了这样一种认识论上的特权地位,即尽管它是经过巨大努力构建起来的,但其本质却不是这样。会计不去探索其产生的自有模式,也不去探究其获得现在的地位的方式,以及它与技术变化的细节相互关联的背景条件,而是想当然地认为那些论述起着动员变化的作用。

这样一种会计发展观也忽视了会计与会计潜能概念之间的相互作用的二重性。无论从历史的还是组织的角度来看,组织化装置在影响我们的组织概念方面起到了重要的作用。有关组织目标、功能和功能化的诸概念是在组织行动和计算的具体方式的发展过程中产生的。同样,组织参加不是被置于其所参与的实践之外的。管理和管理者的概念在特定的社会历史接合点,以特定的方式被积极地构筑起来。这些概念是与管理和计算的实际方法不可分的,而这些实际方法在过去和现在仍然隐含在它们的出现和功能化之中。没有哪个先验的管理者拥有能动员管理实践发展的兴趣和需求。同样,也不存在促成了今天我们所知的会计发展的原始会计概念。会计以一种更为积极的方式出现,而不是仅仅作为一种本质的实现。的确,在一定程度上,会计的现实需要(它们可能而且确实引导会计的发展)产生于会计技艺的实践。按照类似的观点,会计实践应该被看作是在创造有组织的努力方面,而不仅仅是使有组织的努力成为可能方面,发挥更为积极的作用。会计变化既是组织实现和授权的过程,更是组织构建的历史。②

这并非否认会计潜能的外部话语可能而且确实推动了会计的变化。这些

---

① 在财务会计领域,有关通货膨胀会计的争论为研究这样的过程提供了一个很好的舞台。
② Litterer(1963)在他讨论系统的管理在美国制造企业中的出现时,强调了这一点。他指出"事实上,正是那些我们讨论过的系统和许多其他类似的系统构成了管理活动的大部分内容"(参见 p.338 和 p.391)。

话语激励了行动,并且在它们的基础上可以形成对于旨在干预特定的组织目标的理解(Nahapiet,1984)。它们还可以提供既能测定对变化的需求又能解释其效果的尺度和标准。可是对于话语所起到的能够引导和促进变化的诸多作用的理解,仍然不能够帮助我们理解变化的机制和那些推动会计学和会计修辞学发展的动力,也无助于我们理解具体实践的内容、它们所造成的阻力以及它们实际引起的对于组织的影响。因为假定在会计的修辞及话语与组织中的干预行动方案之间存在任何不变的关系都是不适当的。这样一种关系所采取的各种形式应该是一个需要调查研究的问题,而不是一个假定。

会计与建立组织秩序

会计实践本身日益成为人们研究的焦点。认识到关于会计潜能的抽象话语与在组织中发挥作用的会计特征之间的关系尚不明确,会计研究开始更加重视对现实中的会计的分析和理解(Hopwood,1978,1983;Kaplan,1983;Scapens,1983,1984)。但是,这些研究的绝大多数都没有明确地强调会计变化这一现象,只是对现实中会计的多样性和在某一个特别时点上的会计运用进行了初步的探讨。

尽管有些研究已经开始探讨由于会计体系的运用所引起的组织紧张状态,但是却很少有研究涉及它们怎样才能为重新评价会计和会计变化提供基础的问题。虽然有些研究描述了会计的抵抗和机能障碍,但是除了个别的例外(Argyris,1977;Berry et al.,1985),很少有涉及会计精致化和变化的反历史研究,因为人们总是试图保证会计技艺的持续完整性、正当性、有效性和权威性。因此,尽管有些研究开始从组织背景的角度来探讨会计,但是这些研究的基本观点仍旧是一种相对静止的观点。对于会计的多样性所做的分析也基本上是类似的。虽然同一时期会计实践的差异促使人们去分析影响会计形式的某些因素,然而所采用的权变分析法却有许多比较分析的特征(Otley,1980)。人们从会计的过去和现在的形态来认识它,而不是把它视为一个正在形成的过程。而且,暗含在会计适应中的组织计算法仍然是建立在下面的前提之上的,即会计在强化中性的和高度普遍的组织业绩概念方面起着功能性的作用。管理自由决断和选择的作用很少被承认(Child,1972;Thompson,待发表),更不要说积极行使政治和权利的作用了(Cooper,1981;Pettigrew,1972)。会计变化还被看成是一种反映性的而非建构性的组织努力。由于会计被认为只具有使组织事件成为可能,而不是具有更加主动地形成组织事件的作用,因此,其他组织因素虽然对会计产生影响,但是会计却不具有类似的作用。不同的会计被视为不同环境的反映,而不是被视为包含在一种主动的改变会计形态的过程之中。因此,对会计

置于社会与组织环境中的会计研究

多样性的分析只是产生了对于变化的推测,而没有导出对所涉及的过程的具体分析。而这种具体分析对于构成其基础的逻辑和会计技艺的组织作用和结果不做任何事先的假定。

虽然如此,这种对组织的评价一直是有用的。尽管存在着许多的问题(Dent,1986;Otley,1980),但是会计至少被证明是这样一种技艺,它被埋置在组织功能中,并且与组织的其他方面,如战略、结构、工作划分方法和其他组织技术与实践等相互依存。会计不是作为一种独立存在的技艺,而是在一种组织或者国家的特定文化形态、一种特定的组织环境和一套特定的组织任务管理方法之中被建立和使用的一种组织实践(Horovitz,1980)。会计已经至少被建立在某种组织环境的基础之上,并在这种组织环境中发挥它的作用。如果会计被看成是一种与其环境如此相关而且受到其他组织实践影响的现象,那么就至少会存在这样一种可能性,即会计未必适合它的目的(Argyris,1977;Kaplan,1983)。因此,虽然这一观点仍然是初步的和不全面的,会计潜能的抽象概念依然面临着一种对于会计实践新的理解的挑战。

会计与建立社会秩序

尽管只是初步的,从组织的角度对会计的理解仍然将会计视为一种具有某种理论依据的实践。而这种理论依据可以纯粹从(会计在其中起作用的)特定的组织需要和要求的观点来理解。会计可以看成是起源于一些问题,这些问题是在特定的组织约束和目标管理方式的条件下,因协调和管理某个复杂的转换过程的需要而引起的。可是,最近的研究开始质疑这种限定于组织的观点。人们越来越认为会计起源于在组织舞台上展现的各种社会冲突之中(Cooper,1980,1981;Hopper et al. ,1986;Tinker,1980;Tinker et al. ,1982)。人们不是将组织会计视为面向组织管理的、预先给定的经济规则的一种技术性反映,而是将其看作为了在组织中创造一种特别的经济可见性,以及创造一种使得组织的统治和控制纳入经济轨道的方法而主动构筑起来的东西(Clawson,1980)。从这样的观点来看,会计就不是一种技术管理的被动的工具,也不是仅仅揭示事先给定的组织功能的各个方面的中性手段,而是起源于组织内外的社会力量的运用之中。为了创造真正有关经济和社会目的的特别概念,会计参与了在组织内建立经济计算特定制度的过程。

按照这样的观点,与会计实践的交叉方式决定了组织选择、决策和行动等的形态。在可管理组织范围的创造过程中,会计起着一个非常主导性的作用。经济可见性和计算制度促使有助于特定的社会权力概念发挥作用的组织得以产生和运行。通过将经济动机与合理的公认的经济事实相结合,这些经济动机已经成为现实的和富有影响的东西。这样,组织中的工作过程被明示化、有序化,并且按照实物和社会标准进行分配。因而产生的组织事实、策划、日程表和计划使得建立这样一个从工作过程的实际运作中提炼出来的并且与之相分离的管理制度成为可能。

因此,尽管是在组织中起作用,会计最好应被看成是属于社会领域而不是狭窄的组织领域的人工制品。它被包含在社会组织的急剧转变之中。的确,会计被认为是一种使组织融进社会中的重要手段。

从这个角度来看,很明显会计变化是一个令人瞩目的焦点。会计实践的发展不仅被相当明确地论证,而且有时也被强加了一种特别的发展轨道。确实,从这样的观点来看,在某种意义上会计仍然具有动员它自身发展的本质和使命。从这一立场出发,会计仍旧是一种启示性的努力,通过主动地构筑组织来施加影响,而这些影响既独立于会计也独立于其组织代表。按照目前流行的关于会计的比较正统的假设,对于它所致力的目的来说它仍然被看成是一种适当的努力。会计被视为既有目的又有意义的东西。

接近现实中的会计观点

尽管比较缓慢,但是我们对会计变化的理解正在不断加深。人们试图用会计技艺的组织和社会功能分析来对抗传统的会计改进观点。认为会计处在现实组织实践的过程之中,其变化和结果依赖于它如何与其他手法交织在一起创造出可管理的组织方式。人们已经开始在组织和社会领域而不是纯技术的领域探寻会计的结构和功能。

但是,正如我们上面所述,现有的研究探讨仍然是初步的。探讨现实中会计的特性的研究还比较少见。有关讨论往往涉及组织、环境或社会变化的一般倾向的动员潜能(Burchell et al.,1985),几乎没有研究工作对会计变化的精确机制进行揭示和描述。组织与社会仍然是两个相互独立的领域。也很少有研究工作试图描绘出组织和社会之间的互相重叠及互相独立的部分,来理解会计怎样通过社会的关注转变组织,进而创造出影响社会领域形成的组织实践。即使从组织或者社会的观点来看,会计的作用仍旧被定义在会计技艺的实践之外。组织参与者仍然被看作是与其参与的实践相隔离的。或许是由于这种探究与实践的分离,我们目前所知的对会计变化的阐释一直强调会计的反映性倾向而不是它的建构性倾向(Burchell et al.,1985;Hopwood,1985b)。

在这样一个背景之下,我们下面的讨论局限于以下目标。我们试图通过分析会计变化的案例,来弄清在组织层面的某些过程。凭借现实中会计的某些特定的实例,我们试图阐明组织会计在变成与现有形态不同的过程中所隐含的某些要素。但是,我们并不打算建立一个会计变化的替代理论。我们的目标是相当有限的,即描述那些任何理论都必须着力解决的论点和问题。我们的目的仅仅在于扩展概念舞台而不是寻求解答。

将会计放在它不曾有过的位置

一般来说,很难有机会目睹一个新兴的会计的诞生过程。通常我们只好满足于观察一个会计精致化的过程,即某个组织会计被扩展和提炼,并转变成为其他形态的会计的过程。但是,在18世纪英国陶器工匠Josiah Wedgwood的案例中,我们有可能通过被保存下来的大量的信件和记录来间接地观察新兴会计的诞生过程(McKendrick,1960,1961a,1961b,1964,1973)。①

Wedgwood是英国产业革命初期成功的企业家。作为一个既有科学分析能力又有精明商业头脑的人,他创建了英国最早的工业化(与手工陶器作坊不同的)陶器企业之一。他不仅是生产方法(McKendrick,1961a),而且是产品设计、科学研究的应用(Schofield,1956)以及产品的市场开发方面的拓荒者(McKendrick,1960,1961b)。Wedgwood的企业迅速成为面向富裕阶层的陶器供应商,不但盈利丰厚,而且急速扩张。

起初,Wedgwood几乎不使用会计,尤其是出于所谓的管理目的。会计信息没有在其产品、定价决策或者工作方法的选择上发挥作用。正如McKendrick(1973,p.48)所描述的:

> 因为他所能期待的盈利非常丰厚,而且可以定很高的价格,所以对他来说除了日常的成本核算之外,没有什么动力去采用任何其他方法。

确实,Wedgwood承认自己"除了估计成本之外,什么都不会",而且进一步承认"自己试图估算全部成本的努力彻底失败了"(McKendrick,1973,p.49)。

然而,这种状况发生了变化。在1772年,事业的扩张走到了尽头。陶器产业遭遇了一场大的经济衰退。按照Ashton(1959,p.128)的说法,"恐慌蔓延到北欧的大多数城市"。价格、盈利、工资和就业都急速地下降,跟其他行业一样,

---

① 我无意暗示Wedgwood的首创使得成本会计发展成熟起来(Jenks,1960,p.423),或者在他之前没有先例。事实并非如此。虽然早期的成本核算系统没有被很好地记录和分析(参见Jones,1985),但是成本核算技术确实出现了。另外,我认为尤其重要的是一个有力的和更加一般的经济论为创建一种新的可见性提供了动机(Tribe,1978)。成本是可以被谈论的,如果说不能被观察的话。因此,尽管存在这样的事实,即对于每个企业组织,问题是从经验中解决的,这样就形成了一套持续一贯的规范和概念,而且它们之间超出个别企业范围的交流是少见和偶然的(Jenks,1960,p.424),我们仍然应该认识到支撑着这种创新步骤的重要的推理上和实践上的可能性条件。

陶器行业的企业破产也急剧增加。同其他人一样，Wedgwood 在当时也完全意识到了他所面临的困难。

然而，随着需求的疲软从伦敦向周边地区扩散，整个秋季库存增加和销售下降的情况愈加严重。同年 11 月，他记录了在爱丁堡的糟糕的销售情况："从 6 月份以来 Ferrier 先生……没有售出任何产品。"……而且随着销售的下降，在 Eturia 的产量不得不缩减到危险的水平。尽管 Wedgwood 不愿意承认需求的下降，但是他最终不得不承认这一现实。当工人们没有工作可干的时候，他取消了加班时间。即使在那时，他仍然不愿意相信情况已经如此令人绝望以至于必须放走最好的工人。Wedgwood 决心留住他花费了巨大精力培训出来的工人，但是已经有许多工人没有活干了，镀金工们没有一件活干，全都在闲着。伴随着冬季的来临，情况变得更加糟糕。在 9 月 19 日，Wedgwood 写道：我们必须全力寻求任何机会。在节礼日*任何一种琐碎细微的流行样子都被不遗余力地开发出来……两天之后，他欣慰地宣布在圣诞节期间暂时停工。可是，三个星期之后情况更加恶化。"经过三个星期的假期之后，星期一我们又开始工作。如果你有任何订单的话，请赶快交给我。因为我实在不知道该让他们做什么工作。可是他们必须有活干，因为昨天早上他们围攻我，坚决要求要么给他们活干要么允许他们离开"（McKendrick，1973，p.63）。

在这样的危急时期，人们往往会重新估价经营方法。抱着这样一个目的，Wedgwood 开始将其注意力转到生产费用上，也就是在这种背景下，他的成本会计诞生了。

Wedgwood 的想法是这样的：如果能够通过降低其产品的价格而刺激需求的话，或许他的企业就可能在经济萧条时生存下来。但是，实现这样的想法有一个前提条件，就是必须保证降低后的价格仍然要高于成本。这样问题就出现了。因为虽然成本的概念已经进入到商业和贸易的话语之中，而且可以促使行动，但是还没有一种既定的装置来操作这一散漫的概念。成本只是一个概念，而不是一个事实。

Wedgwood 试图发现的正是成本会计的事实。正如他向其经营伙伴 Bentley 指出的那样：

我们需要认真讨论是不是应该大幅度地降低水晶瓶和镀金瓶的价格。为此我制作了一本工艺价格书，它包括每种瓶子从原材料到你的伦敦店铺

---

* 指圣诞节的次日。——译者注

所消耗的每一项成本。我将送给你样本,然后你可以判断我们如何在这方面做得更好些。我们下一步要考虑的问题是什么是最审慎的办法(McKendrick,1973,p.49)。

这不是一项简单的任务。因为没有现成的方法可用来通过会计之眼观察组织内部的运作,而且组织也不是轻易可以看透的。成本会计的事实需要花力气去创造而不仅仅是去揭示。

  Wedgwood 在 1772 年 8 月 23 日给 Bentley 的信中写道:上个星期,我一直在苦苦思考如何找到适当的数据和计算制造费用的方法。将销售和损失分配到我们制造的每一件产品上是一件非常复杂的事情。而且更糟糕的是,我发现目前的做法是错的,某些地方肯定存在着本质性的错误,但是我不知道到底错在哪里以及如何进行修正。我知道这种探索是非常重要的,所以我不会放弃。我现在送给你的材料说明我已经走到了哪一步,依据是什么。希望你有时间坐下来考虑这个问题,并提出好的解决方法。对我们来说,建立测算我们产品的成本的尺度是极为重要的。用这样一种尺度,我们确定产品的价格,使之既不会过高而影响销售,也不会太低而影响盈利(McKendrick,1973,p.49)。

通过这样的努力,建立起了越来越详细的会计。然而,Wedgwood 对自己的努力的结果并不满意。

  我已经把我的某些困难摆在了你的面前。其中最使我困惑的是,虽然我确信我已经考虑到了产品制造和销售的各种成本,但是将一年中的成本与产品的数量加以比较的结果,似乎这些成本只是制造和销售这么多产品的实际费用的一半多一点(McKendrick,1973,p.53)。

但是,不久之后他确实发现了使他困惑的原因。通过比较财务账目和自己的成本核算,他发现两者是不一致的。

  从整体上看,账目是准确无误的,但是具体到每一部分时它就不一致了。对于小的瓷器来说,账目是对的,可是对那些高额瓷器,账目则是不相符的,因为它们的成本似乎是实际金额的 1/10。于是,他开始清查存货并试着采用其他的方法(McKendrick,1973,p.61)。

作为一个好奇心很强的人,Wedgwood 很快发现了为什么成本核算的各个部分不相吻合。他的探求结果揭示了"一部贪污、敲诈、欺骗和奢侈浪费的历史"(McKendrick,1973,p.61)。他的首席秘书 Ben,被证明有问题,这也是

Wedgwood一直担心的事情。Ben的账户总是延迟好几个月,可是当他每次结账时,账目就准确无误了(McKendrick,1973,p.61)。通过进一步的调查,Wedgwood发现办公人员所在的纽波特办公楼对于青年人的成长和社会秩序来说是有害的。管家跟出纳员胡搞,首席秘书腐败,而且奢侈无度(McKendrick,1973,p.61)。

在找出会计数字不一致的根源之后,Wedgwood感到对于企业的经营有了信心。他接着写道:

我们撤换了首席秘书和出纳员。看来现在正好是导入我们认为正确的任何新规定或者改变整个计划的时候。现在我们知道所有被销售掉而没有列在账上的产品必然以库存增加的形式出现,这时我们就有足够的理由来怀疑我们的首席秘书是否忠诚。库存如此迅速的增加是一个使人担心的事情,只有完全消除库存我才会放下心来(McKendrick,1973,p.61)。

为改变上述状况,我们迅速采取了措施。为了"使收集的经营数据保持连续性"(Mckendrick,1973,p.62),我们安排了一个新的秘书,负责每周的日常会计工作。

Wedgwood会计的诞生是困难和费力的。在会计核算的概念与用这一概念在组织中实施特别的干预行动之间从来不存在简单的关系。成本必须被构造出来而不仅仅是被揭示出来。一个以会计事实为基础的组织经济被艰苦地创造出来而不仅仅是被显示出来。

可是,一旦会计被构造起来,Wedgwood就有了用经济观点来观察组织的一个强有力的工具。从记录在危机管理中发挥作用这个战略概念他导出了一种方法,用这种方法可以透视组织内部的运行状况。这样一种新的可见性被创造出来了。组织中被植入了经济事实(Patton,1979)。一种用不同的语言来表达组织功能的计算方法出现了,会计之眼为Wedgwood提供了干预组织的新方法。

事实上,他确实干预了。正如我们所看到的,他改革了财务记录的管理和控制。更为重要的是,在萧条时期,他利用有关成本和利润的新知识主动地对价格进行了调整(McKendrick,1964,1973)。[①] 这样,一个系统的营销策略的基

---

① Wedgwood很清楚在一个不完全的市场,在有明确的产品差异化战略的条件下,在成本和价格之间不存在必然的关系。正如McKendrick(1964,p.29)所指出的:"从他关于定价的信中多次出现'Bentley先生认为价格适当'这样的说法,你会马上意识到这是Wedgwood的一句口头禅。"Wedgwood自己也承认:"当我给任何一件产品定价的时候,请记住与表面的和相对的价值相比,我更加注重工艺的费用。"用McKendrick(1964,p.29)的话来说,Wedgwood先判断生产成本、制作难易度以及可生产的数量,然后Bentley将决定目标市场、价格和生产数量。

置于社会与组织环境中的会计研究

础被建立了起来(McKendrick,1960,1961,1973)。新兴的经济事实为重新评价生产组织过程、大量生产的优势,以及计件工价、工资和奖金的计算提供了一个基础(McKendrick,1960,1961a,1973)。组织的内部运转服从于一种新的经济分析形式。

Wedgwood发现的大规模生产的优势很好地说明了这一点。面对新出现的成本会计事实,Wedgwood这样写道(McKendrick,1973,p.55):

> 如果你注意一下计算栏,看一看造型和模型以及下面的三个栏目在制造费用中所占的份额,并观察一下这些费用的变化规律,就会发现它们基本上是与产品数量无关的。这样你会发现存在于多数制造业中的一个重要规律,即在一个给定的期间内,可以生产最大数量的产品。在此期间内,不管我们生产多少,厂房租金是不变的。无论我们制作20打还是10打花瓶,男工和短工、仓库管理员和记账员等的工资几乎是不变的。对于大多数杂费来说,情况也是类似的。
>
> 我们现有100种以上的瓶制品,它们都有各自的模型、把手和装饰。我们将用它们制造出最新的最实用的产品,而这些产品的成本只是过去的二分之一。假如我们让工人们将每种产品的产量从6打提高到13打时,成本可能会降低到一半以下。
>
> 如果我们不这样做,最初的费用将成为沉入成本。
>
> 贵族们将花瓶放在其宫殿里供中产阶级观赏和赞美。我们知道中产阶级在数量上远远超过贵族阶层。我相信,使花瓶作为宫殿装饰的需求理由已经不存在了。如果花瓶的价格降低的话,中产阶级很有可能购买大量的花瓶。

正像McKendrick(1973,p.54)提到的那样,Wedgwood的成本会计对其经营管理有着更加持久的影响。凭借知识的权威,组织常常以一种预料不到的方式被改变。"通过他的坚持不懈,关注细节,建立(如果不能说是创造的话)领班制度和规则,他把在1765年自己称为拖拉的、醉醺醺的、懒散的、无用的工人转变成十年后非常出色的熟练工"(McKendrick,1961a,p.46)。更为重要的是,Wedgwood现在可以间接地进行监督。他不再需要仅仅依靠在厂里不停地走动,来发现并责骂那些笨手笨脚又不听从指示的工人了(McKendrick,1961a, pp.43—44)。这种观察和监督可以通过在时间和空间上的遥控方式辅助完成。① Wedgwood 现在有了一种匿名的和连续的监控方法。

虽然是在危机和疑问中诞生的,但是 Wedgwood 的会计体系却有着极为深远的影响。它最初的目的是揭示假定已经存在的某种东西,然而它一旦被建立起来,便显著地改变(如果不能说是最终转换的话)着企业的功能。这个新建立的会计体系使得一组不同的动力发挥作用。生产过程的细节可以与作为整体的组织的目的和业绩联系起来。② 组织上层制定的政策可以与组织功能的特定方面联系起来。可以从不同的视角监督和管理组织,也可以试图凭借经济的权威来协调和计划组织的不同部分。这样一门组织经济学便问世了。正像 Patton(1979)从一个非常不同的背景所说的:对于一种实践不能用它后来所起的作用来解释。因为在实践过程中,它可能会被迫承担一些与初始设想无关的新角色。

会计、组织化和组织③

为了更为详细地探讨当组织会计与组织本身相互交织在一起时组织会计的变化过程,我们来考察一个已经有多年会计历史的企业。通过对这个案例的研究,我们将阐述刻画组织特征的要素——过程、实践以及观点——对于会计的影响方式。作为在 Wedgwood 案例的分析中所讨论的主题的一个延伸,我们还将探讨会计反过来影响组织化过程的方式。

M 企业创建于 20 世纪初期,在工业用零部件制造行业,迅速成长为一个国际型企业。它在许多西方国家都设有制造和营销基地。M 企业发展非常迅速,特别是在 20 世纪 50 年代。那个年代经济发展蒸蒸日上,企业的利润丰厚而且资产收益率高。但是 60 年代以后,情况发生了变化。虽然产品需求只是稍微

---

① 在有关 Boultn 和 Watts 创建于 1796 年的 Soho 机械厂历史的详细研究中,Roll(1930,p.250)也指出了工人考勤卡的各种不同作用。除了提供计算工人工资的依据和通过计算生产发动机的劳动成本来确定其价格以外,Roll 说明了新的详细的工资成本的可见性影响工作组织和贡献与报酬之间关系的方式。数据为改变生产方法、加快工作速度和引进新的机器提供了依据。新的记录也有助于建立提高企业效率的标准或规范,使得工资更加与具体的工作业绩相联系。像在 Wedgwood 的案例中那样,在这里新建立起来的经济可见性本身创造出了改变组织的动力。

② Loft(1986b,pp.93—94)指出了生产方法与记录管理之间的相互依存关系。她认为:复杂的成本核算系统是与产品和生产方法的标准化密不可分的。成本核算系统所需要的"事实"难以在工作状态混乱无序的情况下得到,反过来,没有记录也不可能实现复杂的、详细的组织系统的运营。Roll(1930,p.252)也提到了这一点,指出 Boulton 和 Watts 的 Soho 机械厂的重组是为了使任何非文字记录的检查都不再有效。

③ 感谢 John Hughes 在案例研究方面的协助。这里的分析也受益于我和 Sten Jönsson 的讨论。

减弱,但是供给方面发生了明显的变化。日本企业进入国际市场宣告了激烈竞争时代的开始。在 20 世纪 60 年代,日本的生产总值增加了 3.5 倍以上,但是它的出口却增加了将近 17 倍。M 企业被突然地置于激烈竞争的环境之下,而且是竞争最为激烈的量产产品市场,在这部分市场对于某些产品其日本企业的售价甚至低于 M 企业的产品单位成本。

出于对日本企业竞争的危险性的认识和对自己企业业绩表现的不满,M 企业对自己的竞争地位重新进行了全面的评价。在 70 年代初期还成立了多个工作小组,对企业所面临的问题进行了一次彻底的调查。

M 企业发现的第一个问题是企业为顾客提供了"太好的"服务,这听起来或许有点儿自相矛盾。M 企业为顾客服务的宗旨是:以最优惠的价格提供最好的产品,而不是斤斤计较产品的成本。由于子工厂的半自治性质,特别设计部(它是营销职能的一部分)按照顾客的每一项要求生产零部件,而这种活动是通过小范围的工程设计协作来完成的。结果导致了零部件种类的急剧增加,而且,虽然这些零部件基本相似,其生产却分散在不同国家的不同工厂里。此外,组织的分散化战略还导致了在每个国家生产着同样或类似的产品,其后果是设备重复、生产准备和其他间接成本增加,以及由于庞大分散的库存所引起的在产品成本的上升。工厂数量迅速增多,而且常常是在同一个国家内建立了多家工厂,使得这个问题更加恶化。在赢利丰厚的 50 年代,这些问题没有引起太多的注意。可是,当面临着一个完全不同的竞争环境的时候,M 企业决定大幅度削减其产品的种类。

意识到外部市场的威胁,企业开始仔细检查其内部生产业务。在当时,M 企业所采用的批量生产方法赋予生产过程的各个职能很大的独立性。这使得业务流程非常灵活,紧急订单可以很容易地加入生产系统,而且也减少了机器故障的发生。可是,这样的生产方式不适合集中化、大批量的生产。各个操作之间处理设备的缺乏,导致了处理时间延长和库存增加。而且,这种批量生产方法给局部生产控制系统、库存管理人员、操作人员、检查人员以及工厂管理人员造成了很重的负担。因此,该企业积极考虑采用其他的生产方法。

M 企业决定尽可能采取多台机器排列的生产方式。按照这种方式,多台相似的机器与一个相互作业搬运系统单独连接起来。这个系统不但提供运送,而且起到缓冲库的作用,使得机器组能以不同的速度运行,并且相对地限制了故障的影响范围。这种工厂的投资成本是很高的,但是它提高了生产速度,缩短了处理时间,其结果是降低了库存水平。可是,获得上述好处的代价不仅包括很高的资本投资,而且也包括在相当程度上失去了生产的弹性。这个生产系统应该更加自主地应对市场的变化,而市场的急剧变动正是使得生产方式改变的原始动力。

为了满足当地市场的需求，原先 M 企业的每个工厂都生产多种不同的产品。可是，如果要按照国际市场的要求降低生产成本，就必须引进多台机器排列的生产方式。这就意味着如果要实现规模经济，生产工序必须更长。做到这一点的一个方法是减少产品品种数量，但是，在竞争激烈的 20 世纪 60 年代末期和 70 年代初期的市场上，单靠这个方法是不够的。因此，M 企业决定将每一种产品的生产集中在一个地方以实现产量最大化和成本降低。

从这些检查和讨论中渐渐形成了一个新的生产战略，这一生产战略在 1971 年被正式批准。可是，实施和达成这一战略却是非常艰难的。最初的生产分配主要表现为一个平衡问题，有关的讨论持续了好几年。去除那些次要的产品也是一个艰巨的任务，因为要从商业的、财务的和技术的角度评估每一个最终产品的可行性。在 1973 年，M 企业将所有产品按照其销售金额分类，据此来确定那些销售额低且可能不盈利的产品，然后个别地评估每一个候选产品。在进行商业性评估的同时，实施技术性评估。每种产品的设计、质量和材料都被严格地评估。制造和营销方面的内容也被列入评估范围。通过这样的筛选过程，M 企业的产品种类从 1972 年的 5 万种减少到了 1978 年的 2 万种。在同一时期，每种最终产品的平均年销售额增长了 300%。同时增添了叫做"特别产品"的产品种类，目的在于以特别的价格向顾客提供满足其特殊需要的产品。总的来说，M 企业的管理者认为产品范围的集中化仅仅使企业的市场覆盖面缩小了 1%，却去除了那些过去亏损的业务部门。

这样，M 企业以成本的名义彻底地改变了生产方法、产品策略和生产定位。然而，将所有这些战略考虑导入企业的决策过程不仅是通过成本语言，而且是通过使用特别的会计计算而实现的。在这里，首要的目标是导出精确的成本概念。在政策的评议和制定中，成本不仅作为战略语言中的一个重要的抽象概念，而且作为一套特定的会计程序的精确结果而发挥着作用。

以这样的方式，会计的技术实践与 M 企业的管理功能相互交织在一起。因为一套复杂的会计规则给出了成本高低的含义，所以组织政策开始与它们的会计代表物相互依赖。关于"生产性的"和"非生产性的"成本范畴的定义关系到确定和改变某个特定的生产场所，而最终又关系到是否生产某种特定的产品。将间接成本分配到生产业务上的规则和方法，对于所报告的成本水平有重大的影响。就像技术程序对于如何确定标准成本的更新期间以反映通货膨胀和汇率变动因素有着重要影响一样，关于作为间接成本分配对象的生产能力假设在高度详细的成本估算中具有类似的影响。在 M 企业，针对业务变化的会计程序也是非常重要的。因为虽然企业的问题起源于对正在变化的环境的认识，它的会计体系却是在稳定生产状态假设下运作的。生产准备成本、订货成本和业务启动成本的计算与报告处于这样一种情况下：虽然稳定生产的财务结果是清晰可见的，而同样重要的生产变化的含义却远远不是可见的，且业务弹性和非弹性的成本根本没有进入会计计算之中。在所有这些方式中，不仅会计的修辞学在政策评议中开始起到一个重要的中介作用，而且包含在 M 企业的正式会计体系中非常特别的假定和倾向性影响了对于各种生产战略的相对偏好。会计体系不仅成为 M 企业的映像，而且成为其选择和政策的建构物(Burchell *et al.*, 1985)。

可是在当时 M 企业的变化网络是处于这样的情形，即会计本身受到了变化的压力。会计不仅在调解战略变化需求的管理观念和业务反应之间的关系方面起着重要的作用，而且认识到市场危机之后产生的不同的生产策略也明显地改变了 M 企业的信息系统，包括那些具有会计性质的系统。在过去的多局部生产体系下，营销与生产的关系是在局部（国家）层次来处理的。许多联络的进行都是非正式的。虽然存在正式而且系统的信息流，但是从本质上来说它基本上还是局部的。可是，随着生产在地理上的集中，营销与生产被分离开来，上述信息系统就不能满足要求了。为了做好每个工厂的生产能力使用计划，必须找出计算每种产品的预计需求和实际需求的新方法。过去为非正式的东西，现在变成了正式的。新的生产战略引起了对于新的组织模式和完全不同的正式信息流的需求。

为了解决这些问题，设立了两个新的组织机构。设立中央协调委员会是为了判断市场需求并且按照现有的生产能力、库存以及战略和业务政策来决定适当的生产水平。因此，营销与制造的界面更加受到集中控制。为了支持这种新的影响结构，还在总公司设立了新的职能人员小组。而且，因为这些关键性的决策要求精确的、最新的信息，所以又设立了新的管理信息系统，该系统的业务团队的基地设在中央地区。运用协调组制定的预测参数，新的中央信息部决定生产能力、工厂负荷、组装计划和分配指导。为了使这一过程顺畅无阻，需要有关制造、销售和库存的实际信息的反馈。这些信息由 M 企业的各个分厂部门按月整理，并通过计算机数据传输系统传给中央信息部。越来越集中而且相互关联的决策制定和控制过程需要大量的正式信息(Galbraith, 1973)。M 企业当时正处在向更加信息密集和信息依存型组织的转化之中。

这些变化的结果，使得 M 企业的正式组织结构问题也成为考虑的对象。原先该企业是按照国家来设置其制造和营销单位的。作为相对独立的实体，它们构成了有效的业务责任单位。各个单位的业绩用传统的资产负债表和利润表项目的年度指标来衡量。M 企业曾经试图制订较长期的整体性的经营计划，但是结果表明那是一项既困难又不能令人满意的工作。可是现在它是一个更加一体化和集中化的组织,局部的营销和制造之间的关系已经被断绝,当地的销售不再与当地的生产相关,总体业绩更加依赖于中央的决策。出于这种考虑,整个组织开始按照生产线来构建。

在这样的组织变化之中,人们认识到过去那种简单的控制已经远远不够,因而开始考虑更加频繁和更加分散化的报告系统。成本预算愈加成为一个重复且费时的过程。预算完成之后还要按照季度计划定时更新。中央需要有关局部发展和局部预期修正的更加及时的信息。反过来,极为详细的财务、营销、业务和人事的报告取代了过去的总结性财务信息,成为评价局部单位每月业绩的依据。在这样一个集中化的企业,甚至局部的业绩也受到有关转移价格和成本分配的中央会计政策的影响。①

如图 1 所显示的,会计体系和它所引起的问题现在开始成为营销、生产和组织战略的遗留物。正像会计曾经调解某些关键的政策决策一样,现在会计本身受到其自身效果的影响。

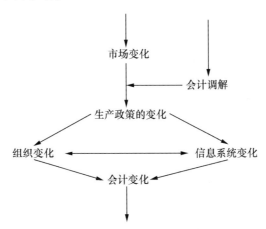

图 1 包含在组织行动中的会计

会计不是与组织相分离的一部分,而是被牢固地埋置在组织之中。组织也不是与其会计相独立的。尽管可以在某个时点上识别会计实践,但是会计实践的功能既以反映的方式又以构建的方式与组织的功能相互交织在一起。组织功能的其他重要方面冲击着会计,对会计的变化造成压力。在这个意义上,会计是一个过去的战略选择、组织模式决策以及政策执行的遗留物,这种政策使

---

① 随着强调的重点越来越放在局部业绩报告的控制功能上,"公平性"而不是决策相关性,成为评价这种会计实践和其中的变化的一个重要尺度。非常感谢 Sten Jönsson 提示我注意到这一点。

置于社会与组织环境中的会计研究

得组织的特定方面具有可见性因而可以控制(Miller and O'Leary,1987)。所以这些活动都起到了逐渐削弱过去的会计和创造今天的会计的可能性的作用。不管怎样,会计从来不是一个被动的现象。它不仅是组织生活的其他方面的一个反映,而且在组织功能中起着相当建设性的作用。会计提供了一种影响和操作经济动机的语言,其计算注入和影响着重要的政策决策,而且它所创造的可见性在特定的组织舞台划分方面起着重要的作用。会计不仅反映组织过去的所有形态,而且在积极地塑造组织现在的形态方面也起着不小的作用。

会计与组织的遗留物

会计的建构性作用提供了一个分析 Q 企业的主要焦点。该企业也是一个制造企业,像 M 企业一样,它也面临着急剧的市场波动和变化。越来越激烈的竞争、顾客预期的变化和利润率的降低等引起了 Q 企业对其组织的危机感。

Q 企业是比 M 企业更加信息密集型的企业。它在正式的信息和控制系统方面投资巨大,而且特别重视财务和会计方面。这些系统的触角深深地渗透到企业的制造、营销、销售和管理职能中。组织的每个细微的方面都具有经济意义上的可见性。在协调与整合这个职能上专业化、地理上分散化的巨大组织方面,标准、预算和计划起着核心作用。实际上,正是通过经济信息的流动,Q 企业的许多重要方面才被认识、管理和评价。企业内不允许有任何局部自治的地盘存在。为企业提供业务管理基础的信息系统不但将巨大而分散的企业的各个部分聚合到一起,而且会计年度循环也成为组织结构和时间管理非常重要的组成部分。①确实,会计之眼是重要的和无处不在的。

Q 企业的信息经济是在企业的成长发展时期被精心建立和完善起来的。虽然这个庞大且昂贵的信息管理机构遇到过许多困难,但是在稳定增长的形势下,这些困难没有成为大的问题。成本和利润的抽象分类提供了组织功能化的完整的描述。只管理一般情况而不管理特殊情况的方法一直没被看成是有问题的。在比较稳定的条件下,关于统治的时期划分也没有造成任何不可克服的困难。由于存在着大量局部一体化的系统,因而要根据特别的问题和需要对这些系统进行微调及扩展。Q 企业的管理制度以这样的方式向前推进,在获得了更多的自治的同时也进一步为一个独立、专门和抽象的管理舞台奠定了基础。而这个管理舞台与企业的个别业务的直接联系似乎越来越少。

可是,市场危机使得这样一个信息管理方式越来越成问题。由于大量不确

---

① 关于会计在建立时间概念中作用的进一步的讨论参见 Hopwood (1986b)。

定性的存在,对于过去未曾收集的信息的需求变得愈加迫切。Q 企业的高层管理人员开始认识到,过去被看成是孤立的和独立的信息源实际上是企业管理及统治体系的一个直接的反映和组成部分。那些过去被控制的东西——成本、利润、差异和产量——都产生了信息剩余。而那些没有被控制但现在被认为需要控制的东西,却没有在组织的信息系统中反映出来。质量、生产过程的功能化的细节、雇员和管理参与以及动机、处理时间和业务库存、技术进步、顾客反映的细节等过去没有管理的东西,仍然属于未知的领域。因此,目前的可见性是不完全的,仅仅反映了过去的问题、过去的控制以及过去的权力模式的所在。不管它有多么重要,在 Q 企业里新体系要想渗入旧体系是非常困难的,因为双方所关心的方面是如此不同。

因此,现在的组织被限制在过去的关心范围之内。Q 企业的信息系统不仅变得如此详细,看起来如此精确和综合,而且与 Q 企业现在的组织如此密切地相互交织在一起,以至于在很长的时间内它们起到了一种否定其他信息系统合理存在的作用。不仅它们的技术质量看起来如此之高且如此包罗万象,以至于感觉不到有什么不足之处,而且现在的信息和控制渠道变为与企业自身共同决定的因素。Q 企业的会计体系以一种重要的方式变得与组织决策同步。两者都发生了变化,结果是其中任何一方既依赖于另一方同时又反映着另一方。过去曾经是直接的和可识别的官僚式控制,随着时间的推移,变成一个比较不引人注目的 Q 企业的核心部分(Perrow,1986)。现在,它们被隐含在决策前提——对作为行动的基础的认识前提(Perrow,1986,p. 129)——的机构之中,在一个基本的层面上决定在组织中的意义和重要性的结构。① 在这样一个环境下,变化是极为困难的。人们要开始设想以不同的方式做任何事情,都会遇到巨大的困难。因为新的东西无法去突破由旧的东西所建立起来的意识。

可是,最终 Q 企业里出现了这样的情形,即人们认识到环境发生了剧烈的变化。即使在传统的指标上,这一点也被慢慢地反映出来。尽管被推迟了,但由此促成的有关调查的结果使得组织的一些成员开始认识到正在发生着的变化的重要意义。

在这种情况下,Q 企业开始意识到过去由信息系统决定的一些重要方面存在着许多问题。人们看出一系列的标准、预算和计划造成了企业缺乏弹性和自我封闭。"分析导致麻痹"一词开始成为组织理论的术语。人们意识到过去管

---

① 正如 Perrow(1986)所指出的,在不引人注目的控制下,即他所谓的"控制的前提",组织的参与者会故意限制激励的范围和可供选择的范围(Perrow,1986,p. 129)。在 Q 企业中,这样的态度确实很普遍。

理的重点放在了正常管理而不是异常管理上。抽象概念的管理造成企业很难对个别情况做出反应。人们也认识到信息系统在 Q 企业的时间观念的创造中起着重要的作用。不但连续的组织行动被以一种非常特别的方式区分,而且例行的计划和报告制度导致了只顾眼前的短期意识的形成。通过大范围的预算和计划过程,把将来带到现在来,似乎变得更加确定、更少偶然和争议之处,而且或许更少在过程中受到影响。在其管理的许多方面强调即时性的时代过去之后,Q 企业现在发现培养一种影响和管理长期未来的积极主动的观念是极端困难的。

像 M 企业一样,组织生活的重要特征已经变得与会计体系的功能相互交织在一起。会计已经被埋置在组织的结构之中,既反映着又创造着其运行的环境。然而,在 Q 企业这个过程走得更远。这些倾向在 M 企业里可以清晰地看出,但在 Q 企业里它们完全变成了现实。虽然在 Q 企业会计体系的设计和功能化中自主的发展可能而且确实发生了,但是企业的会计成为一种在任何意义上都不能被认为是与作为一个整体的企业相分离的现象。

依照经济可见性进行的投资从根本上提高了可以从职能专业化、地理分散和管理协调中获得的诸多经济性。会计之眼已经变得非常具有战略性。凭借着对组织的了解,它将组织动员了起来。经济目标以及为了达成目标的战略被赋予了非常清晰的含义。在这样一种特定的经济知识的环境下,进行了各种投资。其结果是,Q 企业现在由不同的机器和分散在不同的地点、具有不同的技能、被不同的管理制度管理的不同的人所构成。而且,为了像过去一样运行,Q 企业需要其会计体系。这些会计体系实现了它们曾经在创造过程中所起到的作用(Ignatieff,1984)。会计的存在成为目前的组织结构的前提。这些会计体系不再仅仅是一些互不相关的技术程序,而是被注入组织自身之中。

会计遗留物的创造一直是 Q 企业的一个重要部分。这种遗留物反过来在组织创造的过程中起到了作用。可见性成为现实,但是这种可见性并非包含在 Q 企业的功能化中。它诞生于不同的现实之中,所服务的目标与现在要求的目标不同。会计的遗留物被放置在一个与现在的 Q 企业不同的组织中。

新兴的经济可见性的重要特征是在试图控制劳动过程的背景下创造出来的(Clawson,1980)。在 Q 企业里,好争议的和有组织的员工为经济计算及管理制度的出现提供了一个重要的基础。对于受经济导向的有组织的活动如何进行控制是一个涉及动员的问题。在确定工作期待和将努力与回报挂钩以及衡量和控制实际业绩等方面投入了很多。为了使得组织业务的核心功能以一种特定的方式具有可见性,确立了详细的经济计算制度。对工作的社会控制为 Q

企业在提高经济可见性方面的投入提供了重要的激励。① 可是，那个被构建成的社会可见性已经造就出这样一个企业，它在组织上依赖于所必然产生的知识。组织在其知识的名义下被重构。这样，一种基于事实和分析的管理制度出现了（尽管是在一个不同的公司环境下，参见 Geneen，1984）。各个目标被更加精确地表达，而且这些通过会计计算的手段在整个组织中予以普及。新的工作划分被引进到组织中，形成了新的管理专门知识的基础。以社会的名义引进到组织中的东西开始以组织和社会两方面的名义发挥作用。

关于现实中会计的思考

这些案例不仅说明了会计可以看成是某种处在运动中的东西，而且说明这样的观点提供了一个洞察会计的组织实践及其行动结果的手段。传统上一直被看作是处于静止状态的会计技艺，现在被看作是处在某种变化过程之中，而且正在变得与其过去不同。而这样一种描述使得我们可以对会计通过与其他组织过程和实践相交而影响组织的可见性、重要性以及结构和行动的某些方式进行分析。

在 Wedgwood 的案例中，我们观察了一个新的会计的出现过程。经济话语和修辞的范畴与相互关系（McCloskey，1985），刺激了用经济术语来观察组织的实践手段的产生，从而使得原先抽象的东西变成似乎真实的东西。尽管这种手段最初是作为一种决定价格和产量的工具而被创造出来的，但它却成为以新的经济知识的名义干预和转换组织的手段。从我们对 Wedgwood 的案例的思考中，形成了这样的认识，即会计可能成为一种干预和统治组织的更加重要的手段，并且能够在组织发展轨道的形成中发挥更为积极的作用。会计之眼本来是用来揭示那些被假定存在的东西的，但在组织改革中，它却发挥出了建设性的作用。

在 M 企业制定其应付市场危机措施的初期，我们看到了会计的这种积极作用。在过去建立在 M 企业中的会计将经济动机和管理分析的抽象语言加工成评价组织变化的更加精确的计算方法。以这样的方式，会计体系相当特别的性质在传递组织对变化的需要的反应中起到了积极的作用。现在我们看到在早期的 Wedgwood 的成本核算中固有的动员潜力在起作用，它以相当特别的方式促进了 M 企业的营销、生产甚至会计战略的形成。因为埋置在组织中的会计不

---

① 好几个独立而详细的历史研究都支持这个结论。而且，这些研究是从不同的理论角度进行的。然而，因为不能公开 Q 企业的名字，所以在这里没有注明出处。

仅决定了组织生活的其他重要方面,而且反过来也受到它们的影响,从而在创造其自身转变的可能性和条件方面发挥了某些作用。

在 Q 企业,会计在组织中的埋置表现为它在组织功能中起了一个重要而富有影响的作用。虽然会计的产生经历了漫长的时间,而且最初要求的理由也与现在的功能不同,但是会计和与其相关的信息及控制系统却创造出主导性的可见性手段。也就是说,用会计之眼来审视和管理企业。会计可见性的选择模式为动员和改变组织提供了一种方法,这样它不但依赖于而且也几乎与特定的信息流是同义的,而这种信息流与它的发展和现行的功能模式互相交织在一起。

对于上述三个企业,会计在它们的转变中起到了某种作用。它们的会计转变的过程开始或者已经被埋置在其功能的结构之中。它们创造出了对会计事实的特别管理方式,赋予了经济管理范畴与修辞在业务上的意义。将看起来似乎精确而详细的计算方法运用于有关组织的商议和争议中。经过不断的传播和变化,会计已经卷入了组织观念、组织统治和战略动员的广泛过程之中。

由这样一个发展轨道导致的种种结果对于上面的三个企业都很重要。在 M 企业的案例中,它在关键的战略变化时期起到了重要的传达影响的作用;而在 Q 企业中,创造了一种旨在限制从而影响组织对环境变化的反应的组织依赖形式。

这样一些结果使得人们有理由对于管理会计产生普遍的担忧(Hopwood,1985a)。正像前面讨论的那样,现在出现了一种越来越明显的趋势:既从实际的又从预期的组织结果来评价会计体系。现在人们开始讨论会计体系可能对组织产生的所有影响。即使仅仅因为这一点,也非常有必要尝试更加详细地整理和分析这些案例中的某些内在的问题,虽然在有关会计实践的组织性质的知识发展过程的现阶段,这种整理和分析只能是暂时的及局部性的。从这样的观点来看,这些案例会启发我们如何思考现实中的会计和会计的精致化及变化。

或许最重要的是,我们所分析的这些变化没有反映出任何简单、线性的会计发展模式。尽管关于变化的抽象讨论起到了打乱占主导地位的现状的作用,但是没有发现任何单一的动员力量,无论是某种经济合理性、社会意图或者是某种政治目的,被静静地埋置在会计变动轨迹的移动过程中。确实,在 Wedgwood 的案例中,在抽象的经济范畴与以它的名义在组织中实行的干预活动之间不存在简单而明显的关系。在 M 企业,许多相当特殊的问题、原理和制约冲击了它的会计变化的进程,同时提供了一种手段,通过这一手段会计既可以发现和解决问题,而且其本身也可以通过其他组织现象的转换模式而得到调整。在 Q 企业,会计被如此牢固地埋置在组织的结构和意识之中,以至于由它决定什么东西是具有经济意义的。因此,在这三个企业中,都不曾存在某种朝着预期的设想而前进的会计。人们也没有能给出一个自明的会计进步的模式。会计的变化都是特殊的,旨在解决各自的非常特殊的问题。尽管在会计变化的途径中肯定存在着未知的和不确定的因素,但是没有事实表明仅仅由于我们忽视了对某些特别的组织参与者的考虑,而使得某种事先存在的会计秩序难以被觉察。尽管组织功能化的过程有时是复杂而微妙的,难以精确地表达,但是没有事实表明上述过程隐藏着任何会计改进的抽象而先验的途径。

特定的会计的出现已经表明,它既不是某个更为抽象的意图的必然反映,也不是一个突然的发现或者变换。上述案例已经说明了特定的局部起因调节和控制会计发展途径的更为主动的方式,以及引起会计技艺的特别表现形式产生的多重的甚至相互冲突的各个条件。它们已经表明问题的特殊形态与其他组织结构和实践既为特定的会计变化的发展提供了环境,又对特定的会计变化的发展有重大的影响。正如已经阐明了事件、错误和偏差怎样在成长中的会计上留下痕迹一样,上述案例也阐明了会计信息的特殊意义和重要性如何影响会计的转换方式。虽然人们要求一个会计知识和技术实践的实体,要求动员会计和更加广泛的理论基础,但是这些案例却说明需要将因而发生的会计变化看成是上面要求的与存在于组织舞台的不同部分之中的大量的其他微小变化的复合结果,而每一个微小变化自身都是因为局部的、策略的和推测的原因而参与进来的。

尽管会计变化的过程是复杂的,但是这些案例已经说明这样一种关于变化的局部和权变模式是可以理解的。我们可以通过会计所产生的环境来认识和理解其变化。但是,正如上面的讨论试图搞清的那样,可理解性不应同必要性混同起来。在所有这些案例中,没有任何一种必要性导致了某个特定的结果。也没有任何一种必要性建立在导致会计变化的组织环境基础之上。这些案例既没有假定会计必须是什么样,也没有导出关于所发生的事情的必然性的任何结论,而是说明有必要通过更加详尽地了解会计在一个组织中的埋置方式,以及通过了解会计为与其相关的组织问题提供解决方法的过程来理解变化的必要性。它们也说明有必要理解会计是如何改变组织实践和过程的构造,从而为改进和变化提供更加积极的环境的。同样重要的是,它们暗示有必要理解在任何特定的背景下围绕着这些过程的各种情况的偶然性和相互作用性。从这样一个角度来看,我们所寻求的可理解性的提高就取决于我们质询和解释会计技艺的组织功能的方式,从而也取决于那些概念的影响以及调查和分析的方式。上述影响和方式既为理解特殊的会计又为理解一般的会计提供了一个基础,而不是要求任何被视为隐含在会计实践或者强制其改变的环境之中的起支配作用的基本原则。尽管人们认识到组织生活包含着可能和现实之间的持续对话,

置于社会与组织环境中的会计研究

因而有关会计潜力的各种构想可能在动员会计变化中发挥作用,但是这并没有使得那些与会计技艺相关的主张变得显而易见,有某种优先权和必要性,也不给它们任何特权使其在促使会计成为与其过去不同的东西的过程中扮演特殊的角色。这些主张的效果应该看成是来自它们与表现组织生活特征的环境的相互作用,而不是来自一个包罗万象的、强大深刻的且十全十美的逻辑。①

考虑到需要给现实中的会计及其变化的过程一个更加广泛而明确的评价,我们对案例的分析是按照几个主题来进行的。我们重点强调了由会计体系所创造的特殊可见性、转移组织功能、调解问题的认识和可能的解决方案,以及在组织内部注入语言模式、含义和意义。从这样一种立场出发,我们把注意力集中在会计的建构性和反映性作用方面。虽然人们认识到许多其他的因素可能而且确实冲击并影响着会计技艺,有时会引起其关注焦点和组织体现场所的转移,而我们的分析是在意识到会计自身更为能动的性质的基础上展开的。通过构造组织可见性的各种模式,通过扩大组织中影响模式的范围,通过创造不同的相互作用和相互依赖的模式,通过创新组织划分的形式,会计被看成是能够在转变组织变化的前提和影响其结果,甚至包括其自身的转换中起积极作用的东西。通过这样的相互影响过程,会计被设想为埋置在组织中的现象,而不是具有实在意义的独立存在。它所采取的形式及其各种影响无法从其他组织实践、功能或过程的相互交织的背景的外部来理解。它们合在一起反映了一种特殊的调整特性。虽然在某些时候有可能区分一个组织现象在影响另一个组织现象,但是我们的分析是从这样的影响的可能性而不是从其必要性的角度来进行的,因为动员因素常常是如此众多、分散、模糊和不确定的,而且与会计技艺有着不明确的演绎关系,以至于无论是会计变化或者其他变化都被视为是某种被创造出来的东西,而不是被决定的东西。而且,组织实践和过程随着时间一起变化,理解它们所组成的构造似乎是更加重要的,因为任何一个实践的存在都预示着其他实践的存在。或许一点儿也不值得奇怪,这样的分析主题对于那些调节控制会计变化轨道的细微差别和不确定性是很敏感的,同时对必然产生的组织过程的相互依赖性所引起的非故意性、不可意料性和或然性也是很敏感的。

---

① Keat and Urry (1982,pp.245—246)在考虑更加一般的社会现象时提出了类似的观点:……社会实体之间的互相依存是……重要的……(因为)实现重要社会实体的诱发能量所需要的条件存在于其他社会实体和它们的能量至少是部分的实现这一事实之中。这些实体之间的相互依存意味着某些实体的诱发能量构成其他实体实现其能量的基本条件。当然,这意味着实际事件是高度复杂的互相依存的过程的产物……而且,这些过程并非仅仅被列举出来,使得它们可以被合计起来,恰恰相反,它们将被综合起来,使得它们的组合定性地修改每一个构成实体。

会计的建构性作用值得特别关注,因为这些作用一直很少被意识到和被讨论。

正像我们已经看到的,会计有时候可以起到促使其他组织现象变化的重要作用。通过与可解释性和可信赖性等推理概念相交织,会计可以在组织代理的重构方面发挥作用,使得组织安排有不同的构造。通过将会计信息流常规化和将空间加在时间轴上,会计可以改变过去、现在和将来的概念,赋予每一个概念不同的特征,而反过来,这些概念又会节制时间的偏好和偏重,因而节制组织行动。通过将原本模糊、抽象和特殊的有关经济事实的概念具体化,会计不仅可以创造其他组织实践变化条件存在的环境,而且创造出一种方式,通过这一方式特定的组织可见性为获得管理上的关注而竞争。正像 Q 企业那样,如果上述战略成功了,或许甚至会最终排除反映组织环境特点的其他方式的可见性和重要性。如果出现这样的情况,会计的潜在转换能力只会被加强,因为由会计技艺创造的事实会产生一种用经济术语表达和改变组织的一种富有影响的语言和一组范畴。正像 Foucault(1972,p.167)所指出的:"一系列事件可以……成为一个话语的对象,被记录、描述、解释和阐述为概念,从而为理论选择提供机会。"因此,虽然没有得到充分的分析,但是会计的建构性作用的重要性却不应被低估,因为它们代表了会计埋置在组织中的一个重要方式。

正如我们在 M 和 Q 两个企业中所看到的,会计可以成为组织实践的一个必不可少的组成部分,它能够创造某种可能性,为改变动员会计变化的条件提供基础。在 M 企业,会计调解营销和生产战略的选择,为随之而来的组织变化创造出新的信息和会计问题提供了环境。而在 Q 企业,在一系列组织问题的背景之下建立起了特殊的经济可见性管理方法,这种方法在创造一种经济意识方面发挥了作用。这种经济意识转变了组织,并且为组织创造了一个有关会计事实的更加细致的管理方法。这样的解释不但说明了会计转变的潜能,而且显示了会计可能成为影响自身的主要因素的某些方式。

这种会计观点的核心是在会计发展的目的和会计的实际组织结果之间可能存在多义性关系(参见 Burchell et al.,1985;Hopwood,1983,1986b)。尤其因为会计修辞的主体可能会在与组织行动的细节、复杂性、分散性和特殊性相衔接之处存在困难,所以特定的会计干预的某些预期的结果或许不会出现(参见 Hopwood,1986a)。而且,当会计与其他组织实践和过程相交叉时,当它主动地创造一个组织可视性、客观性以及潜在意义时,当它在这样做的过程中引起对战略和干预的抵抗时，所有事先无法预期的结果都可能出现。① 就像上述案例分析所表明的那样，会计干预的结果可能干扰、中断和取代正在形成中的组织舞台，因此，它拥有转变而不仅仅是修改组织变化过程的能力。

从这样一个观点出发，会计也可以被设想为这样一种东西，它创造组织结果的遗留物，而这些遗留物会改变随之而来的组织变化的前提。它好像是组织转换的沉积物，不仅与组织的过去相互作用，而且可能修正组织的现在和将来。在这个意义上，正如 Gross(1981—1982, p.76)所说的："现在确实包含着它之前的过去……这一点或许还未被人们注意到。"暂存的互相依存已经成为组织生活的组成部分，分析工作的一个部分就是要通过挖掘有关组织事务的遗留物，来阐明调节控制会计技艺的各种前提条件。

正是基于这样一个比喻，分析工作才被看成是一种考古工作，仔细而小心地分类整理有关组织历史（无论这个历史距离现在如何地近）的沉积物，以重新构建现在从过去而来的方式。② 可是，按照 Foucault(1972, 1977)的说法，目前的讨论中所使用的分析模式既有系谱学的特征又有考古学的特征。"考古学试图勾勒特定结构的轮廓"(Foucault, 1972, p.157)，以揭示"推理结构和非推理领域的关系(制度的、政治的事件，以及经济实践及其过程)"(p.162)。在目前的分析中，考古学力求将社会组织实践的可能性条件与旨在重建一个关系与效果的多样性系统的知识体分离开来，而这种多样性系统的权变连锁构成了实践形成、进行和发挥效果的基础(Gordon, 1980, p.243)。而且，正是积极构建考古学的行为创造出了一种对于知识、组织、社会实践体所蕴含的权力创造潜力的敏感性。这种知识、组织、社会实践体渐渐开始创造一个它们在其中运行的现实概念。另一方面，系谱学则涉及破裂和转变等，凭借着破裂和转变，当言词、范畴、实践和制度等变得与新的目的和意图相互交织时会获得新的含义和意义。这是目前讨论的另一个同样重要的题目。这种系谱学的观点，通过强调变化向我们发出了警告，即假定存在任何具有潜在的连贯性、趋势或者逻辑（比如进

---

① 在这方面，Hirschman (1977, p.131)的见解是很有趣的：一方面，毫无疑问，人类行为和社会决策往往会导致当初完全没有预料到的结果。但是，另一方面，之所以采取这些行动和决策是因为热切地希望它们会带来某种效果，而结果却没能实现。作为前面那种现象的对应物，后面的现象也很可能是其原因之一；某些社会决策在被采纳时所具有的虚幻的预期可能会隐藏它们真正的未来效果。而且，一旦这些预期的效果未能出现，它们起初曾经被期待这样一个事实往往不仅被遗忘而且被主动地压制。

② 事实上，关于考古学的想象来自最初在 M 企业进行的现场调查，它成为我分析所观察的现象的一个基础。在那时，我尚不了解 Foucault 的理论，只是在一种更加原始的意义上使用这一比喻。在随之而来的对本文和其他相关论文(参见 Burchell et al., 1985)的讨论中，援引了 Foucault(1967, 1972, 1973, 1977, 1979)提出的强有力的分析方法。然而，即使有可能引起一点混乱，我仍然把考古学的比喻保留在题目中，这样做既出于对历史的忠实，也因为它比较恰当。

步),以及朝着某个最终目标或结论前进的历史和组织转换的动员模式都是危险的。正像 Foucault(1977,p.146)所阐明的那样,系谱学并不自命可以复原一个未曾中断的、超越遗忘的历史连续性。

尽管比 Foucault 所做的探索更加集中也更加有限,我们的调查仍然阐明了会计既可能被改变,同时也可能成为转变为更广泛的组织的工具的某些方式。我们将流动性和特殊性引入了对现实中会计的理解。会计所具有的重要性在其变更组成的过程中已经被显示出来。会计被视为逐渐被埋置在不同的组织构造之中,并且在其变化的过程中承担着非常不同的组织功能。这些变化的动员工具被视为存在于众多不同的组织实践之中,尤其是存在于会计之中。

可是,就目前我们的理解而言,很有必要提出一些在解释上的注意,特别是在解释有关可能使会计发挥作用的动员要素方面。因为虽然我们的案例深入地考察了会计精致和变化的某些内部过程,但是所有这些案例并没有对外部因素如何能够重铸内部因素提出足够的解释。尽管从危机——特别是经济危机——的角度对动员潜力进行分析是很有诱惑力的,然而,在据此建立一个过强的理论之前,我们需要非常小心。毋庸置疑,危机和经济的限制可能而且确实导致行动,特别是在会计领域(Khandwalla,1973;Olofsson and Svalander,1975)。可是,对这些案例的分析表明这种关系远不是一种直线关系。在 Wedgwood 的案例中,虽然会计变化的经济论据和变化的实施之间的关系并非没有问题,而且它要求一种知识的运作体和特定组织实践的交叉,但是经济衰退确实刺激了会计变化的发生。在 M 企业的案例中,尽管会计本身是在营销、生产以及组织方面的变化造成了一个新的组织结构和一组新的会计问题之后才发生变化的,但是它传递了对重大市场变化的反应。而在 Q 企业中,会计被如此隐蔽地埋置在组织的结构和意识之中,以至于变成了某种通过掩饰环境动荡的实质来限制变化的东西。所以,我们的三个案例没有为任何有关危机驱动型会计变化的一般理论提供依据。确实,我们所阐明的分析模式应该会缓和任何试图表述上述一般观点的愿望。这种模式应该促进对外部事件的感知或外部事件的现实可能扰乱组织构造进行更加精确和更加仔细的调查(参见 Czarniawska and Hedberg,1985)。从转移组织范围的可能性和组织的可见性来看,动员潜力有它的作用,但它肯定不是侵扰组织的所有因素。除了一个关于危机的作用的更加精细的观点(参见 Brunson,1985),我们需要搞清楚可能为行动和变化提供基础的各个要素,其中包括新的知识体、专家的实践、政府的管理意图、组织治理和秩序的理论及实践,甚至不同的会计修辞的发展等。

显然,有必要做大量的研究,也有必要使理论分析研究的前提更加精确化。但是,我们希望目前的调查至少有助于说明会计变化分析的这样一种可能性,

置于社会与组织环境中的会计研究

即它不依赖关于潜力的抽象概念,也不对行动施加任何统一整合。我们还希望这项调查通过认识到不能将会计所起的作用看成与其实践相分离,以及认识到必须理解构成会计的特定的实践和赋予它们重要性和含义的组织过程,显示了历史(无论它距现在如何地近)分析可以揭示会计动态变化的方法。

参考文献[①]

(卜志强 译)

---

① 参见本文英文参考文献。

Observing the Accounting Craft

ANTHONY G. HOPWOOD

(*London School of Economics and Political Science*)

AN INTRODUCTION

Accounting has always had a certain fascination for me. As a child, I almost left school on two occasions to enter the accountancy profession. Not doing that, I proceeded to study the subject at the London School of Economics and Political Science. Although thereafter I was one of the few who did not seek to enter professional training, I nevertheless decided to continue my probings into accounting at the University of Chicago, in the process first setting aside the possibility of pursuing research in the area of industrial economics and thereafter in the area of finance. And since that time accounting has become a phenomenon for almost continuous observation, curiosity, and inquiry.

The reasons for the fascination are difficult to appreciate, as they are for many things that provide an element of continuity between one's quite distant past and the here and now. The interest arose during a period of rapid accounting development in the United Kingdom. Its involvement with attempts at industrial and financial reconstruction resulted in a certain prominence in media discussions. Accounting was starting to catch the public eye and I might well have been one of those enticed within its web at that time. Its characterization as a seemingly modern and rational form of knowledge and expertise might have influenced the perceptions of a young grammar school boy, not least when a close family member provided a more immediate exemplar of the accountant in action. I remember what might otherwise have been purely social discussions being peppered with tales of new American methods, accounting's involvement in corporate reorganisation, the early stages of the rise of a new breed of financial executives in the United Kingdom, and, not least in significance, the more questionable implications of this for local manufacturing and employment in a relatively poor region of the North of England.

Just such an ambiguity surrounded many of my initial involvements with accounting. Early attempts to join the profession provided some fascinating insights into the social recruitment criteria used by the agents of a seemingly meritocratic occupation. Through family involvements I had the opportunity to witness some of the personal and organizational tensions, anxieties, and contradictions associated with the economic rationalizing concerns of accountants and the other managerial groups with which they were associated. Not only could parts of a local economy be seen as being more readily incorporated into wider patterns of economic forces, but also the management practices with which accounting was associated were seen in ways that provided some insights into how they could shift patterns of influence and discretion within wider organizational settings. Even at that time accounting started to come across as a more multifaceted phenomenon and one that, however technical its procedures might appear, was not isolated from wider patterns of human and social life. Indeed, as I remember it, I was already starting to be aware of the contradictory nature of the accounting task. Despite the aura of professional neutrality and the articulation of its serving a conception of the public interest, accountants were widely known to be the servants of those wishing to follow the letter rather than the spirit of the legislative intent, not least in the area of taxation. Even quite mundane associations with accounting in practice were starting to create an impression of the equivocality of the accountant's craft, if only in terms of the discretionary nature of a final account. There quite obviously was more at stake in accounting than mere financial arithmetic.

My undergraduate years at the London School of Economics only served to increase such impressions. Under the watchful eye of people like Will Baxter, Harold Edey, and Basil Yamey, accounting started to emerge as a more problematic activity. Although the accounting part of a wider study of the social sciences was not extensive at that time, the economic orientation to the subject that was an important part of the intellectual tradition at the LSE (Dev, 1980), provided a means of confronting the technical practice of accounting with a wider framework for its analysis. Costs and profits were portrayed as multifaceted, complex, and conceptual phenomena whose interpretation required a wider, albeit still economic, appreciation of the contexts in which they functioned and had an effect. Whilst certainly not emphasized, some basis for appreciating how political and social concerns might intermingle with and change modes of economic calculation was nevertheless also provided at the LSE at that time, not least in the context of discussions of approaches to forms of social cost-benefit analysis which were then emerging.

In such ways an interest in studying and understanding accounting developed. A more questioning curiosity about accounting started to emerge, providing the basis for an interest in continuing the study *of* accounting rather than seeking a professional indoctrination *in* the subject. In the mid-1960s, however, it was almost impossible to obtain adequate research training in accounting or indeed most other management subjects in the United Kingdom. The major business schools were just about to be established. The research infrastructure was minimal. Being advised of such constraints, I decided to apply to doctoral programmes in the United States. On these grounds the University of Chicago was to become my intellectual base for the next five years.

CHICAGO AND THE EXPLORATION OF ACCOUNTING IN USE

Chicago undoubtedly provided the intellectual basis for the development of my interest in the study of accounting in use. Although the focus of that interest was to change a great deal subsequently, the idea of probing into the actual functioning of the accounting craft originated in and was nurtured by the productive academic environment that Chicago provided. The commitment to the sustained and rigorous study of business phenomena that was such an important part of the intellectual life of the Graduate School of Business at the University of Chicago at that time created an intellectual ethos that was exciting, demanding, and, above all, conducive for experimentation.

It was indeed an exciting time to be studying accounting at Chicago. The rise of an interest in empiricism was still occurring, much fostered by David Green and propagated by him in his doctoral seminars and, not least, in the newly established *Journal of Accounting Research*. New interrelationships were being forged between accounting and economics, quantitative methods, and even the behavioral sciences. Research discussions were couched in philosophical terms. Modern finance theory and its empirical basis were being constructed at the School, amongst other places. Even the student community was itself an exceptionally able and innovative one. Bill Beaver, Philip Brown, Joel Demski, and Mel Greenball, for instance, were all ahead of me on the Doctoral Programme, and Ray Ball and Ross Watts, amongst others, were to join soon afterwards.

In such an environment research, not surprisingly, had a very high profile and priority. For someone recently arrived from the United Kingdom, it was quite obvious that research was perceived as a professional activity rather than a gentlemanly pursuit. Amongst both the faculty and the doctoral students, I think it fair to say, there was a feeling that knowledge itself was in the process of changing. The old was contrasted with the new and the forces driving the new were explicitly discussed and argued.

My own interest in the behavioral and organizational aspects of accounting emerged by chance in an institution devoted to the extension of quite particular conceptions of economic rationality. Forced to take a course on organization theory to satisfy the course distribution requirements of the doctoral programme, that course, so ably and interestingly taught by Paul Goodman (now of Carnegie-Mellon University), provided me with a new vision of how to study accounting. The interest and challenge was such that I restructured my doctoral studies, setting aside a specialization in finance in order to delve further into the behavioral aspects of accounting systems. Of course there were those who thought such a move ill-advised, but the helpful counsels of George Sorter, the director of the doctoral programme at the time, and particularly Dick Hoffman, a social-psychologist who had himself only recently joined the Chicago faculty from the University of Michigan, greatly eased the intellectual transition that was to result in an attempt to forge some understanding of the interrelationship between accounting and the organizational contexts in which it operated.

The dysfunctional consequences of management accounting systems started to be a topic of particular interest to me. Stimulated by Chris Argyris's pioneering study of *The Impact of Budgets on People* (1952), still possibly wondering about my own early exposure to the more equivocal functioning of accounting, certainly influenced by the social-psychological orientation of a great deal of the behavioral science programme at Chicago, and also intrigued by the then emergent contingency formulations of organization theory, I began to think about exploring the factors that influenced the behavioral and organizational consequences of accounting systems, dysfunctional or otherwise.

A commitment to engage in field research also developed at an early stage for reasons now difficult to reconstruct. Perhaps my very early interest in the actual functioning of accounting played some role. I certainly remember holding the view that accounting was an organizational phenomenon and needed to be studied as such. Seen in such terms, I think that there was a quite genuine interest in the development of an action based, more humanistic basis for appreciating the variety of management responses to accounting, with a view to moving towards a more adequate understanding of how accounting functioned as a significant organizational and social practice. I was also quite definitely worried about the validity of laboratory experimentation, a methodology then just starting to be used in accounting research. A trial experiment using friendly subjects reinforced my doubts about the credibility of the exercise as a basis for understanding the functioning of accounting as an organizational practice. By then I was also familiar with and quite worried about a developing body of research on the social psychology of the psychological experiment, work conveniently ignored by the experimental literature. The laboratory appeared to me to be an ever less obvious site for the exploration of accounting in action. Although I was aware of the difficulties of entering the field, not least for a novice Englishman in Chicago, I was nevertheless convinced that this was what I ought to do even though it created a new precedent for accounting research at Chicago and even though there were those who initially did not look on the proposal with favor.

Research access to a suitable organization was far from easy to negotiate, taking nine anxious months in all. As a research orientated institution, the Chicago Business School had relatively few suitable contacts in industrial and commercial circles at that time. I decided I did not wish to study a traditional insurance company, even though access might have been available. However tempting it initially appeared, I also decided that the impracticalities of field work in Florida were too great. And even greater in Chile! Even the efforts of a future Secretary of State failed to get me into one organization. In the end, however, access was gained to a major steel company and Gary, Indiana, amidst its agonising environmental deprivations, was to become a second home for the next couple of years or so.

"You don't need to be a behavioral scientist to understand this lot. You need to be a bloody anthropologist," advised one of my early shop floor contacts. "You're in the jungle now," he went on to add, describing how almost every department in the steel plant had its own ethnic and cultural identity, mirroring the immigration history of the Mid West. The newest arrivals seemingly always started on the shop floor in the dirty and dangerous early processes, slowly being promoted upwards and, over time, moving into the relatively cleaner and safer later processes of steel making. By the time I was around the descendents of the British, the Germans, and the Scandinavians were way down the line and the first black foreman had been appointed in the blast furnaces.

For somewhat different reasons, an anthropologist of sorts I was to become. Entering the field with quite general interests and hypotheses, and almost no prior studies to rely on, a great deal of time was spent on trying to understand how an amazingly complex and quite sophisticated accounting system functioned, how it became involved with wider organizational processes, and how it had the consequences it had. The initial research efforts were exploratory and observational. I worked on the night shift. I had a hole burnt in my jacket in the blast furnace—an initiation of a sort. I spent an amazing amount of time watching, listening, and talking. Later I was to refer to this in terms of tapping into the linguistic culture of the firm. For over time I became increasingly aware of not only the different ways in which the same accounting system was implicated in organizational processes, but also the subtle distinctions in language that both reflected and shaped the patterns of differential use. These distinctions provided a focus for the final study; the linguistic differences were the basis for further exploration by the use of questionnaires. The latter is something that nearly all subsequent users of the research instrument have ignored, merrily but all too ignorantly proceeding with using it in factory like style.

The form of the doctoral research was influenced not only by the problem and the exploration of the research site. With such field research being all very new in an accounting context, not least at Chicago, it was made quite clear that a more structured approach to the final research design was required. So questionnaire design, distribution, and analysis entered the research process, as did the complexities of nonparametric statistics. So much so, in fact, that in those distant days when field explorations were new and little understood by the accounting research establishment, and when accounting itself was less assured of its intellectual bases, the highly significant exploratory research was purged from the final text, the latter thereby having the appearance of a more structured, anticipated, confident, and seemingly scientific work.

The resultant study, published in its entirety as *An Accounting System and Managerial Behaviour* (Hopwood, 1973; see also the papers in section one of the present collection), provided some insights into the managerial processes through which accounting data acquired an organizational meaning and significance. Focusing on the differing ways in which different managers used the same accounting system, it cast some light on the ways in which organizational factors could mediate and shape the consequences associated with an accounting system, thereby providing a way of appreciating a diversity of effects rather than a set of inevitable ones, anticipated or otherwise. The study also provided a basis for appreciating how factors such as participation in the budgetary process and other organizational circumstances could influence the change the processes at work, thereby creating a whole range of new problems for investigation in further studies. In more contemporary terms, the study also provided some insights into how organizational cultures and managerial philosophies might shape the significance attached to accounting systems and play some role in influencing their effects.

Perhaps more significantly for me, however, the study undertaken in Chicago had demonstrated that it was possible and meaningful to probe into the actual functioning of accounting. Although I was never myself to extend the precise form of that analysis, a basis for a more widespread interest in observing and questioning accounting in use had been created. Rather than focusing on the technical analysis and elaboration of accounting in isolation from its organizational context, I had started along a path of inquiry concerned with the observation of accounting rather than its propagation, with an exploration of its organizational and social bases rather than the presumption of a technical autonomy, and with an attempt to appreciate the actual consequences of accounting rather than the unproblematic acceptance of its stated rationales.

THE DEVELOPMENT OF AN ORGANIZATIONAL INTEREST

The culture shock on returning to the United Kingdom in 1970 was intellectual as well as social in nature. Having developed my interest in organizational issues in the United States, I had tended to take for granted the social psychological domination of the subject evident at that time and place, and its resulting individualistic orientation (Kassem, 1976). The contrast with a British perspective therefore could not have been more marked, not least with the vibrant organizational research community at the Manchester Business School, which celebrated its links to the substantive disciplines of anthropology, sociology, and even a version of institutional economics. Accordingly I had to set about merging myself in organizational studies afresh, luckily, however, in an environment noted for its excitement, its innovativeness, and its concern with the scholarly, the practical, and the interface between the two.

Working on the text of *Accounting and Human Behaviour* (Hopwood, 1974) provided a most useful way of thinking through what might be at stake with a wider organisational perspective on accounting. It provided a context in which to explore new literatures, to push existing understandings, and to start raising a somewhat different set of questions related to the organizational embeddedness of accounting. Although the text is now a somewhat dated work (albeit one that is still in use), I am still surprised by the apparent novelty of some of the occasional comments and the extent to which it reflected what was then only the beginning of a new way of attempting to perceive the accounting craft. At times even I wonder how I could possibly have thought that way at that time!

A number of influences were starting to reflect themselves in my work. Not only was an expanding interdisciplinary basis evident but also a growing involvement with accounting in practice. Post-experience management teaching was useful in this respect, as were the opportunities that the Manchester Business School provided to work with a mature, ambitious, and intellectually able group of post-graduate students. In a more complex way I was also stimulated by the intellectual agenda created by the Management Control Research Group at the School. Founded by Morris McInnes and Tony Lowe, the group set itself an impossibly ambitious research agenda of both surveying and categorizing the variety of approaches to management control systems functioning in the United Kingdom. At that time there was little prior work to guide such an endeavor. Existing conceptual frameworks and distinctions were woefully inadequate to reflect the diversity of practices in use. And the methodological problems involved in mapping such diversity were very real. Hardly surprisingly the activities of the group generated a fair amount of conflict, an enormous data bank of observations and recordings, and relatively few publications. Be that as it may, the project exposed all of us to the complexities of management accounting in practice and illuminated very forcefully the inadequacies of many existing understandings of the subject. What findings there were pointed to an appreciation of accounting that recognized its involvement with other organizational practices and the ways in which accounting systems were implicated in the construction of organizations as we know them, rather than being mere reflections of the organizational endeavour.

As a result of such experiences a more organizationally grounded appreciation of accounting started to emerge. The technical practice of accounting increasingly came to be related to the organizational and wider contexts in which it functioned. The interrelationships between accounting and organizational structures, aspects of the technological and competitive environments of the enterprise, and the dynamics of the political processes that characterise organizational life started to be explored. Although I was at this time both aware of and influenced by contingent notions of organization developed in the organizational literature, I think that it is fair to say that even then I found such frameworks useful but inadequate, at least as they were then formulated. They provided one way of characterizing the organizational dependency of accounting systems, but they did this in a way that was too deterministic, offered too limited a view of the more complex patterns of interdependency that I increasingly came to see as influencing accounting's functioning in organizations, and ignored the more subtle ways in which flows of accounting information could shift and disturb patterns of influence, power, meaning, and significance within the organizational realm.

Aware of such limitations of more conventional, albeit still emerging, ways of conceiving accounting in an organizational context, a more open personal agenda for probing into the organizational functioning and significance of accounting started to develop. Much interested in the challenge of deriving an approach to teaching in the area, I became increasingly interested in the articulation of quite general but hopefully useful frameworks that might help to improve our understanding of the organizational construction, functioning, and consequences of accounting. Somewhat in contrast but certainly not in conflict, I also developed an interest in both ways of appreciating the quite specific functioning of accounting systems in specific organizations and the research strategies that might result in a more organizationally grounded insight into accounting as it operated. Earlier interests in the "use" of accounting broadened out into interests in the different ways in which accounting systems could be and were caught up in decision and influence processes in organizations. An interest in the micro politics of accounting started to emerge. I became more sensitive to the ways in which accounting changes could influence managerial vocabularies and the articulation of organizational aims, problems, and possibilities. The ways in which accounting got caught up in wider organizational patterns of transformation and change started to become of particular interest. I started at least to talk about the extent to which the elaboration of accounting systems might be a response to organizational crisis. The management of information flows in circumstances characterized by rapid change and disruption became a topic of growing curiosity. The quite complex ways in which accounting could be influenced by organizational restructurings started to enter my research agenda.

Perhaps unfortunately, most of these interests did not result in specific research projects. Rather together they provided a basis for a growing sense of unease with both existing technical appreciations of the accounting craft and the so-called behavioral insights that had emerged by that time. The autonomy attributed to the former and the constrained notions of organizational rationality that were implicit in discussions of them were an increasing source of dissatisfaction, as were the individualistic emphases that were quite explicit in the rise of a behavioral stance in the accounting research community. The inability of the latter to confront a great deal of what I came to see as being at stake in the organizational practice of accounting provided a basis for an intellectual unease with research developments. Increasingly I also put more emphasis on the limitations that such behavioral views had for guiding even pragmatic interests in accounting system design. Perhaps by then the teaching demands evident in a business school environment were making their impact, although not only was I never aware of a conflict between the scholarly and the practical but, in contrast, I became increasingly interested in some of the quite similar demands that both strands of thinking could make on accounting knowledge.

All too clearly, subsequent interests in understanding the dynamics of accounting change were emergent at this time. A focus on grounded inquiry had already been articulated. A multiplicity of rationales for accounting elaboration and development were starting to be appreciated, providing a rich basis for continuing empirical and theoretical inquiries. Although perhaps not quite so well appreciated at that time, an interest in both the scholarly and the practical roles of accounting knowledge was also starting to be made more evident. All told, an agenda for future research, a quite particular theoretical stance, and a perspective on the roles that knowledge might play were all emerging in ways that continued to have a significant influence on the direction of future enthusiasms and inquiries.

INSTITUTIONAL INVOLVEMENTS

It is most likely quite difficult to appreciate some, at least, of these shifting interests outside of the context of a growing involvement with the institutionalization of accounting research. For reasons that I sense owe more to luck than design, I had the opportunity to become an active contributor to three quite significant advancements in the institutional development of accounting research in the United Kingdom at that time. These were the launching of an accounting research initiative by the then Social Science Research Council, the government funding body for research in the human and social sciences; the development of a programme of European accounting research workshops by the newly established European Institute for Advanced Studies in Management, in Brussels, an activity that subsequently gave rise to the creation of the European Accounting Association; and the establishment of a new specialized international research journal concerned with the behavioral, organizational, and social analyses of accounting, *Accounting, Organizations and Society*. All of these activities consumed a vast amount of my time, and some still do so. Although they considerably constrained my own research and writing endeavors, not only did they not stop them but over the years they also had a very considerable influence upon them.

The development of a European network of accounting researchers brought me into contact with very different research traditions, theoretical ways of appreciating accounting, and strategies for engaging in accounting research. It is always difficult to appreciate and disentangle the influences such awarenesses have had on your own work. They invariably leave few specific residues. But I am very conscious of the cumulative impact, not least with respect to the richness of insight and sheer enthusiasm for grounded organizational inquiry that was such an important part of the Scandinavian, and particularly the Swedish, tradition of research in the areas of accounting and information systems in particular and management more generally. My personal contacts and friendships with Scandinavian researchers provided possibilities for direct theoretical influences; they also prompted a reorientation of my organizational interests, away from a model influenced by the North American academic community and towards one increasingly open to the quite different intellectual traditions of continental Europe. In ways that would be difficult, if not impossible, to chart with precision, I started to develop into a European academic who increasingly could observe both American work and my own earlier inquiries with interest but from a distance.

The full development of a more European tradition of inquiry will, in all probability, be manifested by a younger group of scholars, rather than by those of us who were privileged to have played some role in the creation of a cross-national network of accounting researchers. But I derive a great deal of pleasure from the part I have been able to play in the establishment of that network and I look forward with pleasure to the days when it might result in understandings and insights different from those I personally have been able to utilize.

Different institutional forms can undoubtedly play some role in changing modes of inquiry and the resultant patterns of knowledge and understanding. Indeed it was with just such a view in mind that I sought to establish a new journal that would be exclusively concerned with the organizational, behavioral, and social analyses of accounting. Although it still has an unfinished agenda for intellectual exploration and change, I like to think that *Accounting, Organizations and Society* has already played some role in opening up new areas for inquiry, legitimizing different scholarly traditions, and creating a more international and open research community amongst those interested in probing into the human and social nature of accounting thought and practice.

The initial idea on which *Accounting, Organizations and Society* was based emerged in an educational context. With other colleagues at the Manchester Business School I had designed a role-playing case study based on the affairs of Pergamon Press, an organization that played a not insignificant role in recent British accounting history. Wanting the students to have the opportunity to question actual participants in the affair rather than rely solely on press reports and official documents, key participants were invited to take part in the teaching of the case study. Robert Maxwell, the founder of Pergamon Press, was one of those individuals and, ever the entrepreneur, Mr. Maxwell used the opportunity to inquire into whether I had any ideas for new research journals!

Well, as it happens, I had. At that time I was becoming increasingly conscious of a gap that existed between the potential for an organizational and social understanding of accounting and the editorial policies and concerns of the existing accounting research journals. That idea of a gap gave rise to a proposal for a new journal and after numerous deliberations and consultations *Accounting, Organizations and Society*, the new journal, was launched in 1976.

In retrospect it is interesting to reflect on the enormous gap between the naiveté of the idea and the reality of the journal's establishment. Even getting agreement on the name of the new journal was problematic. Majority opinion was strongly in favor of it being known as the *Journal of Behavioral and Social Accounting*. I, however, was bothered about the constrained view of what would hopefully become a new research area implicit in such a designation. I wanted something more suggestive of the need to openly explore ways in which accounting functioned in organizational and social settings. Whilst the concerns of the 1970s emphasized the specificities of behavioral and social accounting, I envisioned a journal that would encourage the investigation of wider questions relating to the rise of economic calculation in organizations and society. *Accounting, Organizations and Society* emerged as a title that hopefully suggested the possibilities that the new journal might create, rather than being reflective of, the immediate context out of which it emerged.

Now is not the occasion to review the history of *Accounting, Organizations and Society*. I like to think that it has achieved quite a lot, although I am equally conscious of what remains to be achieved. It certainly has consumed an immense amount of my time and energy, and still does so. But my involvement with the journal has been a reciprocal one. Just as I have at least attempted to steer and influence it, so *Accounting, Organizations and Society* has had a very significant influence on me. I have learnt from what it has published; I have gained from the intellectual agendas it has helped to create; and I am wiser as a result of the new networks of enthusiastic researchers that have been associated with the journal. International in scope, the community of those interested in the organizational and social analysis of accounting has established a tradition of open, friendly, and facilitative interchange that has brought together friendship and intellectual curiosity in ways that have been mutually enriching.

THE RISE OF A SOCIAL INTEREST

It was whilst *Accounting, Organizations and Society* was still a very new baby, that I moved to what was then the Oxford Centre for Management Studies (now Templeton College, Oxford) with the explicit brief of establishing a programme of accounting research. Although my stay at Oxford was a relatively short one, it was nevertheless a productive and significant one. An active and successful period of fund raising provided the basis for me to plan a more focused programme of research and to recruit a talented team of researchers that included Stuart Burchell, Colin Clubb, John Hughes, and Janine Nahapiet. Freed from many of the pressures of teaching and academic administration, that newly established research group was quickly able to establish a congenial and very productive mode of operation.

The research agenda of the group was explicit, albeit general. We were all interested in pushing further our understandings of what might be at stake in an organizational and social analysis of accounting. Whilst I and others had pointed to the organizational and social bases and consequences of accounting practices, in many ways such appeals had only served to point to the possibilities of a new way of inquiring into the functioning of accounting. The group was all too aware of this; early discussions focused on "what was at stake" with such a view, which ways of characterizing accounting might enrich the task of directly conceiving accounting within the spheres of the organizational and the social, and what were the theoretical and methodological prerequisites for advancing such a view. The research group was also unanimous that a major focus for such inquiries ought to be the study of accounting change. Rather than seeking to directly explore accounting as it was, we viewed that much more might be gained from exploring accounting in the process of becoming, of changing, of becoming what it was not. In such a context, it was thought, more might be seen of the forces that put accounting into motion and of the organizational and social consequences of disruptions in the accounting craft. Whilst we were well aware that change is a relative matter and that we might, as a consequence, have to focus on accounting elaborations rather than more fundamental shifts, we were nevertheless convinced that even such analyses might provide an empirical richness that would stimulate, provoke, and influence our more theoretical explorations of accounting in the process of becoming what it was not.

The specific empirical interests of the research group were influenced by a mixture of pragmatic and intellectual considerations, as is invariably the case. One project focused on the introduction of budgeting systems into a region of the National Health Service. Another aimed to explore the rise of interest in forms of social accounting in a number of European countries, although given the diversity of such initiatives it also sought to understand the social dynamics that gave rise to social accountings and the different nature of the social significances attached to them. A third project was orientated towards organizational studies of accounting system change. Taken together, the projects resulted in a vast amount of rich empirical material, only some of which has been published as of now. Both the diversity and the depth of the empirical findings served as a vital stimulus to theoretical inquiry, raising, as they did, questions about adequate ways of understanding the forces at work and the ways in which accounting changes emerged out of complex configurations of organizational and social circumstances.

The inquiry resulted in a number of more general contributions to the literature, all of which are collected here. Early concerns to probe into, question, and distance ourselves from many conventional understandings of accounting are reflected in "The Roles of Accounting in Organisations and Society." So aware of the possibilities for different ways of interrogating accounting, some initial statements of our research interests and agenda appeared in "The Development of Accounting in its International Context: Past Concerns and Emergent Issues," a paper that now reads as a very preliminary one indeed, and "'A Message From Mars'—and Other Reminiscences from the Past," a paper that reports on some empirical findings that were to serve as a crucial catalyst for more general theorizing. More mature statements of the research position developed in the group are given in "Accounting in Its Social Context: Towards a History of Value Added in the United Kingdom" and, although written and published appreciably later, in "The Archaeology of Accounting Systems."

Other writings pursue and elaborate upon the approach to the organizational and social analysis of accounting developed in those initial papers. Some of the implications for an organizational understanding of accounting are sketched out in "Management Accounting and Organisational Action: An Introduction" and "Accounting and Organisational Action." Questions of a more explicitly social nature are addressed in the rather brief "Economics and the Regime of the Calculative," a paper that reflects my remaining worries about the unproblematic advance of calculative practices, whether they stem from economic or social rationales for action, and in "The Tale of a Committee that Never Reported: Disagreements on Intertwining Accounting with the Social" and "Accounting Research and Accounting Practice: The Ambiguous Relationship Between the Two." Recognizing the potential for the development of accounting in the public sector in the United Kingdom to illuminate some of the more general issues at stake in an organizational and social analysis of accounting, a number of papers have specifically sought to address this area in a tentative way. "Accounting and the Pursuit of Efficiency" and *Accounting and the Domain of the Public: Some Observations on Current Developments* are illustrative examples. Although based on quite extensive contacts with such public sector developments, such analyses nevertheless remain preliminary, not least because of my own equivocality about the role that economic calculation is called upon to play in the reform of organizations seeking to advance quite particular conceptions of the social.

The research perspective addressed in such writings is all too clearly an emergent one. Individually they provide specific illustrations of the issues at stake and the potential offered. Others attempt to sketch out some of the more general implications for social understanding of accounting practice. However, whilst undoubtedly preliminary, the themes developed in the papers hopefully also have a coherence, not least when contrasted with those evident in other organizational and economic perspectives.

Emphasis is placed on both the reflective and constitutive aspects of accounting. Recognizing that accounting is not an autonomous calculative practice, attention is directed towards improving our understanding, not only of how factors external to accounting can impinge upon and change it, but also of how such interminglings can occur and of how accounting can mediate and reflect other organizational and social circumstances. Equally, however, emphasis is placed on the enabling and productive properties of accounting. Explicitly seeking to recognize how accounting can create quite particular and partial patterns of visibility, the analyses hopefully start to provide at least one basis for understanding how accounting can at times disturb and disrupt other organizational and social circumstances. Emphasizing the specificities of the economic categories and linguistic distinctions that infuse accounting in practice, a basis is provided for appreciating some of the ways in which the calculative practices of accounting can permeate and shape patterns of organizational concerns, influencing conceptions of the problematic, the desirable, and the possible.

In these analyses increasing emphasis is placed on the ways in which accounting is implicated in the wider diffusion of economic priorities and concerns. Greater attention is being given to the organizational and social consequences of the calculative rationality that can be associated with the advance of accounting practices. Not unrelated, more attention is being given to the discursive and theoretical conceptions with which accounting is often implicated. Once again recognizing that the technical practices are not independent of notions of their functioning and rationales, although the relationship between them is neither direct nor uniform, some of the papers reflect a growing interest in the knowledges and understandings capable of being advanced and diffused by them.

In all cases the understanding offered of the dynamics of accounting change is quite a complex one. Simple notions of functionality are questioned. Accounting is not seen as being a mere reflection of unproblematic essences or imperatives. A detailed understanding of the specific contexts in which accounting change occurs demonstrates the diversity of influences that can impinge on accounting and its consequences, the often quite complex and shifting circumstances, issues, and practices with which accounting can be associated, and, of equal significance, the roles played by the unintentional and the unanticipated consequences of accounting change.

All too clearly such emerging understandings reflect a combination of theoretical and empirical interests. Increasingly they emerge from a commitment to grounded inquiry and a concern to address and understand the specificities of accounting in use. Consistent with such a view, I still attempt to invest a great deal of time in trying to observe accounting, always trying to maintain an interest in new accountings, major accounting changes and reforms, and pragmatic attempts to articulate new or expanded rationales for accounting practice. The nature of the research task is such that only a small amount of material emerges in public form, although much of the rest influences the intellectual agendas I maintain and develop. Equally the understandings I have of accounting reflect a view that such appreciations are not implicit in the circumstances being observed but reflect the use of an interpretative theoretical lens. There is little doubt that over the years I have attempted to be more theoretically conscious, equally investing an enormous amount of time trying to inform myself of at least some to the theoretical developments in the wider human and social sciences. I also have possibly become more conscious and careful of the criteria that I seek to impose on my own theorizing. Recognizing that such theorizing is a human endeavor, I have become increasingly aware that the particular understandings I seek to develop should attempt to be consistent with the more general notions of knowledge and theory they themselves articulate. I also often say that theorists should always be willing to be subject to their own theories! I am happy to stand by that test, although I know of many theories of the economic, organizational, and social nature of accounting that I, at least, would oppose being subjected to.

CONCLUSION

Trying to give coherence to a diversity of work is not an easy task. It is equally difficult trying to account for something that so obviously remains open-ended and emergent.

What uniformity there is in the papers that follow reflects a longstanding attempt to delve into accounting, to observe and explore its functioning, to construct a basis for interrogating it in use, and indeed, as I have sometimes said, to account for accounting itself. Rather than accepting accounting, seeking unproblematically to advance its functioning and improve its rationality, I have sought to understand accounting, to appreciate what it is, what it does, and how it does it. My position vis-à-vis accounting has therefore been a more questioning one, always striving to examine it from without rather than from within. Such a stance continues and it therefore still remains appropriate to entitle this collection of papers *Accounting from the Outside*.

REFERENCES

Dev, S., *Accounting and the L. S. E. Tradition* (London School of Economics and Political Science, 1980).

Hopwood, A. G., *Accounting and Human Behavior* (Haymarket, 1975; Prentice Hall, 1976).

Hopwood, A. G., *An Accounting System and Managerial Behavior* (Saxon House, 1973).

Kassem, M. S., Introduction: European versus American Organisation Theories, in G. H. Hofstede and M. S. Kassem, eds., *European Contributions to Organisation Theory* (Van Gorcum, 1976).

Towards an Organizational Perspective for the Study of Accounting and Information Systems[*]

ANTHONY G. HOPWOOD

(*Oxford Centre for Management Studies*)

Many might think that the introduction to a collected series of papers ought to reassure the reader, showing how each sheds light on the others and on the overall accumulation of knowledge, thereby guaranteeing the unity and coherence of the various contributions. Here, however, I believe that it would be unrealistic to attempt an introduction along such lines at this stage of conceptual development. Certainly the following papers, with one exception, were brought together for two workshops at a conference organized in late 1976[①] and all of them focus on the same topic—the relationships between the organization and its accounting and information systems. But the criteria employed in selecting the papers deliberately set out to provide a plurality of theoretical and empirical perspectives. So, it is important to point out right from the beginning that this diversity is not being concealed but, on the contrary, openly stated. It represents, in my opinion at least, not a pathological condition of inquiry into accounting and information systems, but quite the reverse. The diversity of conceptual and research strategies reflects scholarship in action. For understanding in any area of human inquiry has to be constructed through a process of debate, be it explicit or otherwise, between different conceptual systems, reasonings and analytical and methodological approaches. At the very least this collection of papers aims to illustrate the potentiality of such a debate for accounting (and information system) thought and practice.

---

[*] *Accounting, Organizations and Society*, Vol. 3, No. 1, pp. 3—13, 1978.

[①] The original versions of the papers by Bariff & Galbraith, den Hertog and Hedberg & Jönsson were presented at the Workshop on Designing Management Accounting Systems for Organizations in a Changing Environment organized by Anthony Hopwood at the November 10—12, 1976 meetings of the American Institute of Decision Sciences held in San Francisco. The paper by Waterhouse and Tiessen is a revised version of one presented at the Workshop on the Relevance of Modern Organization Theory for the Design of Accounting Systems organized and chaired by Vijay Sathe at the same meetings. A brief report of the latter workshop also appears in this issue.

PAST TRADITIONS AND CONCERNS

So many of the early studies of the way in which accounting systems operate, or might operate, in organizations have concentrated on gaining a rather static understanding of the more psychological and social psychological aspects of the accounting process. A great deal of con-sideration, for instance, has been given to the way in which different accounting methods, configu-rations of data and modes of presentation influence the decision making behaviour and the decision outcomes of individual managers. And this tradition of research now provides the rationale, if not the intellectual basis, for today's increasingly influential and rigorous concerns with the way in which individuals process, interpret and use accounting information. However, it is now being recognized that this and other related research, has tended to study what are admittedly quite crucial aspects of the accounting process in isolation of the ongoing organizational context that provides the very *raison d'être* of the accounting function.

The relationship between individual responses to accounting information and other aspects of the dynamic functioning of the organizations in which individuals manifest their behaviour has rarely been regarded as explicitly problematic. And, in consequence, a great deal of the research on the human processing of accounting information has, of necessity, had to adopt a rather fragmented view of the organizational decision process and the role which information plays in this. Accordingly emphasis has had to be placed on understanding particular individual responses to particular presentations of information and little consideration has been given to either the more specific role that might be played by ongoing managerial learning, and the resulting shiftings of meanings and concerns, or the more general findings of those studies that have sought to investigate the way in which managers make decisions in organizations and the role that formal information systems, such as accounting systems, might or might not play in this process (March & Olsen, 1976; Mintzberg, 1973, 1975; Pettigrew, 1972, 1973, 1977). Although the resulting rather simple view of organizational, as distinct from individual, behaviour, with its emphasis on pro-active, goal directed behaviour in response to the discrete presentation of information (Atkin, 1978), might be implicit rather than explicit, it is nevertheless real.

Even in cases where accounting has been studied in its organizational context, emphasis still has been placed on gaining a comparatively static understanding of the more individual, or at the most group, aspects of the process. So, for instance, the response of the individual manager or employee to different degrees of budget tightness has been studied, at one time, in a great deal of detail. However, this has been done without any consideration of the known social as well as individual influences on such responses, the effects of individual and organizational learning and of the possible relationship between different budget standards and formats and, for example, the distribution and management of organizational power and influence or alternative strategies for coping with uncertainty, even though it has been recognized that the managerial response to budgets might be as dependent, if not more so, on the organizational rather than the overt technical meanings attributed to them.

Studies of participation in the budgeting process, to cite another substantive body of the literature in this area, have also tended to focus on the static relationships between participation and such factors as managerial orientations to the budgeting system, extrinsic and intrinsic motivations to perform, levels of individual satisfaction and the propensity or not to engage in such protective strategies as 'padding' the budget and 'fiddling' the accounts rather than on attempting to gain an appreciation of the organizational process through which such results are achieved or of the relationship between budgeting and other organizational control structures and strategies. Indeed not only have accounting researchers not investigated such dynamic aspects of the process themselves but they have only made symbolic or little or no use of those pioneering studies by other social scientists that have focused on such matters (Argyris, 1952; Bower, 1970; Pettigrew, 1973; Roy, 1969; Whyte, 1955; Wildavsky, 1964). Related static and individualistic concerns are also evident in many of those studies that have focused on the way in which accounting information is actually used where factors such as managerial style and the characteristics of the manager-subordinate relationship have tended to dominate research perspectives.

After striving to identify the partiality of so much of the past research that has sought to understand the ways in which accounting systems operate it *must* be stated that an emerging area of research inquiry cannot hope to provide a comprehensive view, let alone appreciation, of all aspects of its problematic domain. Not only do choices have to be made, and the resulting partialities and incompleteness accepted, but it is more than likely that such choices should be made if enquiry is to be thorough and cumulative. Nevertheless, whilst respecting the inevitability of specialisation in such an embryonic area, it is still appropriate to retrospectively identify what choices have been made, particularly at a time when there are clear pressures for alternative approaches and domains of inquiry, and it is even more appropriate to ponder on those factors that might have influenced the direction of progress to date.

SOME INTELLECTUAL INFLUENCES

Firstly, it should be stated that the static and individualistic orientation of research on the behavioural aspects of accounting reflects much more general influences on the development of social science inquiry. Given that virtually all the pioneering studies in the area, and the vast majority of the subsequent work to date, has emanated from the U. S. A., or at least been strongly influenced by U. S. approaches and concerns, it should not be surprising that the conceptual and methodological approaches that characterise behavioural enquiries undertaken in the accounting area should be related to the dominant concerns in substantive areas of American social science. And this would appear to be the case. For although an adequate understanding of the complex social, political, institutional and philosophical factors that influence the development of social science knowledge remains to be achieved, numerous commentators (Hage, 1978; Karpik, 1978; Kassem, 1976; Lammers, 1976; Wilson, 1977) have pointed to the distinct and often divergent social science traditions and concerns in the U. S. A. and Europe, with the U. K. for this purpose at least, rather ambiguously having a foot on both sides of the intellectual Atlantic!

Such commentators, and particularly Kassem (1976) in his discussion of the contrasting perspectives brought to bear on the study of organizational behaviour, have tended to contrast the more micro American orientation, with its focus on organizational psychology, with the more macro European approaches focusing on questions of organizational sociology. Such comparisons have emphasized the centrality of U. S. concerns with the problems of the individual contributing to the organization, as reflected, for instance, in the human relations movement and the 'radical psychological individualists' (Whitley, 1974) and the consequent study of the organizational mechanisms for relating individual performance, and rewards, to organizational action and goal achievement, whether such mechanisms be seen as ways of increasing organizational rationality or as social and procedural means for managing commitment, motivation and hence achievement. Such pragmatic and functional U. S. concerns have been contrasted with more European interests in the structural and broader environmental influences on organizational processes and actions, which perhaps inevitably, because of the very breadth of the definition of the problematic, have been more oriented towards providing conceptual, interpretative and possibly critical appreciations of the historical and specific influences on organizational action (Hage, 1978; Sandberg, 1976, pp. 29—32).

Broad generalizations of this type are difficult to make for inevitably there are always exceptions, including, in this case, some rather influential ones. In the U.S., for instance, important sociological inquiries have been undertaken, not least the early studies associated with the Chicago School of Sociology, the work of Merton, Gouldner, Blau, Etzioni, Hage, Perrow and others and the more recent contingency formulations. And in Europe exceptions also abound. But the contrasts remain, in general terms, meaningful ones, and particularly in an accounting context if further consideration is given to the filtering processes inherent in the academic system itself. For in many of the major U.S. Business Schools the more micro psychological and social psychological perspectives have been even more dominant than in the social science community at large.

Perhaps related to the above broader intellectual concerns and perhaps, to some extent, independently building on them is another factor which also must be considered when analysing those factors that have influenced the development of research on how accounting systems operate. And this is the view taken of the broader purpose of the research task.

Research can seek to illuminate and elucidate, to provide, thereby, in the hermeneutic tradition (Taylor, 1971) a basis for interpreting and understanding the role played by accounting systems, and accountants, in organizational and social functioning. It can, however, have more pragmatic concerns, immediate or otherwise. Research can be oriented towards improving the functioning of accounting systems as we know them either by aiming to improve the effectiveness of present systems or by providing the basis for the design of accounting systems, possibly moving accounting a little nearer towards what Simon (1969) has called the 'sciences of the artificial'. And lest we forget it, given the present parsity of research, scholarly inquiry can also seek to provide a critical appreciation of the role played by current modes of accounting, questioning, in the process, the role they might play in furthering the influence of economic interests on organizational action, and possibly, on this basis, moving towards the design of alternative accountings.

Different research orientations, and clearly there are others, make very different demands on knowledge. Both the hermeneutic and critical perspectives require a broad appreciation of the social as well as organizational context of accounting, although clearly the critical approach also requires a more thorough insight into the relationship between accounting and social interests and the organizational knowledge that is so essential for any attempt to construct a design orientated perspective, critical or otherwise. Only when research accepts the present body of accounting knowledge as itself being unproblematic in broad outline, merely seeking to improve the effectiveness of present systems, are fewer demands made on knowledge. For with such a research orientation an appreciation of the organizational basis of accounting might be less crucial than understandings of the role played by the more detailed aspects of design, such as formats and modes of presentation, and of those psychological and social psychological processes which mediate the effects of any given system.

A view that as yet the research horizons of a great deal of accounting research might be (perhaps justifiably) constrained by an acceptance of the present functioning of accounting is supported by others (see Jensen, 1976) who have noted the relationship between research orientations and the demands on knowledge and the direction of scholarly inquiry in accounting. Indeed as other areas of accounting research have moved away from more limited research perspectives, shedding, in the process, some of the traditional constraints of accounting givens, in order to provide a basis for understanding the broader organizational, economic or socioeconomic role played by accounting, one can witness the process in operation. This is certainly true for investigations into the role played by accounting information in the capital markets, the economic rationale for information and control system design and the more recent inquiries into the socio-political bases for accounting standard setting.

It is likely, however, that the effects of the broader intellectual traditions discussed above exert their influence on the research community indirectly through more specific and immediate aspects of the institutional context in which research takes place. We have, for example, already referred to the possible exaggeration of the individualistic orientation in the specific context of business schools. Research perspectives that orientate themselves more towards the production of immediately pragmatic and hopefully generalizable understandings, and are less questioning of existing approaches, will also be more acceptable in such contexts, as has already been demonstrated in the case of industrial psychology (Baritz, 1960). Then, as Kassem (1976) points out, the more micro organizational orientation to social research is more amenable to methodologies that are both compatible with the research traditions of academic peers in different disciplines and functional areas, and to the speedy production of research results. Both of these factors are important within the context of the reward structure of the academic community, influencing both individual advancement and what is acceptable to the established channels of communication.

CHANGING INTERESTS AND CONCERNS

However the approaches of a 'normal science' (Kuhn, 1970) carry within themselves the means for their own advancement and eventual succession. So although one can delineate some reasons why past research has focused on certain concerns to the detriment of others, such appreciations do not necessarily provide any basis for thinking that past concerns will continue into the future. Indeed the opposite is more likely to be the case in scientific endeavour. For whilst the institutional embodiment of research perspectives, in terms of reward structures for instance, can be a constraining influence, historical experience provides one with a basis for expecting that many, if not all, of such constraints will be overcome, sometimes with difficulty and delay, but often with amazing facility and speed.

At present there are indications of at least some pressures for change in the behavioural accounting research community. Some of these pressures eminate from within the present, advancing body of knowledge. Others stem from broader, ongoing changes in social science inquiry. Whilst yet other pressures come from the client community, broadly defined; some from the changing interests of existing clients in corporate management and others from the gradual recognition of the legitimacy of the interests of other social groups in accounting knowledge and research.

Certainly the gradual accumulation of psychological and social-psychological understandings of the way in which accounting systems operate in organizational settings has itself provided a basis for regarding more structural and organizational issues as being problematic. Hofstede's (1967) research on the social psychological dimensions of budgeting, for instance, pointed to the role that technological and organizational factors, as reflected in departmental and organizational cost structures, might play in mediating the effectiveness of budgetary procedures. And the comparative analysis of participation in the budgetary process undertaken by Swieringa & Moncur (1975) provided more direct evidence. Even social psychological studies undertaken in single organizational settings are no less suggestive when the differing results of individual studies are set side by side. So, for example, a comparison of the differences, and commonalities, in the findings of Hopwood (1973) and Otley (1978) points to the role that might be played by organizational level differences, particularly when the diverging results are set aside the comparative hypotheses and findings of Baumler (1971).

The presumption that ever more of such pointers will be discovered as empirical research progresses, and it should be remembered that we have precious little as yet, is supported by the findings of those studies that have been more consciously influenced by an organizational rather than an individualistic or group perspective. The early study of the organization of the accounting function undertaken by Simon and his colleagues (1954), which is so frequently cited by textbook writers for its analysis of the alternative modes of using accounting information but just as frequently ignored for its substantive findings, provided a clear indication of the relevance of such an appreciation. And the subsequent studies reported by Khandwalla (1972), Bruns & Waterhouse (1975), Watson (1975), Watson & Baumler (1975) and Hayes (1977), all much more directly influenced by advancing knowledge in the field of organizational behaviour, demonstrate not only the richness, relevance and potential of the approach but also the way in which the gradual development of behavioural accounting research is itself moving towards more explicitly recognizing the importance of understanding organizational questions.

Such an explicit recognition of developments in organizational behaviour research is itself of significance and no doubt we can expect many more explorations of this type. Certainly the emerging pattern of submissions to this and other journals, successful and otherwise, would support such a conclusion. Equally relevant, if not more so, is the growing interest that organizational researchers themselves are taking in questions related to the design and functioning of accounting and information systems. Whilst this is not a new phenomenon, as evidenced by the pioneering and influential studies undertaken by Agyris (1952) and Simon (1954) and the attention given to such issues by Roy (1969), Dalton (1959), Whyte (1955), Blau (1966) and Wildavsky (1964), amongst many others, there is some basis for believing that the critical role played by accounting and information systems in organizations is now being more generally recognized and studied by scholars of organizational behaviour (Pfeffer, 1977; Pettigrew, 1973; Pondy, 1970; Heydebrand, 1977; Connolly, 1977; etc.). If this is indeed the case then it can only add to our understanding of the area, most likely legitimising and encouraging, in the process, the adoption of similar research perspectives and methodologies by accounting scholars.

The pressures for change do not only eminate from within the research community however. For in business and public organizations there is, I think, and here one can only talk in a much more tentative way, drawing on one's own experiences and impressions, a growing appreciation of the need for a more organizational understanding. In part this reflects, inevitably perhaps, a greater awareness of the limitations of present pragmatic perspectives and approaches (Earl, 1978). More significantly, perhaps, it reflects an increasing recognition of the need for accounting and information system innovation and the role that new knowledge might play in this process.

Until recently the development of accounting and information systems was a very pragmatic affair, prodded, no doubt, by the recognition of the inadequacies of prevailing approaches and the possible relevance of known alternatives. Although change was often real and major (Chandler, 1962, 1977), one can only presume that it was guided by practical wisdom, and on occasions ignorance, and shaped by the rules of experience and the lessons of trial and error. Certainly there is little or no evidence of any systematic research being undertaken, least of all in an academic community.

The results of such processes constitute the substantive bulk of management accounting as we now know it (Gardner, 1954; Parker, 1969; Pollard, 1965). Critical as some researchers might be of it, and at least some of such criticism could be tempered by a greater appreciation of some of the radically innovative and seemingly modern marginal and oft forgotten developments made by our entrepreneurial predecessors, it nevertheless provides the basis on which today's more technical research on topics such as divisional performance measurement, costing methods and capital investment appraisal is conducted.

The increasing pace of change and the growing size and complexity of organizations have created a need for more rapid and more sophisticated accounting and information system developments however. And such increases in organizational complexity, in particular, have increased the relevance of and need for a more explicit understanding of the relationship between information (and accounting) systems and organizational design (Galbraith, 1973). Increasingly, therefore, business and public organizations have turned to outside consultants and researchers for help, sometimes also creating their own specialist developmental teams in the area. The growing sophistication of information system technology provides many examples of such a response, as do the increasing difficulties of costing and controlling both major, long term projects and of deciding upon the production and commercial policies for products with increasingly short life cycles. Similarly, and perhaps more significantly, the complexities of designing the information and control systems, including accounting systems, for the massive modern aerospace and defence organizations have engaged the attention of researchers in both universities and specialized institutes such as the RAND Corporation (Chandler & Sayles, 1971). For in this area in particular the need for the joint design of organizational and information structures and processes was real and recognized.

That few accounting researchers *per se* might have been involved in such innovations does not detract from either their pragmatic or intellectual significance for the development of accounting and information system knowledge, although it might point to the isolation of main stream accounting researchers from matters of major organizational concern. But given that the design and functioning of accounting systems, like other information and control systems, are interrelated with wider aspects of organizational design, and that organizational designs have never been and are unlikely to be static, as witnessed, for example, by the growing relevance today of matrix (Knight,

1977), network and loosely coupled (Weick, 1976) organizations, past isolation by itself is unlikely to remove the continued pressures for new understandings of the organizational basis for accounting system design.

Broader social pressures are also likely to add to such pressures. For as recent research has illustrated (Braverman, 1974; Hales, 1974; Heydebrand, 1977; Marglin, 1974; Whitley, 1974), management practices and structures in organizations, including prevalent accounting and information systems (Mumford & Sackman, 1975) are reflections of wider social structures, institutions and ideologies. Although such aspects of our societies certainly do not change rapidly, there is already evidence of interest in the bases, and at times the reality, of alternative approaches as new social groups gain both power and an understanding of the relevance of managerial insights (Sandberg, 1976). For instance, in Europe research is already under way on the design of either more participative forms of information, accounting and control systems (Magnusson, 1974; Stymme, 1977) or even systems that explicitly aim to further the interests of labour rather than capital (Briefs, 1975; Nygaard & Bergo, 1975). And on both the sides of the Atlantic consideration is being given to the design of information and accounting systems that facilitate the management and assessment of new forms of work organization (Hopwood, forthcoming; Mirvis & Macy, 1976).

EMERGING POTENTIAL AND PROBLEMS

The pressures for a greater organizational appreciation of the way in which accounting systems operate are undoubtedly diverse but nonetheless real. Ranging from those that originate within the context of normal scientific development, through those arising out of the changing needs of existing salient interest groups, to those that stem from more questioning or even critical perspectives, all are slowly resulting in research endeavours and new understandings. At this stage, however, the diversity of approaches and concerns, and the relative sparcity of findings, makes any overall assessment a precarious task, and such an assessment certainly is not attempted within the confines of this introductory essay. Already, however, the developments do point to an emerging potential and, perhaps of equal importance, to some of the problems that might have to be met on the routes ahead.

The first and most obvious advantage is that an organizational perspective provides a way of building on research developments that are already in progress. As we have discussed, some scholars have laid a basis for exploring both the organizational processes through which accounting and other information systems effect, or not, the consciousness and actions of members of organizations and those organizational, and even wider environmental, factors that influence, shape and constrain the form that accounting and information systems take and the organizational roles that they perform. The papers by Waterhouse & Tiessen, and Wildavsky, and the report by Sathe, contained in the present issue all highlight such developments and their potential. Furthermore, implicit in such ongoing work, and possibly more explicitly in future concerns, might also be a basis for better understanding some of the differences and contrasts that are now evident when the findings of separate psychologically and social psychologically oriented studies are compared, some examples of which have been mentioned above.

Such developments are important for a number of reasons, not least of which is the potential for achieving an understanding of the accounting function that complements the complexities of accounting in action. Rather than being satisfied with an understanding of accounting that focuses on the generalizations that can be made across organizations, organizational researchers might be able to move towards an understanding that is able to cope with the heterogeneous and changing circumstances that shape the form, significance and effects of accounting in specific organizations and sections of organizations. And, in trying to articulate and substantiate such an understanding, it is also likely that consideration will have to be given to views of the accounting and information function that move beyond today's almost exclusive characterisation in terms of the particular combination of techniques, procedures and technologies in use. For whilst these certainly constitute an important part of the whole, and that part which is most obviously visible, the partiality of such a characterisation will be realised when consideration has to be given to those organizational structures and processes through which the technical aspects of accounting achieve their effect. As Simon and his colleagues sought to illustrate, the organization of the accounting function itself and those organizational linkages through which it relates to the rest of the organization are as essential as the techniques and procedures, and often more problematic in managerial terms. Yet our understanding of the organizational form and locus of the accounting function is minimal and both it and the derivation of a more heterogeneous basis for diagnosing and analysing the functioning of accounting systems can only be advanced if accounting research starts to draw on the perspectives and findings of organizational sociologists and theorists.

Such a closer relationship with wider developments in the social sciences, the potential of which already has been illustrated in other areas of accounting research, would enable the consideration of important topics known to be of significance but so far not systematically investigated.

At present the behavioural understandings so far gained by accounting researchers stand in rather stark contrast with the findings of those other social scientists who have strived to probe into their relationship to the dynamics of the organizational decision making process (Bonini, 1963; Bower, 1970; Crecine, 1971; Pettigrew, 1973; Whyte, 1955; Wildavsky, 1964). The emerging understandings of, for instance, feedback processes (Annett, 1969; Rosenthal & Weiss, 1966), the retrospective interpretations and rationalizations that accompany and shape prospective decision making (March & Olsen, 1976; Weick, 1969), the role of bargaining and negotiation in resource allocation (Bower, 1970; Pondy, 1970; Wildavsky, 1964), the way in which commitments develop and influence both the production and use of information (Bower, 1970; Staw & Ross, 1978) and the relationship between the design of information and accounting systems and the ways in which those with organizational power attempt to manage the attribution of meaning and significance in an organizational context (Jönsson & Lundin, 1977; March & Olsen, 1976; Pettigrew, 1977) are providing interesting and important leads to the understanding of accounting in action. And, as Bariff and Calbraith suggest in this issue, the reemergence of social science inquiry into power and conflict in organizations (Burns & Buckley, 1976; Pfeffer, 1977; Zald, 1970) has obvious relevance for the study of a subject that has overtly recognized its role in organizational control, influence and restrain.

One important aspect of the emerging organizational appreciation, and one that also relates to more immediate pragmatic concerns, is the consequent possibility it offers for moving towards a more explicit design orientation for accounting. For although accounting systems are organizational artifacts (Simon, 1969), consciously designed and adapted, the study of them has tended to focus on generalizable specifics more than either the nature of the design process, and the way in which design choices are constrained, or the manner in which systems are adapted to organizational circumstances. The foundations for a theory of accounting system design, if they do exist, currently remain within the experiential understandings of accounting practitioners and consultants.

But many of the pragmatic pressures for new accounting and information system knowledge require a more explicit appreciation of the factors that influence and constrain system design (Bjørn-Andersen & Hedberg, 1977). In days of moderate change, implicit understandings may suffice. However a more systematic and articulated understanding becomes vital when organizational structures change with increasing regularity, when, as discussed by both den Hertog & Hedberg and Jönsson in the present issue, there is a growing realisation of the constraining influence of past designs and when ever more social interests attempt to influence design options and the design process.

Real though the potential of an organizational appreciation of the accounting function may be however, its achievement will not be unproblematic. For progress will be dependent not only on accounting researchers mastering new methodologies and theoretical perspectives, some, at least, of which will initially be at variance with those which are embodied and valued within the institutions in which such research takes place, but also on the research keeping pace with the evolving nature of organizational thought and research. It is tempting in all interdisciplinary research, to focus on those insights from the neighbouring disciplines that are thought to be firmly established rather than those that are still in the process of being established, or rejected. But however admirable such a tendency might be in theory, in the context of normal let alone revolutionary scientific progress (Kuhn, 1970) the resulting 'citation lag' will not only unnecessarily constrain the development of research but also do little to discourage it from focusing on findings and perspectives that were subsequently questioned, if not discredited. So, for instance, accounting research is starting to investigate the relevance of contingency theories at the very time when their empirical basis and present theoretical formulation is being questioned (Pennings & Tripathi, 1978; Aldrich & Mindlin, 1978; Weick, 1977).

A further difficulty facing organizational research in accounting relates to its very potential for changing our perceptions of the accounting function. Findings related to the relationship between accounting and the management of power and conflict in organizations will be challenging. Evidence of the contingent nature of the accounting system design process will be disturbing to technical universalists. And research oriented towards the specification of accountings that service new values will be regarded as threatening by existing interest groups.

However, even in having to cope with the latter problem as well as the problems stemming from the substantive nature of the research itself, accounting research will be dealing with difficulties that are endemic to most scientific progress.

CONCLUSION

Accounting and information systems play a vital role in organizational functioning. They have, as a result, responded, and still are responding to changing organizational and environmental circumstances and there is no reason whatsoever for thinking that the future will be different. New knowledge and insights are constantly needed and although research might not have played a major role in the past, it does have at least the potential to influence the future.

Research which is oriented towards understanding the organizational basis for the design and operation of accounting and information systems is particularly important in this respect. For despite the pioneering work that has been done, particularly on information systems *per se* where investigations may have advanced more readily in the absence of either such a well articulated set of techniques and procedures or their professional embodiment, we still have only the barest understanding of the factors which shape either the design of information systems or the processes through which they, in turn, influence the consciousness and actions of organizational participants. The challenge to understand accounting in action remains, in other words, a real one, although, as we have discussed, the pressures for change are equally evident.

Perhaps, outside of such a context, the differences between the articles in this issue of *Accounting, Organizations and Society* may appear more evident than any similarities. Certainly very different intellectual, social and pragmatic bases are evident. But in what might be very different ways they jointly illustrate how research on how accounting and information systems are designed and function is now responding to the challenge of organizational understandings and the pressures and circumstances of wider environmental change.

BIBLIOGRAPHY

Aldrich, H. & Mindlin, S., Uncertainty and Dependence: Two Perspectives on Environment, in Karpik, L., ed., *Organization and Environment Theory, Issues and Reality* (Sage, 1978).

Annett, J., *Feedback and Human Behaviour* (Penguin, 1969).

Argyris, C., *The Impact of Budgets on People* (School of Business and Public Administration, Cornell University, 1952).

Atkin, R. S., Review of Information and Control in Organizations, *Administrative Science Quarterly* (March, 1978), pp. 168—171.

Baritz, L., *The Servants of Power: A History of the Use of Social Science in American Industry* (Wesleyan University Press, 1960).

Baumler, J. V., Defined Criteria of Performance in Organizational Control, *Administrative Science Quarterly* (September, 1971), pp. 340—350.

Bjørn-Andersen, N. and Hedberg, B. L. T., Designing Information Systems in an Organizational Perspective, in Nystrom, P. C. & Starbuck, W. H., *Prescriptive Models in Organizations* (North-Holland, 1977), pp. 125—142.

Blau, P. M., *The Dynamics of Bureaucracy: A Study of Interpersonal Relations in Two Government Agencies* (Chicago University Press, 1966).

Bonini, C. P., *Simulation of Information and Decision Systems in the Firm* (Prentice-Hall, 1963).

Bower, J. L., *Managing the Resource Allocation Process* (Division of Research, Graduate School of Business Administration, Harvard University, 1970).

Braverman, H., *Labor and Monopoly Capital* (Monthly Review Press, 1974).

Briefs, U., The Role of Information Processing Systems in Employee Participation in Managerial Decision-Making, in Mumford, E. & Sackman, H., *Human Choice and Computers* (North-Holland, 1975).

Bruns, W. H. & Waterhouse, J. H., Budgetary Control and Organization Structure, *Journal of Accounting Research* (Autumn 1975), pp. 177—203.

Chandler, A. D., *Strategy and Structure* (MIT Press, 1962).

Chandler, A. D., *The Visible Hand: The Managerial Revolution in American Business* (Harvard University Press, 1977).

Chandler, M. R. & Sayles, L. R., *Managing Large Systems* (Harper & Row, 1971).

Connolly, T., Information Processing and Decision Making in Organizations, in Staw, B. M. and Salancik, G. R., eds., *New Directions in Organizational Behaviour* (St. Clair Press, 1977).

Crecine, J. P., Defense Budgeting: Organizational Adaptation to Environmental Constraints, in Byrne, R. F. et al., *Studied in Budgeting* (North-Holland, 1971), pp. 210—261.

Dalton, M., *Men who Manage* (Wiley, 1959).

Earl, M. J., Prototype Systems for Accounting Information and Control, *Accounting, Organizations and Society*, Vol. 3, No. 2 (1978).

Galbraith, J., *Designing Complex Organizations* (Addison-Wesley, 1973).

Gardner, S. P., *Evolution of Cost Accounting to 1925* (University of Alabama Press, 1954).

Hales, M., Management Science and the "Second Industrial Revolution", *Radical Science Journal* (January, 1974), pp. 5—28.

Hage, J., Toward a Synthesis of the Dialectic Between Historical-Specific and Sociological-General Models of the Environment, in Karpik, L., ed., *Organization and Environment: Theory, Issues and Reality* (Sage, 1978).

Hayes, D. C., The Contingency Theory of Managerial Accounting, *The Accounting Review* (January, 1977), pp. 22—39.

Heydebrand, W., Organizational Contradictions in Public Bureaucracies, in Benson, J. K., ed., *Organizational Analysis: Critique and Innovation* (Sage, 1977).

Hofstede, G. H., *The Game of Budget Control* (Van Gorcum, 1967).

Hopwood, A. G., *An Accounting System and Managerial Behaviour* (Saxon House, 1973).

Hopwood, A. G., *Towards Assessing the Economic Costs and Benefits of New Forms of Work Organization* (ILO, forthcoming).

Jensen, M., Reflections on the State of Accounting Research and the Regulation of Accounting, Paper presented at the Stanford University Lectures in Accounting, May 1976.

Jönsson, S. A. & Lundin, R. A., Myths and Wishful Thinking as Management Tools, in Nystrom, P. C. & Starbuck, W. H., *Prescriptive Models of Organizations* (North-Holland, 1977).

Karpik, L., *Organization and Environment: Theory, Issues and Reality* (Sage, 1978).

Kassem, M. S., European versus American Organization Theories, in Hofstede, G. H. & Kassem, M. S., *European Contributions to Organization Theory* (Van Gorcum, 1976).

Khandwalla, P. N., The Effects of Different Types of Competition on the Use of Management Controls, *Journal of Accounting Research* (Autumn, 1972). pp. 275—285.

Knight, K., ed., *Matrix Management* (Gower Press, 1977).

Kuhn, T. S., *The Structure of Scientific Revolutions* (2nd edition; University of Chicago Press, 1970).

Lammers, C. J., Towards the Internationalization of the Organization Sciences, in Hofstede, G. H. & Kassem, M. S., *European Contributions to Organization Theory* (Van Gorcum, 1976).

Magnusson, A., Participation and the Company's Information and Decision Systems, Working Paper 6022, Economic Research Institute, Stockholm School of Economics, 1974.

March, J. G., and Olsen, J. P., *Ambiguity and Choice in Organizations* (Universitetforlaget, 1976).

Marglin, S. A., What Do Bosses Do? The Origins and Functions of Hierarchy in Capitalist Production, *Review of Radical Political Economics* (Summer, 1974), pp. 33—60.

Mintzberg, H., *The Nature of Managerial Work* (Harper & Row, 1973).

Mintzberg, H., *Impediments to the Use of Management Information* (N.A.A., 1975).

Mirvis, P. H. & Macy, B. A., Accounting for the Cost and Benefits of Human Resource Development Programs, *Accounting, Organizations and Society*, Vol. 1, No. 2/3 (1976), pp. 179—194.

Mumford, E. & Sackman, H., *Human Choice and Computers* (North-Holland, 1975).

Nygaard, K. & Bergo, O. T., The Trade Unions—New Users of Research, *Personnel Review* (1975), pp. 5—10.

Otley, D. T., Budget Use and Managerial Performance, *Journal of Accounting Research* (forthcoming, 1978).

Parker, R. H., *Management Accounting: An Historical Perspective* (Macmillan, 1969).

Pennings, J. M. & Tripathi, R. C., The Organization-Environment Relationship: Dimensional Versus Typological Viewpoints, in Karpik, L., *Organization and Environment: Theory, Issues and Reality* (Sage 1978).

Pettigrew, A. M., Information as a Power Resource, *Sociology* (1972), pp. 187—204.

Pettigrew, A. M., *The Politics of Organizational Decision Making* (Tavistock, 1973).

Pettigrew, A. M., The Creation of Organizational Cultures, Working Paper, European Institute for Advanced Studies in Management, Brussels, 1977.

Pfeffer, J., Power and Resource Allocation in Organizations, in Staw, B. M. & Salancik, G. R., *New Directions in Organizational Behaviour* (St. Clair Press, 1977).

Pfeffer, J. & Salancik, G. R., Organizational Decision Making as a Political Process: The Case of a University Budget, *Administrative Science Quarterly* (1976), pp. 227—245.

Pollard, S., *The Genesis of Modern Management* (Edward Arnold, 1965).

Pondy, L. R., Toward a Theory of Internal Resource-Allocation, in Zald, M., ed., *Power in Organization* (Vanderbilt University Press, 1970).

Rosenthal, R. A. & Weiss, R. S., Problems of Organizational Feedback Processes, in Bauer, R. A., *Social Indicators* (MIT Press, 1966).

Roy, D., Making-Out: A Counter-System of Workers' Control of Work Situation and Relationships, in Burns, T., ed., *Industrial Man* (Penguin, 1969).

Sandberg, A., *The Limits to Democratic Planning* (LiberForlag, 1976).

Simon, H. A., *The Sciences of the Artificial* (MIT Press, 1969).

Simon, H. A., Guetzkow, H., Kozmetsky, G. & Tyndall, G., *Centralization Versus Decentralization in Organizing the Controller's Department* (Controllership Foundation, 1954).

Staw, B. M., and Ross, J., Commitment to a Policy Decision: A Multi-Theoretical Perspective, *Administrative Science Quarterly* (March, 1978), pp. 40—64.

Stymme, B., To Organize For Participation, Working Paper, Stockholm School of Economics, 1977.

Swieringa, R., and Moncur, R. H., *Some Effects of Participative Budgeting on Managerial Behaviour* (NAA, 1975).

Taylor, C., Interpretation and the Science of Man, *Review of Metaphysics* (1971), pp. 1—45.

Watson, D. J. H., The Structure of Project Teams Facing a Differentiated Environment: An Exploratory Study in Public Accounting Firms, *The Accounting Review* (April, 1975), pp. 259—273.

Watson, D. J. H. & Baumler, J. U., Transfer Pricing: A Behavioural Context, *The Accounting Review* (July 1975), pp. 466—474.

Weick, K. E., *The Social Psychology of Organizing* (Addison-Wesley, 1969).

Weick, K. E., Educational Organizations as Loosely Coupled Systems, *Administrative Science Quarterly* (March, 1976), pp. 1—19.

Weick, K. E., Enactment Processes in Organizations, in Staw, B. M. & Salancik, G. R., *New Directions in Organizational Behaviour* (St. Clair Press, 1977).

Whitley, R. D., Management Research: The Study and Improvement of Forms of Cooperation in Changing Socio-Economic Structures, in Roberts, N., ed., *Information Sources in the Social Sciences* (Butterworth, 1974).

Whyte, W. F., *Money and Motivation* (Harper & Row, 1955).

Wildavsky, A., *The Politics of the Budgetary Process* (Little, Brown, 1964).

Wilson, H. T., *The American Ideology: Science, Technology and Organization as Modes of Rationality in Advanced Industrial Societies* (Routledge & Kegan Paul, 1977).

Zald, M., ed., *Power in Organizations* (Vanderbilt University Press, 1970).

On Trying to Study Accounting in the Contexts in Which It Operates*

ANTHONY G. HOPWOOD

(*London Graduate School of Business Studies*)

Accounting has come to be seen as playing a key role in organizational functioning. Concerned, as it now is, with such activities as assessing the costs and benefits of organizational actions, the setting of financial standards and norms, the representation and reporting of organizational performance, and financial planning and control, accounting has been used to cast important aspects of the functioning of the modern organization into economic terms. By offering particular economic representations of organizational activities and outcomes to both internal participants and interested external parties, it has come to be involved in the creation of a quite specific organizational order and mission. Accounting is now associated with particular ways of seeing and trying to shape organizational processes and actions, with the maintenance of certain forms of organizational segmentation, hierarchy and control, and with the furtherance of an economic rationale for action (Batstone, 1979). Indeed in many cases the forms taken by decision processes, the structuring of organizational activities and even the specification of an organizational boundary are not independent of the accounting representation of them. Modes of accounting have become not only important and valued management practices but also ones whose existence and consequences are difficult to disentangle from the functioning of organizations as we know them. Accounting, in other words, has become centrally implicated in the modern form of organizing.

With accounting so intertwined with organizational functioning it is surprising that so little is known of the organizational nature of accounting practice. That, however, is the case. Although early studies of accounting in action focused on trying to understand its organizational roles and consequences, many more recent investigations have detached accounting from its organizational setting, preferring instead to study the consequences which it has at the individual rather than the organizational

---

* *Accounting, Organizations and Society*, Vol. 8, No. 2/3, pp. 287—305, 1983.

level. ① Admittedly such studies are providing us with many interesting and useful insights into both the interpretation of accounting information and ways of trying to facilitate its use in decision making situations. Be that as it may, they do not explicitly aim to help us to understand what is at stake in the organizational practice of accounting, even though it is the latter which provides so many of the rationales for the accounting craft. Studies at the individual level can neither illuminate the ways in which accounting intersects with other organizational practices, decision processes and power structures nor the factors which both give rise to the accounting phenomenon and induce it to change. ②

Together the papers collected here aim to provide some perspectives on accounting in an organizational context. As such, they aim to build upon earlier collections (see, for example, *Accounting, Organizations and Society*, Vol. 3, No. 1 (1976)) and contributions to show both the potential of an organizational perspective for the study of accounting practice and some of the range of approaches which might be included within it. However, before trying to summarise some of the key concerns of the papers and the more informal discussions which they stimulated, it is useful to attempt to delineate both some of the distinguishing features of an organizational level interest in accounting and the reasons for its significance.

SOME RATIONALES FOR AN ORGANIZATIONAL FOCUS

Individual level studies of accounting invariably take the accounting phenomenon for granted. Accounting, as such, is not the problematic issue. The primary

---

① Some of the reasons for this are discussed elsewhere (Hopwood, 1976, 1978). An interesting discussion of the general problem is given in Gowler & Legge (1981). Given the relative recency of research into the behavioural and organizational aspects of accounting, the latter's citation of Platt (1976, p. 42) is particularly interesting:

... there are strong institutional forces pulling people towards distinct disciplinary approaches; the pressure to disciplinary conformity is probably particularly strongly felt by younger people who do not yet have a securely established base or identity in a particular field. To the extent that this is so, the effects of different patterns of intellectual training and socialisation are reinforced by personal needs...

I think that a case could be made that such a situation has prevailed in the behavioural study of accounting, the assessment becoming even more appealing when the situation in management accounting is contrasted with that prevailing in the financial accounting area where legitimacy has been provided to institutional (i. e. market) rather than individual level studies.

② For interesting discussions of these and similar points see the papers by Connolly, March & Shapira, Cummings, Pondy and Weick in Ungson and Braunstein (1982).

concerns are with understanding and improving the interpretations which are made of it, with these insights frequently being seen as providing a basis for fine tuning rather than more fundamentally reforming the practice and technology of accounting. Moreover in the vast majority of such studies this emphasis enables accounting to be detached from both its organizational setting and other organizational practices. Accounting is seen to be a relatively independent art, having its roles and consequences primarily moderated by the cognitive properties of its immediate users rather than the setting in which it is placed. Indeed on many occasions the exclusive focus on the cognitive mediation of accounting justifies transferring the settings in which this can be studied to the college classroom and the psychological laboratory.

A more organizational approach would not deny the significance of such cognitive mediation. Indeed, the ways in which accounting influences individual action are a central part of its concern. However, rather than detaching accounting from its organizational setting, organizational researchers aim to understand the meanings which are given to accounting in particular settings, emphasising not the interpretation of an accounting given but the more active ways in which a particular account can shape, mould and even play a role in constructing the setting of which it forms a part. Accounting, to the organizational theorist, cannot be isolated from the processes which give rise either to its presence or to its present significance, be those within or without the particular setting or even organization in which it plays a role.

For the cognitive theorist accounting is primarily an independent variable, although, on the basis of the understandings which are gained from observing the responses to it, he or she also might seek to change, indeed to improve, the accounting representation of what is seen as being an independent organizational reality. The organizational theorist, on the other hand, can see accounting as both a dependent and an independent phenomenon. Some organizational scholars of accounting seek to emphasise the contingent nature of the accounting craft, aiming to provide an understanding of how particular accountings emerge from organizational and social settings. Such theorists do not necessarily remain content with offering an explanation of a particular accounting manifestation, however. Together with those other scholars of the organizational who place primary emphasis on the ways in which accounting both influences and is constrained by the meanings given to the organizational setting in which it operates, they seek to explore the social processes through which accounts of organizational action influence both the meanings and actions which constitute organizational life.

Such distinctions, however, provide only a relatively superficial view of an organizational level interest in accounting. Given the significance of the contrast, not least in the context of the present studies, it is worthwhile to explore in some more detail the ways in which an organizational perspective might view the accounting phenomenon, appealing both to the studies which are collected here and others which are now available.

Accounting repeatedly becomes what it was not

Accounting is neither a static nor a homogeneous phenomenon. Over time, all forms of accounting have changed, repeatedly becoming what they were not. Accounting, moreover, is not a homogeneous craft. Both management and financial accounts are characterised by an amazing diversity, both within a national culture and even more so across different national contexts (Horovitz, 1980). All too apparently accounting is a phenomenon which is what it isn't and can become what it wasn't!

Unfortunately we have a very limited understanding of the forces that either influence accounting change or help to shape the different forms that the accounting craft can take. Although a great deal of work has been done on the history of accounting, many of the studies that are available have adopted a rather technical perspective, seeking not only to emphasise the developments that have occurred rather than also probing into the rationales for them (Hopwood et al., 1980) but also, even when raising questions about the underlying forces at work, all too readily presuming a functionalist and even progressive interest. Indeed, until recently, both historical and comparative analyses of the accounting phenomenon have adopted a most atheoretical stance, only rarely seeking to relate their insights to broader understandings of the development of the corporate form, its social and economic setting, and the roles which organizational accounts might have played in the emergence of both the organization as we know it now and the relationships which it has to other bodies and interests.

These questions are now starting to be addressed by accounting and other scholars however, as the papers and comments by Johnson (1983), D. Flamholtz (1983), Meyer (1983) and Tiessen & Waterhouse (1983) illustrate.

On the historical side, studies of accounting development are beginning to utilise more theoretical analyses of the emergence of the corporate form and the particular roles which procedures for both internal control and the maintenance of external legitimacy have played. Interestingly, scholars from other social science disciplines also have started to be intrigued by the processes underlying the growing significance of the accounting craft and the roles which it may have served in the emergence of modern institutional forms. Consideration has been given to the roles played by economic record keeping in the construction of forms of organizational visibility which can further particular organizational interests, to the ways in which accounting and other forms of management practices became implicated in the resolution of the conflicts which characterised the emergence of today's organizational forms, and to the contribution which accounting has made to the articulation and propagation of a legitimate myth of disinterested administrative rationality and order.

From an organizational perspective, studies of accounting diversity have drawn on the precarious but nevertheless useful understandings available from contingency theory (Otley, 1980). Consideration has been given to the implications which organizational environments, technologies and tasks and management structures have had for the development of accounting practice. Illuminating though such perspectives have been, however, there is now an increasing recognition of the need to move beyond the restrictive static and often functionalist presumptions which have characterised past forms of contingent analysis. More direct interest is now being expressed in trying to understand the nature of the organizational processes through which accounting becomes what it was not. Albeit slowly, there are signs that consideration is being given to appreciating the ways in which both other management practices and external phenomenon intersect with accounting practices to create pressures for change and the difficulties raised by attempts to understand the implications for accounting of the multiple contingencies which characterise organizational life. Attention is also slowly being given to how accounting can be changed in the context of organizational and social conflicts and debates in order to create different but still persuasive images of organizational aims and achievements. Not least in significance, there are signs that the roles which accounting plays in shaping its own development also are being recognised, be these seen in terms of the implications stemming from the professionalisation of the body of knowledge that has emerged around the practice of the craft or of the ways in which accounting actively shapes the perception of and salience attached to some of the very phenomena which are supposed to put pressures on it to change.

Interestingly, questions related to the emergence of organizational forms and the controls which go with them now attract the attention of the economist as well. Rather than being content to view the organization as an unproblematic "black box", economists have started to explore some of the rationales that may be implicit in prevailing organizational forms, appealing to both the comparative advantages of markets, hierarchies and other organizational forms, and the ways in which modes of organization can moderate and further patterns of economic interest and accountability. As Johnson (1983), Tiessen & Waterhouse (1983) and others (Baiman, 1982; Spicer & Bellew, 1983) illustrate, both of these perspectives emphasise the important roles that procedures for monitoring and control can play, helping, thereby, to cast some light on some of the origins of the accounting function. As of yet, however, most of this work has emphasised the role of technical and economic interests. In contrast to historical and organizational inquiries, economists, to date, have given little or no attention to either the ways in which the economic intersects with the social and the political or the more particular questions involved in how accounting itself may have come to be involved in the very specification of those economic interests in the name of which it is changed.

At present all such explorations of the rationales that might be implicit in the accounting craft remain at an early stage of development. The perspectives of the historical, the organizational and the economic remain largely independent, each tending to offer relatively self-contained explanations of the emergence of organizational accountings and the pressures for them to change, and few studies have been made of the emergence and development of particular modes of accounting practice. Nevertheless such attempts to understand the processes of accounting change are of significance, not least because of their potential to provide us with a very different perspective, or more likely, series of perspectives, for understanding what might be at stake in the accounting endeavour.

Conventional understandings of accounting view it from a relatively unproblematic technical perspective. It is presumed that accountings are there to facilitate organizational and social action (see Burchell et al., 1980 for a further discussion of this point). Only rarely, if ever, is the nature of that facilitation and the ends that might be so served examined. Although notions of cost, profit and other indices of financial performance may not be seen as being unproblematic, the difficulties which they give rise to stem, according to such a conventional view, from the problems of operationalizing pre-given aspects of organizational and social reality and achievement. Accounting, so conceived, is essentially a revelatory endeavour, aiming merely to reflect rather than more actively to construct a view of organizational reality and ends. Seeking, albeit often with difficulty, to explicate and make visible an unproblematic view of the means for organizational achievement, accounting is seen as a phenomenon divorced from the social, as distinct from technical, struggles and innovations that have resulted in its emergence.

All too clearly alternative views of the accounting endeavour will not be appealing to those who have invested in articulating and propagating such a conventional perspective. However for those who are willing to consider them, they offer at least the potential of a way of understanding accounting and its problems that is consonant with the historical conditions which have resulted in its emergence and development and those current organizational forces which contribute to its significance.

Accounting and organizational action

Accounting gains much of its contemporary significance from the ways in which it helps to shape and guide organizational processes and actions. However although accounting texts, pronouncements and recommendations repeatedly emphasise the ways in which it contributes to organizational efficiency, the improvement of managerial and employee motivation and performance, and the more effective allocation of resources, little is known of if and how such ends are achieved. Compared with the extent of the technical ediface of accounting, very little is known of the organizational processes which this seeks to activate and through which the technical achieves its potential.

What roles does accounting play in the construction of organizational participants' views of the desirable and the possible? Does accounting get implicated in the creation of particular conceptions of organizational time? And if so, with what effects? How and when do accountings of organizational performance provide an incentive for action? How does accounting contribute to the articulation of an organizational mission and through what means do the particular and very partial patterns of organizational visibility that accounting creates facilitate the achievement of control within the organization, be that seen in either social or technical terms? How does the routinized provision of information which accounting emphasises relate to the multitude of informal decision arenas which characterise organizational life? Just how, in other words, does accounting achieve and maintain a position of organizational significance?

Such questioning could be extended. For although a great deal of effort has been invested in extending and refining the technical basis of accounting in the name of its organizational roles and consequences, very little is known about the ways in which the potential which is claimed on behalf of accounting is realised. For some, at least, that is a paradoxical situation for a craft that has continually sought to emphasise the pragmatic organizational implications of its technical endeavours.

An organizational view of accounting has enormous potential to illuminate some of the more problematic aspects of the accounting craft. For instance, it could help us to understand the roles which accounting plays in the creation of particular patterns of organizational segmentation and the consequences which this has, not least in those circumstances where the requirements of the task point to the provision of lateral flows of information which are at variance with the vertical ones which accounting more usually emphasises. Equally, greater insights into the ways in which accounts of organizational performance provide particular mappings of both the organizational environment and its internal processes and outcomes could help those concerned with the design of more effective information provision in times of change and discontinuity. Many also would find it helpful to understand the roles which different, and often conflicting, assessments of organizational performance, both past and prospective, play in the determination of decisions and the allocation of scarce resources. Just how does accounting's emphasis on the economic relate to the interests and practices of those who seek to extend the visibility of the technical, the human and the wider environmental characterisation of organizational performance? And how does accounting's commitment to the detached, analytical consideration of the new relate to the need to generate the commitment which may play a determining role in the realisation of the actual? Together insights of this nature could provide at least a basis for trying to ground the technical apparatus of the accounting craft in the specifics of organizational action, thereby hopefully trying to realise the pragmatic potential that is so frequently claimed on accounting's behalf. At present, however, such insights reside in the realm of experience, only rarely being set aside the abstract and highly generalised claims that grace the manuals of technical accounting practice.

Accounting and the achievement of the accounting mission

Conventional discussions of accounting invariably presume that the craft is capable of achieving the claims that are made on its behalf. Accounting, so we are told, is capable of enhancing organizational efficiency and performance (forgetting, of course, the role that it also plays in the definition of the very ends it is trying to further). It can play a positive role in increasing managerial and employee motivations to perform. And accounting can provide the type of information that can facilitate managerial decision making, not least in environments characterised by uncertainty and doubt.

Increasingly, however, some, at least, of such highly generalised claims are being compared with the more equivocal impressions emerging from both research and practice.

There is a long tradition of scholarly inquiry which has sought to illuminate the dysfunctional as well as functional consequences, both latent and manifest, of the accounting craft. More recently, there have been studies which at least have pointed to the ways in which accountings appear to proliferate amidst concerns with organizational crisis and decline rather than in the less problematic days of growth and success. Sometimes such research even has pointed to the ways in which the consequent desire for greater control can result in organizational procedures which detract from rather than enhance the flexibility of managerial response in such conditions.

Such concerns with the actual rather than the claimed achievements of accounting now have started to be articulated by some of the practitioners of the accounting craft. Faced with economic restraint and often with increased competitive pressures, such practitioners have started to become concerned about the limitations of the routinized flows of information which accounting so often provides.

Sometimes seeing how accountings of the present reflect crises of the past, such practitioners have come to appreciate the need for new understandings of how accounting systems emerge in practice rather than in theory and the potential, or otherwise, which they offer for managerial decision making. Although such worries, let alone their causes, have yet to be systematically documented, it is not unusual for such people to express their concerns over the rigidities which routinized controls endow to organizational processes and the contracted time horizons which conventional accountings can often instil. Many also are worried about the problems which result from accounting's almost exclusive emphasis on the economic and the financial, and it is not unusual to hear even quite conventional practitioners articulate their concern for the inefficiencies which might have been legitimised by repeated annual cycles of budgetary review and authorisation. At a more general level, there are now some organizations that are starting to express concern over the full range of implications that might have stemmed from the ways in which accounting and other control practices have resulted in an abstract process of control removed and often distanced from the practice of the task that is being controlled.

All too clearly such concerns are not the worry of the average practitioner. Whilst often concentrated in large organizations, an era of very real economic restraint nevertheless has resulted in at least some accounting practitioners and their managerial colleagues probing into what their investment in accounting has and has not achieved. Although rarely, if ever, expressed in ways other than the immediate set of implications for their own organizations, such questionings have resulted in a new awareness of the interdependency between the technology of the accounting craft and the human and social processes through which the objectives which are set for it are achieved. Moreover that awareness is often expressed in much more subtle terms than those used by the academic practitioners of accounting who have come to see behavioural and organizational studies as providing only a base for their more esoteric colleagues who only deem it worthwhile to worry about the icing on top of the accounting cake.

Unfortunately research on the organizational aspects of accounting is presently not in a position to fully address such practitioner worries. What studies are available have tended to focus on particular aspects of the accounting domain, often seeking to further the missions of accounting as conventionally defined rather than provide a more questioning account of accounting's consequences. Only rarely has research on the behavioural and organizational aspects of accounting concerned itself with investigating those wider linkages between accounting and other organizational processes and practices that provide the basis for some, at least, of the concerns currently emanating from practice.

Be that as it may, an organizational perspective can provide a basis for appreciating the practitioners' worries. It can contrast, for instance, the conventional organizational rationales for accounting which are detached from other organizational processes and concerns with a much more interactive view of organizational life (Ashton, 1976). From the latter perspective, the consequences of interventions in the name of one practice can be seen to be dependent on factors other than the intentions and means of organizational action which are consciously articulated and mobilised. It can be seen that actual outcomes also depend on the practical capacity of accounting procedures to encapsulate, penetrate and then influence the complex fabric of modern organizations, on the ways in which they intersect with both other organizational practices and the wider aims and actions of organizational participants, and, in the latter respect, on the resistances which specific attempts to mobilise one set of organizational practices induce. When seen in such terms there is at least the potential for the aims of any particular intervention in organizational life, be it of an accounting or any other nature, to remain partly or even totally unfulfilled (indeed even resulting in consequences which were wholly unanticipated) since the eventual outcomes are influenced by phenomena which did not enter into its original justification (Merton, 1936; Boudon, 1982). In the words of Hindess (1982, p.498):

> Outcomes ... may or may not conform to the intentions or objectives of any of the agents concerned. They are produced in the course of practices which take place under definite conditions and which confront definite obstacles, including the practices of others. ①

Perhaps when seen in such a light it is not surprising that some consideration is

---

① Hindess (1982) goes on to argue that "the securing of outcomes should always be seen as problematic, that it is subject to definite and specifiable conditions in at least two respects. First, the means of action of agents are dependent on conditions that are not in their hands. Secondly, the deployment of these means of action invariably confronts obstacles, which often include the opposing practices of others. Success in overcoming those obstacles cannot in general be guaranteed" (p.501). He concludes his argument by suggesting the need to take "seriously the particular conditions in which these practices and struggles take place and in which their outcomes are produced" (p.509).

now starting to be given to the circumstances under which accounting does and does not realise the aims that are articulated on behalf of it. The organizationally detached discourses that permeate accounting texts and manuals are being compared with the ways in which accounting has to relate to the practices and underlying bodies of knowledge of other approaches to organizational control. Accounting is being related to questions of organizational design and consideration is being given to how it functions alongside the interrelated practices of production, personnel and even financial management. Finally the resistances to accounting also are now being investigated, be they seen in terms of the behavioural processes which determine the actual use of the accounting craft or the social struggles within the organization in which accounting becomes intertwined. Be that as it may, it must be recognised that an organizational view of accounting in action is still emergent. There remains a very real need for further reflection and inquiry if we are to understand those processes through which accounting achieves the consequences which it both seeks to have and does in fact have.

AN ORGANIZATIONAL AGENDA

No doubt numerous other rationales could have been provided for an interest in the organizational nature of accounting practice. More emphasis could have been placed on the ways in which accounting becomes implicated in the construction of prevailing conceptions of organizational power and the furtherance of particular organizational interests. Greater consideration could have been given to the nature of the organizational order which accounting attempts to maintain and the roles which it plays in creating a particular pattern of economic and financial visibility within the enterprise. Equally, more stress could have been placed on the need for organizationally orientated accounting research to facilitate the decision roles of information within the organization, with consideration even being given to the need to construct new organizational accounts which can positively illuminate different aspects of organizational functioning. In part, at least, such additional factors have been alluded to. More importantly, the discussion of the organizational nature of accounting has sought only to provide a basis for a different view of the accounting craft. Even though it may be partial, it nevertheless has hope fully outlined an area that is of some significance to all interested in the accounting endeavour and an area that is in urgent need of further study and inquiry. Indeed the conference itself was designed to help pursue this latter aim.

The papers presented at the conference focused on a number of different issues, drawing, in the process, on a range of very different organizational perspectives. Rather than striving to attempt to present *an* organizational view, a conscious aim of the conference was to provide an opportunity for the presentation and discussion of a number of different ways of analysing and trying to understand the organizational world in which accounting is embedded.

Together Johnson (1983), D. Flamholtz (1983), as discussant and Tiessen & Waterhouse (1983) provided a number of different perspectives on the processes by which accounting has become what it now is. Attempting to relate both social and economic views of the organization, they provided some bases for appreciating how accounting has become implicated in the construction of the modern business organization and how, in so doing, accounting has provided one means by which the organization can be related to wider economic and social interests, including, in the context of D. Flamholtz's remarks, those of the State. However, although the aims might be related, the approaches adopted by Johnson and Tiessen & Waterhouse are very different. Johnson presents a historical view of the ways in which accounting contributed to the emergence of the modern business enterprise. In part, at least, such a historical perspective provides us with an opportunity for seeing how accounting is both influenced by and in turn shapes the organizational form adopted by the enterprise. Tiessen & Waterhouse, in contrast, attempt to build upon a contingent view of management accounting by seeking to understand how accounting is used to construct a calculative interface between organizational management and those outside the enterprise who seek to pursue an interest in it. By appealing to economic conceptions of organizational rationality, they show how accounting plays a role by making visible a particular view of economic order. Johnson, on the other hand, at least points to the possibility that the resultant order is as much constructed as it is revealed by accounting means. From such a perspective it is possible to see the internally controlled domain of opportunities that is the firm as being a product of both the historical struggles out of which such domains emerged and the present as well as past use of management practices, such as accounting, for their preservation and development.

The papers by Birnberg *et al.* (1983), E. Flamholtz (1983) (and his discussant Kerr, 1983), Boland & Pondy (1983), Markus & Pfeffer (1983) and Hayes (1983) focus on ways of trying to understand how accounting is implicated in the ongoing processes of organizational functioning. In some respects this group of papers is notable for its diversity rather than for its convergence on any single viewpoint or issue. Indeed Hayes explicitly aims to present a number of different ways of accounting for the organizational significance of the accounting phenomenon. However beneath the seeming diversity a number of themes emerge.

Albeit in very different ways, both E. Flamholtz and Markus & Pfeffer discuss accounting's relationship to the bases of organizational power. Indeed in both papers not only the fact of that relationship but also the legitimacy of the present mode of articulation is accepted. With Flamholtz, however, accounting's contribution to mobilizing the powerful and power based organization is accepted implicitly, this seemingly being an unproblematic part of the accounting task. The challenge is to forge sufficient organizational linkages for the power potential of accounting to be realised. Whilst appearing to accept the ways in which accounting (and other forms of information and control systems) further particular conceptions of organizational power, Markus & Pfeffer explicitly discuss, although do little to appraise, the plurality of the bases of power in organizations, the ways in which accountings relate to the exercise of power and the strategies which an explicit recognition of this suggests for the design and implementation of new accounting and information and control systems. So although the organization is seen as having some aspects of a "contested terraine" (Edwards, 1979), strategies seemingly are available to further the contribution which accounting can make to the exercise of a particular powerful interest. Both papers therefore recognise that the accounting endeavour cannot be seen in purely technical terms. Equally, both suggest how the organizational might be mobilized in the name of the technical.

The tension between the technical and the organizational bases of the accounting task is a theme which pervades other papers. Birnberg and his colleagues contrast the stated aims of accounting with some aspects of its organizational achievements. Hayes seeks to ground the artifacts of accounting in the context of the symbolic, linguistic and legitimising roles which they serve. A more direct discussion is provided by Boland & Pondy, however, in terms of the perspectives of the rational and the natural, the former being related to the technical view of an objective accounting that permeates conventional discussions of the subject whilst the latter focuses on the ways in which accountings arise out of processes of social interaction, both reflecting and creating the symbolic structures that give meaning and significance to organizational life. Although outlining two very different views of how accounting is implicated in organizational functioning, Boland & Pondy nevertheless seek to demonstrate the utility of both perspectives. They consciously aim to illustrate how the rational provides a framework for the natural and how the natural can serve as a basis for the emergence and elaboration of the rational. Indeed, by so doing, they focus quite explicitly on the very real tensions that can be created by the juxtaposition of the two; tensions which create the very basis for the development of the accounting craft and the attribution of meanings to it.

Reflecting on such discussions, both Meyer (1983) and Cooper (1983) point to some of the wider issues involved. Meyer focuses on the symbolic domain that is created by accounting fictions, a domain that is important for creating the type of legitimate and seemingly coherent entities that are demanded by the agencies of the modern world. Although acknowledging the ways in which the rational domain so constructed is sometimes only loosely related to the ongoing processes of organizational life, Meyer nevertheless emphasises how the abstract fictions that permeate the accounting craft can nevertheless have a very real impact on organizational decision making and action. Not only does the symbolic define the real, but the reality so created can be and often is changed in the name of the symbolic. With what might initially appear to be the loosely coupled thereby having a very real possibility of becoming quite tightly coupled, Meyer therefore not only asks for a greater understanding of the processes through which this takes place but also suggests the very real need for a greater appreciation of the broader social and ideological factors that are implicated in these processes. Cooper also emphasises this latter point. He too is aware that the technical and the rational can come to be seen as natural; that, in other words, a new view of a seemingly natural order can be created in the name of the technical. However to Cooper, and indeed increasingly to others, such new organizational orders are neither unproblematic nor fully understandable in terms of the technical. Like Meyer, Cooper emphasises how important it is for accounting research both to recognise the wider social nature of the technical and the organizational world that it can in part create. He asks us to analyse much more consciously and systematically than has been the case in the past the social, institutional and ideological factors that are implicated in the emergence of particular conceptions of the technical and the rational, and the implications which they have for organizational and social functioning.

Although such wider debates only had an indirect relationship to the final group of papers presented at the conference, the interests of both Mirvis & Lawler (1983) and Mitroff & Mason (1983) were in part at least mobilised by their dissatisfaction with both the prevailing rationalities incorporated into the accounting craft and some of the organizational consequences of today's accounts. Mitroff & Mason emphasise the dilemmas facing the designers of information and accounting systems in an increasingly complex and uncertain world. Unhappy with the unitary logic which structures today's accounts of organizational action and performance, they argue for an approach to system design which more consciously attempts to map the contradictions, tensions and dilemmas which characterise organizational life. Like Mirvis & Lawler, however, they recognise the resistance which seemingly faces their new organizational order. For Mitroff & Mason such resistance resides in the realms of the cultural, the psychological and the social, all sources, apparently, of an irrational response to the different rationality which they seek to instil. Mirvis & Lawler, on the other hand, at least start to probe into the wider organizational forces which might be implicated in the resilience of the old organizational order which they initially sought to reform—the very same resilience which provided the basis for the wider questionings of both Meyer and Cooper.

By any stretch of the imagination the papers presented at the conference on "Accounting in Its Organizational Context" provided a rich insight into some of the issues that might be at stake in analysing the accounting phenomenon from an organizational perspective. Given this, in the above remarks I have not attempted to provide an overview of all that was said or even the most important things that were on the agenda. I merely have sought to emphasise some similarities, differences, trends and implications from a personal point of view. The task of conducting a detailed assessment remains in the hands of the reader.

SOME EMERGENT ISSUES

The value of almost any conference rests not only on the papers that are formally prepared and presented but also on the informal discussions which these stimulate. This conference was no exception. It therefore might be useful to conclude with a brief presentation of some of the issues, worries, concerns and possibilities that emerged during the course of the conference deliberations.

Accounting as a changing phenomenon

Repeatedly consideration was given to how accounting had become what it now is and to the strategies that might be used for changing it. Stimulated no doubt by the historical perspectives offered by both Johnson (1983) and D. Flamholtz (1983), and by the socio-economic approach of Tiessen & Waterhouse (1983), the conference discussions often tended to focus on the changing nature of both the accounting domain and the accounting craft—on both what was accounted for and the means through which that was achieved. There was an ever conscious awareness of the fact that accounting changes: it becomes what it was not. Equally, however, there was a recognition of the paucity of our understandings of the processes through which this takes place, the broader issues that might be at stake and the consequences of the changes that do occur. Not only was the latter seen in terms of our own inadequate basis for accounting as we now know it, but also, and more generally, the discussions often emphasised our present inability to confront what might be at stake, both in terms of its antecedents and its consequences, in the seemingly ever increasing pervasiveness of the accounting phenomenon.

Dissatisfaction was voiced over the ability of conventional analyses of accounting history to address such questions. Seemingly it was more concerned with documenting the changing accounting phenomenon and the technologies that are at its deployment than providing an insight into the underlying social, institutional, economic and political forces at work. Indeed it was recognised that a great deal of research into accounting history had adopted, consciously or otherwise, a very atheoretical stance, ignoring, in the process, the problems involved in trying to provide an adequate social understanding of the accounting craft. The roles of accounting had been seen in relatively unproblematic and often very contemporary terms. The juxtaposition of accounting innovations in the *nexi* of relationships between the organization, the markets for both labour and capital, and the State had not been emphasised. And accounting scholars of the historical had seemingly distanced themselves from the concerns of both social theorists of the corporation and the corporate state and more recent theoretical advances in historical inquiry.

Equally, dissatisfaction was expressed with organizational attempts to account for accounting change. Although it was recognised that contingency approaches had provided some insights into the nature of accounting diversity, the relatively static and functionalist presumptions of such perspectives also were discussed. Contingency theory had difficulty confronting the dynamics of organizational and accounting change. In adopting a narrowly organizational perspective, it restricted the range of factors which it could consider in its pursuit of the origins of both difference and change. And its concern with more unitary conceptions of organizational aims and achievement foreclosed too many possibilities for inquiring into how organizational accounts emerged from political processes endemic to the organization rather than from the dictates of a more rational economic order.

In criticising the efforts of the past, and it should be said, the present as well, conference participants were aware of the very real conceptual and empirical difficulties involved in trying to provide more adequate and illuminating insights into the processes of accounting change. Indeed it was quite explicitly recognised that the issues involved reside at the frontiers of scholarly inquiries in the social sciences generally. Even so, although aware that research into accounting was not necessarily backward or too far behind that in other social science disciplines, it nevertheless was thought that much could be gained if accounting scholars were prepared to recognise more explicitly the organizational and social issues at stake and the range of theoretical perspectives that are at least available. It was thought that at the very least such a reorientation in perspective might encourage them to undertake a more sustained series of analyses of the emergence and development of accounting systems and practices. These, in turn, might provide a richer empirical basis for reflecting on those factors that might be implicated in accounting change and the processes through which this takes place.

Accounting as a heterogeneous phenomenon

Similar discussions also focused on the diverse nature of the accounting craft, particularly in respect of the practices of management accounting. Not only was there an awareness of the enormous range of technical practices in use (summarised by one participant in the terms of "you name it; somebody is using it!") but also consideration was given to the diversity of those organizational linkages which ground accounting and other information and control systems into the ongoing processes of organizational life, Accounting and control departments are variously organized. Planning, budgeting and performance monitoring procedures operate at different organizational levels, are subject to different degrees of participation, have different expectations and practices for their revision, and even can consider very different time periods. Accounting systems also serve to establish very different patterns of organizational segmentation and relate to the practices for the management of organizational interdependence in a variety of ways. From these and many other viewpoints the accounting domain was seen to exhibit a diversity that seemingly was at odds with the myth of a more generalised phenomenon that permeates accounting texts and those manuals that seek to guide accounting change and reform.

Yet again consideration was given to the inadequate state of our understanding of not only the factors underlying such diversity but also the implications that this might, and perhaps should, have for both the evaluation and change of accounting practice.

Perhaps in this context more sympathy was expressed with at least the aims of contingency approaches. In discussions of the heterogeneous accounting domain at least the contingent nature of the practices was recognised. The roles played by differing technologies, environments, management structures, corporate cultures and other factors were all alluded to. However it was recognised that not only had research from this perspective not progressed as far as it might but also that not sufficient consideration had been given to some of those difficulties of contingent approaches which already have been discussed. The problems raised by multiple contingencies were seen to be important; concern was expressed about the rather deterministic nature of present contingency theories; attention was focused on the need to understand the interplay between management choices and whatever constraints might be deemed to be imposed by the organizational context; and some, at least, wanted research to address more directly the interactive nature of the accounting craft by recognising not only how accounting might be shaped by its context but also how at least some aspects of that very same context might in turn be shaped by accounting itself.

More generally it was recognised that research which could provide insights into both accounting diversity and change had a very real potential to illuminate many key problems of accounting in practice. For the issues which such questions raise about the relationship of accounting to the context in which it operates are ones that are high on the problem agendas of accounting practitioners and consultants. By trying to disentangle the processes by which particular accountings arise, function and change, such research offers the potential to relate knowledge to the specifics of the accounting condition with which such practitioners have to deal.

Competing accounts of the organizational terrain

Albeit less explicitly, consideration nevertheless was given to the diverse accounts which seek to characterise organizational life and its outcomes. At the individual level, all organizational participants construct their own maps of the organizational terrain, delineating the significant, the problematic and the possible, accounting in their own terms for significant organizational boundaries, what they see to be the centres of power and influence, and those rationales which they think do and ought to influence choices and actions. Even in the sphere of rationalised systems of information and management, a multitude of accounts pervade organizational life. Physical and technical mappings are provided by engineers and production management; their systems also seek to shape and influence the physical reality of the organization in terms of volumes, flows, qualities, stocks and tolerances for performance. The personnel, marketing, financial and distribution functions (and others) also all impose their own accounts on the organization. Like the accountant, these practitioners also have invested in complex procedures for delineating the organizational world which they seek to manage and change, for recording those attributes which they have assigned to it and for influencing the cognitions and social behaviours of other organizational participants. Therefore the accountant's *Account* is merely one of many that attempt to make visible and salient particular aspects of organizational life and the constraints that are deemed to apply to it. Rather than existing in isolation, *Accounting* was seen as being in a state of tension with the multitude of other organizational accounts, seeking to impose a particular perspective, order and mission on a domain that is characterised not by the absence of maps for its exploration and explitation but rather by the sheer richness of the competing surveys of its problematic terrain.

When the accounting phenomenon was seen in such terms it invariably raised questions about the means through which a particular account had become enshrined as *Accounting* practice. Questions also were asked about the interplay of the diverse accountings, those factors that might have influenced their relative power, their differential consequences and the relationship which the mobilisation of particular accounts had to the patterns of organizational choice and action over time.

To date accounting research has adopted all too parochial a perspective. A very special significance has been attached to the economic and financial mappings provided by the professionalised practitioners of the accounting craft. As a result, a particular account has been accepted as *the Accozuzt*. Whilst there are good reasons for some specialisation of interest (not least in a world characterised by increasing system diversity, complexity and technical sophistication), the unproblematic acceptance of the priority accorded to such a partial ordering of organizational life undoubtedly has not only restricted the nature of the inquiries undertaken into the organizational nature of accounting practice and the problems which it faces but also, and perhaps more fundamentally, prevented people from exploring the organizational and the wider social factors which have resulted in one account being attributed with so much significance and power—in the world of action as well as in that of scholarly inquiry. It was thought that at least some investigations of the latter set of issues might help to illuminate some key aspects of the accounting condition, those organizational roles which accounting is expected to serve and the tensions which its implementation and use so often engender.

The tension between organizational order and disorder

Such a perspective of competing organizational accounts helped to focus attention on the often precarious nature of the organizational order which accounting seeks to create. Only rarely, if ever, is accounting elaboration and change an unproblematic endeavour of charting an organization anew. More frequently, organizational participants already hold their own views of the significant and the desirable, and usually these have been shaped by the practices of other practitioners who have sought to change the organization in the name of their own particular missions and aims. Accounting, accordingly, enters into a disputed terrain. Its consequences have to be achieved by contesting the dominance of pre-existing conceptions of organizational order and purpose. Accounting therefore can be characterised not only in terms of the aims that are attributed to it but also in terms of the resistances which it engenders. Indeed it is just such resistances which already have stimulated behavioural inquiries and the concerns and worries of those practitioners of the accounting craft who have reflected on the consequences which it has not achieved as well as those which it has achieved but which did not enter into its original justification.

The organizational world in which accounting operates therefore can be seen in terms of the order which accounting seeks to implement and the disorder which its implementation both confronts and, in part, engenders. Moreover both dimensions of such a perspective can be elaborated in terms of what might over simplistically be called the vertical and the horizontal axes of organizational action. Operating vertically, accounting seeks to reinforce a particular conception of organizational power. It aims to create a partial but influential pattern of visibility which can facilitate the operation of the organizational hierarchy by creating a form of organizational segmentation, by channelling down through that an objective for action and subsequently by monitoring actual performance. Seen in such terms, accounting is a tool in the hands of the powerful. Viewed horizontally, accounting also can be seen as being implicated in the propogation of a financial and economic rationale for action, seeking either to contest those alternative conceptions of organizational mission that can be advanced in the name of the technical, the market, the social and whatever or to serve as a means for converting (and invariably modifying in the process) such aims into the language of the economic. On both axes of organizational life accounting can be seen as trying to create a particular conception of organizational order. Equally, however, on both axes that conception of order is invariably contested and challenged, albeit with differing degrees of effectiveness.

In emphasising only the order which accounting seeks to advance rather than the contexts in which it operates there is an ever present danger that accounting scholars of the behavioural merely seek to expose the defects in the present apparatus of accounting and move towards its reform without appreciating the diverse and contested nature of the organizational regime in which accounting operates.

Perhaps somewhat paradoxically, attention also was focused on those circumstances in which accounting had succeeded in imposing its own particular order. Rather than greeting this achievement with acclamation, however, at least some conference participants were concerned with the organizational consequences which might result, with the latter seen in terms of both more general notions of organizational effectiveness and the particular regimes of power that accounting serves to reinforce.

Concerns were expressed about the potential problems which might stem from trying to guide and manage a complex and diverse organization on the basis of a single perspective. In part such worries reflected an awareness of the dangers of the bureaucratic rigidity which could result from a singular emphasis on the routinised procedures for inducing a particular organizational visibility which are so often associated with the accounting craft. In addition, however, the discussions of the organizational context in which accounting operates had resulted in a recognition of the need for a diversity of accounts to map into the organization the very different but equally salient aspects of both its external and internal environments. Even an approximation towards a singular informational order was seen as too narrowly restricting the messages, the options and, thereby, the actions that were available to organizational members. Thought therefore was given to the need for a more organizationally grounded view of accounting that would be compatible with a role as a complementary rather than over-reaching information and control system—a view that would be content with the disorders as well as with the ordering of organizational life.

Of course the concerns with the power potential of accounting also questioned such notions of a unitary organizational order. Accounting, when seen from such a perspective, was centrally implicated in the construction of particular notions of organizational ends and achievements. Rather than merely reflecting in a neutral manner the constraints and imperatives that impinge on organizations as we now know them, accounting was seen as being involved in the specification and articulation of a specific organizational mission. As such, it could not be seen as a disinterested endeavour. Accounting was at least related to the propagation of a particular set of interests, even though that relationship may be moderated by some aspects of the autonomous nature of the craft, the complex of institutional structures in which its practice is embedded and the diverse agents which call upon its practices and procedures. According to this view a questioning of accounting would necessitate an examination of the interests in the name of which it is mobilised, its effectiveness to serve these ends and the strategies that might be available if other interests wished either to challenge or themselves to utilise the accounting craft.

Conceptions of order and disorder therefore were seen to be far from unproblematic terms, appealing both to views of organizational achievement and those political regimes which might underlie accounting practice. Different though they may be, however, it was recognised that both viewpoints had had little impact on accounting inquiry.

The reflective and constitutive role of accounting

To date organizational research in accounting has emphasised the ways in which accounting systems reflect other aspects of the environments in which they are embedded. As has been indicated already, consideration has been given to the impact which technologies and markets have on accounting, to the relationship between organizational structure and the design and use of accounting systems, and some initial interest has been expressed in examining the broader cultural influences on the form taken by accounting and other types of control systems. In such ways accounting has been shown to be a contingent phenomenon, designed and used in the context of other important features of the organizational environment.

Although concern has been expressed about the adequacy of our present conceptual and empirical skills for handling such contingent relationships, the general notion of an interdependent accounting has not been contested. At the conference it was seen to be a partial view however. For although accounting plays a role in mapping into the organization other salient aspects of the managerial, task and external environments, it also has the power to shape and influence organizational life on its own accord.

The environments that are mapped into the organization can become defined in accounting terms. They can become "profitable" or "costly", "cash cows" or "rising stars". Similarly the organization structures which impinge on accounting practice invariably do not have a manifestation that is completely independent of their accounting reflection. Modes of organizational decentralization are defined in terms of cost, profit and investment centres; organizational units have accounting as well as managerial boundaries; and accounting mechanisms for the monitoring of subunit performance help to make real the powerful potential that is reflected within the organization chart. Equally, accounting plays a role not only in shaping the visible map of what is known of organizational functioning but also in expressing and thereby influencing the objectives that are stated for organized action. An operational definition of profit has been a particularly powerful notion. However consideration must also be given to the mobilising potential of concepts such as cash, working capital, assets and, not least, cost. All provide illustrations of where accounting has made operational, and therefore powerful, more abstract notions of economic discourse.

In ways such as these accounting has come to play a positive role in creating our present conceptions of organized endeavour. Whilst in part reflecting many other parameters of organizational life, accounting also has played a more active role in constructing the organizational world in which it is now embedded, shaping views of both the constraints on organized action and the ends which it seeks to serve. There is, in other words, a complex interplay between the reflective and the constitutive roles of accounting,① the former serving to create accounting's dependency on the organizations in which it is embedded and the latter often constraining organizations in the name of the possibilities and potentialities of the accounting craft.

The external origins of internal accounts

The conference had explicitly aimed to focus on the organizational nature of the accounting craft. The objective had been to provide some bases for appreciating how accounting was implicated with other aspects of organizational functioning.

At an early stage in the proceedings, however, such an aim was seen to be a partial one. Just as accounting could not be disentangled from the organizational, so the organizational could not be disassociated from the wider social context in which it in turn was embedded. Accounting, thereby, increasingly came to be seen as a phenomenon subject to the influences of both the particular organization and the wider social fabric in which it functioned.

Many of the organizational influences on accounting were seen to be specific manifestations of social influences, pressures and tensions. The State, for instance, in trying to further its own missions had repeatedly provided a basis for the elaboration of calculative endeavours within the enterprise. Its strategies for the control of prices and wages had resulted in the furtherance of those accounting procedures which sought to define, examine, restrain and plan within the organization those phenomenon which had a macro-economic significance at the national level. In the name of both economic crisis and growth the State had sought to further a regime of economic awareness within both organizations and those constituencies, such as the labour movement, which were deemed to have an interest in them. Calling upon conceptions of economic efficiency and effectiveness (and more recently "value for money"), the State repeatedly had tried to reform both its own administrative apparatus and the management practices of those organizations which were thought to play a significant role in the national economy.

Wider social agencies, including those of the State, the media and the professional institutions of the accounting craft, also could play a significant role in establishing a view of both the prevailing technical state of the accounting art and those managerial practices which were regarded as legitimate and in order. A view of the current, the modern, the desirable and the achievable could be propogated with some autonomy from the particular needs and histories of specific organizations. Ac-

---

① A further discussion of the reflective and constitutive roles of accounting is contained in Burchell *et al.* (forthcoming).

counting, particularly when professionalised, could achieve, and indeed had achieved, some degree of independent action. Solutions could indeed hunt for problems. The craft itself could influence the organizational. Equally significantly, organizations seeking to respond to the pressures of their environments could seek to utilise particular accounting and management practices in the name of the external legitimacy they could endow rather than on the basis of any presumed internal consequences. Indeed with the social thereby becoming the organizational, management might even uncouple their internal procedures and actions from the externally orientated practices of a rational management regime. So although influenced by the social, the organizational might even live in a state of flux with it.

The internal tensions and conflicts within organizations also cannot be detached from broader social movements. Concerns with the humanization of management practices in particular organizations have rarely existed in isolation of social movements which have provided a basis for their rhetoric and aims. The emphasis on the social in accounting itself has been a manifestation of the broader mobilisation of attempts to construct the organization in different terms. Equally, the ways in which accounting has sought to further a particular hierarchical order within organizations cannot be seen outside of the context of the conflicts between different social groups. In this sense accounting has both mirrored the context in which it has operated and enabled it to function in the ways it has. Only certain phenomenon have been regarded as costly. Particular conceptions of time have been emphasised. The benefits that have been incorporated into accounting calculations have not occurred in isolation of the socio-economic fabric to which they seek to relate. Accounting, in other words, has played a not insignificant role in embedding the social into the organizational. Accordingly its practice can never be seen in purely organizational terms.

Such a conclusion is a paradoxical one to emerge from a conference dedicated to exploring the organizational nature of the accounting craft. It reflects, however, the highly interdependent nature of our social world and the complex ways in which accounting has come to be embedded in our everyday lives. The social is not and cannot be isolated from the organizational. Indeed, in part at least, the social is manifest in the organizational and the organizational, in turn, constitutes a significant part of the social. It might even be useful to see the social as passing through the organizational, with both wider and more localised concerns calling upon practices such as accounting to create an ambiguous but nevertheless tethered conception of reality.

The methodologies of accounting research

The paucity of empirical studies of accounting in action was a major constraint on the conference deliberations. Repeatedly it had to be recognised how little was known of the accounting endeavour.

Our organizational colleagues had assumed that accounting researchers would be applied social scientists, committed to exploring the intricacies of accounting in practice. They had presumed that by now behavioural and organizational enquiries would have resulted in a mass of insights into the ways in which accounting was related to the fabric of organizational life. Indeed they had come to be illuminated on the relationship of accounting to the organizational, the strategic and the social. Those expectations could not be met however. The simple fact is that accounting research has tended to isolate itself from accounting in practice, if not accounting practice. The vast majority of efforts have been devoted to furthering the technical ediface of the accounting craft rather than seeking to illuminate the ways in which accounting intersects with the organizational and comes to have the significance it now has.

All too clearly if accounting researchers are to advance our understanding of the accounting context very different methodological perspectives will be required. There is a very real need for theoretically informed studies of both the use and design of accounting systems. Much more needs to be known of the ways in which accounting reflects, reinforces or even constrains the strategic postures adopted by particular organizations and of the ways in which accounting relates to the structures that are created for ensuring a coherent and vertically responsible organization. Studies of accounting changes also could do much to illustrate the nature of the diverse forces, both internal and external to the organization, that are operating on the accounting craft. Such studies also might help to cast some light on the ways in which the ambiguities that so often pervade accounting practice might play a positive role on bridging different, if not conflicting, pressures on accounting to change.

Of course all such investigations require the very commitment that is missing in accounting research to-date—a commitment to study, analyse and interpret accounting in the contexts in which it operates. The fact that so little of this work has been done suggests that change will not be easy. The constraints on organizational empirical inquiry must be very real indeed. To-date the difficulties of access and the inexperience of accounting researchers have been important factors. More significant, however, may be those pressures of the academic reward structure which push for speedy and voluminous research, the very low legitimacy which somewhat paradoxically has been given to grounded empirical inquiry, and the marginal commitment which many academic accountants have to the research endeavour. Unfortunate though these constraints may be, they nevertheless are very real ones. Accordingly change will not occur by mere enunciation. Demonstration is a much more likely route. We can only hope that slowly, but surely, new precedents can be established by adventurous researchers seeking to explore what lies behind today's accounting condition.

CONCLUSION

Organizational inquiry remains a new area of investigation for accounting research. Despite accounting being given an organizational rationale, we have few insights into the factors which influence accounting systems in the contexts in which they operate.

When one reviews the organizational research on accounting that has been undertaken to-date, it is clear that much of it has been limited in scope, fragmentary and essentially atheoretical. The primary concerns often have tended to be the the laudable but nevertheless constraining ones of exposing defects in the accounting craft and seeking a basis for the reform of prevailing practice. Useful though such inquiries often may be, there nevertheless is a very real danger that if too fragmentary in nature they can serve to perpetuate or even to foster myths about the organizational practice of accounting. What is needed are more substantive investigations orientated towards providing bases for understanding or explaining the workings of accounting in action. Yet it is precisely such studies that have been neglected to-date.

However, as the studies collected in this issue illustrate, there are signs of an emergence of interest in the organizational nature of accounting. The origins of this are diverse, spanning economics, organization theory and sociology. Frequently non-accountants have taken the lead. Economists, for instance, have started to probe into the roles served by accounting in the construction of modern organizational forms and their links to external agents. Organization theorists recently have become much more interested in questions of information and control, in the process exploring into not only the taken for granted roles which such practices are presumed to serve but also the symbolic and even political aspects of organizational life with which they can become intertwined. And sociologists too have started to recognise the research potential offered by the accounting craft, asking questions about how accounting might be related to the more general elaboration of calculative practices in modern society, the ways in which accounts have provided a powerful calculus for forging a new visibility which can facilitate specific modes of control within the business enterprise in particular, and the more legitimising functions of the accounting craft.

Most of these influences are reflected in the present collection. The result is an impression of an area in motion. Together the papers (and the discussant's remarks) provide both a useful insight into research in progress and a helpful agenda for future inquiries.

BIBLIOGRAPHY

Ashton, R. H., Deviation-Amplifying Feedback and Unintended Consequences of Management Accounting Systems, *Accounting, Organizations and Society* (1976), pp. 289—300.

Baiman, S., Agency Theory in Management Accounting: A Survey, *Journal of Accounting Literature* (Spring 1982), pp. 154—213.

Batstone, E., Systems of Domination, Accommodation, and Industrial Democracy, in Burns, T. R., Karlsson, L. E. & Rus, V. (eds.) *Work and Power: The Liberation of Work and Control of Political Power* (London: Sage, 1979), pp. 249—272.

Birnberg, J. C., Turpolec, L. & Young, S. M., The Organizational Context of Accounting, *Accounting, Organizations and Society* (1983), pp. 111—129.

Boland, R. J. & Pondy, L. R., Accounting in Organizations: A Union of Natural and Rational Perspectives, *Accounting, Organizations and Society* (1983), pp. 223—224.

Burchell, S., Clubb, C., Hopwood, A., Hughes, J. & Nahapiet, J., The Roles of Accounting in Organizations and Society, *Accounting, Organizations and Society* (1980), pp. 5—27.

Burchell, S., Hopwood, A. G. & Clubb, C., Accounting in Its Social Context: Towards a History of Value Added in the UK, *Accounting, Organizations and Society* (forthcoming).

Connolly, T., On Taking Action Seriously: Cognitive Fixation in Behavioural Decision Theory, in Ungson, G. R. & Braunstein, D. N. (eds.) *Decision Making: An Interdisciplinary Inquiry*, pp. 42—47 (Kent, 1982).

Cooper, D., Tidiness, Muddle and Things: Commonalities and Divergencies in Two Approaches to Management Accounting Research, *Accounting, Organizations and Society* (1983), pp. 269—286.

Cummings, L. L., A Framework for Decision Analysis and Critique, in Ungson, G. R. & Braunstein, D. N. (eds.) *Decision Making: An Interdisciplinary Inquiry* (Kent, 1982), pp. 298—308.

Edwards, R., *Contested Terrain: The Transformation of the Workplace in the Twentieth Century* (New York: Basic Books, 1979).

Flamholtz, D., The Markets and Hierarchies Framework: A Critique of the Models Applicability to Accounting and Economic Development, *Accounting, Organizations and Society* (1983), pp. 147—151.

Flamholtz, E., Accounting, Budgeting and Control Systems in Their Organizational Context: Theoretical and Empirical Perspectives, *Accounting, Organizations and Society* (1983), pp. 153—169.

Gowler, D. & Legge, K., The Integration of Disciplinary Perspectives and Levels of Analysis in Problem Oriented Organizational Research, Working Paper 81/3, Oxford Centre for Management Studies (1981).

Hayes, D. C., Accounting for Accounting: A Story about Managerial Accounting, *Accounting, Organizations and Society* (1983), pp. 241—249.

Hindess, B., Power, Interests and the Outcomes of Struggles, *Sociology* (November 1982), pp.

498—511.

Hopwood, A. G., The Path Ahead, *Accounting, Organizations and Society* (1976), pp. 1—4.

Hopwood, A. G., Towards an Organizational Perspective for the Study of Accounting and Information Systems, *Accounting, Organizations and Society* (1978), pp. 3—13.

Hopwood, A. G., Burchell, S. & Clubb, C., The Development of Accounting in Its International Context: Past Concerns and Emergent Issues, in Roberts, A. (ed.) *A Historical and Contemporary Review of the Development of International Accounting* (Georgia State University, 1980).

Horovitz, J. H., *Top Management Control in Europe* (London: Macmillan, 1980).

Johnson, T., The Search for Gain in Markets and Firms: A Review of the Historical Emergence of Management Accounting Systems, *Accounting, Organizations and Society* (1983), pp. 139—146.

Kerr, S., Accounting, Budgeting and Control Systems in Their Organizational Context: Comments by the Discussant, *Accounting, Organizations and Society* (1983), pp. 171—174.

March, J. G. & Shapra, Z., Behavioural Decision Theory and Organizational Decision Theory, in Ungson, G. R. & Braunstein, D. N. (eds.) *Decision Making: An Interdisciplinary Inquiry* (Kent, 1982), pp. 92—115.

Markus, M. L. & Pfeffer, J., Power and the Design and Implementation of Accounting and Control Systems, *Accounting, Organizations and Society* (1983), pp. 205—218.

Merton, R., The Unanticipated Consequences of Purposive Social Action, *American Sociological Review* (1936), pp. 894—904.

Meyer, J. W., On the Celebration of Rationality: Some Comments on Boland and Pondy, *Accounting, Organizations and Society* (1983), pp. 235—240.

Mirvis, P. H. & Lauter, E. E. III, Systems are not Solutions: Issues in Creating Information Systems That Account for the Human Organization, *Accounting, Organizations and Society* (1983), pp. 175—190.

Mitroff, I. I. & Mason, R. O., Can We Design Systems for Managing Messes? Or, Why So Many Management Information Systems are Uninformative, *Accounting, Organizations and Society* (1983), pp. 195—203.

Otley, D. T., The Contingency Theory of Management Accounting: Achievements and Prognosis, *Accounting, Organizations and Society* (1980), pp. 413—428.

Platt, J., *Realities of Social Research: An Empirical Study of British Sociologists* (London: Sussex University Press and Chatto and Windus, 1976).

Pondy, L., On Real Decisions, in Ungson, G. R. & Braunstein, D. N. (eds.) *Decision Making: An Interdisciplinary Inquiry* (Kent, 1982), pp. 309—311.

Spicer, B. H. & Ballew, V., Management Accounting Systems and the Economics of Internal Organization, *Accounting, Organizations and Society* (1983), pp. 73—96.

Tiessen, P. & Waterhouse, J. H., Towards a Descriptive Theory of Management Accounting, *Accounting, Organizations and Society* (1983), pp. 251—267.

Weick, K. E., Rethinking Research on Decision Making, in Ungson, G. R. & Braunstein, D. N. (eds.) *Decision Making: An Interdisciplinay Inquiry* (Kent, 1982), pp. 325—332.

The Roles of Accounting in Organizations and Society[*]

STUART BURCHELL, COLIN CLUBB, ANTHONY HOPWOOD, JOHN HUGHES
(*London Graduate School of Business Studies*)

and

JANINE NAHAPIET
(*Oxford Centre for Management Studies*)

Abstract: The paper seeks to contrast the roles that have been claimed on behalf of accounting with the ways in which accounting functions in practice. It starts by examining the context in which rationales for practice are articulated and the adequacy of such claims. Thereafter consideration is given to how accounting is implicated in both organizational and social practice. The paper concludes with a discussion of the implications for accounting research.

Accounting has come to occupy an ever more significant position in the functioning of modern industrial societies. Emerging from the management practices of the estate, the trader and the embryonic corporation (Chatfield, 1977) it has developed into an influential component of modern organizational and social management. Within the organization, be it in the private or the public sector, accounting developments now are seen as being increasingly associated not only with the management of financial resources but also with the creation of particular patterns of organizational visibility (Becker & Neuheuser, 1975), the articulation of forms of management structure and organizational segmentation (Chandler & Daems, 1979) and the reinforcement or indeed creation of particular patterns of power and influence (Bariff & Galbraith, 1978; Heydebrand, 1977). What is accounted for can shape organizational participants' views of what is important, with the categories of dominant economic discourse and organizational functioning that are implicit within the accounting framework helping to create a particular conception of organizational reality. At a broader social level, accounting has become no less influential as it has come to function in a

---

[*] *Accounting, Organizations and Society*, Vol. 5, No. 1, pp. 5—27, 1980. We would like to acknowledge the financial support of the Anglo-German Foundation for the Study of Industrial Society and the Foundation for Management Education.

multitude of different and ever changing institutional areas. The emergence of the modern state has been particularly important in this respect. The economic calculations provided by enterprise level accounting systems have come to be used not only as a basis for government taxation but also as a means for enabling the more general economic management policies of the state to grow in significance and impact (Hopwood et al. ,1979; Kendrick, 1970; and Studentski, 1958). Accounting data are now used in the derivation and implementation of policies for economic stabilization, price and wage control, the regulation of particular industrial and commercial sectors and the planning of national economic resources in conditions of war and peace and prosperity and depression. Indeed in its continuing search for greater economic and social efficiency (Bowe, 1977; Haber, 1964; Hays, 1959; and Searle, 1971) the state has been an active agent both for the continued development of accounting systems in industrial and commercial enterprises (Hopwood et al. ,1979) and for their introduction into more sectors of society (Gandhi, 1976).

Such extensions of the accounting domain have had major implications for the development of both accounting thought and practice. As the theorists of management control (Anthony, 1965) now recognize, accounting can no longer be regarded as a mere collection of techniques for the assessment of individual economic magnitudes. Whilst procedures for the derivation of various categories of cost and economic surplus are still important, the growth of the modern business enterprise has resulted in their incorporation into more all embracing forms of organizational practice which can enable the co-ordinated and centralized control of the functional (Litterer, 1961 and 1963), divisionalized (Johnson, 1978) and now, the matrix and project oriented organization (Ansari, 1979; Chapman, 1973; Sayles & Chandler, 1971). Similarly the increasing demands for financial information made by the capital markets, agencies of the state and organizations within the accounting profession itself have resulted in more extensive and rigorous approaches to financial reporting and disclosure (Benston, 1976; Hawkins, 1963). Accounting problems have seemingly got ever more detailed, precise and interdependent, resulting not only in the need to articulate new practice but also to formally explicate what previously had been implicit in practice.

As a result of such developments accounting has gained its current organizational and social significance. No longer seen as a mere assembly of calculative routines, it now functions as a cohesive and influential mechanism for economic and social management. But why should this be the case? Why should accounting have grown in complexity and significance? What have been the underlying pressures for its growth and development? Just what roles has it come to serve in organizations and societies? And why? All too unfortunately such questions very easily take one into uncharted terrain. For although there has been an enormous investment of effort in improving the accounting craft and even in charting its technical development, very few attempts have been made to probe into the rationales for the existence and development of accounting itself. Be that as it may, the present paper will attempt to make a preliminary excursion into the field of the unknown. Whilst recognizing that with so few prior studies to appeal to our conclusions can be tentative at best, we nevertheless believe that it is important at least to start questioning what has not been questioned and thereby possibly to make problematic what may have been taken for granted.

Our argument starts with a discussion of two important tendencies underlying the development of accounting as we now know it: the increasing institutionalization of the accounting craft and the growing abstraction or objectification of accounting knowledge. On this basis we consider how these and other pressures might have stimulated a search for explicitly stated rationales for accounting—for expressions of the roles which it serves in organizations and societies. After discussing at least some of the more commonly articulated roles which accounting is claimed to perform, we attempt to analyse the adequacy of such functional imperatives, using both observations and the research studies that are available to demonstrate how purposes are implicated in action rather than being essential to the craft itself. To reinforce these arguments more particular consideration is given to the variety of roles which are created for accounting both within organizations and the societies of which they are a part. The paper concludes with a discussion of the implications of our arguments for the future study of accounting.

INSTITUTIONALIZATION, ABSTRACTION AND THE SEARCH FOR RATIONALES

It is possible to identify many tendencies underlying the development of the accounting craft. One could point to particular aspects of the emerging bodies of knowledge and practice or to the changing patterns of influence on them. Alternatively one could highlight developments in the organizational and social significance which accounting has had or changes in the organization of accounting itself. For the purpose of the present argument two particular tendencies are identified: the increasing institutionalization of the craft and the growing objectification and abstraction of accounting knowledge.① Both of these tendencies are important for gaining an understanding of the present state of accounting, the roles which it serves and those which are claimed for it. Moreover together they have resulted in the creation of new forums both for accounting deliberation and debate and for the introduction of accounting change, forms of occupational specialization within organizations which have provided bases on which accounting practitioners have searched for as well as responded to organizational needs and meanings, and the continued extension of the domains of both accounting practice and thought.

The institutionalization of accounting has occurred at both the organizational and societal levels. Within both business and governmental organizations, bookkeeping came to take on a new significance and influence as accounting became a more all embracing form of organizational practice (Garner, 1954; Pollard, 1965). Implicated in budgeting and standard costing, organizational segmentation and control, and planning and resource allocation, the accountant came to be an increasingly respected member of the management cadre. Accounting departments were created, specialist staff recruited, emergent accounting systems formalized, standardized and codified, and links with other forms of management practice established. Moreover, accounting itself came to be a more fragmented endeavour with the growing separation of the preparation of the financial accounts from the presentation of internal financial information and the management of corporate liquidity and financial structure.

Such organizational developments were themselves intertwined with the professionalization of the accounting craft. Almost from their birth, the professional institutes provided an interface between the growing agencies of the state and business enterprises. In continental Europe accountants were involved with the administration of the early commercial codes (ten Have, 1976) and in England and Wales the profession derived a large part of its initial rationale from those extensions to the accounting domain which had been created by successive companies and bankruptcy acts and legislation which provided for the regulation of sectors such as railways, building societies and municipal utilities (Brown, 1905; Chatfield, 1977; Edey & Panitpakdi,

---

① The distinction between institutionalization, and objectification and abstraction parallels similar distinctions made by Popper, Kuhn and Foucault. Popper (1972), for instance, characterises objective knowledge ("that massive fabric of statements which exists in journals and books stored in libraries, discussions, computer memories, etc.") as a world—"world 3"—which is largely autonomous of the world of the senses—"world 2"—and the physical world—"world 1". See also Hacking (1975). Similarly Kuhn (1970) distinguishes between paradigms 1 and 2, the former relating to the logical, conceptual and discursive aspects of a science and the latter to the social and institutional conditions under which the science exists. Foucault (1977) likewise operates with a distinction between knowledge and power, with the latter referring to the complex of social relations—the "regime"—in which knowledge is embedded.

1956; Littleton, 1933). And although the U. S. context was not so regulated in the earliest days of the profession, the latter nevertheless came to flourish on the basis of subsequent governmental interventions (Chatfield, 1977). Indeed with the establishment of professional accounting institutes, many of the subsequent institutional innovations in the accounting area in the U. S. A. and the U. K. were to arise at the interface between them and the expanding regulatory agencies of the state. So, initially at least, the Securities and Exchange Commission in the U. S. A. made rather limited use of its regulatory powers in the accounting area, allowing the profession to invest in that chain of institutional mechanisms for the explication, standardization and codification of financial accounting practice which would progress through the Accounting Principles Board to the Financial Accounting Standards Board. Not dissimilar developments occurred later in the U. K. with the Accounting Standards Steering Committee being created in response to governmental pressure and the desire of the professional institutes to preserve their powers of selfregulation. Elsewhere, however, the institutionalization of accounting was a more direct result of the activities of the state. In pre-war Germany, for example, legal and institutional mechanisms for the standardization of enterprise accounting were introduced in the context of the mobilization of the national economy for war (Singer, 1943) and in France these innovations were adapted after the war to provide the information which was required for microeconomic planning by agencies of the state.

Important though such a pattern of institutionalized development may be in its own right, we are particularly interested in a number of the implications which it has had for the functioning of accounting and for understanding the roles which it has come to serve. First, the emergence of accounting as is recognized and influential occupational specialization in organizations gave some measure of autonomy to accounting practice. With the creation of accounting departments and the recruitment of cosmopolitan (Gouldner, 1957) specialists who were receptive to accounting developments elsewhere, the development of accounting systems could become intertwined with the management and growth of the accounting function in an organization. Accounting could take its place in the organizational "garbage can" (Cohen *et al.*, 1972), with its development stemming, in part at least from the fact that it existed. Rather than merely having to respond to preconceived organizational needs, accounting practitioners could search for organizational opportunities for the expansion of accounting practice. Roles could now be created for accounting, with accountants pointing to the potential of their systems and seeking to establish connections between accounting and other forms of organizational practice, particularly that of production management. Second, the emergence of professional institutes and specialized bodies for the standardization and codification of accounting practice provided new forums in which accounting deliberations and debates could take place and from which changes in accounting practice could emanate. Developments in financial accounting were no longer necessarily an outcome of the direct interplay between business enterprises and the institutions of the capital market or even the state. Pressures for change could stem from the relationships between the professional institutes, the bodies concerned with the regulation of accounting practice, the dominant partnerships of the accounting profession and the interested agencies of the state, and then be imposed, comfortably or otherwise, on business or other organizations. So yet again the creation of roles for accounting practice became a much more complex endeavour, with the pressures for change being quite capable of stemming from very different institutional arenas than those in which the new practices were to function. Thirdly the changing institutional structure within which accounting operated created new possibilities for the autonomous development of accounting knowledge.① Within organizations, accounting procedures came to be codified in charts and manuals. With their interests in training, examining and regulating, the professional institutes provided a further stimulus for an interest in accounting discourse that could be separated from the practice of the craft. And the growing interest of the state in enterprise accounting also resulted in the formalization of the craft as disclosure requirements started to be laid down and concerns with accounting standardization emerge. As Chatfield (1977, p. 121) notes:

> In coming to grips with problems of capital, income and asset created by the industrial corporation and absentee ownership, the auditor was forced to reason beyond existing rules of thumb and finally to elaborate his ideas of proper treatment into accounting principles. His scrutiny of financial statements ultimately rationalized bookkeeping itself, not only through the use of internal control procedures but more directly by refining transaction analysis, account classifications, and the rules of financial statement disclosure. English social condi-

---

① The relationship between the institutional setting of accounting and the development of accounting knowledge is very complex, particularly when one considers that institutions are no less discursive in nature than knowledge itself. A profession, for example, can be conceived as a mass of regulations, categories, procedures, norms and laws, etc. The differentiation and relationship between the two levels of analysis therefore needs to be handled with care. As both Popper (1972) and Foucault (1977) point out in their different ways, it is all too easy to seek to explain "abstractions", "paradigm 1" or "knowledge" by reference to "institutions", "paradigm 2" or "power". Rather than arguing that institutionalization gives rise to abstraction, or vice versa, we prefer to observe the conjuncture of the two. So, for example, formalized accounting knowledge can be seen as a condition for the possibility of the professionalization of accounting, and that professionalization in turn changes the conditions underlying the elaboration and development of accounting knowledge.

tions had created a need for audit services and had produced accountants more highly skilled than any before them. By subjecting customary methods to analysis, these auditors gave accounting theory some of its earliest practical applications. And in attempting to standardize British practice, Parliament through the companies acts codified parts of this theory.

In such ways accounting became an identifiable form of organizational and social practice. It could be described and codified, debated and challenged, and ultimately changed. The discourse of accounting could be influenced by pressures very different from those which impinged on its practical application. Other bodies of thought which had no necessary *a priori* relationship to the accounting craft could influence the development of accounting thought, often in institutions which were far removed from the practices of accounting. So, for example, accounting thought could come to be intertwined with that of economics (Baxter, 1978) and production engineering (Wells, 1978), and with the concerns of the scientific management movement (Epstein, 1973). And such discursive developments could provide a basis for changing the practice of accounting itself, either by direct application or through the influences which they had on the requirements and pronouncements of the state, the professional institutes and the bodies concerned with the standardization of the craft and independent commentators and analysts.

Together the institutionalization and abstraction of accounting also provided bases on which people might seek to formally explicate roles which accounting served. As in other areas of human endeavour (Hacking, 1975; Popper, 1972), the existence of an abstract and objective body of thought stimulates a search for its nature and rationale.① Just what is accounting and what functions does it serve were questions that started to be considered. And with the growing significance of the craft and the increasing complexity of the institutional processes through which changes emerged, such questions might have had a particular relevance for many of those concerned with its practice, regulation and development.

Given that the sources of accounting change were increasingly distant from the arenas in which the new practices were to function, there was no reason to expect why those rationales which had been used in the initial justification and development of any change should provide effective rationales for its public implementation. For in a social context, public actions need to have either a political means for their enforcement (Moonitz, 1974) or a wider social significance and legitimacy (Posner,

---

① Equally the explication of roles for accounting can serve as an inducement for the elaboration of accounting knowledge and practice in particular directions.

1974). In the latter case, they need to be seen as being orientated towards some desirable or acceptable social end or ends. Action needs, in other words, to have an explicit and public rationale (Watts & Zimmerman, 1979)—a formal expression of the aims and intentions that might be regarded as being embodied within it.

Certainly the state came to act on accounting in the name of both accountability and the furtherance of organizational and social efficiency (Searle, 1971). Professional institutes and those agencies concerned with accounting regulation adopted a similar stance, although they also emphasised the role which accounting could serve in improving the flow of information useful for the investment decisions of shareholders. And those practicing accounting within organizations came to point to its relevancy in improving organizational efficiency and the maintenance of organizational control.

Such roles were not necessarily mere interpretations of accounting practice. Roles could emerge at a distance from practice, often shaped by very different institutional contexts and bodies of thought, and thereafter serve as bases for changing practice. Providing the imperatives for accounting, their relationship to the practice of accounting need be only indirect.

THE IMPERATIVES OF ACCOUNTING

We are all familiar with those stated roles of accounting which grace the introductions to accounting texts, professional pronouncements and the statements of those concerned with the regulation and development of the craft. Latterday equivalents of the preambles of old which appealed more directly to Heavenly virtue and authority (Yamey, 1974), they attempt to provide a more secular basis for the accounting mission. In such contexts, accounting is seen to have an essence, a core of functional claims and pretensions.① It is, or so we are led to believe, essentially concerned with the provision of "relevant information for decision making", with the achievement of a "rational allocation of resources" and with the maintenance of institutional "accountability" and "stewardship". Such functional attributes are seen as being fundamental to the accounting endeavour. Justifying the existence of the craft, they provide rationales for continued accounting action.

Another rather different set of imperatives for accounting has originated from

---

① The search for a rationale in progress is illustrated by Littleton (1953, p. 18): "There *must* be some basic concept which makes accounting different from all other methods of quantitative analysis, there *must* be some central idea which expresses better than others the objectives, effects, results, ends, aims that are characteristic of accounting—a 'centre of gravity' so to speak" (emphasis added).

those scholars who have seen accounting systems as mirrors of the societies or organizations in which they are implicated. At the societal level, this has involved seeing accounting as essentially reflective of the organization of social relationships. Feudal societies are seen to require feudal accounting systems; capitalist societies, capitalist modes of accounting (Rose, 1977); and the era of the post-industrial society necessitates a new framework for the accounting craft (Gandhi, 1976). The translation of such thinking to the organizational level has been more recent, influenced by the emergence of contingency schools of thought in the study of organizational behaviour (Bruns & Waterhouse, 1975; Hopwood, 1974; Sathe, 1975; Waterhouse & Tiessen, 1978; Watson, 1975). However some would now see accounting systems as being essential products of such characteristics as the complexity, noxity or uncertainty of the organizational environment (Galbraith, 1973; Khandwalla, 1972) the technology of the enterprise (Daft & Macintosh, 1978) or the strategy of corporate management (Chandler, 1962). Although the evidence in support of such broad normative theories of accounting is either non-existent or equivocal at best (see Hopwood, 1978), this has not prevented their growing popularity and influence. The fact that they are largely silent about the mechanisms that might create such an essential relationship between accounting and its presumed organizational and social determinants has not been seen as problematic by those who wish to point to either the necessity for change or the elegance of design which underlies accounting in action. Nor has the fact that so many of the underlying organizational theories depend for their validity on the presumption that such contingent designs further the achievement of higher order but defined, consistent and agreed organizational goals—goals which are in part made objective by the very accounting systems which they are supposed to explain (Pfeffer, 1978).

However rather than further delineating either the particular or the more general normative claims for accounting, we choose to focus on a number of their characteristics.

The stated roles of accounting have served to provide a normative structure for accounting thought. Addressing themselves to the accounting mission, they have provided a statement of what accounting is and ought to be about. And, on this basis, they have facilitated the appraisal of accounting practice. Accounting has been challenged and changed in the name of the roles which it is seen as serving. People have sought to extend accounting in order to promote "corporate accountability" and to further "rational decision making". Others have pointed to the challenges which social change necessarily creates for accounting practice (Gilling, 1976). Recognizing, however, the equivocal relationship between the roles and practices of accounting, the former have been used as vehicles for identifying the disparity of the latter and, on this basis, for correcting what have been seen to be errors in practice.

Indeed many of the functional claims that have been made for accounting have emerged at a distance from the practice of accounting. Emanating from professional institutes, bodies concerned with the regulation of the accounting craft, agencies of the state and not least in importance, the academy itself, they very often reflect the pressures on those bodies and their need for a public legitimacy and rationale for action. Formulated in the context of particular institutional needs and actions, the functional claims attempt to provide rather particular interpretations of the accounting mission. In the academy in particular the public roles that have been articulated have often reflected the influence of other bodies of thought and practice with which accounting as an autonomous body of knowledge has become intertwined. The influences of conventional economic discourse and administrative theory have been particularly important in this respect.

In fact it should be borne in mind that there is little in the development of accounting as practised that would lead one to describe its essential rationale in terms of the furtherance of economic efficiency or rationality. Not only are the concepts which it is claimed to further extremely difficult to define (Winston & Hall, 1959) but also it has been the practice of accounting which has itself provided some of the operational understandings of the pre-given economic ends which it is supposed to serve.① What relationships there are between accounting thought and economic discourse have stemmed from those accounting, management and economic theorists who have sought to analyse and guide the accounting task rather than from any pre-given essential attributes of either of the two bodies of knowledge and practice.

Finally it is worth noting that although the publically stated roles of accounting have been used to identify errors in practice, that very divergence of practice has rarely problematized the roles which are stated for it. Emanating from very different social contexts, the roles have remained absolute. Acting like guardians of the secular accounting mission, they have seemingly defied questioning and rarely been brought into confrontation with accounting as it is.

Hence we can tentatively conclude that the roles which have been attributed to accounting may tell us a great deal about how people have come to see accounting, the influences on accounting discourse and the bases from which people have sought publically to influence accounting. The roles of accounting have been used to change

---

① The latter was particularly the case in the context of the efficiency and scientific management movements at the turn of the present century. See Haber, 1964; Hayes, 1959; and Searle, 1971.

the practice of accounting and no doubt they have been influenced by practice. However that is not to say that they are descriptive of practice. As Argyris and Schon (1974) have pointed out in another context, espoused theories are very different from theories in use. At best the roles of accounting and the practice of accounting would appear to have a rather equivocal relationship.

THE COMPLEXITIES OF ACCOUNTING PRACTICE

More recently, however, we have witnessed what might be the beginning of a reappraisal of the pregiven imperatives of the accounting mission. Pressures stemming from both academic inquiry and the problems of practical action have encouraged some observers to recognize and analyse the complexities of accounting in action and, on this basis, to start questioning what has not been questioned and make problematic what so far has been taken for granted. For different reasons and on different bases these tendencies have been evident in both the financial and management accounting areas.

The sustained and influential body of research on the impact of accounting data on the capital markets (Dyckman, Downes & Magee, 1975) has provided one basis on which the actual functioning of accounting has come to be reconsidered. The findings that investors do not necessarily take accounting data at their face value and that much of the information content of corporate annual reports and accounts is reflected in share prices prior to their public announcement (Ball & Brown, 1968) have highlighted the existence of a highly competitive market in information on corporate performance, of which accounting reports are only a part. Investors appraise, question and corroborate accounting information. Rather than being mere passive recipients, they inquire into its significance for the decisions they are taking, bringing to bear their own standards of relevancy. Now other research is starting to recognize the multiplicity of interests in accounting information within even the investor community, let alone elsewhere. Based on conceptions drawn from the study of the economics of information search and use, it is pointing to the difficulty, if not the impossibility (Demski, 1973), of operationalizing general conceptions of decision relevancy and incorporating them into the selection of a body of information prior to its use in an actual decision situation. Like the empirical research on actual investor behaviours, it too suggests that the relevancy of information is determined within the context in which it is used rather than by the foresight of those who determine the form which it should take.

In which case what influences the nature of the accounting information which is provided, if not used? Unfortunately very little is known about this at the level of the individual enterprise. Whilst consideration is being given to the ways in which information disclosure might be implicated in the formation and operation of agency relationships, the empirical adequacy of such views remains to be tested. However one set of observations which is starting to provide us with at least a partial appreciation of the forces at work at the level of the regulatory institution rather than the individual enterprise has stemmed from analyses of accounting policy formulation. Both Moonitz (1974) and Horngren (1973) have provided insider views which have emphasised the political dimensions of the process. The technical components of accounting regulation and specification were seen as being embodied within a complex pattern of institutional and other influences and the search for technical solutions as being complemented by a search for institutional and political support. Arising from these studies, there is now a growing awareness of the need to understand the bases on which interests in accounting are determined, articulated and deliberated (Watts & Zimmerman, 1978, 1979). For instance, consideration is now being given to how such interests might stem from the ways in which an accounting of the corporate economy of the past can influence the economy of the future (Zeff, 1978). And with the capital markets no longer being seen as the only or indeed the most significant users of accounting data, more emphasis is also being given to the roles played by agencies of the state.

Financial accounting and reporting are coming to be seen as outgrowths of institutional processes of enormous and still uncharted complexity (Burchell *et al.*, forthcoming). More importantly for the present argument, the roles which they serve are starting to be recognized as being shaped by the pressures which give rise to accounting innovation and change rather than any essence of the accounting mission.

A similar problematization of the accounting craft is slowly starting to emerge from organizational and behavioural inquiries into the ways in which management accounting systems function. Some have questioned the extent to which accounting information is actually used in organizations (Mintzberg, 1973, 1975). Others have pointed to their symbolic rather than technical uses (Gambling, 1977; Meyer & Rowan, 1978). And yet others have emphasised the ways in which uses are created for accounting systems within the context of particular organizational environments (Cammann, 1976; Hopwood, 1973; Otley, 1978; Rahman & McCosh, 1976). Rather than the consequences of accounting systems being determined by their mere existence, they are now being seen as stemming from those organizational processes which give them a particular meaning and significance (Pettigrew, 1973, 1977). Already consideration has been given to the roles played by management styles and philosophies (Argyris, 1977; Hedberg & Mumford, 1975; Hopwood, 1973), organizational normative environments (Otley, 1978), power and influence structures (Argyris, 1971; Pettigrew, 1973, 1977), organizational mechanisms for the diffusion of information (Shortell & Brown, 1976), organizational mechanisms for the diffusion of information (Shortell & Brown, 1976) and external pressures and constraints (Meyer & Rowan, 1978; Olofsson & Svalander, 1975). Other researchers have given more attention to how accounting systems both arise from and function within the context of those micropolitical processes which constitute the organization as we know it (Pfeffer, 1978). Wildavsky (1965, 1978), for instance, has provided us with particularly vivid insights into how political processes influence how sophisticated budgeting systems function in practice. Equally detailed descriptions of the ways in which organizational resource allocations are a product of the intertwining of budgeting and planning systems and political processes have been provided by Pfeffer and Salancik (1974) and Dalton (1959), and similar findings in the context of the capital budgeting process have been reported by Bower (1970).

Organizational research is also starting to question those automatic presumptions of a positive and causal relationship between accounting systems and effective organizational performance which implicitly or explicitly grace accounting texts and the pronouncements of practitioners and consultants. Albeit slowly, we are starting to move beyond those questioning pleas from the heart that were uttered by Ackoff (1967) over a decade ago. Whilst accounting systems are most certainly centrally implicated in the design and functioning of organizations as we know them, even enabling the existence of particular forms of organizational segmentation and management (Braverman, 1974; Johnson, 1978), some all too tentative studies (Child, 1973, 1974, 1975; Rosner, 1968; Turcotte, 1974) would at the very least suggest that the financially successful might well avoid many of the rigors of the more sophisticated accounting, information and control systems. Seemingly they revel and flourish within the context of informal planning and assessment practices (Child, 1974) multiple and overlapping flows of information (Baumler, 1971; Grinyer & Norburn, 1975) and continually renegotiated exchanges between organizational participants (Georgiou, 1973). Indeed it might be 13 the "newly poor" (Olofsson & Svalander, 1975) or the externally threatened (Khandwalla, 1978; Meyer & Rowan, 1978) that invest heavily in additional mechanisms for internal visibility and control as they attempt both to allocate their ever more scarce resources or to negotiate a new legitimacy with external agents.

Although we still know all too little about how accounting systems function in practice, the studies that are available do enable us to question the descriptive accuracy of many of the functional imperatives that are claimed on behalf of both financial and management accounting systems. Whilst they may be introduced in the name of particular conceptions of social and organizational efficiency, rationality and relevance, in practice accounting systems function in a diversity of ways, intertwined with institutional political processes and the operation of other forms of organizational and calculative practice. Accounting, it would appear, is made to be purposive rather than being inherently purposeful. At the very least research suggests that in laying down the pretentions of the accounting craft we have uncritically adopted a rather particular set of views of human, organizational and social rationality and the relationships between accounting, decision making and organizational action. Whilst such presumptions might have legitimized the accounting mission, provided the means for acting on accounting and simplified the accounting system design and implementation process, their relationship to the realities of organizational and social life is questionable at best.

Unfortunately the tentativeness of our knowledge of accounting in action precludes any comprehensive and analytical discussion of the way in which accounting systems function in practice. In this essay we can do no more than be suggestive of the roles which they serve. We do this by first focusing on how accounting systems are implicated in organizational practice, choosing to pay particular attention to their involvement in organizational decision making processes. Thereafter we made some even more tentative observations on the social as distinct from organizational functioning of accounting.

ACCOUNTING SYSTEMS AND ORGANIZATIONAL PRACTICE

The relationship between accounting and organizational decision making has been an influential basis for the analysis, development and articulation of normative accounting roles and "solutions". So many writers have pointed to the roles which accounting systems can and should play in providing relevant information for decision making, improving the rationality of the decision making process and maintaining the organization in what is seen as a state of control. However one problem with such a perspective is that the relationship between accounting information and decision making rarely has been examined critically. The link has, in other words, been presumed rather than described. It has been assumed, for instance, that the specification, design and use of accounting systems precedes decision making, that the roles played by accounting systems in decision making can be invariate across a multitude

THE ROLES OF ACCOUNTING IN ORGANIZATIONS AND SOCIETY

of different decision situations and that accounting information is there to facilitate and ease rather than more actively to influence and shape the decision making process. However whilst such assumptions might point to the potential of the accounting mission, they have a much more complex relationship to the ways in which accounting functions in practice.

Recognizing that the present state of knowledge precludes either a comprehensive or an authoritative account of the ways in which accounting information is implicated in the processes of organizational decision making, we base our own analysis on the rather particular understandings of decision making in organizations formulated by Thompson and Tuden (1959). Whilst overly simple, their perspective nevertheless added to the traditional view by characterizing various states of uncertainty and, as a consequence, a range of possible approaches to decision making. By so doing it provides a basis for discussing at least some of the diverse ways in which interests in accounting can arise out of the processes of organizational decision making.

As can be seen in Fig. 1, Thompson and Tuden distinguished between uncertainty (or disagreement, for that has the same effects at the organizational level) over the objectives for organizational action and uncertainty over the patterns of causation which determine the consequences of action. When objectives are clear and undisputed, and the consequences of action are presumed to be known, Thompson and Tuden highlighted the potential for decision making by computation. In such circumstances it is possible to compute whether the consequence of the action or set of actions being considered will or will not satisfy the objectives that have been laid down and agreed beforehand. As cause and effect relationships become more uncertain however, the potential for computation diminishes. Thompson and Tuden then saw decisions being made in a judgemental manner, with organizational participants subjectively appraising the array of possible consequences in the light of the relatively certain objectives. Just as the introduction of uncertainty into the specification of the consequences of action resulted in a different approach to decision making, so did the acknowledgement of debate or uncertainty over the objectives themselves. With cause and effect relationships presumed to be known, Thompson and Tuden thought that disagreement or uncertainty over the objectives of action would result in a political rather than computational rationale for the decision making process. A range of interests in action are articulated in such circumstances and decision making, as a result, tends to be characterized by bargaining and compromise. When even patterns of causation are uncertain, Thompson and Tuden pointed out that decision making tends to be of an inspirational nature. With so little known beforehand rationales for action were seen as emerging in the course of the decision making process itself.

		Uncertainty of objectives	
		Low	High
Uncertainty of cause and effect	Low	Decision by computation	Decision by compromise
	High	Decision by judgement	Decision by inspiration

Fig. 1 Decision making and the location of organizational uncertainty

By being based on a richer characterization of the ways in which uncertainties and indeed conflicts are perceived and located in organizations the array of approaches to decision making articulated by Thompson and Tuden offers some possibility for trying to understand the different roles which accounting and other information systems serve in organizations. Moreover their framework, whilst simple, does relate to the views of those who have seen information processing mechanisms as means for uncertainty reduction (Galbraith, 1973) and information value as the degree to which uncertainty is reduced. However rather than presuming any such link between information and uncertainty, let us consider the roles which accounting systems might play in the different decision situations. How, in other words, does accounting relate to the computational, the judgemental, the political and the inspirational?

Using an all too unsatisfactory "machine" analogy, Fig. 2 outlines a set of organizational roles which might help us to appreciate some of the ways in which accounting systems function in practice (Earl & Hopwood, 1979; Hopwood, forthcoming). Given low uncertainty over both the consequences of action and the objectives for action, we approach the management scientist's definition of certainty, where algorithms, formulae and rules can be derived to solve problems by computation. Alternatively this situation might represent what Simon (1960) has called structured decision making, where the intelligence, design and choice phases are all programmable. In either case, accounting systems can serve as "answer machines", providing the simple investment appraisal methods, stock control systems and credit control routines which grace many management accounting texts.

		Uncertainty of objectives	
		Low	High
Uncertainty of cause and effect	Low	Answer machines	Ammunition machines
	High	Answer machines / Learning machines	Rationalization machines

Fig. 2 Uncertainty, decision making and the roles of accounting practice

With clear objectives but uncertain causation, the situation is more complex. One might expect that this is where organizational participants would need to explore problems, ask questions, explicate presumptions, analyse the analysable and finally resort to judgement. Rather than providing answers, accounting systems might be expected to provide assistance through what Gorry and Scott-Morton (1971) have called decision support systems and Churchman (1971) calls inquiry systems. In fact we do find such "learning machine" uses of the accounting function: access facilities, *ad hoc* analyses, what-if models and sensitivity analyses are available and used in organizations. However this is also the area of decision making where we have seen enormous extensions of more traditional approaches to computation practice. For the uncertainty, some would claim, has been seen as a threatening but not inevitable state of the world, needing to be masked, if not reduced, by an investment in the advancement of calculative systems. Accordingly the accountant has devised systems which can themselves absorb rather than convey the surrounding uncertainties. Together with the management scientist, optimizing models and modes of probabilistic and risk analysis have been developed and applied. Often trying to inculcate an aura of relative certainty, the "answer machine" extensions to the accounting craft often have presumed or imposed particular forms of economic and scientific rationality which have an equivocal relationship at best to those rationalities which are implicated in the processes of organizational decision making.

Given uncertainty or disagreement over objectives but relative certainty over causation, values, principles, perspectives and interests conflict. Standards for appraisal and criteria for guiding the organizational task are inherently problematic. Here political processes are important in the decision making process and modes of accounting can arise as "ammunition machines" by which and through which interested parties seek to promote their own particular positions. Striving to articulate the desirability of particular conceptions of the organizational mission (Batstone, 1978) and to selectively channel the distribution of information (Pettigrew, 1973), parties implicated in organized action can introduce new mechanisms for organizational control and the management of information flows.

Similarly we suspect that the uncertainties inherent in decision making by inspiration can create the need for accounting systems to serve as organizational "rationalization machines". Seeking to legitimize and justify actions that already have been decided upon, in such circumstances an accounting for the past can have a rather particular organizational significance and value.

Admittedly simplistic, our framework of accounting roles is nonetheless suggestive. By pointing to the different ways in which the accounting craft might be used to create particular conceptions of organizational clarity, it enables us to articulate a variety of roles which accounting systems might serve. However rather than discussing all of these, we will assume that at least the "answer machine" and "learning machine" roles are adequately covered in the existing literature. Our subsequent discussion therefore focusses on those extensions of computational practice which seemingly have extended the scope of "answer machine" approaches, the emergence and use of organizational "ammunition machines" and the roles which accounting might play in the rationalization of organizational action.

The extension of computational practice

The reasons behind the extension of computational practice into the realms of the judgemental remain largely uncharted. However we can point to at least two underlying factors. The first stems from the increasing formalization and objectification of management knowledge and the second from the growing extent to which accounting practices have become implicated in the development of new and more complex forms of organizational segmentation and management.

Organizational management has become the focus of a great deal of abstract investigation in the last few decades. Drawing on the perspectives and methods of economics, mathematics and statistics, in particular, formal representations have been made of management problems. Searching for algorithms, formulae and standardized rules, the investigations of an array of practitioners, consultants and scholars increasingly have enabled the reconstitution of significant portions of organizational decision making into programmed, highly specified forms (Galbraith, 1967; Simon, 1960). To varying extents, computational practices have been developed which can complement, if not replace, the exercise of human judgement.

Accounting has been implicated in the design and implementation of many of these changes in management practice. The increasing formalization of investment appraisals and planning processes has increased the sphere and extent of financial calculation. On occasions the financial risks and uncertainties which were important foci for managerial judgement are now being quantified, with the decisions taking more of a computational form. Developments in accounting practice have enabled the operationalization of particular conceptions of organizational efficiency and performance, allowing the objectives for action to be stated in seemingly less ambiguous terms. Advances in the practice of budgeting and planning have provided means for the coordination of organizational activities by computational means. Production and marketing operations, for instance, can be integrated in rather particular ways, inventory policies evaluated and amended in the light of envisaged organizational circumstances, and the consequences of planned actions for particular organizational resources, such as cash, calculated and evaluated. Similarly the introduction of production and inventory control procedures has resulted in demands for far more detailed financial and other information as the domain of computational practice has been extended.

The extension of computational practice has also been implicated in the development of other approaches to organizational management. The emergence of particular forms of organizational segmentation, for instance, has been enabled by extensions of the accounting craft. Certainly the creation of the divisionalized (Chandler, 1962; Johnson, 1978) and the project orientated (Sayles & Chandler, 1971) organization has been facilitated by the ability to create accounting representations of the newly emergent organizational maps, to measure the performance of organizational sub-units in ways which could be seen as relating to the objectives articulated by central management and to cope in informative and reporting terms with the complex array of organizational interdependencies created by such strategies of segmentation. The use of organization designs to isolate the technical core of the organization from environmental fluctuations (Thompson, 1967) also has enabled and often required the development of computational practices to aid both the control of the technical and the management of organizational buffers such as inventory. Similarly the emergence of accounting procedures for the measurement and assessment of performance has been intertwined with the development of practices for the evaluation and reward of organizational participants, with the emphasis which accounting has allowed to be put on operational concepts of efficiency and productivity being particularly important in this respect. In ways such as these the organizational rationales for accounting have stemmed increasingly from what it can achieve in conjunction with other approaches to the management task. Rather than having an independent and essential role to play, accounting systems have become ever more implicated with the functioning of more all-embracing forms of organizational practice.

Whilst a discussion of the wider organizational, let alone social, conditions which have facilitated the extension of computational practice is beyond the scope of the present discussion[①], some of the dynamics which are inherent in the development of such practice at least can be noted. The growing extent of the computational domain, for instance, has resulted in the recruitment of specialists who can search for, as well as respond to, organizational roles. More importantly, however, computational developments can themselves provide the conditions for subsequent changes

---

[①] Clearly the technical possibility for an accounting is not a sufficient condition for its organizational implementation and use. For discussions of some of the organizational and social considerations involved in the process of accounting change see the literature on the efficiency movement (Haber, 1964; Hayes, 1959; and Searle, 1971) and our analysis ot the emergence of value added accounting in the U. K. (Burchell et al., forthcoming).

in both accounting and organizational practice which need be related only tenuously to the rationales in the name of which the initial changes were introduced. By creating a new pattern of organizational visibility, for instance, computational practices can often significantly change organizational participants' perceptions of the problematic and the possible. As a result, new systems of computation might emerge to complement the perceived inadequacies of the old (Jones & Lakin, 1978, pp.89—96). Of possibly greater significance, however, the new patterns of visibility can change the conditions underlying the existence and functioning of other management practices. Measures of efficiency, for instance, can create possibilities for new targets for managerial intervention and new bases for organizational rewards. Similarly, means for the accounting representation of organizational segments can provide the conditions for the reorganization of the enterprise and the changing locus of power and influence. In ways such as these a rather complex dynamic can be introduced into the development of computational practice. New practices can themselves create possibilities for the development of yet further practices, the emergence and functioning of which may be governed by entirely different forces than those which guided the original changes.

Organizational "ammunition machines"

Rather than creating a basis for dialogue and interchange in situations where objectives are uncertain or in dispute, accounting systems are often used to articulate and promote particular interested positions and values. For the organization is almost invariably characterized by conflicts over both basic orientations and the organizational means which are likely to achieve particular ends. Rather than being cohesive mechanisms for rational action, organizations are constituted as coalitions of interests (Cyert & March, 1963). They are arenas in which people and groups participate with a diversity of interests with political processes being an endemic feature of organizational life. The mobilization and control of the organization, in the name of any interest, are problematic endeavours.

Mechanisms for organizational control are now starting to be seen as arising out of the political and conflictive nature of organizational life. As Pfeffer (1978) has stated:

> Structure, it would appear, is not just the outcome of a managerial process in which (organizational) designs are selected to ensure higher profit. Structure, rather, is itself the outcome of a process in which conflicting interests are mediated so that decisions emerge as to what criteria the organization will seek to satisfy. Organizational structures can be viewed as the outcome of a contest

for control and influence occurring within the organization. Organizational structural arrangements are as likely to be the outcomes of political processes as are organizational resource allocation decisions.

The design of information and accounting systems are also implicated in the management of these political processes.

For out of the mass of organizational actions and their consequences, accounting systems can influence those which become relatively more visible (Becker & Neuheuser, 1975), particularly to senior management groups. And the visibility so established is very often an asymmetric one. The powerful are helped to observe the less powerful, but not vice versa, as a rather particular mode of surveillance is established, The centralized coordination of activities can thereby be established. Equally, however, demands, requirements, pressures and influences can be more readily passed down the organization, particularly in the spheres of the financial and the economic because of the disaggregative arithmetical properties of the accounting art (Hopwood, 1973). Budgeting, planning and reporting practices can together provide a framework within which a measured and observed delegation of authority can take place. A pattern of expectations can be articulated and even motivations influenced, as the visibility which is created provides a basis for organizational rewards and sanctions. Moreover by influencing the accepted language of negotiation and debate, accounting systems can help to shape what is regarded as problematic, what can be deemed a credible solution and, perhaps most important of all, the criteria which are used in their selection. For rather than being solely orientated towards the provision of information for decision making, accounting systems can influence the criteria by which other information is sifted, marshalled and evaluated.

However the consequences which accounting systems have cannot be considered to be simple reflections of the interests which might have given rise to their creation. New systems certainly can arise out of particular interests and concerns. They can be designed to make particular phenomena visible, to inculcate a particular mission or form of organizational consciousness and to help establish a particular chain of command. Indeed accountants themselves use a language which is suggestive of such ends. Nevertheless the rationales underlying their operation and functioning can differ from those which entered into their design and implementation. For once in operation, accounting systems are organizational phenomena. Indeed having their own *modus operandi* they themselves can impose constraints on organizational functioning, often contributing in the process to the effective definition of interests rather than simply expressing those which are pregiven. So although they might be able to be influenced by particular participants, accounting systems can rarely, if ever, be the exclusive domain of a single interest. Rather they become mechanisms around which interests are negotiated, counter claims articulated and political processes explicated. They may influence the language, categories, form and even timing of debate, but they can rarely exclusively influence its outcomes.

Accounting and the rationalization of action

The imperatives of the accounting mission have focused exclusively on roles for accounting which precede decision making. Even accountings for the past have been given a future rationale. However in organizations, decisions, once made, need to be justified, legitimized and rationalized. Often arising out of complex organizational processes of which few, if any, organizational participants have a comprehensive understanding (Veick, 1979) or out of those inspirational situations where both aims and causal relationships are in a state of flux (Thompson & Tuden, 1959) there is often a need for a retrospective understanding of the emergence of action, for an expression of a more synoptic organizational rationale or at least one which is seemingly consistent with formal expressions of organizational aims. And this particularly might be the case where there are dominant external interests in the decision making process (Meyer & Rowan, 1978).

Accounting systems can be and often are implicated in such organizational processes. As Bower (1970) and others have discovered, the widespread use of capital budgeting procedures has resulted in the availability of justification devices for proposals for organizational action which have gained early commitment and support as well as the simple provision of information for and prior to decision making for those proposals which remain problematic to the end. Similarly budgets and plans can be built around what is to be. Arguing more generally Meyer and Rowan (1978) note that:

> Much of the irrationality of life in modern organizations arises because the organization itself must maintain a rational corporate persona: We find planners and. economists who will waste their time legitimizing plans we have already made, accounts to justify our prices, and human relations professionals to deflect blame from our conflicts. Life in modern organizations is a constant interplay between the activities that we need to carry on and the organizational accounts we need to give.

Indeed our own inquiries and those of others suggest that quite complex accounting developments can arise out of the need to justify and legitimize. For instance Pringle (1978) has described how the pioneering work on cost-benefit analysis by British officials in mid-nineteenth century India was orientated towards justifying rather than deciding what was to be done.

Then, as now, the main *raison d'être* of cost benefit analysis, as practised, has been aimed at justifying projects rather than as a tool for investment planning... The main impetus seems to have come from the need of British civil servants in India to make a case for state investment. Given a relatively interventionist economic role recommended to the state, the development of a methodology for project evaluation was essential. It was necessary to show and to take into account the gains from state investment which did not accrue to the investing authority. Thus cost-benefit analysis served, in the case of nineteenth century India, to convince a sceptical government of the benefits, both to investors and to the society, of infra-structural projects.

In such circumstances an accounting rose to mediate between divergent interests in an organized endeavour, to legitimize and justify particular stances and, above all, to create a symbolic structure within which discourse could take place and through which action could be achieved.

Our discussion of the organizational functioning of accounting has been partial. Utilizing a particular frame of reference and a limited number of rather simple organizational metaphors, we have sought to illustrate some of the ways in which accounting is implicated in organizational action, but ignored others which might be equally vital. We have also focused on the organizational roles which accounting serves in a piecemeal fashion, discussing them sequentially rather than in combination, yet it is conceivable and indeed probable that within an organizational coalition support for accounting developments and change emerges from a variety of rationales (Banbury & Nahapiet, 1979) and that once implemented, the same accounting system can be used to serve even a different variety of ends as it is used by different actors in different ways (Hopwood, 1973). Moreover our discussion also has been restricted by the sheer lack of studies of accounting as it operates in organizations: there is so much that we do not know.

Hopefully, however, we have succeeded in demonstrating the divergence between the functional claims that are made on behalf of the accounting craft and the roles which it serves in practice. Whilst accounting can be and is acted upon in the name of its essential imperatives, it functions within that complex of political processes which constitute the organization. We have at least pointed to how the pressures to account can arise out of organizational functioning, how accounting can strive to shape conceptions of organizational reality and, in turn, how accountings and accounting systems can reflect as well as shape the pressures of action. Rather than being essential to the accounting mission, the roles which accounting serves in organizations are created, shaped and changed by the pressures of organizational life. They are implicated in action, rather than being prior to it.

ACCOUNTING AND SOCIAL PRACTICE

Accounting cannot be conceived as purely an organizational phenomenon however. Whilst arising out of organizational and institutional pressures, it is also a prevalent feature of the societies in which we live. Few accounting systems are unique to particular organizations for very long. Indeed many of the more important accounting innovations have occurred within numerous organizations at more or less the same time (Burchell *et al.*, forthcoming). Seemingly they satisfy more general searches for the extension of calculative practice which are embodied within the societies of which organizations are a part. Certainly the development of accounting itself has paralleled the emergence of numerous other specialized mechanisms for information processing and social and economic calculation, including *stat(e)* istics, the compilation of information for social and economic administration, and instruments for social and economic categorization in medicine, psychiatry, education, law and business and economic life (Baritz, 1960; Cullen, 1975; Kamin, 1974; Kendrick, 1970; Sutherland, 1977). Moreover accounting change increasingly emanates from the interplay between a series of institutions which claim a broader social significance. Often operating at a distance from the arenas in which their innovations function, those regulatory bodies, professional institutes, formal representatives of social interests and agencies of the state which increasingly shape the accounting domain are open to a very different array of social, political and economic pressures than those which directly impact on the business corporation.

Accounting, it would appear, can be intertwined with social as well as organizational practice. Unfortunately, however, very little is known about either the social nature of accounting thought and practice or the interplay between the social and the organizational. Some scholars have made occasional comments which have pointed to the social origins and significance of the accounting craft, although these have either not remained uncontested for very long or else have not been subjected to further inquiry. Yet other insights have been provided in more general historical studies of social and economic development (Kula, 1976), but those of direct relevance to accounting rarely have been explicated at length. So being all too conscious of such uncertainties, we do not intend to venture too far into the field of the unknown. Our comments on the social in accounting are brief, focusing first on the suggestions of those who have tried to appreciate the social significance of the accounting craft and thereafter on some of the implications for the development of accounting of those bodies which have claimed to have a broader social rationale.

The social significance of accounting

A multitude of different social significances have been attached to accounting. For Marx, accounting served as an ideological phenomenon. Perpetrating a form of false consciousness, it provided a means for mystifying rather than revealing the true nature of the social relationships which constitute productive endeavour.① Others, whilst adopting a less dogmatic stance, have nonetheless pointed to the mythical, symbolic and ritualistic roles of accounting (Coppock, 1977; Douglas, 1977; Gambling, 1977; Meyer, 1979; Wildavsky, 1976). In such a context accounting has been seen as implicated in the operationalization of dominant economic and social distinctions, the creation of symbolic boundaries between competing social agents and the provision of a basis on which rationales and missions can be constructed and furthered. Conveying a pattern of economic and social meanings, it has been seen to be at least partially fulfilling demands for the construction of a symbolic order within which social agents can interact.

The contribution which accounting has made to the emergence and maintenance of the particular order inherent in economic rationality was emphasised by Weber (1969) to whom (Vol. 1, p. 86):

> From a purely technical point of view, money is the most "perfect" means of economic calculation. That is, it is formally the most rational means of orienting economic activity.

In fact Weber went so far as to see rationality in terms of the calculative means which might bring it about, defining the "formal rationality of economic action" as "the extent of quantitative calculation or accounting which is technically possible and

---

① Marx saw accounting as a perfectly adequate tool for rational decision-making on the part of capitalists. This is the aspect of his thinking taken up by Most (1963) and Bailey (1978), Most even lamenting that Marx did not jetison his ideological baggage and concentrate on management accounting. However, it is important to note that Marx claimed to reveal the *social* rationality of accounting which, as is pointed out in the text, consists of its mystification of the true nature of social relationships. In *Capital*, Vol. III, Part I, p. 45, Marx states:

"The way in which surplus value is transformed into the form of profit by way of the rate of profit is, however, a further development of the inversion of subject and object that takes place already in the process of production. In the latter, we have seen, the subjective productive forces of labour appear as productive forces of capital. On the one hand, the value, or the past labour which dominates living labour, is incarnated in the capitalist. On the other hand, the labourer appears as bare material labour-power, as a commodity. Even in the simple relations of production this inverted relationship necessarily produces certain correspondingly inverted conceptions..."

which is actually applied" (1969, Vol. 1, p. 85). Whilst distinguishing between such a formal rationality and the "substantive rationality" which is implicit in action, Weber thought that the former provided an adequate means to achieve the latter. In the words of a recent commentator (Hirst, 1976, pp. 98—99):

> Only formal rationality can adjust means to ends in terms of efficiency since it provides a quantitative measure of efficiency; a *qualitative* measure of the *efficiency* of use of resources is logically impossible. *All* economic action therefore requires formal rationality and is modelled on formal rationality; resources cannot be "rationally oriented" to economic ends without quantitative calculation. *The definition of economic action defines it in terms of formal rationality.* Formal and substantive rationality are not alternative and equally "rational" calculations; end-rational action in the economic sphere requires formal calculation (emphasis in original).

The implications of that economic rationality which might be embodied within the perspectives and practices of accounting are more uncertain however. Whilst for Weber it was most likely an achievement for the good,[①] for Schumpeter (1950) it might contain the germs of the decline of the business civilization as we know it. That rational, calculating frame of mind which had served capitalism well when its rise was opposed by the "irrational" privileges of an aristocratic order could, he thought, undermine it as its critical intellectuality continued to develop, revealing "the pretensions of property to be as empty as those of the nobility" (Heilbroner, 1977). In his own words (1950, pp. 123—124):

> Once hammered in, the rational habit spreads under the pedagogic influence of favourable experiences to ... other spheres and there also opens eyes for that amazing thing, the Fact... capitalist practice turns the unit of money into a tool of rational cost-profit calculations, of which the towering monument is double entry bookkeeping ... primarily a product of the evolution of economic

---

① It may be noted that Weber did allow for the possibility of formal calculative rationality actually subverting substantive rationality by reducing the world to an arid, soulless domain of mechanical calculation. In *The Protestant Ethic and the Spirit of Capitalism* (1958, p. 182) he commented:

"In the field of its highest development, in the United States, the pursuit of wealth, stripped of its religious and ethical meaning, tends to become associated with purely mundane passions, which often actually give it the character of sport. No-one knows who will live in this cage in the future, or whether at the end of this tremendous development entirely new prophets will arise, or there will be a great rebirth of old ideas and ideals, or, if neither, mechanized petrification, embellished with a sort of convulsive self-importance. For at the last stage of this cultural development, it might well be truly said: 'Specialists without spirit, sensualists without heart; this nullity imagines that it has attained a level of civilization never before achieved.'"

rationality, the cost-profit calculus in turn reacts upon that rationality; by crystallizing and defining numerically, it powerfully propels the logic of enterprise. And thus defined and quantified for the economic sector, this type of logic or attitude or method then starts upon its conqueror's career subjugating—rationalizing—man's tools and philosophies, his medical practice, his picture of the cosmos, his outlook on life, everything in fact including his concepts of beauty and justice and his spiritual ambitions.

Other commentators on the social roles and significance of accounting have adopted a less macroscopic stance, often emphasising the enabling functions of the accounting craft. Although some have stressed the roles which it plays in allowing the devolution and decentralization of economic decision making, others have pointed to the rather different internal pressures to account when decision making is centralized, either in the hands of the monolithic enterprise (Chandler, 1962) or the state (Bettleheim, 1976). And consideration has been given to the ways in which accounting has enabled the operationalization and furtherance of particular concepts of efficiency through the introduction of management methods which have reconstituted the enterprise, separating the conception and control of the task from its practical execution (Braverman, 1974).

In this arena of inquiry the thoughts of a few undoubtedly have constructed an agenda of enormous complexity and potential significance, the validity of a lot of which remains to be tested. Looking beyond the immediate implications of the accounting craft, they have searched for a more general social significance, often, as non accountants, seeing accounting as an agent for the furtherance of particular concepts of rational action. Accounting has been seen as both reflecting and enabling the construction of society as we now know it, with both institutional forms and modes of social action intertwined with its emergence and development.

Accounting and the institutions for the regulation of the accounting craft

Very different aspects of the social functioning of accounting have been highlighted by our growing awareness of the processes inherent in accounting regulation. At one time seen in terms of technical elucidation and standardization, attention has now been devoted to the institutional and political components of the regulatory endeavour. For operating as they do at the nexus between the institutions of a professionalized craft, centralized bodies for the representation of social interests, the dominant partnerships of the accounting profession and the interested agencies of the state, those organizations which have a claim to regulate and standardize accounting are open to very different pressures from those which impinge on the organizations in which accounting is practiced. With the locus and form of regulation being subject to debate and change, the technical components of standardization have become intertwined with the desire to gain institutional legitimacy and support. Attention has had to be given to the origins of a diverse array of interests in the development of accounting and, as this has happened, the roles embodied in accounting change have been seen as being ever more implicated in the political pressures which have given rise to its emergence.

In the United Kingdom, for instance, we have witnessed how the institutional mechanisms for accounting regulation arose at the interface between a critical media, concerned agencies of the state and a profession concerned with preserving its powers of self-regulation and control (Zeff, 1972). And although often formally advocated in the name of the user's interests, the articulation of accounting standards has continued to reflect the dynamics of the institutional context of which they are an outgrowth.

The case of inflation accounting is a particularly interesting example of such forces at work. Here the fact of an inflationary economy was certainly a stimulus for change (Mumford, 1979). But that fact alone is not enough to provide an understanding of the emergence of the issue, the processes of the debate or its provisional outcomes. For arising out of the questioning of the state of accounting regulation and the emergent relationships between the accounting profession, the agencies of the state and industrial and commercial interests, the development of methods for the adjustment of financial accounting in an inflationary context has been influenced by a varied and changing number of issues and interests which either stimulated action or were called upon to legitimize particular stances and proposals. In this constellation, the changing interests of the state have been particularly important. At first inflation accounting was of interest to those administrative agencies which were concerned with the taxation of corporate income and the formulation of policies for macro-economic management. In those contexts, it was seen as being able to play rather particular roles, which could be favourably or unfavourably evaluated. Thereafter, however, other agencies of the state started to devote more explicit attention to the roles which inflation accounting might play in the implementation and furtherance of micro-economic policies for industrial recovery and growth. During its turbulent career other interested parties also have devoted attention to the roles which inflation accounting might or might not play in coping with both an economic crisis and a concurrent threat of a changing social power structure. Embodied within such a context, the inflation accounting debate has reflected pressures at both the social and the organizational levels. Some of the issues with which it has become implicated had no *a prioti* relationship to the accounting craft and others have stemmed from the pressures of accounting regulation rather than its organizational practice. In such ways the potential roles which have at times given momentum to the debate have changed in both scope and level of institutional significance. Indeed only together rather than singly can they offer some basis for gaining an appreciation of the dynamics of the debate and those technical changes in accounting which are (or are not) likely to emerge.

Other accounting changes have had not dissimilar patterns of development. In some European countries, for instance, the centralization of accounting policy making has both enhanced and been enabled by the growing interest of the organized labour movement in information disclosure. And elsewhere we have noted the pressures which have created roles for accounting and accounting changes in the context of the conduct of war and the management of the national economy (Hopwood *et al.*, 1979).

In a regulatory environment, the conditions for accounting change are complex indeed. Whilst both technical and conceptual developments are required, to be influential they have to root themselves in a dynamic constellation of issues which constitutes the accounting context. In that constellation, both practice and the roles and functions which it serves and is seen as serving are subject to change as new issues emerge, new linkages to accounting established and new needs for the standardization of accounting practice arise. With so many of these pressures emerging from institutions which at least claim a broader social significance, the roles which can be associated with an accounting change can be different from those which subsequently might be implicated with its actual operation and use.

CONCLUSION AND IMPLICATIONS FOR THE PURSUIT OF ACCOUNTING RESEARCH

Our discussion of the organizational and social roles of accounting has tried to identify an area of enormous and largely uncharted complexity. Whilst the development of accounting has resulted in the attribution of formal roles for accounting which can be and are used to evaluate and change the accounting craft, our analyses have attempted to show how the actual practice of accounting can be implicated with the furtherance of many and very different sets of human and social ends. At the organizational level, we have emphasised how roles can be created for accounting within the context of the development of other forms of management practice, how accounting systems, as modes of organizational control, can arise out of the interplay of political processes both within the organization and at its interface with dominant external agents, and how accountings can emerge out of decisions rather than necessarily having to precede them. At the societal level, our discussion has been more tentative. However we have at least considered some of the views of those who have attributed quite a substantive social significance to the functioning of accounting. In a far more provisional manner, consideration also has been given to the roles which accounting change can play in a regulatory context.

In these ways we have chosen to give particular emphasis to the distinction between the imperatives which are articulated on behalf of accounting and those roles which it is made to serve in the context of organizational and social functioning. Whilst the former are inherently purposeful, often being used to give rise to accounting change, we have emphasised how organizational and social actors making accounting purposive. Seeing thereby the roles which accounting serves as being intertwined in the contexts in which it operates, we also have pointed to the diversity of functions which can be associated with even a single accounting. The pressures which give rise to its existence can themselves be both numerous and conflicting, and different from those which are used for its formal justification. Once implemented, an accounting becomes an organizational and social phenomenon, there to be used for a variety of ends by a range of actors in an organization.

Unfortunately our thoughts have had to remain tentative and suggestive for as yet all too little is known about accounting in action. The number of empirical studies of the organizational operation of accounting systems is few indeed, and even less is known about either the operation of regulatory bodies in the accounting area or the broader social context of accounting development and change. Until recently scholars interested in accounting have been seemingly content to accept the ends which have been claimed on its behalf, focusing their efforts on the further refinement of the craft. We do not necessarily criticize such an orientation, but we would claim that a case also can be made for the study *of* accounting as a social and organizational phenomenon to complement the more prevalent analyses which operate *within* the accounting context.

Not that such studies would be without problems. As we are already becoming aware, a questioning of what has not been questioned can be challenging to existing interests. Like other modes of inquiry, it too has the potential to change our conceptions of the accounting craft.

However, assuming that there is some willingness to investigate accounting as it functions, what types of inquiries might be required? There is, we think, a real need for more historical studies of the development of accounting. Just how has accounting

THE ROLES OF ACCOUNTING IN ORGANIZATIONS AND SOCIETY

come to function as we now know it? What social issues and agents have been involved with its emergence and development? How has it become intertwined with other aspects of social life? And what consequences might it be seen as having had? For until recently, we should remember, there have been relatively few social analyses of accounting change and the emergence of the new. Rather than inquiring into the mechanisms of change, scholars apparently have been more interested in studying the sequence and correlates of change. More emphasis has been placed on chronological accounts of technical developments *per se* than on the processes which gave rise to their existence and significance. And similar needs exist at the organizational level. In fact it is quite staggering to reflect on how few studies there are of the organizational functioning of accounting, particularly in light of the fact that most of what do exist have adopted a relatively short time horizon, focusing on the uses which are made and not made of accounting systems rather than the conditions which gave rise to their existence. Just how, we wonder, has accounting become implicated in the functioning of the modern large scale, hierarchical organization? How have particular systems arisen out of organizational processes and actions? What actions have been involved with their design, implementation and operation? And what have been the mechanisms for innovation, change and diffusion?

Such inquiries call for theoretical as well as methodological innovation. Scholars of the behavioural in accounting, for instance, would have to be prepared to move beyond the social psychological perspectives which have dominated their inquiries to date. In searching for the organizational and social significance rather than the human use of their craft they would have to be willing to confront those uncertainties which still characterize our knowledge of organizational behaviour and social action. Consideration would need to be given to the roles which information and accounting play in the political processes which characterize organizational and social life, to those forces which have constituted the organization as we now know it and to the ways in which the social and the organization in accounting intertwine with each other. Appeals would have to be made to very different frames of reference and bodies of knowledge. And above all it would have to be recognized that for the foreseeable future at least the different perspectives which are conceivable and available would produce very different insights, problems and leads.

Initially such developments cannot help but produce enormous uncertainties for accounting inquiry. And for that reason alone, some may not want to venture along the route. We nevertheless believe that such changes in orientation are required if scholarly inquiry is to explicate theories of accounting which can help us to appreciate the social and organizational significances which it has had and is capable of having.

BIBLIOGRAPHY

Ackoff, R. L., Management Misinformation Systems, *Management Science* (October, 1967), pp. B147—156.

Ansari, S. L., Towards an Open Systems Approach to Budgeting, *Accounting, Organizations and Society* (1979), pp. 149—161;

Anthony, R. N., *Planning and Control Systems: A Framework for Analysis* (Harvard Business School, 1965).

Argyris, C., Management Information Systems: The Challenge to Rationality and Emotionality, *Management Science* (1971), pp. B275—292.

Argyris, C., Single Loop and Double Loop Models in Research on Decision Making, *Administrative Science Quarterly* (September, 1976), pp. 363—375.

Argyris, C., Organizational Learning and Management Information Systems, *Accounting, Organizations and Society* (1977), pp. 113—123.

Argyris, C. & Schon, D. A., *Organizational Learning: A Theory of Action Perspective* (Addison-Wesley, 1974).

Bailey, D. T., Marx on Accounting, *The Accountant* (January 5th, 1978).

Ball, R. & Brown, P., An Empirical Evaluation of Accounting Income Numbers, *Journal of Accounting Research* (Autumn, 1968), pp. 159—178.

Banbury, J. & Nahapiet, J. E., Towards a Framework for the Study of the Antecedents and Consequences of Information Systems in Organizations, *Accounting, Organizations and Society* (1979), pp. 163—177.

Bariff, M. L. & Galbraith, J., Intraorganizational Power Considerations for Designing Information Systems, *Accounting, Organizations and Society*, (1978), pp. 15—28.

Baritz, L., *The Servants of Power* (Wesleyn University Press, 1960).

Batstone, E., Management and Industrial Democracy, in *Industrial Democracy: International Views* (Industrial Relations Research Unit, Warwick University, 1978).

Baumler, J. V., Defined Criteria of Performance in Organizational Control, *Administrative Science Quarterly* (September, 1971), pp. 340—350.

Baxter, W. T., Introduction, in W. T. Baxter (ed.) *Selected Papers on Accounting* (Arno Press, 1978).

Becker, S. W. & Neuheuser, D., *The Efficient Organization* (North-Holland, 1975).

Benston, G. J., *Corporate Financial Disclosure in the UK and the USA* (Saxon House, 1976).

Bettleheim, C., *Economic Calculation and Forms of Property* (Routledge & Kegan Paul, 1976).

Bowe, C. (ed.), *Industrial Efficiency and the Role of Government* (London, H.M.S.O., 1977).

Bower, J., *Managing the Resource Allocation Process* (Graduate School of Business Administration, Harvard University, 1970).

Braverman, H., *Labour and Monopoly Capital* (Monthly Review Press, 1974).

Brown, R. (ed.), *History of Accounting and Accountants* (Jack, 1905).

Bruns, W. J. & Waterhouse, J. H., Budgetary Control and Organization Structure, *Journal of*

Accounting Research (Autumn, 1975), pp. 177—203.

Burchell, S., Clubb, C. & Hopwood, A. G., Accounting in Its Social Context: Towards a History of Value Added in the UK (forthcoming).

Cammann, C., Effects of the Use of Control Systems, *Accounting, Organizations and Society* (1976), pp. 301—313.

Chandler, A., *Strategy and Structure* (MIT Press, 1962).

Chandler, A. & Daems, H., Administrative Co-ordination, Allocation and Monitoring: A Comparative Analysis of the Emergence of Accounting and Organization in the USA and Europe, *Accounting, Organizations and Society* (1979), pp. 3—20.

Chapman, R. L., *Project Management in NASA: The System and the Men* (NASA, 1973).

Chatfield, M., *The History of Accounting Thought* (Krieger, 1977).

Child, J., Strategies of Control and Organization Behaviour, *Administrative Science Quarterly* (1973), pp. 1—17.

Child, J., Management and Organizational Factors Associated with Company Performance—Part I, *Journal of Management Studies* (1974), pp. 175—189.

Child, J., Management and Organizational Factors Associated with Company Performance—Part II, *Journal of Management Studies* (1975), pp. 12—27.

Churchman, C. W., *The Design of Inquiring Systems* (Basic Books, 1971).

Cohen, M. D., March, J. G. & Olsen, J. P., A Garbage Can Model of Organizational Choice, *Administrative Science Quarterly* (March, 1972), pp. 1—25.

Coppock, R., Life Among the Environmentalists, *Accounting, Organizations and Society* (1977), pp. 125—130.

Cullen, M. J., *The Statistical Movement in Early Victorian Britain* (Harvester, 1975).

Cyert, R. M. & March, J. G., *A Behavioural Theory of the Firm* (Prentice-Hall, 1963).

Daft, R. L. & MacIntosh, N. B., A New Approach to Design and Use of Management Information, *California Mananement Review* (Fall, 1978), pp. 82—92.

Dalton, M., *Men Who Manage* (Wiley, 1959).

Demski, J. S., The General Impossibility of Normative Accounting Standards, *The Accounting Review* (October, 1973), pp. 718—723.

Douglas, M., Accounting and Anthropology, Unpublished opening address to the Social Science Research Council Conference on Accounting Research, Oxford, 1977.

Dyckman, T., Downes, D. & Magee, R. P., *Efficient Capital Markets and Accounting: A Critical Analysis* (Prentice-Hall, 1975).

Earl, M. J. & Hopwood, A. G., From Management Information to Information Management, A paper presented to the IFIP TCR-WG8.2 Working Conference on the Information Systems Environment, Bonn, 1979.

Edey, H. C. & Panitpakdi, P., British Company Accounting and the Law, in A. C. Littleton and B. S. Yamey, *Studies in the History of Accounting* (Irwin, 1956).

Epstein, M. J., *The Effect of Scientific Management on the Development of the Standard Cost System*, Doctoral Dissertation, University of Oregon, 1973.

Foucault, M., *Discipline and Punish* (Allen Lane, 1977).

Galbraith, J., *Designing Complex Organizations* (Addison-Wesley, 1973).

Galbraith, J. K., *The New Industrial State* (Houghton Mifflin, 1967).

Gambling, T., Magic, Accounting and Morale, *Accounting, Organizations and Society* (1977), pp. 141—153.

Gandhi, N. W., The Emergence of the Postindustrial Society and the Future of the Accounting Function, *The International Journal of Accounting Education and Research* (Spring, 1976), pp. 33—50.

Garner, S. P., *Evolution of Cost Accounting to 1925* (University of Alabama Press, 1954).

Georgiou, P., The Goal Paradigm and Notes Towards a Counter Paradigm, *Administrative Science Quarterly* (1973), pp. 291—310.

Gilling, D. M., Accounting and Social Change, *The International Journal of Accounting Education and Research* (Spring, 1976), pp. 59—72.

Gorry, G. A. & Scott-Morton, M. S., A Framework for Management Information Systems, *Sloan Management Review* (Fall, 1971).

Gouldner, A. W., Cosmopolitans and Locals: Toward an Analysis of Latent Social Roles, *Administrative Science Quarterly* (1957), pp. 281—306.

Grinyer, P. & Norburn, D., Planning for Existing Markets: Perceptions of Executive and Financial Performance, *Journal of the Royal Statistical Society* (Series A, 1975), pp. 70—97.

Haber, S., *Efficiency and Uplift* (University of Chicago Press, 1964).

Hacking, I., *Why Does Language Matter to Philosophy?* (Cambridge University Press, 1975).

Hawkins, D. F., The Development of Modern Financial Reporting Practices Among American Manufacturing Corporations, *Business History Review* (Autumn, 1963), pp. 135—168.

Hays, S., *Conservation and the Gospel of Efficiency* (Harvard University Press, 1959).

Hedberg, B. & Mumford, E., The Design of Computer Systems: Man's Vision of Man as an Integral Part of the System Design Process, in E. Mumford and H. Sackman (eds.), *Human Choice and Computers* (North-Holland, 1975).

Heilbroner, R. L., *Business Civilization in Decline* (Penguin Books, 1977).

Heydebrand, W., Organizational Contradictions in Public Bureaucracies: Toward a Marxian Theory of Organizations, in J. K. Benson (ed.), *Organizational Analysis: Critique and Innovation* (Sage Publications, 1977).

Hirst, P. Q., *Social Evolution and Sociological Categories* (George Allen and Unwin, 1976).

Hopwood, A. G., *An Accounting System and Managerial Behaviour* (Saxon House and Lexington, 1973).

Hopwood, A. G., *Accounting and Human Behaviour* (Haymarket Publishing, 1974).

Hopwood, A. G., Towards an Organizational Perspective for the Study of Accounting and Information Systems, *Accounting, Organizations and Society* (1978), pp. 3—14.

Hopwood, A. G., Information Systems and Organizational Reality, Occasional Paper No. 5, Thames Valley Regional Management Centre, forthcoming.

Hopwood, A. G., Burchell, S., Clubb, C., The Development of Accounting in its International Context: Past Concerns and Emergent Issues, A paper presented at the Third Charles Waldo Haskins Seminar on Accounting History, Atlanta, April 20, 1979.

Horngren, C. T., The Marketing of Accounting Standards, *The Journal of Accountancy* (October, 1973).

Johnson, H. T., Management Accounting in an Early Multinational Organization: General Motors in the 1920's, *Business History Review* (*1978*), pp. 490—517.

Jones, R. & Lain, C., *The Carpetmakers* (McGraw-Hill, 1978).

Kamin, L. J., *The Science and Politics of IQ* (Penguin, 1974).

Kendrick, J. W., The Historical Development of National Income Accounts, *History of Political Economy* (1970), Vol. 2, No. 3.

Khandwalla, P. N., The Effect of Different Types of Competition on the Use of Management Controls, *Journal of Accounting Research* (Autumn, 1972), pp. 275—285.

Khandwalla, P., Crisis Responses of Competing Versus Noncompeting Organizations, in C. F. Smart and W. T. Stanbury (eds.), *Studies in Crisis Management* (Institute for Research on Public Policy, Toronto, 1978), pp. 151—178.

Kuhn, T., *The Structure of Scientific Revolutions* (2nd Edition, enlarged; University of Chicago Press, 1970).

Kula, W., *An Economic Theory of the Feudal System* (New Left Books, 1976).

Litterer, J. A., Systematic Management: The Search for Order and Integration, *Business History Review* (1961), pp. 461—476.

Litterer, J. A., Systematic Management: Design for Organizational Recoupling in American Manufacturing Firms, *Business History-Review* (1963), pp. 369—391.

Littleton, A. C., *Accounting Evolution to 1900* (American Institute Publishing Co., 1933).

Littleton, A. C., *Structure of Accounting Theory* (American Accounting Association, 1953).

Meyer, J. & Rowan, B., The Structure of Educational Organizations, in M. W. Meyer *et al.* (eds.), *Environments and Organizations* (Jossey-Bass, 1978).

Meyer, J., Environmental and Internal Origins of Symbolic Structure in Organizations, Paper presented at the Seminar on, Organizations as Ideological Systems, Stockholm, 1979.

Mintzberg, H., *The Nature of Managerial Work* (Harper and Row, 1973).

Mitzberg, H., *Impediments to the Use of Management Information* (NAA, 1975).

Moonitz, M., *Obtaining Agreement on Standards in the Accounting Profession* (American Accounting Association, 1974).

Most, K. S., Marx and Management Accounting, *The Accountant* (August 17, 1963).

Mumford, M., The End of a Familiar Inflation Accounting Cycle, *Accounting and Business Research* (Spring, 1979), pp. 98—104.

Otley, D. T., Budget Use and Managerial Performance, *Journal of Accounting Research* (Spring, 1978), pp. 122—149.

Olofsson, C. & Svalander, P. A., The Medical Services Change Over to a Poor Environment— "New Poor" Behaviour, Unpublished working paper, University of Linköping, 1975.

Pettigrew, A. M., *The Politics of Organizational Decision Making* (Tavistock, 1973).

Pettigrew, A. M., The Creation of Organizational Cultures, Working Paper, European Institute for Advanced Studies in Management, Brussels, 1977.

Pfeffer, J., The Micropolitics of Organizations, in M. W. Meyer, *Environment and Organizations* (Jossey-Bass, 1978).

Pfeffer, J. & Salancik, G. R., Organizational Decision Making as a Political Process, *Administrative Science Quarterly* (June, 1974), pp. 135—151.

Pollard, S., *The Genesis of Modern Management* (Edward Arnold, 1965).

Popper, K. P., *Objective Knowledge: An Evolutionary Approach* (Oxford University Press, 1972).

Posner, R. A., Theories of Economic Regulation, *The Bell Journal of Economics and Management Science* (Autumn, 1974), pp. 335—359.

Pringle, G., The Early Development of Cost-Benefit Analysis, *Journal of Agricultural Economics* (January, 1978), pp. 63—71.

Rahman, M. & McCosh, A. M., The Influence of Organizational and Personal Factors on the Use of Accounting Information: An Empirical Study, *Accounting, Organizations and Society* (1976), pp. 339—355.

Rose, N., Fetishism and Ideology: A Review of Theoretical Problems, *Ideology and Consciousness* (Autumn, 1977).

Rosner, M. M., Administrative Controls and Innovation, *Behavioural Science* (1968), pp. 36—43.

Sathe, V., Contemporary Theory of Organization Structure, in J. L. Livingstone (ed.), *Managerial Accounting: The Behavioural Foundations* (Grid Publishing, 1975).

Sayles, L., & Chandler, M. K., *Managing Large Systems* (Harper and Row, 1971).

Schumpeter, J. A., *Capitalism, Socialism and Democracy* (3rd ed.; Harper and Row, 1950).

Searle, G. R., *The Quest for National Efficiency* (Blackwell, 1971).

Shortell, S. M. & Brown, M. (eds.), *Organizational Research in Hospitals* (Blue Cross, 1976).

Simon, H. A., *The New Science of Management Decision* (Harper and Row, 1960).

Singer, H. W., *Standardized Accounting in Germany* (National Institute for Economic and Social Research Occasional Paper V; Cambridge University Press, 1943).

Studenski, P., *The Income of Nations* (New York: 1959).

Sutherland, G., The Magic of Measurement, *Transactions of the Royal Historical Society* (1977), 5th Series, Vol. 27.

ten Have, O., *The History of Accountancy* (Bay Books, 1976).

Thompson, J. D., *Organizations in Action* (McGraw-Hill, 1967).

Thompson, J. D. & Tuden, A., Strategies, Structures and Processes of Organizational Decision, in J. D. Thompson et al. (eds.), *Comparative Studies in Administration* (University of Pittsburgh Press, 1959).

Turcotte, W. E., Control Systems, Performance and Satisfaction in Two State Agencies, *Administrative Science Quarterly* (1974), pp. 60—73.

Waterhouse, J. H. & Teissen, P., A Contingency Framework for Management Accounting Systems Research, *Accounting, Organizations and Society* (1978), pp. 65—76.

Watson, D. J. H., Contingency Formulations of Organizational Structure: Implications for Managerial Accounting, in J. L. Livingstone, *Managerial Accounting: The Behavioural Foundations* (Grid, 1975).

Watts, R. & Zimmerman, J. L., Towards a Positive Theory of the Determination of Accounting Standards, *The Accounting Review* (January, 1978), pp. 112—134.

Watts, R. & Zimmerman, J. L., The Demand for and Supply of Accounting Theories: The Market for Excuses, *The Accounting Review* (April, 1979), pp. 273—305.

Weber, M., *The Protestant Ethic and the Spirit of Capitalism* (Charles Scribner & Sons, 1958).

Weber, M., *Economy and Society* (3 Vols) (Bedminster Press, 1969).

Weick, K., *The Social Psychology of Organizing* (2nd ed., Addison-Wesley, 1979).

Wells, M. C., *Accounting for Common Costs* (International Centre for Accounting Education and Research, 1978).

Wildavsky, A., The *Politics of the Budgetary Process* (Little, Brown, 1965).

Wildavsky, A., Economy and Environment/Rationality and Ritual: A Review Essay, *Accounting, Organizations and Society* (1976), pp. 117—129.

Wildavsky, A., Policy Analysis is What Information Systems are Not, *Accounting, Organizations and Society* (1978), pp. 77—88.

Winston, C. & Hall, M., The Ambiguous Notion of Efficiency, The *Economic Journal* (1959).

Yamey, B. S., Pious Inscriptions: Confused Accounts; Classification of Accounts: Three Historical Notes, in H. Edey and B. S. Yamey (eds.), *Debits, Credits, Finance and Profits* (Sweet and Maxwell, 1974).

Zeff, S. A., *Forging Accounting Principles in Five Countries: A History and an Analysis of Trends* (Stipes Publishing Company, 1972).

Zeff, S. A., The Rise of Economic Consequences, *The Journal of Accountancy* (December, 1978), pp. 56—63.

Accounting in Its Social Context:

Towards a History of Value Added in the United Kingdom*

STUART BURCHELL

(Borough of Greenwich)

COLIN CLUBB

(Department of Management Science, Imperial College, London)

and

ANTHONY G. HOPWOOD

(London Business School)

Abstract: Although the relationship between accounting and society has been posited frequently, it has been subjected to little systematic analysis. This paper reviews some existing theories of the social nature of accounting practice and, by so doing, identifies a number of significant conceptual problems. Using the case of the rise of interest in value added accounting in the United Kingdom in the 1970s, the paper conducts a social analysis of this particular event and then seeks to draw out the theoretical issues and problems which emerge from this exercise. Finally, the implications of these for the social analysis of accounting are discussed.

Accounting is coming to be seen as a social rather than a purely technical phenomenon. The social contexts of the accounting craft are starting to be both recognised and made more problematic. Albeit slowly, the ways in which accounting both emerges from and itself gives rise to the wider contexts in which it operates are starting to be appreciated. Accounting, in turn, also has come to be more actively and explicitly recognised as an instrument for social management and change. Attempts

---

* *Accounting, Organizations and Society*, Vol. 10, No. 4, pp. 381—413, 1985. We wish to acknowledge the helpful comments of George Benston, Wai Fong Chua, David Cooper, Jeremy Dent, Dick Hoffman, John Hughes, Janine Nahapiet and Ted O'Leary. The financial support of the Anglo-German Foundation for the Study of Industrial Society is gratefully appreciated. One of the authors wishes to acknowledge the facilitative and supportive environment provided by the College of Business Administration, Pennsylvania State University, which greatly eased the final writing up of this study.

have been made to reform accounting in the name of its social potential. Proposals have been made for accounting to embrace the realm of the social as well as the economic, to objectify, quantify and thereby give a particular insight into the social functioning of organizations. To this end, attempts have been made to orchestrate social accountings, social reports, social audits, socioeconomic statements, social cost-benefit analyses and accountings of the human resource.

However, despite such apparent manifestations of an intertwining of accounting with the social, relatively little is known of the social functioning of the accounting craft (Hopwood, 1985). Accounting seemingly remains embedded in the realm of the technical. Although it is now recognised that the social can influence the technical practice of accounting and that that, in turn. can mobilise and change the world of the social. the processes by which these intersections take place have been subject to hardly any investigation. Accounting has not been explored in the name of its social functioning or potential. The social has been brought into contact with accounting but the intermingling of the two has not been explored. As a result, little is known of how the technical practices of accounting are tethered to the social, of how wider social forces can impinge upon and change accounting, and of how accounting itself functions in the realm of the social, influencing as well as merely reacting to it. For to date the relationship of accounting to the social has tended to be stated and presumed rather than described and analysed. [1]

Recognising the very significant gap in present understandings, the present discussion merely aims to illustrate and discuss one specific instance of the intertwining of accounting and the social, namely the rise of interest in value added accounting in the United Kingdom during the 1970s. The contours of this event are outlined and an analysis conducted of the wider arenas in which such a form of accounting came to function. Drawing on this analysis, an attempt thereafter is made to explicate some of the implications for an understanding of the emergence of value added accounting in particular and the social functioning of accounting more generally. Initially, however, we discuss some existing understandings of accounting's relationship to the social. Our aim in so doing is to provide a basis for appreciating both the possibilities for and the difficulties of conducting a social investigation of the accounting craft.

---

[1] One noteworthy exception to this tendency has been the work of Tinker. See Tinker (1980). Tinker et al. (1982). Tinker (1984) and Neimark & Tinker (forthcoming). Although there are a number of significant differences between the work of Tinker and ourselves, we nevertheless recognise the pioneering attempts he and his colleagues have made to investigate the social origins and functioning of accounting practice. Also see Cooper (1981).

ACCOUNTING AND SOCIAL CHANGE

No doubt reflecting the more general concerns of the social responsibility movement (Ackerman & Bauer, 1976; Vogel, 1978), a literature emerged during the 1970s which concerned itself more or less directly with the impact of social change on accounting (e.g. Bedford, 1970; Estes, 1973; Gambling, 1974; Gordon, 1978; Livingstone & Gunn, 1974; Vangermeersch, 1972). However, although a social challenge to accounting thereby was recognised. most of this literature accepted both the fact of social change and its relevance to accounting, seeking primarily to change and reform accounting in the name of its social context. Despite a proliferation in pleas, suggestions and possibilities for different accountings, very few attempts were made to explicate and develop any general description and characterisation of the processes involved in the interaction of accounting with its social context. Technical reform took precedence over social understanding once a necessity for change had been stated.

Gilling (1976) was one exception to this tendency. Although he too notes the fact of and argues the necessity for accounting change under the impact of environmental (social and technical) change, Gilling also attempted to provide some understanding of the underlying social and institutional forces at work. His animating concern was the lag that he perceived to have arisen in the adaptation process. Gilling argued that accounting change was lagging behind environmental change as a consequence of the incapacity of the accounting professions to decide, or rather agree, on the appropriate modifications to be made in accounting practice. This immobilisation of the agency of accounting change stemmed in turn from the absence of any one dominant point of view on accounting, or of what Gilling termed accounting "ideology"①. Thus the process of adjustment of accounting practice to changes in its environment was blocked not because accounting theory was in some sense inadequate but because of the clash of interests as they were represented by the different ac-

---

① Gilling (1976, p.69) defined ideology in the following terms:

All professions have a defining ideology. which in a general sense establishes a pattern of thought and a way of looking at the world for the profession. This pattern of thought defines the activity of the profession, its problems, and appropriate ways of approaching those problems. The behaviour of a profession towards its environment is a matter of perception of that environment. Once an image of that environment has been established, then behaviour will be determined by that image and the frame of reference that it creates. As long as image and perception are appropriate to the real world. behaviour will be appropriate to the real world. If perception does not correspond to the real world, behaviour will be inappropriate and irrelevant.

ACCOUNTING IN ITS SOCIAL CONTEXT

counting ideologies. Each of these alone "could provide order and direction to accounting endeavour" (p. 70) but each also "provides little possibility of reconciliation or comprise with other views". According to Gilling the net effect of this impasse was that both the autonomy and the expertise of the accounting professions were under challenge—there existed a crisis:

> As a result of its failure to react to new environmental circumstances the accounting profession is facing something of a crisis; a crisis in part of public confidence and in part of identity (Gilling, 1976, p. 64).

Thus within Gilling's framework, accounting appears as something marked off from its environment. With the passage of time, the latter requires the former to change. Accounting thereby is seen to be something that is and certainly should be a reflective phenomenon. As the environment develops or evolves it requires accounting to fulfil different needs. The process of accounting change passes through the accounting professions and depends on their perceptions to determine precisely what adjustment is necessary. These perceptions are, in turn, structured by particular world views or ideologies which amongst other things are characterised by a number of assumptions concerning the basic properties, purposes and functions of accounting. ①

Such a contingent perspective of accounting change is common to most discussions of the topic (see, for example, Bedford, 1970; Chambers, 1966; Flint, 1971). It is, however, open to enormous variation in its details, with considerable differences in the specification of the environmental changes to which accounting must respond. ② Gilling's own specification was not very precise. He argued that the principal environment change in the last forty years has been "the recognition of the

---

① Gilling (1976, p. 69) elaborated his views on the different and conflicting ideologies of accounting in the following way:

> Within accounting there is a latent ideological clash, frequently on issues of topical and lasting concern, between those who support the utilitarian view of accounting with its consequent piecemeal, case-by-case approach to the development of principles and practices, and those who seek to provide a sound, consistent theoretical base, to which all principles and practices can be related. Within those who are theory-orientated there exists further considerable differences of opinion between the current cash equivalents, the value to the owner, and the replacement cost schools of thought. To further cloud the issues there is the clash between those who see accounting as technology and those who see it as policy making.

② Even when there is some agreement over the specification of the environmental change, the significance attached to it may vary. There is, for example, no sense of threat or crisis in Churchill's (1973) comments on the search for corporate social responsibility and the concomitant emergence of a plethora of different social indicators and measurement techniques. There is rather a sense of an opportunity for the expansion of the accounting domain.

public character of accounting information" (Gilling, 1976, p. 65). This, he continued, had arisen out of public concern over the activities of the business corporation, as evidenced at the time of his writing by the debate over corporate social responsibility. The consequent search by the accounting profession for ways to improve the accuracy and utility of published financial statements resulted in, amongst other things, the creation of institutions for accounting standardization and regulation, themselves a significant new part of the accounting environment.① Others have identified the growing power of labour (Barratt Brown, 1978; Carlsson et al., 1978; Gold et al., 1979; Hird, 1975) the increasing recognition of consumer rights (Medawar, 1978; Vogel, 1978) the acknowledgment of significant enternalities associated with the conduct of business (Estes, 1976; Frankel, 1978; Ramanathan, 1976) and changing political conceptions of corporate accountability as being amongst the important environmental changes which have influenced or should influence accounting theory and practice. Moreover for Gandhi (1976, 1978) environmental developments were characterised in terms of the emergence of the non-market economy. For him, the significance of this development was that it has increasingly made accounting an inadequate means of rational action given its unidimensional monetary character. Gandhi exhorted accountants to "come to a collective realization that there is more to performance evaluation than financial indicators" (Gandhi, 1978).

The notion of the environment implicit in such contingent theories of accounting change is therefore a diffuse and only partially articulated one. Given the significance attached to accounting being or desirably being a reflective phenomenon, this introduces a large element of indeterminacy into such understandings of accounting change. Whilst, imperatives for change are recognised②, the means for their explication and influence remain imprecise and relatively unexamined.

A different perspective on accounting change is provided by Wells (1976). In

---

① Other commentators and theorists would fully agree with Gilling in identifying the emergence of such institutions of accounting regulation as being crucial for the subsequent development of accounting practice. However, different analyses would put the functioning of these bodies in an altogether different light. For Watts & Zimmerman (1978,1979), for instance, accounting regulation appears as a wasteful and ill-fated maladaption (Also see Watts, 1977). The search for an agreed set of accounting principles on which to base regulation is doomed to failure because the different accounting ideologies discussed by Gilling mask a mass of necessarily different interests which are rooted in the different positions individuals occupy in the business environment. Further, the accounting standards actually reduce social welfare because of the existence of significant political transactions costs which mean that bureaucrats cannot in general be assumed to act in the public interest. Also see Benston (1969, 1976, 1983). For a different view of the emergence and functioning of these bodies and their interest in and utilization of knowledge, see Hopwood (1984).

② For a critique of the notion of accounting imperatives see Burchell et al. (1980).

a sense Wells turns the contingency model on its head. He argues that the present crisis in accounting is less a question of a lack of adaption, on the part of accounting, to a changing environment, but more a product of virtually autonomous developments within accounting theory. Basing his analysis on the work of Kuhn (1970), Wells argues that a distinct, identifiable accounting disciplinary matrix emerged for the first time in the 1940s. This disciplinary matrix provided the framework for the work of normal science which subsequently, under the impact of criticism "by scholars, businessmen and in the courts", brought to light a number of anomalies within the body of accounting theory and it is these anomalies which engendered a crisis. During the 1960s and 1970s so the argument goes, a series of *ad hoc* attempts were made to deal with the anomalies and criticisms. In part, at least, this resulted in a more general concern for the theoretical basis of accounting which, amongst other things, led to the 1960s being described as the "golden age in the history of *a priori* research in accounting" (Nelson, 1973, p. 4). However, far from resolving difficulties, these works of high theory instead served to "highlight the defects of the disciplinary matrix and loosen the grip of tradition". As a result there emerged a number of different schools of thought which tended to have different axiomatic starting points and were thus difficult to compare.① Each of these schools is in principle a candidate for a new disciplinary matrix, however, and Wells looks forward to the next stage in the development of accounting thought in which, according to Kuhn's schema, there "will be 'an increasing shift in allegiances' in favour of one of the alternatives" (Wells, 1976, p. 480).

Wells' arguments are suggestive of the constitutive capacities of accounting. Rather than simply reflecting the context in which it operates, accounting has a power to influence its own context. Difficulties and disputes within accounting can engender accounting developments and a perception of crisis both internal and external to the specifically accounting domain. Accounting thereby is seen to give rise to developments which shape the context in which it operates. The environment of accounting can become, in part, at least, contingent upon the accountings of it.

In fact both Gilling (1976) and Wells (1976) move towards recognising the duality of accounting change. For although it is the constitutive capacities of accounting that tend to be stressed by Wells as compared to the reflective capacities which are highlighted in Gilling, both these writers offer some initial insights into a dialec-

---

① One important aspect of the differences between the different approaches is that members of competing schools have different views of the phenomena which were the subject of their discipline. In particular, there were represented in the different schools of accounting theory, different conceptions of the business enterprise.

tic of accounting (in the case of Wells, accounting theory) and its environment. The environment, having previously partly been created by accounting, calls for changes in accounting:

> He [Kuhn] argues that the change takes place only after a serious malfunction has occurred in the sense that "existing institutions (or practices) have ceased adequately to meet the problems posed by an environment that they have in part created" (Wells, 1976, p. 472).

The interdependency of accounting and its environment results in change being brought about by a process of mutual adaption. Environmental demands lead to changes in accounting practice and changes in accounting practice lead to changes in environmental demands and expectations (Gilling, 1976, p. 61).

It would appear that however the tale is told, the environment-accounting contingency model cannot avoid tackling the seemingly indeterminate dualistic character of the process of accounting change that it proposes.①

Our study of value added accounting attempts to cast a little more light on the character of just such an accounting-society interdependence. In our case, however, it would perhaps be better to speak of an accounting-society interpenetration. In the discussion of value added accounting which follows we have not employed the categories of "accounting" and "society" as if they denoted two distinct, mutually exclusive domains. Rather attention has been focused on the specific practices and institutions in which the category "value added" appeared and functioned and on the contexts and the manner in which it has been mentioned and discussed. It will be seen that the social, or the environment, as it were, passes through accounting. Conversely, accounting ramifies, extends and shapes the social.

THE VALUE ADDED EVENT

The particular object of interest in this paper is "the sudden upsurge of interest in value added" (Cameron, 1977b) that occurred in the United Kingdom during the

---

① A further discussion of the reflective and constitutive aspects of accounting change is given in Hopwood (1985). Also see Roberts & Scapens (1985).

ACCOUNTING IN ITS SOCIAL CONTEXT

late 1970s.① The general contours of this event appear to be fairly uncontroversial and they therefore compromise the basic facts of the matter. These facts are that the concept "value added" appeared as an indicator of the value created by the activities of an enterprise in a number of different sites (private companies, newspapers, government bodies, trade unions, employer associations, professional accountancy bodies, etc.), functioning in a number of different practices (financial reporting, payment systems, profit sharing schemes, economic analyses, information disclosure to employees and trade unions, etc.), where before it had been largely absent or, at the most, an object of very limited sectional interest.

The widespread discussion of value added within the ranks of professional accountants commenced with its appearance in *The Corporate Report*, a discussion paper prepared by a working party drawn from the accountancy bodies, which was published by the Accounting Standards Steering Committee (now the Accounting Standards Committee) in August 1975. At least for accountants, this was the official debut of value added.

The Corporate Report recommended, amongst other things, a "statement of value added, showing how the benefits of the efforts of an enterprise are shared between employees, providers of capital, the state and reinvestment" (ASSC, 1975, p. 48). Subsequently a first draft of a consultative document entitled "Aims and scope of company reports", prepared by the Department of Trade, was issued on 9 June, 1976 for comment. This paper, which reads very much as a commentary on *The Corporate Report*, states:

> ... our preliminary view is that the subjects identified in *The Corporate Report* which should be given highest priority for further consideration as candidates for new statutory disclosure requirements are:
> (a) Added Value;
> (b) Employee Report;
> (c) Future Prospects;
> (d) Corporate Objectives (*The Accountant*, 1 July, 1976, p. 13).

When the Government's Green Paper on *The Future of Company Reports* finally appeared in July 1977, one of the legislative proposals contained in it was for a state-

---

① The discussion in this paper focuses on value added accounting in the U.K. However, at the same time attention also was being given to it in other European countries. See McLeay (1983). For developments in German see Dierkes (1979). Reichmann & Lange (1981). Schreuder (1979) and Ullmann (1979). For the Netherlands see Dijksma & Vander Wal (1984). In France interest was expressed in the idea of surplus accounting (see Maitre, 1978; Rey, 1978, pp. 132—134).

ment of value added (Department of Trade, 1977b, pp. 7—8).

This policy debate in the realm of accounting regulation was paralleled by the phenomena of a number of companies using value added statements in their company reports and for reporting to employees. Fourteen companies (out of 300) in the Institute of Chartered Accountants in England and Wales' *Survey of Published Accounts* included value added statements in their annual reports for the year 1975—76 (ICAEW, 1978). This figure grew to 67 for 1977—1978, 84 for 1978—1979 and 90 for 1979—1980 before declining to 88 in 1980—1981, 77 for 1981—1982 and 64 for 1982—1983 (ICAEW, 1980; Skerratt & Tonkin, 1982; Tonkin & Skerratt, 1983). Other surveys indicate that more than one-fifth of the largest U. K. companies produced value added statements in the late 1970s (Gray & Maunders, 1980).

The exact incidence of the use of added value in employee reports is unclear, although several commentators mentioned its popularity in this context (e. g. Fanning, 1978). It also is of interest to note its use by several winners of the *Accountancy Age* competition for the best employee report, its advocacy for the purposes of explaining company performance to employees by the Engineering Employers' Federation (EEF, 1977) and its mention by the Trades Union Congress as a possible performance indicator in the context of a discussion of information disclosure to employees (TUC, 1974).

The Engineering Employers' Federation's advocacy of value added was a development of its position as presented in an earlier document, *Business Performance and Industrial Relations*: *Added Value as an Instrument of Management Discipline*, published by the Federation in 1972. As the title suggests, added value appears in this document as part of a discussion concerned with its use "as a practical tool of management" rather than simply as a form of presentation of financial information in company and employee reports. The particular area of decision making in which it was envisaged this "practical tool" could be brought into play was the one concerned with the utilisation of and payment for labour:

> The Federation therefore aims to encourage the use of added value as a discipline, so that all managers, with or without experience of accounting practices will appreciate the financial environment within which decisions affecting manpower are taken (EFF,1972).

In the later 1977 EEF pamphlet the discussion of the applications of value added is taken further. Examination of its uses has shifted from simply describing how it may serve as a guide to management when formulating wages policy to describing how it may be linked more directly to earnings when serving as the basis of a value added incentive payment scheme (VAIPS). Moreover it should be noted that VAIPS's themselves became the focus of considerable interest. It has been estimated that 200—300 companies were operating, or about to operate, added value schemes in 1978 (Woodmansay, 1978).

In addition to the above uses of value added as a vehicle for information disclosure and as a basis for determining rewards at the level of the enterprise, the category also has appeared on several occasions in the context of policy discussions concerned with the performance of British industry (Jones, 1976, 1978; New, 1978). In addition it has been canvassed as the means of reforming company wide profit sharing schemes (Cameron, 1977a) and appears in stockbroker reports (Vickers da Costa, 1979) as a means of faciliating financial performance analysis.

The value added event, as we term it, already has stimulated some research and analytical reflection. In particular, four of the leading U. K. accountancy bodies— the Institute of Chartered Accountants in England and Wales, The Institute of Chartered Accountants of Scotland, the Institute of Cost and Management Accountants and the Association of Certified Accountants, commissioned and issued research reports on the subject of value added (respectively, Renshall et al., 1979; Morley, 1978; Cox, 1979; Gray & Maunders, 1980). Our concerns however are somewhat different from those which motivated and characterise these reports. In each they very largely take for granted "the sudden upsurge of interest in value added". Value added is discussed in terms of its possible uses and the principles of measurement and forms of presentation that may be employed. As such, this discussion may be considered to be as much part or continuation of the value added event as it is a reflection on it. Insofar as an attempt is made to explain why this event took place, its occurrence is attributed to the phenomenon of social change:

> Accountants have reported on profit for many centuries. Why do we now need to report on Value Added as well? One answer is that the Value Added Statement reflects a social change: shareholders have become less powerful and central Government and organized labour have become more powerful (Morley, 1978, p. 3).

Indeed in the case of value added this is not an uncommon theme (see Pakenham-Walsh, 1964; Wilsher, 1974; Robertson, 1974) and it is precisely our interest in the relation between accounting change and social change that motivates this study of value added.

VALUE ADDED AND THE SOCLAL

On the face of it, the basic facts of the value added event appear clear enough.

However, on closer inspection the picture becomes more complex and somewhat enigmatic. To begin with just what is value added? Rutherford (1977) responds to this question by advancing a definition drawn from Ruggles & Ruggles (1965, p. 50):

> The value added by a firm; i. e. the value created by the activities of the firm and its employees, can be measured by the difference between the market value of the goods that have been turned out by the firm and the cost of those goods and materials purchased from other producers. This measure will exclude the contribution made by other producers to the total value of this firm's production, so that it is essentially equal to the market value created by this firm. The value added measure assesses the net contribution made by each firm to the total value of production; by adding up all these contributions. therefore it is possible to arrive at a total for the whole economy.

However, as Rutherford goes on to point out, this definition does not provide a detailed prescription for the *calculation* of valued added. Indeed, he has pointed out elsewhere (Rutherford, 1978) as have other writers (Vickers da Costa, 1979; Morley, 1978) that calculative practice is very diverse. The treatment of depreciation varies (McLeay, 1983). A great deal of discretion exists as to the treatment of taxation, and so on. Futhermore, this calculative diversity is compounded by the fact that value added statements are presented in a number of different formats (tables, graphs, pie charts, pictures, etc.) which in turn bear a variety of different names ("value added", "wealth created", "where the money goes", etc.) (see Fanning, 1978). There are clearly very many different value addeds.

Another curious feature emerges on inspecting the purported advantages of using value added. We already have indicated that the uses of value added are multiple—payment systems, company reporting, information disclosure to employees and trade unions, economic analysis, etc. What, however, is only rarely discussed is that the descriptions or specifications of the functioning of value added in any given organizational practice are commonly characterised by a form of duality. Value added is seen as a system of both determination and representation.

In the case of, for example, an incentive payment system (see Bentley Associates, 1975; Smith, 1978) value added is specified as a clearly defined financial category, the magnitude of which determines, according to certain well defined calculative procedures, a component of labour income. However, in addition to such a description of a particular system of *determination* there is usually associated a description of a system of *representation*, albeit that the latter is usually thoroughly intertwined with the former. The system of representation is itself composed of two strands. On the one hand, value added, it is argued, represents wealth; to be precise it represents the wealth created in the accounting entity concerned. Furthermore, so the argument goes, this representational property provides a basis for the improved calculation of certain important indices of enterprise performance, namely efficiency and productivity (e.g. Ball, 1968). On the other hand, it also is claimed that value added has the property of revealing (or representing) something about the social character of production, something which is occluded by traditional profit and loss accounting. Value added reveals that the wealth created in production is the consequence of the combined efforts of a number of agents who together form a cooperating team: "Value Added measures the wealth creation which has been built up by the cooperative efforts of shareholders, lenders, workers and the Government" (Morley, 1978, p. 3). It follows, therefore. that value added "puts profit into proper perspective vis-avis the whole enterprise as a collective effort by capital, management and employees" (ASSC, 1975, p. 49). Together these representational properties of value added are presumed to make it a means for both the more rational control of production and the achievement of a more harmonious and cooperative productive endeavour.

Now these expressive properties of value added, properties which provide it with both a technical and a social rationality, create a dilemma. For in order for value added to be able to represent the company as a cooperating team, the company must first have been constituted as such. On further investigation, however, it transpires that value added is seen as being able to serve as one means to this end. Value added therefore does not simply represent the company as a cooperating team, it also is seen as playing a positive role in the creation of this cooperative harmony. This is a point that was made very clearly some time before value added became such a widespread object of interest:

> The growth we are interested in is a growth of the national product, growth of the national product is achieved by making changes which lead to increased production by business undertakings. This will not be realised until production is seen by managers to be the central purpose of business and until the accounting profession re-orients its practices to this view. The profit and loss orientations of accounts, and notably of published accounts, is inimical to the improvement of industrial relations without which the growth in production desired will he attenuated.
>
> Although the antagonism between capital and labour has declined in recent years, the basic division of interest between maximising profits and providing maximum rewards for labour will continue to afflict industrial relations, unless

we cease to see profits as the objective (Pakenham-Walsh, 1964, p. 268).

In such a context accounting is seen as a means of vision. A change in accounting implies a change in what is seen and hence a change in action. Social harmony might therefore not so much be revealed by value added as constituted by it. We are on the horns of the very dilemma which, as we already have indicated, is central to the society-accounting contingency model. On the one hand, it is asserted that value added may be accounted for by reference to wider changes and shifts in society (see Morley, 1978; Robertson, 1974; Wilsher, 1974). On the other hand, it now appears that this same social change might not be independent of the existence of value added. Value added is thus called upon to provide at least some of its own preconditions.

Whatever may be the logical problems that arise from the circularity that characterises attempts to explain accounting innovations in terms of their purported roles (also see Burchell *et al.*, 1980), it also is important to note that there does not exist any unanimous agreement over what the roles of value added are in the first place. The roles we have described above by no means exhaust the significance of this particular accounting innovation. In respect of its social rationality—value added as an expression of production as team production—it has been pointed out by Stolliday & Attwood (1978) that there is no obvious logical reason why the use of value added should not serve as a spur to workers in their attempts to totally eliminate the claims of others in its distribution. In this case value added still functions to reveal a "truth" about production, albeit a rather different one from production as teamwork. From yet another standpoint, the use of value added is viewed as a way of "misleading the workers" in an attempt to gloss "over the problem of profits" (see Hird, 1980; *Labour Research*, 1978). In this case value added serves as a device for *misrepresenting* reality. It presents a picture of a unity of interests in the financial performance of a given business organization, whereas in fact there exists a basic conflict of interests. Value added, it seems, is a distinctly equivocal social indicator.

There is yet another problem concerning the roles of value added and the statuses attributed to them. We have already pointed to calculative diversity as an important feature of the event we are seeking to unravel. Virtually all those writers who comment on it see this calculative diversity as subversive of those very properties that are often deemed to characterise value added:

> ... published statements of value added have, to date, been characterised by ambiguous terminology and by the treatment of items in ways inconsistent with the model of value added, and inconsistent within and between individual statements. The impression received by lay users of SVAS must be one of confu-

sion—together possibly, with a conviction that value added, like profit can be made to mean whatever the accountant wishes it to mean (Rutherford, 1978, p. 52).

The advantages offered by the Value Added Statement are. however. currently jeopardised by great diversity of practice (Morley, 1978, p. 141).

Most of those [value-added statements] available seem to be designed to show, often by a "sales-cake" diagram, how much of the value-added goes to the employees themselves. how much the Government absorbs and how little the shareholder receives (Vickers da Costa, 1979).

Rather than shedding light, reducing conflict, etc. value added statements appear to be equally conducive to confusion, doubt and suspicion. This state of affairs problematises not only the social rationality. of value added but also its technical rationality. Clearly there may be as many productivities and efficiencies as there are added values. Thus value added is always more or less inadequate to its roles and the value added event cannot therefore be viewed simply as either the dawning of economic enlightenment or the expression of a particular social transformation.

The general upshot of this discussion is that the roles of value added do not of themselves provide a very satisfactory explanation of "the sudden upsurge of interest in value added". To summarise the argument so far: we encounter logical problems if we attempt to explain the widespread use of value added in terms of its roles; in any case, the precise specification of these roles is controversial; and, finally, the value addeds we actually encounter do not function flawlessly to achieve their appointed end. It is therefore suggested that these roles would be better considered as part of the phenomena to be explained and with this idea in mind it is possible to specify in rather greater detail our object of investigation and certain problems in respect of it which we wish to solve.

To the basic facts of the value added event we now have to add that it was not a sudden and massive outbreak of a single, unambiguous concept of value added that occurred during the 1970s. There occurred instead the widespread discussion and use of a range of very particular, differentiated value addeds. These value addeds vary in definition and form of presentation and they came into the world in association with a number of properties. However historically contingent this association may be, the value addeds that we are interested in do not exist independently of these, their properties—namely the various roles that are imputed to value added and in the name of which it is frequently advanced. Although there is no unanimity in respect of these roles (or rationales), two have tended to predominate in the discussion and debate surrounding value added. It is frequently argued that value added is a superior means of the measurement, and hence pursuit, of wealth, productivity and efficiency. In addition it is also argued that it is the measure of income appropriate to production seen as a process involving the action of a team of cooperators. Finally, the circularity which is involved when seeking to explain the appearance of value added in terms of its roles coupled with the lack of general agreement over the specification of these roles enables value added to serve as the focus of a widely differentiated field of political interest. The very ambiguity of value added might, in other words, be implicated in its emergence and functioning. Depending on the point at which the circle of reasoning is entered, value added may be seen as a determining factor in the process of social change, a harbinger of social change or a consequence of social change. As Morley (1978, pp. 5—6) has expressed it:

> In saying that the Value Added Statement reflects social change one does not necessarily approve of the phenomenon. Indeed, one can distinguish three very different views on this:
>
> (i) One might report Value Added in order to hurry the change along and to give impetus to the movement of power from capital owners towards labour and *central Government.*
>
> (ii) One might report Value Added in order to alert the business community to this change, hoping that it may thereby be reversed.
>
> (iii) One might report Value Added in the hope that it would help one's new masters to make sensible decisions.
>
> These three attitudes may perhaps explain why Value Added enthusiasts are to be found at both ends of the political spectrum. One encounters both left and right wingers who support this new Statement though their expectations from it differ greatly.

It is precisely this high differentiated social space within which the value added event took place that is our object of investigation. In what follows we have attempted to discover some of its preconditions—the factors that made possible the value added event. This work of description and analysis has been carried out by delineating three arenas, or complexes of issues, institutions, bodies of knowledge, practices and actions, within each of which there may be traced a descent—a succession of phases in the trajectory of a social movement. These movements intersected in the 1970s with value added serving as an important element in the triple conjuncture. No doubt arenas other than the ones that we have outlined could be constructed. However the aim of this paper is *not* to provide an exhaustive description of the genesis and development of value added. Such a study would in any case take us back to before the Industrial Revolution and is therefore a task beyond the scope of the present paper (see, for example, Crum, 1982). The aim here is more modest: it is merely to shed a little descriptive and analytical light on the processes of accounting change.

THREE ARENAS

Each of the three arenas discussed below marks out a particular field of operations, namely the explication of standards for corporate financial reporting, the management of the national economy and the functioning of the system of industrial relations. Within each arena there has been charted the shifting patterns of relations between the various agencies functioning in these fields, e. g. the government, trade unions, the accounting profession, and the changes in their modes of operation and objects of concern, e. g. productivity, strikes, accounting standards. In each case some emphasis is placed on the interest in economic calculation and reporting in general and in value added in particular.

At this stage in the argument the movement in each arena, along with its associated "problems" and "solutions", has been handled as if it had a trajectory which was largely independent of those in the other arenas. This is no doubt an oversimplification. Clearly, macro-economic management concerns with payment systems were not without their implications for industrial relations. Conversely, the interest in industrial relations reform was not unrelated to certain postulated negative consequences of the existing structure of industrial relations for national economic performance. Similarly developments in accounting standardisation were related to both macro-economic issues, not least in the context of the inflation prevailing in the period, and the management of industrial relations in a time of a perceived growth in the power of the trade union movement. However the approach which we adopt at this stage does in our opinion have the merits not only of enabling the field of social relations in each of the arenas to be analysed more readily, allowing, in the process, both their autonomies and their interdependencies to be recognised, but also of facilitating an investigation of how issues such as economic performance and calculation were brought into relation with those of the status of employees and trade unions rather than presuming any *a priori* necessity for this to happen. [1]

The debate surrounding economic performance and industrial relations spilled

---

[1] We would argue that there is after all no obvious way in which notions of efficiency should be related to those of democracy. The nature of such a relationship has been subject to very little analysis and investigation, with the two notions inhabiting two distinct orders of discourse, namely those of economic and political theory. The same point applies to the relationship between the various practices concerned with the measurement and pursuit of efficiency and those concerned with the representation of interests.

over into a *pre-existing* debate in the area of corporate reporting which was concerned with determining the appropriate categories, principles and forms of presentation and distribution of corporate reports. While our treatment of accounting as a separate domain or arena has been motivated by a prior commitment not to handle accounting solely in a reductive or reflective manner, the discussion below goes some way towards indicating in a more positive fashion not only the components of this domain but also its articulations with other fields of action.

Accounting standards

As we already have observed, value added is characterised by considerable calculative diversity.① In a survey of published value added statements it was concluded that "It is difficult to capture systematically the degree of diversity present in the construction of statements of Value Added" (Rutherford, 1980). Moreover, such a heterogeneity of practice was seen as problematic for the roles, rationales and purposes that value added was seen and mobilised to serve. Rather than promoting efficient, harmonious, productive activity, the motley collection of value addeds was seen as subverting the very roles allocated to them precisely as a consequence of their variegated character. Amongst other things, the calculative diversity opened management to the charge of manipulation and bias. In the case of employee newsletters, for example, it was asserted that "most of those available seem to be designed to show ... how much of the value added goes to the employees themselves, how much the Government absorbs and how little the shareholder receives" (*The Accountant*, 1978, p. 373).

One consequence of the perception that the practice of value added was not adequate to the roles commonly attributed to it was a call for its standardisation (Fanning, 1979; Vickers da Costa, 1979). The relevant agency in this respect was the Accounting Standards Committee. As a result of these and other② pressures, four of the accountancy bodies represented on the Accounting Standards Committee commissioned research studies of value added. The reports issued by both the Institute of Chartered Accountants in England and Wales (Renshall *et al.*, 1979) and the Insti-

---

① We would not wish to claim that value added is unusual in this respect. Most other key accounting indicators are subject to a similar ambiguity of definition and diversity of practice. In fact this characteristic of so seemingly an objective phenomenon could provide an interesting perspective for both technical and social analyses of the accounting craft.

② By initiating these research studies at least three of the four accountancy bodies also were responding to the Labour Government's threat of legislation requiring the reporting of value added. Given that the concept was *a* new part of the official accounting discourse, they were quite strategically investing in enhancing their understanding of the category.

tute of Chartered Accountants in Scotland (Morley, 1978) conclude in favour of value added reporting but add the caveat that "Standardisation of practice is a necessary precondition to any formal requirement" (Renshall *et al.*, 1979, p. 38) so as "to bring comparability to Value Added Statements and so safeguard the confidence of readers in the Statement" (Morley, 1978, p. 141). The study prepared for the Institute of Cost and Management Accountants was notably less enthusiastic and presented value added as just one more addition to the kitbag of management tools which may be usefully employed in connection with employee payment systems and public relations (Cox, 1979). The issue of standardisation was not raised in the report. The Association of Certified Accountants' study investigated the information needs of potential users of value added statements and reviewed existing corporate practice in the area before discussing measurement and disclosure policy (Gray & Maunders, 1980). Two approaches to the measurement of value added were identified, and although it was stated that "conceptually it would seem desirable that a consistent approach be adopted one way or the other" (p. 28), it also was argued that value added reporting should be "placed outside the restrictions established by convention" in order to facilitate its "imaginative development" according to the decision requirements of its potential users (p. 37).

There are two points of note concerning these four research studies. First, although all the reports commented on the sudden growth of interest in value added, an interest which provided the pretext for their discussions, none of them investigated the factors underlying this phenomenon. They all provided some sort of inventory of the various alleged advantages of using value added but none of them asked why these should have been perceived so suddenly or so late in the day. This point is important because if it can be shown that the emergence of value added was deeply implicated in certain wider socio-economic processes peculiar to a particular historical conjuncture, processes which moreover might have imbued value added with a particular historically contingent significance, then under different conditions debating the potential uses and advantages of value added might well be quite irrelevant. The second point relates to the fact that accounting policy in relation to the formulation of financial accounting standards has been fairly narrowly constrained to issues of measurement and forms of presentation. Until recently (Zeff, 1978) these problems have been deliberated very largely without reference to the likely implications of introducing particular standards. Indeed, in relation to the American experience, it has been argued that the dominant means of discourse in this domain—those furnished by accounting theory—have served to obscure the political character of the standard setting process and thereby have rendered ineffectual certain procedural reforms and research initiatives aimed at resolving the problem of obtaining agreement on accounting standards (Moonitz, 1974; Watts & Zimmerman, 1979; Zeff, 1978). In this sense it is ironic that the difficulties encountered by the Accounting Standards Committee in its standard setting programme—difficulties which could well have extended to any attempt to standardize value added should that ever have appeared on the agenda—provided an important impetus to the publication of *The Corporate Report* in which value added first entered the ranks of the accountancy profession.

The present arrangements for setting accounting standards in the U. K. were established at the end of the 1960s in the aftermath of the considerable controversy and debate surrounding a series of company collapses and take-over battles (Zeff, 1972). The standards setting programme very quickly ran into trouble however, not least in relation to its stated aim of narrowing the areas of difference and variety in accounting practice (JCAEW, 1969). This was most dramatically exemplified in the case of the inflation accounting debate (Whittington, 1983) but the same difficulties also applied to a number of other areas of accounting standardisation.

Although initiated to maintain professional control over accounting standardisation, the inflation accounting proposals of the then Accounting Standards Steering Committee quickly engendered such a breadth and intensity of debate that the Conservative Government of the time established a committee of inquiry in the area—the Sandiland's Committee (1975) (for an initial analysis of the context see Hopwood et al., 1980; Hopwood, 1984). That in itself was perceived by the profession as a threat to the traditional division of responsibility between the professional bodies and the government concerning the determination of the content and form of presentation of and the measurement principles employed in corporate reports. The sense of professional crisis was further intensified by the fact that the committee was anticipated to report in a not uncritical manner during a new Labour administration whose opposition Green Paper, *The Community and the Company* (1974) had also threatened the existing framework of professional self-regulation with its proposals for the setting up of a powerful Companies Commission for regulating companies and financial institutions.

In anticipation of the report of the Sandilands Committee, the Accounting Standards Steering Committee established a committee to reexamine "the scope and aims of published financial reports in the light of modern needs and conditions" (ASSC, 1975)—something which had until then been ignored by the standard setters. ①The

---

① In-depth research had been mentioned as one aspect of the standard setting programme, but no concrete steps had been taken in this area until the establishment of *The Corporate Report* Working Party. For an insider's comments on the establishment and functioning of this group see Stamp (1985).

committee's findings were published as *The Corporate Report*. In appraising current reporting practices, *The Corporate Report* evinces some concern for what it considers to be an over-emphasis on profit and goes on to argue that:

> The simplest and most immediate way of putting profit into proper perspective vis-a-vis the whole enterprise as a collective effort by capital, management and employees is by the presentation of a statement of value added (that is, sales income less materials and services purchased). Value added is the wealth the reporting entity has been able to create by its own and its employees efforts. This statement would show how value added has been used to pay those contributing to its creation. It usefully elaborates on the profit and loss account and in time may come to be regarded as a preferable way of describing performance (ASSC, 1975, p. 49).

In this way value added entered the discourse of accounting policy making. ①

Value added was seen as a performance criterion that put employees on a par with other interests in the enterprise. Moreover this claim for an equality of status was reinforced by the stakeholder model adopted in *The Corporate Report*. Where before there only existed the shareholder (Sharp, 1971) there now stood a number of stakeholders, each of which is deemed to have "a reasonable right to information concerning the reporting entity" (ASSC, 1975, p. 17). The employee group constituted one such stakeholder. The report makes the point that "it is likely that employees will more suitably obtain the information they need by means of special purpose reports at plant or site level" (p. 22). However, it goes on to argue that corporate reports could be used as a check on the reliability of these special purpose documents and could be useful to employees in evaluating managerial efficiency, estimating the future prospects of the entity and of individual establishments within a group.

The merits of value added as an alternative or complementary performance indicator had not been advanced in a vacuum, however. Two very important contextual considerations that should be borne in mind in connection with conditions in the United Kingdom during the second half of the 1970s were the debates, legislation and practical initiatives concerned with incomes policy and information disclosure to employees and trades unions. Although value added was new to the accounting policy making arena, it was functioning as a practice in both of these other two contexts.

---

① One reviewer suggested that further effort be put into tracing the origins of the interest in value added by *The Corporate Report* Working Party. Our investigations revealed that one of the authors of the present paper might have been influential in this respect! If this is so, it further reinforces our concluding observations on the non-monolithic and unanticipated nature of accounting change.

Macro-economic management

Income policies have been linked to the use of the value added category by a number of writers (Beddoe, 1978; Cameron, 1978; IDS, 1977; Low, 1977). In every case the connection has been made via a discussion of value added incentive payment schemes (VAIPSs). VAIPSs are group bonus schemes which are usually operated on a plant basis, thus covering both blue- and whitecollar employees. The bonus pool available for distribution to the employees is related to the value added of the plant. This pool may, for example, be determined by a certain agreed percentage of any increase in the value added per pound of payroll costs, over some agreed base figure for this ratio. These schemes came very much to the fore during the period of the 1974—1979 Labour Government. With the inception of Stage Ⅲ of that Government's pay policy in August 1977 there was imposed a 10% limit on wage settlements with the provision for agreements above this level where self-financing productivity deals had been implemented. VAIPSs. which had been introduced into the U. K. during the 1950s, were already functioning in a number of firms and were strongly advocated by a number of management consultants, are almost by definition self-financing and thus were well placed under Stage Ⅲ to become more widely adopted.

One of the most important conditions of this particular conjuncture of value added and national incomes policy was that constituted by the practices of government management of the national economy. The "national economy" as an object of government intervention and "macro-economic policy" as a domain wherein this intervention is deliberated, planned and conducted were only constituted in the U. K., in the sense that we understand them today, during and immediately after the Second World War (Tomlinson, 1981). For a long time this field of action remained very much as it was initially structured by the conditions under which it emerged. This was particularly the case for the problem of productivity. "Before the war productivity was largely confined to academic discussion", Leyland (1953, p. 381) observed. "Today," he went on to add, "it is common currency". Such an interest is not hard to understand. Under conditions of full employment, improving productivity had been the only source of economic growth. It also faciliated the maintenance of an external balance without reducing domestic consumption or investment—both painful exercises with hazardous side effects for the government of the day. Moreover productivity also provided an indicator for gauging the competitive position of the manufac-

turing sector—a factor given continuing attention in the U. K. in the post-war era. ①
In short, productivity growth appeared to be a key to economic success.

While productivity and, more generally, economic efficiency have been continuing concerns of government, as evidenced by agencies such as the National Economic Development Office and earlier, the Anglo-American Productivity Council, neither these bodies nor the means of intervention associated with monetary and fiscal policy afforded governments a very effective purchase on these key economic variables. However, a rather more direct form of intervention has been provided from time to time by government incomes policies. These have been introduced, usually reluctantly and *in extremis*, in order to attempt to resolve one of the central presumed dilemmas of modern demand management, namely how is it possible to reconcile the objectives of price stability and full employment using only the instruments of fiscal and monetary policy. What is interesting here is that productivity growth has re-occurred as an important criterion for judging wage increase throughout the various phases of the post-war history of incomes policies.

Productivity was so emphasised during the incomes policies of 1961 and 1962. The theme re-emerged during the life of the National Board of Prices and Incomes (NBPI) established by the Labour Government in 1965 and wound up on 31 March, 1971. The NBPI was assigned the task of examining "particular cases in order to advise whether or not the behaviour of prices, salaries or other money incomes was in the national interest ... " (see Fels, 1972, Chapter 3). "The national interest" was first specified in the White Paper, *Prices and Incomes Policy*, of April 1965 and was subsequently elaborated and modified in a series of White Papers until 1970. Initially it required that there should be an incomes "norm", i. e. a maximum percentage by which the wages and salaries of individuals should increase. A figure of 3%—$3\frac{1}{2}\%$ per annum was derived from the expected annual rate of growth of productivity per head. In addition certain exceptional circumstances in which increases above the norm were considered justifiable were also defined. Amongst these there was one which allowed for above-norm increases in pay where employees had made a direct contribution towards an increase in productivity. For certain periods during the life of

---

① In the second half of the 1970s value added was itself increasingly used in political and media discussions of national economic performance and policy (Jones, 1976, 1978; New, 1978). Indeed productivity tended to be seen as something that was, if not synonymous with value added, at least very closely related to it. From this perspective discussions focused on the need for income policies. increased investment, particularly in "high value added sectors", and policies on the proportion of value added devoted to industrial research and development. In these ways value added appeared to simultaneously function as a way of describing the economy, elucidating policy problems and, in the context of VAIPSs, facilitating the solution of the problems so identified.

the NBPI there was imposed a zero norm and the exceptional criteria became the only permissable grounds for obtaining an increase in pay. It was under this regime that productivity agreements became very popular. The NBPI's third report on productivity agreements showed that 25% of all workers had been involved in productivity agreements, mainly in 1968 and 1969 (NBPI, 1968).

Subsequent investigation of these productivity deals led certain commentators to conclude that many of them were bogus, i. e. "the productivity increase was mostly that which would have happened in any case; so that what many socalled 'productivity bargains' really did was to use this to justify an exceptional wage increase" (Turner, 1970, p. 203). This experience plus the *ad hoc*, piecemeal character of many productivity deals which tended to be self-perpetuating thereafter (Elliott, 1978) and, perhaps more importantly, the lack of any mechanism relating the increases in hourly rates paid to the increase in productivity actually achieved were the cause of some concern on the part of both Government and the Confederation of British Industry in the discussions over the arrangements to be brought into effect with the expiry of Stage II of the 1974—1979 Labour Government's incomes policy. At that time the Government was keen to build a productivity element into the provisions for Stage III. In this context VAIPSs could be presented as model schemes. They were comprehensive in character and maintained a continuous link between performance and reward. VAIPSs therefore involved the use of a measurement technology that offered a solution to many of the problems that had created difficulties for the NBPI in its attempts to audit the productivity deals of the late sixties. However, it is important to note that the force of the claims made on behalf of VAIPSs did not rest on these features alone.

In discussions of VAIPSs it is rare to find their merits presented solely in terms of their scope, self-financing character or measurement technology. In a number of different ways, the point was nearly always made that the effective functioning of these schemes presupposes a number of changes in the intra-organisational relations of the enterprise concerned. Further, it was often made clear that these changes were considered to be of positive value in their own right. The relevant organisational changes were usually discussed in terms of "information disclosure" and "participation". As one leading management consultant in this area put it:

> the contribution of Added Value requires: (a) an open management style that will "open the books" and welcome the increased questioning that will ensure; (b) a preference for a more participative and less autocratic way of getting results (Binder, Hamlyn, Fry & Co., 1978, p. 18).

The underlying reasoning appears to be that given that the relevant unit of performance for determining bonus is a company or plant rather than a single machine, improved performance and hence bonus presupposes cooperation across functions and different activities and occupational groups within functions. This cooperation, so the argument goes, can only be achieved by means of the widespread disclosure of detailed company information which then provides the basis for discussion and agreement on the appropriate action for attempting to improve performance. Thus, in the case of the Bentley plan—a particular British varient of the VAIPS—the scheme "is initiated through a fully representative employee management council. A structure which will establish employee involvement and participation in a wider range of problems and enable profits, productivity and earnings to be rationally discussed and improved" (Bentley Associates, 1975, p.12). In one group of companies in which a VAIPS was introduced the scheme in each company in the group was administered by a company consultative council. These bodies included representatives from senior and junior management and from all shop floor departments. Each council was given the details of its company's performance for the preceding month. Council members then reported back on the figures to colleagues in their own sectors (Cameron, 1977b; also see Woodmansay, 1978, p.13). It is interesting to note that although the trade union response to VAIPSs was somewhat guarded it was suggested that if unions did enter such schemes they would require, amongst other things, complete access to all the relevant data (Beddoe, 1978).

The positive value of all these changes was generally seen in terms of the improvement in industrial relations that they were said to effect. It was argued that flexible working arrangements would become more likely and employees would become positively motivated to cut costs and improve efficiency. As a result there would be some amelioration in the repeated confrontation between workers and managers over working practices (Marchington, 1977; Cameron, 1977b). Now it was for very similar reasons that the NBPI was earlier so interested in productivity deals. It has been argued that the "NBPI's recommendations on pay policy often required changes in the machinery of wage determination; in addition, the incomes policy was often used as a Trojan horse to bring about reforms in collective bargaining institutions" (Fels, 1972, p.150). The productivity deal was one of the principle means whereby the NBPI sought to supplant the hold of traditional factors in income determination and give practical effect to its own criteria.

However, in the 1970s there occurred a significant change in the character of the discussion surrounding the intra-organizational changes associated with the reform of payment systems. The productivity deals of the NBPI period were discussed wholly in terms of the rhetoric of management control:

> ... genuine productivity agreements. for example, would have very useful side effects, such as improving management by increasing cost-consciousness. by providing new information about performance and information about performance and new methods of assessing it, and by directing attention to the possibility of changing methods of work. Management negotiations were brought into closer touch with unions, and more managers became aware of the implications for industrial relations of technical and financial decisions. The experience of applying the agreements with their provisions on overtime, flexibility, manning and so on often brought a revolution in managerial control over working hours and practices. There were changes in organisation, personnel and the provision of training, and senior and other managers were better informed and organised than before the agreements (Fels, 1972, p. 133).

While the discussion of VAIPSs during the second half of the 1970s still contained this thread concerned with management control and the efficiency of enterprise operations, it was also conducted according to the rhetoric of employee participation and industrial democracy. Indeed it became possible to completely invert the normal order of presentation and use the issue of industrial democracy as a springboard for advancing the claims of VAIPSs (e. g. Marchington, 1977). The significance acquired by and emphasis placed on the participative characteristics of VAIPSs at this time was rooted in a number of parallel developments occurring within the area of industrial relations.

Industrial relations and information disclosure

During the 1960s there commenced a significant shift in the conditions of trade union activity in the U. K. The pre-existing voluntary system of "free collective bargaining" was displaced by a progressively elaborated object of government intervention—an object increasingly overlaid by a network of legal relations and inset with a variety of new institutions concerned with the investigation, regulation and normalisation of industrial relations (see Crouch, 1979). This shift was preceded by two events of some interest. In 1961 there commenced the production of a record of unofficial strikes and in 1965 the Labour Government appointed a Royal Commission on Trade Unions and Employers' Associations—the Donovan Commission (Donovan, 1968). Thus there occurred the production of a key statistic, to be read a little later as a sign of a "central defect in British industrial relations" (Crouch, 1979, p. 264). In addition to its work of diagnosis, the Donovan Report contained a clearly articulated conceptual framework which would serve as a means of generating programmes of intervention designed to rectify this "defect".

A singular feature of the interventions into industrial relations that occurred during the period of the 1974—1979 Labour Government was the degree to which the discussions and debates surrounding them were organised around the theme of industrial democracy (Elliott, 1978). Despite its apparent centrality, "industrial democracy" is an extremely difficult concept to pin down. According to one commentator "the term 'industrial democracy' is incapable of definition" (Kahn-Freund, 1977) and Elliott (1978, p.6) has noted that:

> Despite its central semi-political theme of increasing the role and status of workers in an industrial society, industrial democracy means different things to different people. To some on the far left it is perceived as a path to full workers' control, while for many employers and Conservative politicians, who dislike its political connotations, it should be called simply "employee participation" and only involve a partnership between employer and employee in making the company and the present social and economic system work more efficiently and productively, without any changes in power relationships.

As for value added itself, it is perhaps precisely *because* of its equivocal character that industrial democracy was able to serve as a key point of articulation between a number of distinct conceptions of enterprise and industrial relations reform. The ambiguity might be required if the concept is to orchestrate the considerable number of positions that can be argued concerning the specification of individual and group interests and their political representations (Pitkin, 1967). [1]

An inquiry into industrial democracy chaired by Lord Bullock (Department of Trade, 1977a) and the enactment of the Employment Protection Act of 1975 were important elements in the programme of industrial relations reform of the 1974—1979 Labour Government. However its democratic content may be judged, this programme implied a change in the information economies of private companies. Amongst other things it entailed the creation of new agents and bodies for the receipt and relay of in-

---

[1] "Industrial democracy" may be thought of as functioning in two different ways. Firstly it is the name attached to particular palpable regimes of industrial democracy. For example, in the name of industrial democracy, the Trades Union Congress advanced a comprehensive set of proposals for developing trade union activity at the level of the economy, industry, company and the plant (TUC, 1974). A rather different set of proposals are to be found in the evidence of the Confederation of British Industry to the Bullock Committee. There is thus a wide range of institutional and procedural arrangements that can lay claim to being democratic. In its second mode of functioning industrial democracy serves as a criterion for critically evaluating given institutions and procedures for their democratic content—the extent to which the arrangements in question may be considered to represent the interests of all the persons concerned. Thus Gospel appraises the provisions of the Employment Protection Act 1975 (Gospel, 1976) and the signatories of the minority report take their stand in relation to the majority report of the Bullock Committee (Department of Trade, 1977a, p.175, para. 23).

formation, new rights of access for certain existing bodies and the setting up of certain national agencies to oversee and supervise the implementation and functioning of the new provisions. The Employment Protection Act of 1975 gave statutory form to the Advisory, Conciliation and Arbitration Service (ACAS)① which was "charged with the general duty of promoting the improvement of industrial relations". To this end it was empowered to issue Codes of Practice containing practical guidance for promoting the improvement of industrial relations. A Code of Practice on the disclosure of information to trade unions was issued by ACAS and came into effect on 22 August 1977. The disclosure provisions placed a general duty on an employer to disclose information to representatives of independent recognised trade unions, "(a) without which the trade union representatives would be to a material extent impeded in carrying on with him... collective bargaining, and (b) which it would be in accordance with good industrial relations practice that he would disclose to them for the purposes of collective bargaining". Although the Bullock Report did not result in any legislation, parallel developments in the areas of occupational pension schemes (Lucas, 1979) and health and safety took some steps towards taking workers into the sphere of management decision-making. The Health and Safety at Work Act was enacted in 1975. It provided for the appointment of employee safety representatives with functions of representation and consultation, workplace inspection and investigation and rights of access to certain documents and information. As one writer put it: "For the first time in law, the Regulations have given trade unions decision-making rights in their workplaces" (Stuttard, 1979).

It was in this context, in which the relative status of management personnel vis-a-vis trade unionists had come under considerable pressure, both in respect of information access and decision-making, that there developed a considerable amount of interest in employee reporting. Popular versions of companies' annual reports to shareholders were prepared in an attempt to make them understandable to employees (Hussey, 1978, 1979; Holmes, 1977). Around these corporate initiatives there had in turn grown up a parallel literature of prescription and advice emanating from such bodies as the Institute of Personnel Management, the ICAEW and the CBI. In addition to the use of employee reports, information also was disseminated to employees by means of personal presentations by company chairmen to mass meetings, slide and video presentations and small group briefing sessions. It was within this area of corporate communication with employees that value added frequently appeared and was discussed as a preferred form of presentation (Hopkins, 1975; EEF, 1977;

---

① ACAS was first established on an administrative basis in 1974.

Smith, 1978; Hilton, 1978). The Trades Union Congress, in its statement of policy on industrial democracy, had itself suggested that companies should provide information on value added to their employees (TUC, 1974, p. 33).

One final strand of interest in the industrial democracy debate is that of profit sharing. As a result of undertakings made to the Liberal Party during the formation of the "Lib-Lab" alliance, profit sharing was encouraged by provisions introduced in the Finance Act 1978 (Elliott, 1978). This particular innovation is one that was continued under the Conservative administration which came to power in 1979. The Confederation of British Industry viewed financial participation schemes as a means of obtaining a "sense of purpose, at least at company level" and "as a useful contribution to an employee participation programme" (CBI, 1978). Of particular interest here are the changes introduced by ICI into its own profit sharing scheme. This scheme had been running since 1953 and covered nearly 100,000 monthly and weekly paid staff who received an annual profit related share allocation. In 1976 an ICI working party report proposed that the right of the ICI board to unilaterally fix the annual bonus should be replaced by a formula based on an added value concept (Cameron, 1977a). This scheme differed from a VAIPS in that it operated at the company level as opposed to the plant level and it was not viewed as a major productivity incentive. The stated objectives were "(1) to help encourage the cooperation and involvement of all employees in improving the business performance of the company; (2) to provide tangible evidence of the unity of interests of employees and stockholders in the continued existence of ICI as a strong and financially viable company; (3) to help focus the interest of the employees towards being part of a more effective company, by being involved as stockholders" (Wellens, 1977).

It is perhaps no surprise therefore that VAIPSs having been introduced into the U. K. during the 1950s and effectively incubated during the 1960s then came into their own in the 1970s. While the topics of information disclosure to employees and economic performance were by no means new (see for example BIM, 1957; Searle, 1971), the discussion of them took place within and was driven forward by the rhetoric of industrial democracy which tended to place in the foreground the issue of the relative status of economic agents. It is precisely under these conditions, formed by the intersection of a number of different developments in the fields of setting accounting standards, the management of the national economy and the regulation and reform of industrial relations, that profit and its associated connotations could appear as a problem—an "awkward term"—and value added could establish its claim as an alternative performance indicator.

THE ACCOUNTING CONSTELLATION

Our concern is to discover the pre-conditions of the social space within which the value added event took place. As we indicated earlier, this particular social space is, amongst other things, characterised by the fact that the discussions concerning efficiency and productivity that took place within it during the second half of the 1970s were extensively intertwined with those concerning employee participation. The language of economic performance was strongly inflected with that of industrial representation and democracy. In the literature of the period concerned with such enterprise administrative practices as accounting and payments systems, problems were diagnosed and solutions proposed according to the terms of a discourse which was organized around the notions of efficiency and democracy. However these two ideas function as a pair of values the commensurability of which is far from clear. Just how is "efficiency" to be brought into relation with "democracy"? One solution to this problem seemingly was offered by value added. Value added was repeatedly presented as a means of achieving a felicitous combination of participation, if not democracy, and efficiency. Within the network of statements generated by the efficiency-democracy discourse, value added functioned as one strategic node or point of inter-relation.

Notions of efficiency and participation did not exist as a pair of pre-given, disembodied categories however. Nor did the debates and discussions concerning them simply consist of a series of words and statements, lacking any historical or contextual specification save that of the dates between which they occurred. In our discussion of the three arenas we have attempted to outline a three branched genealogy (Foucault, 1977) of the specific social space within which value added appeared and developed. As a consequence of tracing this genealogy, the space which the value added event occupied is seen to be comprised of a very particular field of relations which existed between certain institutions, economic and administrative processes, bodies of knowledge, systems of norms and measurement, and classification techniques. We have called such a field an accounting constellation. It was in the network of intersecting practices, processes and institutions which constituted this constellation that value added was caught and it was this network that governed how it might function as a calculative, administrative and discursive practice. In this latter sense the constellation also operates as a regime—one which governs the production, distribution and use of value added statements. Business organizations themselves appear within this regime as dense concentrations of social relations—a chain or archipelago of individual information economies set into a web of more dispersed, loosely knit relations.

We have described the development of activities along three strands of this web and how these three strands or arenas together made it possible for a number of mutually reinforcing interventions to be relayed into the information economies of individual enterprises during the 1970s in the United Kingdom. These interventions associated with incomes policies and the management of the national economy, company and labour law and the reform of industrial relations, accounting regulation and the standardisation of financial reporting, simultaneously affected a number of different aspects of the business enterprise. For example, productivity deals in general and VAIPSs in particular resulted in a significant elaboration of a firm's administrative apparatus. Moreover this elaboration was aimed at increasing its pervasiveness in order to secure greater unity in the combined action of the component parts of the enterprise. It also has been argued that productivity deals were seen to offer workers the scope for greater involvement and participation in decision making giving rise to the application of wage-work rules (McKersie & Hunter, 1973, pp. 21—23). an implication that was particularly apparent in many of the discourses that were associated with VAIPSs. Overall, therefore, these diverse strategies and interventions together had the possibility to intensify the regime of economic information within an enterprise and to move towards some reconstitution of the patterns of social relations. One interesting index of such an overall change was the widespread concern shown for the general level of financial and commercial literacy. Indeed the disclosure of corporate information to employees was often discussed as if it were part and parcel of an exercise in business education. A shift in the pattern of distribution and consumption of corporate information implied, or at least in this particular case was becoming increasingly associated with, a change in the distribution of the cultural resources commonly associated with the receipt and use of this information.

In many respects the appearance of value added statements in company annual reports was merely the tip of the iceberg in relation to the more general shift which had taken place in and around the enterprise in the processing of information. Although further investigation undoubtedly would provide interesting insights, we have not sought to uncover the precise mechanisms whereby value added was written into *The Corporate Report*, for instance. Instead we have attempted to indicate how it was necessary to speak about value added, to adopt a certain style of discourse, if what was basically a very marginal calculative elaboration of existing accounting practice was to generate such widespread interest and debate. Ours, therefore, is a history of possibilities, an account of how and why value added came to be a significant even if technically marginal accounting elaboration. From our perspective the necessity of talking about value added in a particular way arose as a result of the conditions that made the value added event possible—conditions we wish to encapsulate within our notion of an accounting constellation.

It is this idea of an accounting constellation, along with the processes of its formation, modification and dissolution which now appears as our prime object of interest. As yet, however, it remains a vague and ill-specified idea. The series of interconnected observations which follow seek to clarify certain of its more general features.

The specificity of the constellation

It is important to note first of all that the accounting constellation discussed here has been constructed in response to a particular problem concerning the value added event. There is no presupposition whatsoever that it encompasses the field of relations governing the production distribution and use of all accounting statements. An examination of, for example, the conditions of possibility of the debates surrounding accounting for depreciation, deferred taxation or inflation accounting[①] would no doubt reveal an accounting constellation that only partly coincided with that associated with value added. Indeed, this might also be true if one examined an aspect of the value added event other than the one addressed here, e. g. the appearance of value added in a particular firm.

To so argue for the specificity of a particular accounting constellation does not reduce the significance of our general method of analysis. It is merely to recognise the diverse and changing factors that can intermingle with the processes of accounting change (also see Hopwood, forthcoming). However, although advising caution on the transference of any specific accounting constellation to the domains of other ac-

---

① For some brief but related comments on the emergence and functioning of the inflation accounting debate see Burchell *et al.* (1980) and Hopwood (1984). Inflation accounting occupies some of the same accounting constellation as the value added event, albeit that different aspects are emphasised. Indeed in the accounting standards arena discussions of the two were intertwined at particular junctures in the politics surrounding the processes of accounting regulation. Inflation accounting also was implicated in debates on macro-economic management, although in somewhat different policy arenas than those which explicitly related to value added. (The emphasis was on questions of indexation, albeit a problem that had arisen in the context of incomes policies, and the performance of the manufacturing sector.) Moreover in the context of a wider politics surrounding the techniques for surplus declaration, the inflation accounting debate became intertwined with industrial relations issues. In addition to such partial overlaps, however, other significant arenas also became involved with the development and functioning of inflation accounting, including questions of taxation policy, debates on the relative performance of different sectors of the U. K. economy, a questioning of the high levels of profitability of financial institutions and discussions and developments within the academic community.

counting innovations and changes, we nevertheless would seek to argue for the general mode of analysis adopted in the present study, not least in respect of its genealogical emphasis, its mobilising theoretical and practical concerns, and the very real theoretical cautions which resulted in the use of this approach rather than any other.

The pursuit of interests and unintended consequences

The accounting constellation as we have described it was very much an *unintended* phenomenon. The field of action that we have outlined in relation to value added was not designed by anyone, and no blueprint for its construction can be found. It was produced as the consequence of the intersection of a great many events, some famous, and, as a consequence, well documented, and others unnoticed and possibly lost to history forever. Most of these events were produced by people with clear views of what they were doing—negotiating a wages settlement; conforming to an Act of Parliament; fighting inflation; seeking information; informing workers of the facts of economic reality—and no thought at all for an accounting constellation. Although there were identifiable causes to that which eventually emerged, they were ones which operated without any reference to certain of their effects.

Admittedly such a view differs from other notions of the interested nature of accounting practice. While, as we have stated, we do not seek to deny the purposive nature of accounting action, we are concerned to emphasise the potential multitude of different actors acting on accounting in purposive ways in an array of different arenas, each having specific, often nonoverlapping and sometimes conflicting interests in the accounting practice they are utilising and only partial knowledge of both its consequences and the resistance that its use will engender (Hindess, 1982). Although at any particular moment of time there may be some mobilisation of consequences that relates to the interests in the name of which accounting is advanced, in our analysis there is no assumption as to either any functional orchestration of these diverse initiatives or their precise effectivity in realising the objectives which were stated for them. Accounting may, in other words, be purposive but whether it is purposeful is a matter for detailed and careful investigation across the diverse arenas in which specific accountings can become intertwined.

A non-monolithic constellation

One consequence of being the unintended product of a large number of different purposive actions is that the accounting constellation is non-monolithic in character. Although an accounting constellation may well govern the form of reasoning concerning certain of the decisions confronting enterprise management, such as, for example, the choice of the form of accounting and payment system to be adopted, there still remains considerable scope for conflict and disagreement. It is possible to imagine a situation in which workers and management of a firm are both agreed on the desirability of introducing VAIPS and yet for both sides to violently disagree on virtually all the procedural and organizational details which would effectively constitute the new payment system. In an analogous way, a particular mode of reasoning and institutional milieu can be said to organise the conflictual debates that have occurred in the area of accounting standard setting (Zeff, 1978). In the case of value added, we have indicated how a field of action was laid down by the intersection of developments in three distinct arenas—developments which in each case proceeded without reference to certain of the possibilities and consequences of their interaction in mind. One aspect of this meshing of these developments, in fact one of the very ways in which they were articulated with one another, was that certain systems such as VAIPSs and certain categories such as value added functioned as the vehicle for a number of different interests and purposes. They were overdetermined phenomena, equivocality and ambiguity being central to their functioning. Seen in such terms an accounting constellation is less a system or an entity which is usually understood in relation to some unambiguous governing principle, role or function, than a garbage can (Cohen et al., 1972).

Accounting's embeddedness in the organisational and the social

Our model of accounting change is still in many ways a contingency model. We have not suggested or discovered any general theory of accounting change. Everything all depends on the circumstances under which change occurs. There are, however, important differences with the accounting-environment contingency model of change discussed earlier. For a start, we have not attempted to separate out two domains called accounting and the environment and then conduct the analysis in terms of this prior distinction. Instead we have attempted to outline a network of social relations throughout which there may be found in the process of their emergence and functioning a certain class of statements—value added statements, company reports, employee reports, financial statements, statements concerning financial statements, etc. Within this network accounting can be found providing the conditions of existence of certain social relations, such as helping to define the rights, duties and field of action of certain agents and playing a role in the specification of both organizational boundaries and intra-organizational segments. Accounting, so seen, is intimately implicated in the construction and facilitation of the contexts in which it operates. It cannot be extracted from its environment like an individual organism from its habitat. Of course it is possible to discuss categories such as profit and indeed value added in a general abstract manner without any reference to the law, organizational rules and functioning, and the rights and duties of agents. However the added values we are interested in, the added values featuring in the value added event, did not exist thus. To attempt to investigate them in such an abstract fashion would be to investigate a different problem. We have been concerned to capture and analyse the way value added exists and functions as an integral part of and inscribed within certain social relations. [1]

The accounting constellation and networks of social relations and organizational practices

We have frequently described the set of social relations pertinent to the emergence and functioning of value added as a network. Our use of this term is very similar to the way in which it is deployed in organizational theory (Aldrich, 1979). There the idea of a network of organizations has opened up research perspectives which tend to cut across the organization—environment dichotomy. Interest focusses less on the intra-organizational problems of adaptation to a changing environment than of the properties of a network of inter-organizational relations.

In our analysis the formation of a network of social relations has been described as a means of accounting for the outbreak of value added which during the 1970s characterised financial statements emerging from a wide range of sources. Although we have not analysed the properties of this network in any detail, it is important to note that in certain respects we conceive the accounting constellation rather differently from the way networks are specified in organizational theory. The main components of our network are not individual organizations, but rather particular systems or processes—payment systems, financial reporting systems, information systems. We

---

[1] In a very different context (that of the emergence of prisons), Patton (1979) similarly noted that "... the abstract machine, however, can only function by means of concrete social machines which give it content". He elaborated this idea in the following way: "... each concrete social machine is composed of both discursive and non-discursive elements. While the abstract machine only functions through its concrete forms, it is nevertheless that which renders possible the emergence of those concrete social machines. It plays the role of immanent cause, which 'selects' a particular machine according to its own design". In the case of value added the actual historical emergence of the abstract discursive category is so intimately bound up with its social functioning that it is difficult to disentangle the two. In other areas of accounting, however, it might be possible to more readily conduct an analysis of the interrelationship between the discursive and non-discursive components. Inflation accounting comes to mind in this respect.

have indicated how these systems are caught up and elaborated in networks of relations existing between various agents, agencies and the systems themselves. Moreover these networks were uncovered by studying developments in three arenas, each of which could be characterised in terms of specific fields of action, and targets and agents of intervention, along with their means of surveillance and intervention and associated bodies of knowledge. The developments within each arena were then seen as involving the formation of relations between particular agents, agencies and administrative practices as a consequence of the various interventions taking place. Finally, the accounting constellation was itself specified as a network by noting the often unintended interdependencies between the processes and the practices in the separate arenas.

In this way we provided an account of the emergence and functioning of value added across a diverse social space with developments in particular fields of action both changing the preconditions for developments elsewhere and enabling or constraining specific innovations to take place. Thus the arena of accounting standard setting was shown not to be independent of developments taking place in the arenas of macro-economic management and the conduct of industrial relations. Although each of these arenas had its own trajectory of change, the notion of a network enabled us to locate the possibilities for their interpenetration and mutually dependent functioning.

We attempted to use such a perspective in order to avoid giving a privileged ontological status to the notion of an organization as a discrete bounded entity with a well defined interior and exterior. Clearly such notions do exist and certain agents act in their name and are engaged in their fabrication and maintenance. What is important to note, however, is that the conditions of possibility for the actions of organization builders are *not* contained in that which they are attempting to build. An organization can hardly be presupposed as a means for its own (auto-) generation. Aware of such problems, by focussing on certain administrative systems and their position within each of the arenas we have studied, we hope to have indicated how the very substance of organizations is constructed by processes which cut across any single distinction that might be made between organizational members and non-members. In a similar way Litterer (1961, 1963) has indicated how the organizational phenomenon of "Big Business" (Chandler, 1962) was made possible by the emplacement of cost accounting, production and inventory control systems as joint effects of the systematic management movement. ①

In a similar manner the developments in each of our arenas also amount to the elaboration and development of certain dimensions of those complex entities we call the economy, society and the environment (see Donzeiot, 1979). The interventions within the different arenas, which are conducted according to a variety of different principles, single out and privilege certain agents and their means of action. In the process of being used to intervene in the organization, practices for the management of the social and the economic are elaborated and changed. "The organization" thereby designates a particular site of intersection of practices conducted in the name of the social and the economic, amongst other things. It represents a common nodal point in a number of different networks, each having different objects and means of intervention. And it also represents a site where people in attempting to draw boundaries seek to coordinate the actions of those enclosed within them, striving to fashion out of the diverse processes and interventions at work a machine for pursuing certain goals and performing certain functions. Seen in such terms the organization and society and the economy are not independent realms. Rather than residing without, the social and the economic pass through the organization in the course of their own formation, as we have seen in the case of the value added event.

The mode of investigation

Finally, it is worth making some comments concerning the mode of investigation that we employed. The choice of arenas around which the investigation has been organized was a product of the particular origins and history of a more general inquiry of which this paper is one (unintended) outcome. It was not determined at the beginning on 'the basis of any general theoretical principles or model. However the de-

---

① Unlike Chandler (1962, 1977) who merely provides a rationale for certain organizational forms by reference to general economic developments (railways, markets, etc.), Litterer (and others) describe some of the processes and mechanisms at work in the construction of the large bureaucratic firm. The systematic and scientific management movements and the welfare movement were very specific, describable forms of intervention in the enterprise involving very specific agents (engineers. welfare secretaries, foremen) which coalesced around a number of measurement techniques and administrative procedures (cost accounting, inventory and production control systems. measurement of efficiency and personnel turnover) and emerged and functioned under very specific social, political and economic conditions. These different movements were not unitied in their goals and encountered resistance to their attempts to implement their programmes, clashing with one another and with certain of the agents they attempted to (re-) construct (the foreman, the labourer, etc.). As Jenks (1960, p.421) has said: "The contemporary institutionalization of business management development through the convergence of an indeterminate number of distinct movements of thought and action." He went on to add: "Perhaps it would be well to think of several origins for the management movement, each of limited scope hut some possible overlap..." (p.427). Such a form of analysis is very consistent with our own.

cision to attempt to divide the accounting context into a number of arenas—whatever they might have been—and to consider the process of development within each as *sui generis* marching to its own drummer, was motivated by a prior theoretical concern to attempt to avoid the problems entailed in adopting an enterprise-environment and/or an accounting-environment model of change.

Having identified three arenas, our mode of investigation was in many ways very similar to those conducted by the authorities—Department of Trade Inspectors—when investigating irregularities in the affairs of a company. The irregularity that we set out to investigate was the outbreak of added value during the second half of the 1970s. How was this phenomenon or event possible? What did it signify? Now Department of Trade Inspectors in their investigations presuppose and attempt to reconstruct the accounting regime—system of book-keeping, accounting and internal control—existing in the particular company under investigation. Such a regime must have served as the condition of possibility for the irregularities which precipitated the investigation. We have been concerned with a considerably more widespread and heterogeneous set of phenomena than those normally addressed by Department of Trade Inspectors. However we have argued that certain features of the value added event were only possible given the existence of a set of conditions—the accounting constellation—which together also comprise a regime of sorts. It is however a regime which no one designed, and is never audited.

The enquiries of the authorities are also of interest because they must of necessity study accounting systems in terms other than the roles or functions, e. g. stewardship, that are commonly attributed to them. It is not enough merely to register the fact of irregularities, errors, and anomalies in the operation of an accounting system. In order to refine and elaborate accounting systems so as to prevent such irregularities occurring again in the future it is necessary to discover the positive determinants of errors and anomalies. How is it that something that is assumed to function as a means of accountability, served instead as a mechanism for financial irregularity? In the case of the value added event we have pointed to the multiplicity of roles attributed to value added statements and commented on the seeming inadequacy of any given statement as to its purported role(s). Our genealogical study of the event attempts to show how certain roles came to be attributed to a number of processes within which value added could be found functioning. We have attempted throughout to avoid making any assumptions concerning the essential or proper functions of accounting practice.

ON EMERGENCE AND DECLINE

Having discussed the nature, significance and specificity of the constellation which provided the conditions for the value added event, it is now of interest to note that the attention given to value added subsequently waned during the early 1980s. With the election of a new Conservative Government in 1979 the three arenas of the value added constellation were suddenly ruptured and transformed. Different policies were introduced for the management of the national economy. Industrial relations came quite quickly to be seen and conducted in fundamentally different terms. And albeit with a lag, the specification of accounting standards was no longer seen to be subject to so real a possibility of government intervention. In these ways the specific significances which had been attached to value added were no longer salient. With its context so radically changed, the functioning of value added in social relations started to approximate to its technical marginality. Value added started to become a phenomenon of the past.

Although the state of the British economy was still such that economic performance remained a fundamental governmental policy concern, the new administration attempted to deal with this in very different ways. Emphasis was placed on the roles that could be served by monetary policies, financial stringency and the enhancement of competitive pressures. The level of wage settlements was still seen as problematic, but incomes policies did not enter into the explicit political repertoire. Market pressures in an increasingly high unemployment economy were seen to offer more effective means for income control. Productivity and efficiency also remained important objects of government attention. Here too, however, very different interventionist strategies were used. A reemergence of the managerial prerogative was seen as being capable of enhancing the efficiency of British industry. Gone were the days when conceptions of cooperation and participation were interwoven into the vocabulary and practice of economic management. Stress was placed on the positive roles that could be played by a reemphasis of competitive pressures, increased training, the shedding of "surplus" labour and increased investment, particularly in areas of high technology and capital intensity. Related changes were taking place in the industrial relations arena. Discussions of industrial democracy, participation and the enhancement of worker rights ceased. Indeed efforts were made to repeal or not to enforce legislative rights conveyed by the previous administration. The relevance of a relationship between democracy and efficiency was no longer seen. The vocabulary of change focussed on competition, free markets and the ending of restrictive practices and monopoly powers. Certain economic rather than more widespread social and political rights came to be emphasised. More significance was attached to decisive and entrepreneurial action rather than cooperation and persuasion. Leadership rather than participation was the order of the day.

The accounting profession was slow to recognise the relevance of the changes taking place. The fear of government intervention had been a very deeply felt and widely articulated one. Eventually, however, it came to realise that it was no longer subject to the same intensity of threat. Although still very much concerned with very visible remnants of an era past in the form of inflation accounting, the profession in general and the Accounting Standards Committee in particular started to adjust itself to the new political situation. Representatives of wider industrial and financial constituencies were brought on to the Accounting Standards Committee now that its legitimacy as a protector of the profession from an interventionist State was no longer apparent. New investments were made in the potential legitimising roles of knowledge (see Hopwood, 1984). And the agenda of future areas of standard setting was radically curtailed. Amongst other things, value added was removed from the agenda for future deliberation and action.

The time for value added was no longer. The specific constellation which had resulted in its emergence, significance and development had been ruptured. The arenas out of which value added had emerged had been subject to signiticant discontinuities. The social context of value added had mutated. Devoid of its specific social conditions of possibility, value added was little more than a mere technical accounting possibility—perhaps something to be mentioned in the footnotes of accounting texts. The factors that had endowed it with a wider significance and momentum for development had disappeared.

Such a waning of interest in value added was not a new phenomenon however. Value added also had had a period of temporary significance in the United Kingdom in the late 1940s and early 1950s. Then, as in the mid 1970s, there also was conjoined a considerable interest in employee communication and information disclosure and a concern for the performance of the British economy. It was in this context that value added also appeared in company reporting practices in a way which also completely anticipated the practices of the late 1970s (Burchell *et al.*, 1981). Between those two periods there was little if any discussion of value added however.

The immediate backcloth to this earlier, proto-value added event was the Second World War. War-time mobilization resulted in trade unionists being heavily involved at all levels in the administration of social and economic policy (Pelling, 1971). Many of these war-time arrangements continued after the war when the problems of post-war reconstruction and the sudden ending of American "lend-lease" assistance led to a continued concentration on production and productivity. The winter fuel crisis of 1947 brought things to a head. In response to the Government's call for cooperation, the General Council of the Trades Union Congress urged the reconstitution of the joint production committees in the factories, most of which had faded away after the war. In addition, the issue of wage restraint came very much to the fore. One aspect of this period, as evidenced by the work of the Anglo-American Productivity Council and the contents of *Target*, a Central Office of Information publication, was the extent to which attempts were made to propagate the value of more systematic management practices. What is particularly interesting is that this discussion of enterprise practices was shot through with the imagery of cooperative endeavour. Cooperation and participation were presented as the means of underpinning improved economic performance and were to be secured by the disclosure of information. In the words of a *Target* editorial statement (*Target*, 1948):

> There is undoubtedly widespread misapprehension among working men and women upon the subject of wages and profits. The points made by the Chancellor of the Exchequer... at the recent Trades Union Congress need further elaboration and emphasis. The subject must be dealt with fully and frankly if workers generally are to be satisfied on the issues involved... the worker, who suspects that the shareholders are reaping large rewards while he, the man who produces the goods, is denied his dues, should be given the facts. More often than not a full and frank explanation will remove such misconceptions... if we are going to stand on our own feet by the time American aid comes to an end—by 1952 at the latest—we must concentrate on productivity... if workers can be made to feel that they really are partners in this all-out effort to put this country of ours on its feet again, they are surely entitled to the full facts?

Target functioned as a means of communication between companies on the problems of raising productivity. During the first eight months of its existence it focussed on works information schemes before being designated the official means of communication between the Anglo- American Productivity Council and British industry in February, 1949. Before this happened readers of the publication were greeted by such headlines as "Telling workers the facts"; "Scottish firm tells the workers 'what and why'"; "More firms who say where the money goes"; "The facts about factory economics"; and even "Workers had all the facts—up went efficiency".

Many of the employee communication schemes of companies featured in *Target* were organised around forms of distribution accounting, very reminiscent of the value added statements used nowadays in employee newspapers. Information was presented in order to reveal "how each pound of revenue... is paid out to the various costs of manufacture or remain as profits". It was at this juncture that value added made its entry in a booklet entitled *Added Value* produced by Metal Box Company Ltd (written by Sir Robert Barlow, the company's chairman). "In spite of paper difficulties", a copy of *Added Value* was sent to every man and woman on the weekly staff and to hourly-paid workers in certain long service grades. Its publication was timed to coincide with the issue of the company's 1948 annual report which was sent to every member of each factory's work committee. Writing in the booklet, Sir Robert commented that:

> There is... a great deal of misconception about profits, or, as they might properly be called, earnings. There is even a danger that they may be regarded as evil in themselves—hence that those who earn them are engaged in anti-social activities.
>
> Writing from the standpoint of productive industry, we say that this is the opposite of truth: that a profit which arises from the efficient working of a worthwhile enterprise is legitimate, desirable and necessary. For the alternative to a profit is a loss, and who, may it be asked, will be the better for that? Not the shareholders, not the employees, not the management, nor the State, for all of these benefit from a profit and would suffer from a loss. Least of all, perhaps, the customer: for no enterprise. operating at a loss, can supply him with what he will need in a market competitive in quality and price.
>
> The object of this booklet is to demonstrate this from facts: to go further and to show that from the operations of an industrial concern there arises an added value which is shared by all. For when a man performs a useful piece of work he creates wealth in its real sense. Once a body of men are actuated to perform their part of a common task in a better than normal way, and when from their efforts there flows a continually expanding activity, wealth is created to a considerably increased degree. Profit ceases to be, if indeed it ever has been, the dominating motive, and pride in work and an ensuing sense of responsibility takes its place (Metal Box Company Ltd., 1948).

In the name of such ideas, Metal Box introduced a whole array of strategies and practices to communicate the facts of business life to the workers in order "to explain the significance of... various points, their impact on the company, what the organization as a whole and the men and women who make it work, can do to help."①

---

① For a discussion of other related schemes at this time see Burchell *et al*. (1981).

The existence of such a proto-value added enables us to reinforce the point concerning the way the functioning and very existence of accounting categories is conditioned by a complex set of circumstances. It also enables us to emphasise the highly specific and contingent nature of those circumstances. For in the early 1950s, as in the early 1980s, interest in value added was to wane. Again with a different political context and, in this case, the emergence of relative economic prosperity rather than the use of very different policies for the continued management of adversity, the value added constellation was ruptured and subjected to significant discontinuities. The very decline of interest in value added thereby serves to reinforce the theoretical perspective developed in this paper.

CONCLUSION

We have sought to indicate how the value added event arose out of a complex interplay of institutions, issues and processes. The study of this particular accounting change has enabled us not only to move towards grounding accounting in the specific social contexts in which it operates but also to raise and discuss what we see to be some important theoretical issues which have to be faced when seeking to understand the social functioning of the accounting craft.

Zeff (1978) albeit in a different way from ourselves, is another who has pointed to the need for such richer and more contextual appreciations of accounting in action. Focussing solely on the setting of accounting standards he points to the myriad political factors which have intruded in the setting (and subsequent criticism) of standards, factors the impact of which is not registered in the accounting model which has traditionally provided the dominant frame of reference for discussing accounting practices and the reasons for adopting them. Zeff argues that the economic and social consequences of accounting practices "may no longer be ignored as a substantive issue in the setting of accounting standards" (Zeff, 1978) and *inter alia* points to the importance of developing our theoretical resources in order to be able to adequately confront this issue.

Recently there has been developed a theoretical approach to accounting based on the agency model of the firm (Jensen & Meckling, 1976) which may be seen as a direct response to the problem articulated by Zeff. This approach has been employed in the analysis of the standard setting process (Watts & Zimmerman, 1978), the status and form of accounting theory (Watts & Zimmerman, 1979) and the form of particular accounting procedures (Zimmerman, 1979). By way of concluding, it is worthwhile to indicate briefly in what ways the approach we have adopted differs from that of the agency theorists and the associated implications for accounting research.

In general terms the differences between the two approaches can be clearly stated. In the case of the agency theorists, financial statements are viewed as economic goods for which there exists a certain demand and the production of which entails certain costs. The function of financial statements is that of a means of determining the magnitude of certain wealth transfers such as dividends, tax credits, loan payments, management renumeration and agency costs. Accounting procedures differ in their impact on these wealth transfers, and it is argued that individuals and groups are therefore not indifferent as to the particular procedures used. These individuals and groups calculate the effect on their wealth of using any given procedure and take up positions accordingly—whether it be in an unregulated market for financial statements or in relation to some regulatory agency. We do not doubt that individual agents do attempt to estimate the financial effects of proposed changes in accounting practice as part of their process of decision-making in relation to the choice of accounting procedures. We, however, are more interested in the processes whereby a particular configuration of interest groups, or rather groups with an interest in accounting, comes into existence. The agency theorists only distinguish between such configurations to the extent that they distinguish between regulated and unregulated economies. Clearly state intervention into the economy has been of enormous importance for the development of accounting (see Hopwood et al., 1980). This, however, does not mean that it is impossible to construct a more nuanced picture than that which the dichotomy between a regulated and unregulated state allows and, at the same time, study in greater detail the processes of change. Amongst other things we would include amongst these processes those whereby accounting, or particular categories and statements, came to feature within the field of interest of certain agents and the *means* whereby the position of these agents with respect to these novel objects is deliberated and calculated: how was it that value added surfaced within the field of industrial relations and how was it evaluated once it had appeared there?

Thus our focus rests on the processes of change whereas the agency theorists attempt to establish correlations between certain classes of action, such as positions adopted on proposed accounting standards, and estimates of the interests of those adopting the positions. The agency theorists present their model as a self-interest theory whereas we are concerned to discover how self-interests, or particular policy positions, are in fact established—including the role which specific economic calculations and accountings rather than the generality of an economic calculus play in this process. The agency theorists privilege a particular mode of calculating (self-) interests derived from economic theory and a particular role for financial statements. Their analysis presupposes the existence of a meta-accounting which somehow guides rational economic action and their studies seek to explore specific explications and elaborations of such an accounting. Our analysis aims to make no such presumption of a primaeval account. Rather than being viewed by us as revelatory of particular administrative and policy making practices, the role and mode of calculation are instead viewed as functioning discursive components *within* these practices.

We have in this paper adopted a historical, genealogical approach as a device to avoid the assumption that accounting has some essential role or function. Our working principle in this has been that "the cause of the origin of a thing and its eventual unity, its actual employment and place in a system of purposes, are worlds apart" (Nietzsche, 1969, p. 77 as quoted in Minson, 1980). It has been suggested elsewhere that the organization of our concepts and the philosophical difficulties that arise from them, have to do with their historical origins. When there occurs a transformation of ideas, whatever made the transformation possible leaves its mark on subsequent reasoning. It is as if concepts have memories (Hacking, 1981). Indeed the study by Wells of the origins of accounting for overhead costs is written in just such a vein (Wells, 1978). In a similar way we have attempted to indicate how the processes underlying the value added event determined the character of discourse bearing the category value added.

BIBLIOGRAPHY

Aims and Scope of Company Reports, *The Accountant* (1 July, 1976), pp. 12—14.

Accounting Standards Steering Committee, *The Corporate Report* (ASSC, 1975).

Ackerman, R. & Bauer, R., *Corporate Social Responsiveness: The Modern Dilemma* (Englewood Cliffs, NJ: Prentice-Hall, 1976).

Aldrich, H. E., *Organizations and their Environments* (Englewood Cliffs, NJ: Prentice-Hall, 1979).

Ball, R. J., The Use of Value Added in Measuring Managerial Efficiency, *Business Ratios* (*Summer* 1968), pp. 5—11.

Barratt Brown, M., *Information at Work* (Arrow Books, 1978).

Beddoc, R., *Value Added and Payment Systems*, Technical note no. 42 (Oxford: The Trade Union Research Unit. Ruskin College, 1978).

Bedford, N. M., *The Future of Accounting in a Changing Society* (Champaign, IL: Stipes. 1970).

Benston, G. J., An Analysis of the Role of Accounting Standards for Enhancing Corporate Governance and Social Responsibility, in Bromwich, M., and Hopwood, A. G. (eds) *Accounting Standard Setting: An International Perspective* (Pitman, 1983).

置于社会与组织环境中的会计研究

Benston, G. J. , *Corporate Financial Disclosure in the UK and the USA* (Saxon House, 1976).

Benston, G. J. , The Value of the SEC's Accounting Disclosure Requirements, *The Accounting Review* (July 1969) , pp. 515—532.

Bentley Associates, *A Dynamic Pay Policy for Growth* (Brighton: Bentley Associates, 1975).

Binder, Hamlyn and Fry & Co. , *Added Value as a Concept* (Binder, Hamlyn and Fry, 1978).

British Institute of Management, *The Disclosure of Financial Information to Employees* (BIM, 1957).

Burchell, S. , Clubb, C. & Hopwood, A. , "A Message From Mars"—and other Reminiscences From the Past, *Accountancy* (October 1981) , pp. 96, 98, 100.

Burchell, S. , Clubb, C. , Hopwood, A. G. , Hughes, J. & Nahapiet, J. , The Roles of Accounting in Organizations and Society, *Accounting, Organizations and Society* (1980), pp. 5—27.

Cameron, S. , Added Value Plan for Distributing ICI's Wealth, *Financial Times* (7 January, 1977a).

Cameron, S. , Adding Value to Britain, *Financial Times* (31 May, 1977b).

Cameron, S. , Breeding a New Type of Productivity Deal, *Financial Times* (3 April, 1978).

Carlsson, J. , Ehn, P. , Erlander, B. , Perby, M-L. & Sandberg, A. , Planning and Control from the Perspective of Labour: A Short Presentation of the DEMOS Project, *Accounting, Organizations and Society* (1978), pp. 249—260.

Chambers, R. J. , *Accounting Evaluation and Economic Behaviour* (Englewood Cliffs, NJ: Prentice-Hall, 1966).

Chandler, A. D. , *Strategy and Structure* (Cambridge, MA: M. I. T. Press, 1962).

Chandler, A. D. , The *Visible Hand: The Managerial Revolution in American Business* (Harvard University Press, 1977).

Churchill, N. C. , The Accountant's Role in Social Responsibility, in Stone, W. E. , *The Accountant in a Changing Business Environment* (University of Florida Press, 1973), pp. 14—27.

Cohen, M. D. , March, J. G. , Olsen, J. P. , A Garbage Can Model of Organizational Choice, *Administrative Science Quarterly* (March 1972) , pp. 1—25.

Confederation of British Industry, *Financial Participation in Companies: An Introductory Booklet* (CBI, 1978).

Cooper, D. , A Social and Organizational View of Management Accounting, in Bromwich, M. and Hopwood, A. G. (eds) *Essays in British Accounting Research* (Pitman, 1981).

Cox, B. , *Value Added: An Appreciation for the Accountant Concerned with Industry* (Heinemann in association with the Institute of Cost and Management Accountants, 1979).

Crouch, C. , *The Politics of Industrial Relations* (Fontana, 1979).

Crum, R. P. , Added-Value Taxation: The Roots Run Deep into Colonial and Early America, *The Accounting Historians Journal* (Fall 1982) , pp. 25—42.

Department of Trade, *Committee of Inquiry on Industrial Democracy* (Chairman: Lord Bullock) Cmnd 6706 (1977a).

Department of Trade, *The Future of Company Reports* (London: H. M. S. O. , 1977b).

Dierkes, M. , Corporate Social Reporting in Germany: Conceptual Developments and Practical

Experience, *Accounting Organizations and Society* (1979), pp. 87—100.

Dijksma, J. & Van der Wal, R., Value Added in Dutch Corporate Annual Reports 1980—1982, Working paper of the Faculteit der Economische Wetenschappen, Erasmus University, Rotterdam (1984).

Donovan, Lord, *Royal Commission on Trade Unions* (Cmnd 3623, London: H.M.S.O., 1968).

Donzelot, J., *The Policing of Families* (Pantheon, 1979).

Elliot, J., The Liberals Make Their Point, *Financial Times* (3 February, 1978).

Engineering Employers Federation, *Business Performance and Industrial Relations* (Kogan Page, 1972).

Engineering Employers Federation, *Practical Applications of Added Value* (Archway Press, 1977).

Estes, R., *Accounting and Society* (Melville Publishing Company, 1973).

Estes, R. W., *Corporate Social Accounting* (New York: John Wiley, 1976).

Fanning, D., Banishing Confusion from the Added Value Equation, *Financial Times* (13 December, 1978) p. 11.

Fels, A., *The British Prices and Incomes Board* (Cambridge University Press, 1972).

Flint, D., The Role of the Auditor in Modern Society: An Exploratory Essay, *Accounting and Bussiness Research* (Autumn 1971), pp. 287—293.

Foucault, M., Nietzsche, Genealogy, History, in Foucault M., (ed. by D. F. Bouchard). *Language, Counter Memory Practice* (Oxford: Basil Blackwell, 1977).

Frankel, M., *The Social Audit Pollution Handbook* (Macmillan, 1978).

Gambling, T., *Societal Accounting* (Macmillan, 1974).

Gandhi, N. M., The Emergence of the Postindustrial Society and the Future of the Accounting Function, *International Journal of Accounting* (Spring 1976), pp. 33—49.

Gandhi, N. M., Accounting in a Non Market Economy: A Futuristic Look, in Gordon, L. A. (ed.), *Accounting and Corporate Responsibility* (University of Kansas, 1978).

Gilling, D. M., Accounting and Social Change, *International Journal of Accounting* (Spring 1976), pp. 59—71.

Gold, M., Levie, H. & Moore, R., *The Shop Stewards' Guide to the use of Company Information* (Spokesman Books, 1979).

Gordon, L. A. (ed) *Accounting and Corporate Social Responsibility* (University of Kansas, 1978).

Gospel, H., Disclosure of Information to Trade Unions, *Industrial Law Journal* (1976).

Gray, S. I. & Maunders, K. T., *Value Added Reporting: Uses and Measurement* (Association of Certified Accountants, 1980).

Hacking, I., How Should We do the History of Statistics, *Ideology and Consciousness* (Spring 1981), pp. 15—26.

Hilton, A., *Employee Reports: How to Communicate Financial Information to Employees* (Woodhead-Faulkner, 1978).

Hindess, B., Power, Interests and the Outcomes of Struggles, *Sociology* (November 1982), pp. 498—511.

Hird, C., Beware of Added Value, *New Statesman* (4 August, 1980).

Hird, C., *Your Employers' Profits* (Pluto Press, 1975).

Holmes, G., How UK Companies Report Their Employees, *Accountancy* (November 1977), pp. 64—68.

Hopkins, L., Value Added, *Accountancy Age* (7 November, 1975).

Hopwood, A. G., Accounting Research and Accounting Practice: The Ambiguous Relationship Between the Two, Paper presentation to the conference on New Challenges for Management Research, Leuven, Belgium (1984).

Hopwood, A. G., The Tale of a Committee that Never Reported: Disagreements on Intertwining Accounting with the Social, *Accounting, Organizations and Society* (1985), pp. 361—377.

Hopwood, A. G., The Archeology of Accounting Systems, *Accounting Organizations and Society* (forthcoming).

Hopwood, A. G., Burchell, S. & Clubb, C., The Development of Accounting in Its International Context: Past Concerns and Emergent Issues, In A. Roberts, ed., *A Historical and Contemporary Review of the Development of International Accounting* (Georgia State University, 1980).

Hussey, R., *Employees and the Employment Report—A Research Paper* (Touche Ross & Co., 1978).

Hussey, R., *Who Reads Employee Reports?* (Touche Ross & Co., 1979).

Incomes Data Report, New Thoughts on Profit Sharing at ICI, Report 251 (February 1977) p.21.

Institute of Chartered Accountants in England and Wales, Statement of Intent on Accounting Standards in the 1970s, *The Accountant* (18 December, 1969), pp. 842—843.

Institute of Chartered Accountants in England and Wales (ICAEW), *Survey of Published Accounts 1977* (ICAEW, 1978).

Institute of Chartered Accountants in England and Wales (ICAEW), *Survey of Published Accounts 1979* (ICAEW, 1980).

Jenks, L. H., Early Phases of the Management Movement, *Administrative Science Quarterly* (1960), pp. 421—447.

Jensen, M. C. & Meckling, W. H., Theory of the Firm: Managerial Behaviour, Agency Costs and Ownership Structure, *Journal of Financial Economics* (1976), pp. 305—360.

Jones, F. C., The *Economic Ingredients of Industrial Success* (James Clayton Lecture, The Institution of Mechanical Engineers, 1976).

Jones, F. T., Our Manufacturing Industry—The Missing £ 100.000 million, *National Westminster Bank Quarterly Review* (May 1978), pp. 8—17.

Kahn-Freud, O., Industrial Democracy, *Industrial Law Journal* (1977), pp. 75—76.

Kuhn, T., *The Structure of Scientific Revolutions*, 2nd Ed. (University of Chicago Press, 1970).

Labour Party, *The Community and the Company* (1974).

Value Added, *Labour Research* (February, 1978).

Leyland, N. H., Productivity, in Warswick and Ady, *The British Economy 1945—1950* (Oxford: The Clarendon Press, 1952).

Litterer, J., Systematic Management: Design for Organizational Recoupling in American Manufacturing Firms, *Business History Review* (1963), pp. 369—391.

Litterer, J., Systematic Management: The Search for Order and Integration, *Business History Review* (1961), pp. 461—476.

Livingstone, J. L. & Gunn. S. C., *Accounting for Social Goals: Budgeting and Analysis of Non*

Market Projects (Harper & Row, 1974).

Low, E., Forget Piecework and Develop a Fair Way to Reward Employees, *Accountants Weekly* (6 May, 1977), pp. 16—17.

Lucas, R. J., *Pension Planning Within a Major Company: A Case Study of the Negotiation of the British Leyland Pension Plan for Manual Workers* (Oxford: Pergamon Press, 1979).

Maitre, P., The Measurement of the Creation and Distribution of Wealth in a Firm by the Method of Surplus Accounts, *Accounting, Organizations and Society* (1978), pp. 227—236.

Marchington, M. P., Worker Participation and Plant-wide Incentive Systems, *Personnel Review* (Summer 1977), pp. 35—38.

McKersie, R. B. & Hunter, L. C., *Pay Productivity and Collective Bargaining* (Macmillan, 1973).

McLeay, S., Value Added: A Comparative Study, *Accounting, Organizations and Society* (1983), pp. 31—56.

Medawar, C., *The Social Audit Consumer Handbook* (Macmillan, 1978).

Metal Box Company Limited, *Added Value* (London: Metal Box Company Ltd., 1948).

Minson, J., Stragegies for Socialists? Foucault's Conception of Power, *Economy and Society* (1980).

Moonitz, M., *Obtaining Agreement on Standards in the Accounting Profession*, Studies in Accounting Research No. 8 (American Accounting Association, 1974).

Morley, M. F., *The Value Added Statement* (Gee & Co. for the Institute of Chartered Accountants of Scotland, 1978).

National Board for Prices and Incomes, *General Report*, August 1967—July 1968, (Cmnd 3715 London: H. M. S. O., 1968).

Neimark, M. D. & Tinker, A. M., The Social Construction of Management Control Systems, *Accounting, Organizations and Society* (forthcoming).

Nelson, C. L., A *Priori* Research in Accounting, in Dopuch, N. and Revsine, L. (eds) *Accounting Research 1960—1970: A Critical Evaluation* (Center for International Education and Research in Accounting, 1973).

New, C., Factors in Productivity that Should Not be Overlooked, *The Times* (1 February, 1978).

Nietzsche, F., *On the Genealogy of Morals*, Kaufmann, W. (trans.) (Vintage Books, 1969).

Pakenham-Walsh, A. A., Spanners in the Growth Engine, *The Cost Accountant* (July 1964), pp. 260—268.

Patton, P., Of Power and Prisons, in Morris, M. & Patton, P. (eds.) *Michel Foucault: Power, Truth, Strategy* (Sydney: Feral Publications, 1979).

Pelling, A., *A History of British Trade Unionism* (Harmondsworth: Penguin Books, 1971)

Pitkin, H. F., *The Concept of Representation* (University of California Press, 1967).

Ramanathan, K. V., Theory of Corporate Social Accounting, *The Accounting Review* (July 1976), pp. 516—528.

Reichmann, T. & Lange, C., The Value Added Statement as Part of Corporate Social Reporting, *Management International Review* (1981).

Renshall, M., Allan, R. & Nicholson, K., *Added Value in External Financial Reporting* (Institute of Chartered Accountants in England and Wales, 1979).

Rey, F., *Introduction a la Comptabilite Sociale: Domaines. Techniques et Applications* (Paris: Enterprise Moderne d'Edition, 1978).

Roberts, J., & Scapens, R., Accounting Systems and Systems of Accountability—Understanding Accounting Practices in Their Organizational Contexts, *Accounting, Organizations and Society* (1985), pp. 443—456.

Robertson, J., Can we have a Non-Profit Society, *The Sunday Times* (19 May, 1974).

Ruggles, R. & Ruggles, N. D., *National Income Accounts and Income Analysis*, 2nd Ed. (New York: McGraw Hill, 1965).

Rutherford, B. A., Value Added as a Focus of Attention for Financial Reporting: Some Conceptual Problems, *Accounting and Business Research* (Summer 1977), pp. 215—220.

Rutherford, B. A., Examining Some Value Added Statements, *Accountancy* (July 1978), pp. 48—52.

Rutherford, B. A., Published Statements of Value Added: A Survey of Three Year's Experience, *Accounting and Business Review* (Winter, 1980), pp. 15—28.

Sandilands Committee, *Inflation Accounting: Report of the Inflation Accounting Committee* (Cmnd 6225 London: H. M. S. O., 1975).

Schreuder, H., Corporate Social Reporting in the Federal Republic of Germany: an Overview, *Accounting Organizations and Society* (1979), pp. 109—122.

Searle, G. R., *The Quest for National Efficiency* (Oxford: Basil Blackwell, 1971).

Sharp, K., Accounting Standards After 12 months, *Accountancy* (May 1971), pp. 239—245.

Skerratt, L. C. L. & Tonkin, D. J., *Financial Reporting 1982—1983: A Survey of U. K. Published Accounts* (Institute of Chartered Accountants in England and Wales, 1982).

Smith, G., *Wealth Creation—the Added Value Concept* (Institute of Practitioners in Work Study, Organizations and Methods, 1978).

Stamp, E., The Politics of Professional Accounting Research: Some Personal Reflections, *Accounting, Organizations and Society* (1985).

Stolliday, I. & Attwood, M., Financial Inducement and Productivity Bargaining, *Industrial and Commercial Training* (1978).

Stuttard, G., Industrial Democracy by the Back Door, *Financial Times* (21 March, 1979).

Target, The Facts About Factory Economics (November 1948).

Tinker, A. M., The Naturalization of Accounting: Social Ideology and the Genesis of Agency Theory Working paper, New York University (1984).

Tinker, A. M., Towards a Political Economy of Accounting: An Empirical Illustration of the Cambridge Controversies, *Accounting Organizations and Society* (1980), pp. 147—160.

Tinker, A. M., Merino, B. D. & Neimark, M. D., The Normative Origins of Positive Theories: Ideology and Accounting Thought, *Accounting, Organizations and Society* (1982), pp. 167—200.

Tomlinson, J., *Problems of British Economic Policy, 1870—1945* (Metheun, 1981).

Tonkin, D. J. & Skerratt, L. C. L., *Financial Reporting 1983—1984: A Survey of U. K Published Accounts* (Institute of Chartered Accountants in England and Wales, 1983).

Trades Union Congress, *Industrial Democracy* (TUC, 1974).

Turner, H. A., Collective Bargaining and the Eclipse of Incomes Policies: Retrospect, Prospect and Possibilities, *British Journal of Industrial Relations* (July 1970).

Ullman, A. A., Corporate Social Reporting: Political Interests and Conflicts in Germany, *Accounting Organizations and Society* (1979), pp. 123—133.

Vangermeersch, R. G. J., *Accounting: Social Responsible and Socially Relevant* (Harper and Row, 1972).

Vickers da Costa, *Testing for Success* (London: Mimeo, 1979).

Vogel, D., *Lobbying the Corporation: Citizen Challenges to Business Authority* (Basic Books, 1978).

Watts, R. L., Corporate Financial Statements: A Product of the Market and Political Processes, *Australian Journal of Management* (April 1977), pp. 53—75.

Watts, R. L., & Zimmerman, J. L., The Demand for the Supply of Accounting Theories: The Market for Excuses, *The Accounting Review* (April 1979), pp. 273—305.

Watts, R. L. & Zimmerman, J. L., Towards a Positive Theory of the Determination of Accounting Standards, *The Accounting Review* (January 1978), pp. 112—134.

Wellens, J., An ICI Experiment in Company-wide Communication, *Industrial and Commercial Training* (July 1977), pp. 271—278.

Wells, M. C., *Accounting for Common Costs* (International Centre for Accounting Education and Research, University of Illinois, 1978).

Wells, M. C., A Revolution in Accounting Thought, *The Accounting Review* (July 1976), pp. 471—482.

Whittington, G., *Inflation Accounting: An Introduction to the Debate* (Cambridge University Press, 1983).

Wilsher, P., How do you cut your Profit and Save Prosperity, *Sunday Times* (30 June, 1974).

Woodmansay, M., *Added Value: An Introduction to Productivity Schemes* (British Institute of Management, 1978).

Zeff, S. A., *Forging Accounting Principles in Five Countries* (Stipes, 1972).

Zeff, S. A., The Rise of Economic Consequences, *Journal of Accountancy* (December 1978).

Zimmerman, J. L., The Cost and Benefits of Cost Allocations. *The Accounting Review* (1979), pp. 504—521.

The Archaeology of Accounting Systems*

ANTHONY G. HOPWOOD

(*London School of Economics and Political Science*)

Abstract: Accounting systems change over time. However relatively little is known of the preconditions for such change, the process of change or its organisational consequences. Existing perspectives on accounting change are reviewed and evaluated in this article. Thereafter three examples of accounting change are discussed. Based on these cases, a number of theoretical issues relating to the understanding of the process of accounting change are examined. Emphasis is placed on the diversity of factors implicated in accounting change, the constitutive as well as reflective roles of accounting and the ways in which accounting change can shift the preconditions for subsequent organisational changes.

Accounting is not a static phenomenon. Over time, it repeatedly has changed. New techniques have been incorporated into the accounting craft. It has been called upon to serve an ever greater variety of different and changing purposes. Different accounts have been provided of organisational activities, processes and outcomes. Different emphases have been incorporated into accounting practices. Over time, accounting has been implicated in the creation of very different patterns of organisational segmentation. New patterns of organisational autonomy and interdependency have been highlighted, if not more actively created by accounting means. Different managerial functions have come to be emphasized by the changing accounting representation of them.

When seen in such terms, accounting continually has had a tendency to become what it was not. A fluid and emergent craft, its techniques and their attendant perspectives have been implicated in a number of very different ways in organisational and social transformations. Unfortunately, however, very little is known of the

---

* *Accounting, Organizations and Society*, Vol. 12, No. 3, pp. 207—234, 1987. The financial support of the Anglo-German Foundation for the Study of Industrial Society and the Foundation for Management Education is greatly acknowledged. The paper has benefited enormously from discussions with Stuart Burchell, Colin Clubb, John Hughes and Janine Nahapiet. The more specific comments of Shahid Ansari, Simon Archer, Mark Covaleski, Mark Dirsmith, Graeme Harrison, Pat Keating, Brendan McSweeney, Peter Miller, Ted O'Leary, Charles Perrow and Ross Stewart have greatly assisted in the revision process. Finally, I wish to acknowledge the facilitative environment provided by my Summer colleagues at Pennsylvania State University which helped the preparation of the final draft of the article.

processes of accounting change. As of now we have only a limited understanding of the conditions which provide the possibility for particular conceptions of the accounting craft, the forces that put accounting into motion, the processes accompanying accounting elaboration and diffusion, and the varied human, organisational and social consequences that can stem from changing accounting regimes.

Although a great deal of attention has been devoted to the history of accounting (American Accounting Association, 1970; Baladouni, 1977; Parker, 1977, 1981), most of the studies that are available have adopted a rather technical perspective delineating the residues of the accounting past rather than more actively probing into the underlying processes and forces at work. Antiquarianism has reigned supreme. Much of the significance for accounting of the wider economic and social setting of the organisation has been ignored. The roles which organisational accounts might have played in the emergence of organisations as we now know them, the external and internal boundaries which they are conceived of having, and the relationships which they have to other bodies and interests have been subjected to very little investigation. Relatively little consideration has been given to the ways in which accounting has become implicated in, and, in turn, shaped by, the emergence of processes of organisational governance and management. For until recently (Armstrong, 1985, 1987; Hoskin & Macve, 1986; Loft, 1986a; Merino & Neimark, 1982; Miller & O'Leary, 1987), most historical analyses of the accounting phenomenon, if not adopting a quite atheoretical stance, have been content to see accounting change as a process of technical elaboration and, almost invariably, improvement.

Rather than being perceived as an outcome of processes that could make accounting what it was not, accounting has more frequently been seen as becoming what it should be. A teleological trajectory of development has provided a basis for understanding changes in the accounting craft. Discursive conceptions of technical or economic rationality and purpose have been called upon to make sense of the emergence of practical developments in the accounting arena.[①] Instead of being interroga-

---

[①] For a somewhat more detailed discussion of the relationship between accounting (and related) discourses and accounting practice see Hopwood (1984b). Also see Miller & O'Leary (1986, 1987). A fuller consideration of the practical consequences of accounting discourse also would probe into the discursive cohesion given to disparate accounting practices by textbooks and manuals, the diffusion roles served by these sources, and the significance for the development of an accounting rhetoric of the extension of accounting discourse into the arena of the organizational and, particularly, the managerial uses of accounting techniques. Accounting discourses also have played an influential role in interpreting the heterogeneous nature of practice, isolating from amongst the diversity examples of both "good" and "bad". By so appealing to conceptions of practice that are not in any sense implicit in the craft itself, the accounting discourse articulates a normalising logic that concerns itself with the achievement of what is seen to be accounting and organizational improvement. For a further discussion of these points see Hopwood (1986a).

ted in the name of the factors that either impinge upon accounting or are changed as a result of it, a relatively unproblematic progressive and functionalist interest has been imposed all too readily on the residues of the accounting past.

A not dissimilar perspective also has tended to pervade many of the attempts that have been made to gain a more explicit organisational understanding of the accounting phenomenon. Relatively little has been done to advance our understanding of the pressures that impinge on accounting in practice; we have few insights into how the very practice of accounting might itself create a dynamic for accounting change and reform; and little is known of the precarious and often uncertain relationships which the practice of accounting has with the potential in the name of which it is advanced.① Despite the fact that accounting has and still does become what it is not, despite the fact that accounting can be quite centrally implicated in wider processes of organisational functioning, and despite the fact that accounting gets mobilised in the name of ends that do not enter into its own justification (Burchell et al., 1980), many organisational enquiries into accounting have tended to see and study it in ways that are disconnected from the contexts in which it operates. It is still perceived as a relatively static technical phenomenon that enables rather than more actively shapes organisational functioning as we now know it.

The need for an alternative view of accounting in action is now a very real one, however. On the other hand, there are a number of quite significant pressures on accounting to change. Questions are being raised about the relationship which accounting might have to different organisational forms and processes (den Hertog, 1978; Hedberg & Jönsson, 1978; Hopwood, 1977, 1979). Increasingly accounting is being interrogated in the name of a more strategic conception of organisational management (Goold, 1986; Simmonds, 1983). Accounts are being demanded of different organisations, not least those residing outside the domain of the "private" (Hopwood, 1984a). Different information technologies are creating the potential for con-

---

① Although many enquiries have sought to identify the dysfunctional aspects of accounting functioning, these usually have been seen as phenomena to be confronted and changed in the name of an accounting potential rather than manifestations of the organizational tensions and conflicts created by the increasing encroachment of the accounting craft on other aspects of organizational life. As such, analyses of dysfunctions have tended to tell us much about the conceptions of the ideal from which practice is deemed to have deviated as they do about the functioning of accounting systems in practice. Indeed such a primary concern with the accounting potential rather than its actuality also is reflected in the increasingly sophisticated attempts that have been made to utilize behavioural understandings to fine-tune the sociotechnical practice of accounting. Rather than seeking to confront the technical practice of accounting, and the aims that are attributed to it, with insights gained from an appreciation of its organizational emergence, functioning and consequences, many behavioural and organizational studies have tended to be used to mobilize the technical interest.

tinued shifts in the locus and organisational significance of the accounting craft. And, not least in significance, increasingly accounting is being examined in terms of the consequences which it actually has rather than those to which it continues to aspire (Hopwood, 1986; Kaplan, 1985). So albeit slowly, the factors implicated in accounting change, its organisational advancement and the actual consequences of the accounting craft are startingto enter the research agenda. On the other hand, the research perspectives from which accounting is examined also are starting to change. Rather than necessarily seeking to advance only the technical rationality of the craft, there are signs of both more appreciative and more critical stances emerging within the research community. Not unrelated to this, very different questions are starting to be asked of accounting. Rather than accepting its technical rationality, such research is beginning to probe into the wider organisational and social origins of accounting as we now know it. Questions are being asked of the variety of organisational pressures and rationales underlying the accounting craft. Consideration is being given to the ways in which conflicting interests are intertwined with the development of forms of economic calculation, such as accounting. And with accounting no longer seen as a disinterested endeavour, but as one that creates a very particular visibility and pattern of organisational significance, more explicit attention is being given to its consequences for both organisational and social action.

When seen in such terms, the agenda for research is a large one. The technical and static emphases of the past stand in stark contrast to the emerging interest in a wider view of accounting dynamics. Recognising, however, that such an agenda is beyond the scope of any single analysis and review, the present discussion has a number of more particular objectives. Initially some existing perspectives, both explicit and implicit, on accounting change are examined. The aim is to consider their adequacy for understanding both the forces that put accounting into motion and the ways in which the accounting craft becomes intertwined with organisational and social action. Thereafter, an appeal is made to a number of illustrative cases, both historical and contemporary, in order to illuminate at least some of the pressures and processes involved in accounting change. Rather than striving to present comprehensive analyses of accounting becoming what it was not, the objective of the case discussions is the more tentative one of trying to tease out some bases for an alternative questioning of the accounting craft. Based on these case analyses, a number of important issues relevant for an understanding of accounting change are identified and discussed. The aim of the analysis as a whole is to move towards a more questioning, a more organisationally grounded and a more dynamic understanding of the accounting craft.

置于社会与组织环境中的会计研究

SOME PERSPECTIVES ON ACCOUNTING CHANGE

Accounting and organisational improvement

As has been made clear already, the majority of conventional discussions of accounting change see it in terms of organisational reform and improvement. Accounting is changed in order to get better. Albeit slowly, the craft is seen as having progressed. Analysis, enquiry and experiential learning together are seen as having resulted in the increasing realisation of an accounting potential. In becoming what it was not, accounting has been seen to be in the process of becoming what it should be.

Such characterisations of accounting change invariably appeal to the role which accounting is seen as playing in the enhancement of organisational performance. Organisational economy, efficiency and effectiveness are seen not only as being capable of being improved by accounting means but also as having an existence independent of the accounting or other calculative representations of them. Moreover, the positive roles which accounting plays in organisational functioning also tend to be defined prior to and independently of the specific organisational practices by which they are effected. Accounting is seen as being implicated in processes of direction, planning, decision making, co-ordination, control and the management of motivation, amongst other things. In all of these areas specific practices of accounting can be, and indeed are, compared with abstract conceptualisations of what they essentially should be about.

In such ways conceptual bodies of knowledge play a powerful role in informing our understandings of the accounting craft. Accounting, even in the conventional view, is not a mere technique. Knowledge does not stand outside of accounting. Our appreciations of the technical nature of accounting are infused by a rhetoric of economic and managerial rationality and functioning. Appeals are made to a "conceptual network" (Foucault, 1972) of ideas, categories and theories that are seen to illuminate and give guidance to the pragmatic accounting task. Actual accounting practices thereby can be seen as manifestations of the realisation or frustration of these abstract imperatives. They can be seen as being more or less adequate in ways that are not solely dependent on their specific functioning in specific organisations. And because of this, attempts can be made to improve accounting in the name of what it should be rather than what it is.

As a discipline, accounting has invested a great deal in the articulation of abstract bodies of knowledge concerned with what it should be.① Ideas exist as to good, indeed, "best", costing practice, good planning, good modes of management reporting and good approaches to the appraisal of new investment possibilities. Attempts have been made to tease out the abstract characteristics of good co-ordination and direction, and their implications for the reform of accounting practice. Both economic and cognitive conceptions of decision making and its rationality have been related to the accounting concrete. Regimes of thought thereby have been developed which have an existence and dynamic of change which are not dependent on the practice of the accounting craft. By drawing on bodies of knowledge from such more autonomous discourses as economics, political theory, public administration and psychology or emergent notions of strategic management, as well as by abstracting from the practice and functioning of the craft itself, accounting can be evaluated in terms of what it is not. Specific practices can be appraised on the basis of their conformity to more general notions of management and the manageable. An abstract external body of knowledge can be imposed on them in order both to assess their adequacy and to reform them so that they can become what they really should be. Accounting is seen as being able to be mobilised and changed in the name of an abstract image of its real potential.②

Undoubtedly much accounting change has resulted from such conceptions of an accounting potential. However, as a basis for understanding either the process or the consequences of such change, conventional views are severely limited. For rather than providing a history of the emergence of accounting as it now is, they provide the basis for the compilation of a history of inadequacy, ignorance and obsolescence when accounting was not what it should be, peppered with only occasional moments of enlightenment when accounting moved nearer to realising its potential. Presuming that the functions of accounting exist independently of its practice, that its practice is orientated towards particular goals that themselves are autonomous of the accountings that are made of them and that the problem of practice is to reform organisational procedures so that their intrinsic goals are achieved, accounting change is described and evaluated by reference to a body of knowledge that is assumed to be external to ac-

---

① Such understandings are not only future orientated. Very particular appreciations of the past also have informed our view of what accounting is and might become. As has been discussed already, quite specific trajectories of emergence have been imposed on accounting developments, at times creating a basis for a powerful continuity between what accounting was and what it should become. For more general discussions of the mobilization of understandings of the past see Hobsbawm & Ranger (1983), Lowenthal (1985) and Wright (1985).

② In the area of financial accounting, the debates over inflation accounting would provide an interesting arena in which to study such processes at work.

counting itself. So, whilst the realisation of the accounting potential may be problematic, the potential itself is only rarely, if ever, seen in either problematic or emergent terms. It is endowed with a privileged epistemological status such that although accounting is seen as being laboriously constructed, its essence is not. Rather than enquiring into their own patterns of emergence, the means by which they have gained a current significance and the circumstances under which they come to be intertwined with the specifics of technical change, accounting has taken for granted the discourses that are credited with mobilising change.

Such a view of accounting development also ignores the duality of the interactions between accounting and ideas of its potential. In both historical and organisational terms the apparatus of organising has played a profound role in influencing our conceptions of the organisation. Ideas about organisational goals, functions and functioning have emerged amidst the development of specific means of organisational action and calculation. Equally, organisational participants have not been defined externally to the practices in which they are engaged. The concepts of management and the manager were actively constructed in a particular way at a particular socio-historical juncture and are inseparable from the practical means of administration and calculation which were, and still are, implicated in their emergence and functioning. There was no *a priori* manager to whom one can appeal as having interests and needs which can mobilise the development of management practices. Equally, there was no primeval concept of accounting which shaped the development of accounting as we now know it. Accounting has emerged in a more positive way than the mere realisation of an essence. Indeed, in part, the present imperatives of accounting which can and do guide its development have emerged from the practice of the craft. And, in similar terms, accounting practice needs to be seen as playing a more active role in creating rather than merely enabling organised endeavour. Accounting change is as much a history of organisational construction as organisation realisation and enablement. ①

That is not to deny that external discourses of an accounting potential can and do mobilise accounting change. They provide an incentive for action and an understanding of specific organisational targets for intervention can be constructed on their bases (Nahapiet, 1984). They can also provide criteria for both gauging the presumed need for change and reading its effects. But such appreciations of the roles

---

① Such a point is emphasized by Litterer (1963) in his discussion of the emergence of systematic management in American manufacturing firms. He states that "in fact, it is systems such as those we have been discussing and many others like them which constitute the great bulk of managerial activities" (p. 388, also see p.391).

served by discourses which can direct and facilitate change still do not help us to understand the mechanisms of change, the forces mobilising the deployment of different accountings and different accounting rhetorics, the precise practices involved, the resistances which they engender and the actual organisational consequences which they gave rise to. For it would be inappropriate to assume that there is any invariant relationship between a rhetoric and discourse of accounting and a programme of intervention in the organisation conducted in the name of it. The variety of forms that such a relationship can take should be a problem for investigation rather than presumption.

Accounting and the construction of an organisational order

Increasingly accounting practice has itself become the focus of research interest. Realising the ambiguous relationship between the abstract discourse of an accounting potential and the specifics of accounting as it functions in organisations, research has come to be more concerned with analysing and understanding accounting in action (Hopwood, 1978, 1983; Kaplan, 1983; Scapens, 1983, 1984). In the vast majority of such investigations, however, the phenomenon of accounting change has not been emphasized explicitly. Primary consideration has been given to the present diversity of the accounting craft and the use made of the resultant accountings at any particular point in time.

Although studies have started to investigate the organisational tensions engendered by the use of accounting systems, comparatively little consideration has been given to how these might provide bases for a re-appraisal and change of the accounting craft. Some histories of accounting resistance and dysfunctions have been written, but, with relatively few exceptions (Argyris, 1977; Berry et al., 1985), little or no consideration has been given to the counter histories of accounting elaboration and change as attempts are made to ensure the continued integrity, legitimacy, effectiveness and power of the craft. So, although accounting is starting to be examined in its organisational context, the underlying perspective remains a relatively static one. The analyses that have been made of accounting diversity are not dissimilar. Although the differences in the contemporaneous practice of the craft have provided an incentive for the analysis of some of the factors that impinge on the forms that accounting takes, the resultant contingent analyses have many of the characteristics of an exercise in comparative studies (Otley, 1980). Accounting is seen as it was and as it is rather than in the process of becoming. Moreover the organisational calculus implicit in accounting adaptation is still one that is posited on the functional roles that accounting plays in the enhancement of a neutral and highly generalised concept of organisational performance. Little role is acknowledged for management discretion and choice (Child, 1972; Thompson, forthcoming), let alone the active exercise of politics and power (Cooper, 1981; Pettigrew, 1972). Accounting change also is seen as a reflective rather than a constructive organisational endeavour. With accounting conceived of as enabling rather than more actively shaping organisational affairs, other organisational factors are seen as impinging on it, but accounting seemingly is seen as having no similarly active role to play. Different accountings are seen as reflecting different circumstances rather than themselves being implicated in a more positive process by which accounting becomes what it was not. The analysis of accounting diversity thereby has resulted only in a presumption of change rather than more specific analyses of the processes involved which make no prior assumptions as to either the underlying logics at work or the organisational roles and consequences of the accounting craft.

Still, such organisational appreciations have been useful. Despite the many problems to which they are subject (Dent, 1986; Otley, 1980), accounting at least is being shown as a craft that is embedded in the functioning of the organisation, co-existing and interdependent with such other aspects of the organisation as its strategy, structure, approaches to the segmentation of work and other organisational technologies and practices. Not existing as an isolated craft, accounting is shown as being an organisational practice that is constructed and used amidst the configuration of a specific culture, be it organisational or national (Horovitz, 1980), a specific organisational environment and a specific set of approaches to the management of the organisational task. Accounting has at least been grounded in the organisational contexts in which it operates. And by being seen as a phenomenon that is so interdependent with its context and subject thereby to the vicissitudes of other organisational practices and concerns, the possibility is at least opened up that accounting is not necessarily adequate to the ends in the name of which it is advanced (Argyris, 1977; Kaplan, 1983). So although the perspectives remain preliminary and partial, abstract conceptions of the potential of the craft are nevertheless being faced by a growing understanding of its practices.

Accounting and the construction of a social order

Preliminary though they are, organisational insights into accounting all still see accounting as a practice that has a rationale that can be understood purely in terms of the needs and requirements of the specific organisations in which it functions. Accounting is seen as having its origins within the problems created by the need to coordinate and manage a complex process of transformation within the context of a particular regime of organisational constraints and objectives. More recent inquiries are starting to question such an organisationally isolated view however. Increasingly accounting is coming to be seen as having some of its origins in the social conflicts which are enacted in the organisational arena (Cooper, 1980, 1981; Hopper et al., 1986; Tinker, 1980; Tinker et al., 1982). Rather than seeing organisational accounts as a technical reflection of the pregiven economic imperatives facing organisational administration, they are now being seen to be more actively constructed in order to create a particular economic visibility within the organisation and a powerful means for positively enabling the governance and control of the organisation along economic lines (Clawson, 1980). Accounting, when seen in such terms, is not a passive instrument of technical administration, a neutral means for merely revealing the pregiven aspects of organisational functioning. Instead its origins are seen to reside in the exercising of social power both within and without the organisation. It is seen as being implicated in the forging, indeed the active creation, of a particular regime of economic calculation within the organisation in order to make real and powerful quite particular conceptions of economic and social ends.

From such a perspective, organisational options, decisions and actions are seen as being positively shaped by the ways in which they intersect with accounting practices. Accounting is seen as having played a very positive role in the creation of a manageable organisational domain. A regime of economic visibility and calculation has positively enabled the creation and operation of an organisation which facilitates the exercising of particular social conceptions of power. Economic motives have been made real and influential by their incorporation into legitimate and accepted economic facts. The labour process in the organisation has been exposed, ordered and physically and socially distributed. The resultant organisational facts, calculations, schedules and plans have positively enabled the construction of a management regime abstracted and distanced from the operation of the work process itself.

So, although functioning within the organisation, accounting is best seen from such a perspective as an artifact residing in the domain of the social rather than the narrowly organisational. It has been implicated in the radical transformation of the organisation in the name of the social. Indeed, accounting is considered as one of the important means by which the organisation is incorporated into the social domain.

Accounting change is clearly a specific focus of attention from such a viewpoint. Not only has the development of accounting practice been addressed quite explicitly but also a particular trajectory of development sometimes has been imposed upon it. Indeed, in some senses, accounting, when seen from such a perspective, still has an essence, a mission which mobilises its development. Accounting, from such a stance, is still a revelatory endeavour, making real, by the active construction of the organisation as we know it, interests which are independent of both the accounting and the organisational representation of them. And, like the more conventional presumptions of accounting in motion, it can still be seen as an endeavour that is adequate to the ends in the name of which it is advanced. Accounting is seen to be both purposive and purposeful.

Towards a view of accounting in motion

Albeit slowly, our understanding of accounting change nevertheless is advancing. Attempts are being made to confront the conventional view of accounting improvement with insights from analyses of the organisational and social functioning of the craft. Accounting is in the process of being seen as an organisational practice in motion, the changes and consequences of which are dependent on its intertwining with other approaches to the creation of a manageable organisational regime. A very real start has been made on locating the construction and functioning of accounting in the domains of the organisational and the social rather than purely the technical.

As has been discussed above, existing approaches are still preliminary however. Relatively few attempts have been made to confront the specifics of accounting in action. Reference still tends to be made to the mobilising potential of general tendencies for organisational, environmental or social change (Burchell et al., 1985). Little has been done to uncover and describe the precise mechanisms of accounting change. The domains of the organisational and the social also have tended to remain independent ones. Few attempts have been made to delineate the both overlapping and interdependent spheres of the two, to appreciate how accounting might enable the concerns of the social to pass through and thereby transform the organisation and, in turn, to create organisational practices which can be influential in the construction of the world of the social as we know it. Be it from an organisational or social perspective, the roles of accounting are still defined externally to the practice of the craft. Organisational agents are still seen as existing in isolation of the practices in which they are engaged. Possibly because of the distancing of inquiry from practice, only the reflective rather than the constitutive tendencies of accounting (Burchell et al., 1985; Hopwood, 1985b) have been emphasised in the accounts that we now have of accounting change.

In the context of such an agenda for development, the subsequent discussion has only a modest aim. Using some instances of accounting change, an attempt is made to tease out some of the processes at work at the organisational level. By drawing on some specific illustrations of accounting in action, the aim is to illuminate some of the factors that are implicated in the processes by which organisational accountings become what they are not. No attempt is made to construct an alternative theory of accounting change however. The aim is the much more modest one of delineating a few of the issues and problems that any such theory or theories would need to address. The intention is merely one of expanding the conceptual arena rather than of seeking its resolution.

ON PUTTING ACCOUNTING WHERE ACCOUNTING WAS NOT

It rarely is possible to witness the birth pains of a newly emergent accounting. Normally we have to content ourselves with observing the process of accounting elaboration, as one organisational account is extended and refined as it becomes transformed into another. However, in the case of Josiah Wedgwood, the eighteenth century English potter, is is possible to do this indirectly by means of the extensive correspondence and records that have been preserved (McKendrick, 1960, 1961a, 1961b, 1964, 1973). ①

Wedgwood was a successful entrepreneur in the early days of the British industrial revolution. A man of scientific and analytical temperament, as well as acute commercial acumen, he created one of the first British industrial (as distinct from craft) manufactures of pottery, pioneering not only in production methods (McKendrick, 1961a) but also in product design, the application of scientific research (Schofield, 1956) and the commercial exploitation of his products (McKendrick, 1960, 1961b), Wedgwood quickly established himself as the supplier of pottery to the wealthy. His business quickly became a very profitable and rapidly expanding one.

Initially Wedgwood made little use of accounting, particularly for what would

---

① I do not wish to imply in any way whatsoever that the "protean manifestations" of cost accounting "sprang full-grown" from Wedgwood's initiatives (Jenks, 1960, p. 423), nor that there were no precedents. That clearly was not the case. Although earlier costing systems have been poorly documented and analysed (see, however, Jones, 1985), a costing craft was emergent. In addition, and of particular significance, I think, a relevant more general economic discourse was available to serve as an incentive for the production of a new visibility (Tribe, 1978). Costs could be talked about, if not observed. So despite the fact that, to use Jenks' (1960) characterization of the process of change in a somewhat later era, "problems of organization . . . were solved *ad hoc* empirically for each establishment", resulting in the development of "little clusters of socially sustained norms and concepts, whose communication beyond the individual firm was rare, accidental, or the result of individual transfer of employment" (p. 424), we nevertheless should recognize the important discursive and practical conditions of possibility underlying such innovative steps.

now be seen as management purposes. Accounting information did not inform his product and pricing decisions or the selection of his methods of work. As McKendrick (1973, p. 48) has observed:

> So handsome were the profit margins which he could normally expect, and so high the prices which he could regularly charge, that the incentives towards anything more than routine costing were usually rather slight.

Indeed Wedgwood himself admitted that "he could do little more than guess at costs" and "further conceded that his attempts at total costing were out by a factor of two" (McKendrick, 1973, p. 49).

That situation was to change however. In 1772 the expansion came to an abrupt end. The pottery industry was caught in a major economic recession. "Panic spread through most of the cities of northern Europe", according to Ashton (1959, p. 128). Prices, profits, wages and employment all fell sharply, and bankruptcies soared in the pottery industry as elsewhere. Wedgwood, like others, was well aware of the impending difficulty:

> The evidence of accumulating stock and falling sales mounted miserably through the autumn, as the slackening demand, so evident in London, spread farther afield. In November he reported very poor sales in Edinburgh. "Mr. Ferrier... has sold nothing at all since the month of June"... And as sales slackened, production at Eturia had to be cut back to a dangerous level. Reluctant as Wedgwood was to recognise the drop in demand, he finally *had* to recognise it. He stopped overtime only when "we have not work for them the common hours". At this stage Wedgwood refused to believe that the situation was "in such a desperate way and that we should set our best hands adrift to the establishment of our antagonists"... Wedgwood was determined to hang on to the men he had taken such pains to train but already many of his men were out of work—"our Gilders have not a piece to do and are all at play". With the coming of Winter things grew steadily worse. On 19 September Wedgwood wrote that "any opening" should "be pursued with all our might". On Boxing Day any trivial aspect of fashion was being frantically exploited... Two days later he announced with relief that he was laying off the men for Christmas, but three weeks later the situation was even worse. "We begin, after 3 weeks rest, to work again on Monday. If yon can make us any orders pray send them, for I really do not know what to set them to work upon, however they must begin for they attacked me in a body yesterday morning and insisted on being either employed or discharged" (McKendrick, 1973, p. 63).

In times of such crisis business methods often are re-examined. With such an aim in mind, Wedgwood started to turn his attention to the level of his production expenses. And it was in this context that his cost accounts were born.

Wedgwood had the idea that he might better survive the recession if he could lower his prices in order to stimulate demand. Such a view was conditioned, however, by the need to ensure that the price still exceeded the cost. And there the problem arose. For although a concept of cost entered into the discourse of commerce and trade, and could thereby mobilise action, there was no well established apparatus for operationalising the discursive category. Cost remained an idea, not a fact.

It was the facts of costing that Wedgwood set out to discover. As he noted to Bentley, his business partner:

> It will deserve our serious discussion whether we should not lower the prices of Pebble and Gilt Vases very considerably, for this purpose I am forming a price book of Workmanship which is to include every expense of Vase making as near as possible from the Crude materials to your Counter in London, upon each sort of Vases, of this we will send you a specimen & you will then be able to judge better what we can do in this respect, what will be most prudent is the next question for our Consideration (McKendrick, 1973, p.49).

The task was not an easy one. No established procedures were available for observing the inner workings of the organisation through the accounting eye. The organisation could not be readily penetrated. The facts of costing had to be laboriously created rather than merely revealed.

> I have been puzzling my brains all the last week (Wedgwood wrote to Bentley on 23 August 1772) to find out proper data, and methods of calculating the expense of manufacturing, Sale, loss &c to be laid upon each article of our Manufacture & a very tedious business it has been, but what is worse I find what I have done is wrong—somewhere, very essentially so, but do not know where or how to amend it though I shall not give up being sensible of the importance of the enquiry, and what I now send you is only to shew you what steps I have taken & the grounds I have gone upon, & to desire you will sit down some morning & consider the subject & try to put me in a better way, for it will be of the greatest use for us to establish some such scale as I have now been attempting to examine all our new articles by, that we may not fix the prices so high as to prevent sale, nor so low as to leave no profit upon them (McKendrick, 1973, p.49).

Such endeavours resulted in the construction of an increasingly detailed account. Still, however, Wedgwood was not satisfied with his efforts.

> Some of my difficulties I have laid before you, but what perplexeth me most is, that although I am very positive what I have allowed for the expenses of making & selling our goods is quite enough yet it appears from comparing this expense of Manufacture for a year, with the amot of goods made, to be little more than half the real expense attending the making & selling so many goods (McKendrick, 1973, p. 53).

Shortly thereafter, however, he was to obtain some insight into some of the reasons for his uneasiness. Comparing his financial accounts with his emergent costings, he found that the two did not agree.

> This Acc^t is very exact as to the *whole* but we cannot make it agree with its parts viz the separate pieces— It agrees with the small Vases very well but those we sell at 2 or 3 G-s do not appear to cost us 1/10 of that money. We are now taking a stock & shall then try another method (McKendrick, 1973, p. 61).

Being of a curious disposition, Wedgwood soon discovered why the various parts of his accounting experiments did not mesh together. His inquiries revealed "a history of embezzlement, blackmail, chicanery, and what Wedgwood called 'extravagance and dissipation'" (McKendrick, 1973, p. 61). His head clerk, Ben, whom he had "long been uneasy on this account being fully perswaded (*sic*) that matters were not right with... His Case ace^{ts} being always several months behind, & yet to jump exactly right when he did Ballance them" (McKendrick, 1973, p. 61), had had his hand in the till. On further investigation, Wedgwood found that "the plan of our House in Newport St.", where the clerks resided, "is rather unfavourable to Virtue & good order in young men", "that the housekeeper was frolicking with the cashier", "that the head clerk was ill with 'the foul Disease' and had 'long been in a course of extravagance and dissipation far beyond anything he has from us (in a lawfull way) wd. be able to support'" (McKendrick, 1973, p. 61).

Only after such revelations as to the sources of accounting inconsistency did Wedgwood feel confident in his newly fledged facts. As he went on to report:

> Our House may be looked upon as unfixed, & afloat, the first Clerk and Cashier being removed, it seems the properest time to introduce any new regulations we may think proper, or to change the whole plan if we can adopt a better... now we know that all goods *sold for money* & not *brought to account* must appear as *increase of* stock in *stating the* acc^{ts} & we have such strong reasons for suspecting our Head Clerks fidelity such an amazing increase of stock is an alarming circumstance & I shall not be easy' till the stock is taken to clear my

doubts in this respect (McKendrick, 1973, p. 61, emphasis in original).

Immediate steps were taken to correct the matter. A new clerk was installed and, in order "to put the necessary business of collecting into a way *of perpetual motion*" (McKendrick, 1973, p. 62, emphasis in original), a routine of weekly accounts implemented.

The birth of Wedgwood's accounts had been difficult and laborious. There had been no easy relationship between the idea of costing and a specific programme of intervention in the organisation conducted in the name of that idea. Costs had had to be constructed rather than merely revealed. An organisational economy grounded in a domain of accounting facts had to be forged painstakingly rather than merely exposed.

Once constructed, however, Wedgwood had a powerful instrument for observing the organisation in economic terms. His strategic conception of the role which records could play in the management of crisis had resulted in a means by which he could penetrate the inner workings of the organisation. A new visibility had been created. The organisation had been colonised by economic facts (Patton, 1979). A calculative means had been found for conceiving the functioning of the organisation in different terms. An accounting eye had provided Wedgwood with a new means for intervening in the organisation.

And intervene he did. As we have seen, the administration and control of the financial records was reformed. More substantially, during the depression, prices were actively changed in the name of the new knowledge of costs and profits[①](McKendrick, 1964, 1973). A basis for a more systematic consideration of marketing policies was created (McKendrick, 1960, 1961, 1973). The newly emergent facts of the economic provided a basis for re-appraising the organisation of the manufacturing processes, the advantages of large volume production, and the calculation of piece rates, wages and bonus's (McKendrick, 1960, 1961a, 1973). The inner workings of the organisation had been made amenable to a new form of economic analysis.

Wedgwood's discovery of the advantages of large scale production illustrates this

---

[①] Outside periods of depression, Wedgwood was well aware that in an imperfect market, with explicit strategies for product differentiation, there was no necessary relationship between cost and price. As McKendrick (1964, p. 29) points out: "The phrase 'The prices Mr Bentley will regulate as he thinks proper' occurs so frequently in letters on pricing that one soon recognizes it as a familiar refrain". As Wedgwood himself put it, "When I fix a price upon any new article, please to remember that I have more regard to the *Expense of workmanship* than/the *apparent and comparative value* with other things so you'll correct it by the latter which is often most essential" (emphasis in original). In McKendrick's (1964, p. 29) words, Wedgwood judged "the cost of production, the difficulty of making, and the number he could easily make, and then Bentley would decide at which market to aim them, at what price to charge them and in what quantities to make them".

well. Faced with his newly emergent costing facts, Wedgwood noted that:

If you turn to the columns of calculation & see how large a share, Modeling and Moulds, & the three next columns bear in the expense of Manufacturing out goods, & consider that these expenses move like clockwork, & are much the same whether the quantity of goods be large or small, you will see the vast consequence in most manufacturers of *making the greatest quantity possible at a given time* (Wedgwood's italics). Rent goes on whether we do much or little in the time. Wages to the Boys and Odd Men, Warehouse Men & Book-keeper who are a kind of Satalites to the Makers (Throwers, Turners &c.) is nearly the same whether we make 20 doz of Vases or 10 doz per week & will therefore be a double expense upon the later number. The same may be said in regard to most of the incidental expenses....

We now have upwards of 100 Good forms of Vases, for all of which we have the moulds, handles & ornaments & we cd. make them almost as currently as useful ware, & at half the expense we have hitherto done, provided I durst set the Men to make abo' 6 to 13 doz of a sort; perhaps (as the first expense of all these apparatus's is over, & our Men in full practice, and many have some fears of losing a good branch of business) at much less than half.

The first expense will be all sunk if we do not proceed in the business this apparatus is adapted for.

The Great People have had these Vases in their Palaces long enough for them to be seen & admired by the Middling Classes of People, which Class we know are vastly, I had almost said, infinitely superior in number to the Great, & though a great *price* was, I believe, at first necessary to make the Vases esteemed *Ornament for Palaces*, that reason no longer exists. Their character is established, & the Middling People wd. probably by [sic] quantitys of them at a reduced price (McKendrick, 1973, p.55).

As McKendrick (1973, p.54) notes, Wedgwood's costing "had other more permanent repercussions on his business management". In often unanticipated ways, the organisation was changed in the name of the knowledge of it. For "by his own persistence, by an unfailing attention to detail, by founding, if not creating, the traditions of a foreman class and equipping it with rules and regulations, he transformed a collection of what in 1765 he called, 'dilatory, drunken, idle, worthless workmen' into what ten years later he allowed to be 'a very good set of hands'" (McKendrick, 1961a, p.46). What is more, Wedgwood's observations could now be conducted indirectly. No longer did he have to rely solely on walking around the pottery constantly on the lookout for "unhandiness", scolding those individuals who did not follow his instructions (McKendrick, 1961a, pp. 43—44). Such personal observation and supervision could start to be complemented by the exercising of control at a distance, both in time and space. ① Wedgwood now had available to him the basis of a more anonymous and continuous means of surveillance.

Although born amidst crisis and doubt, the consequences of Wedgwood's accounting system started to be quite profound. Initiated to reveal what had been presumed to be there already, once established, it provided a basis for significantly changing, if not eventually transforming, the functioning of the enterprise. The newly established accounting system enabled a different set of dynamics to be set into motion. The fine details of the production process could now be related to the aims and performance of the organisation as a whole. ② Policies created at the top of the organisation could be related to specific aspects of organisational functioning. The organisation could be observed and managed in terms different from those in which it functioned. Attempts could be made to co-ordinate and plan divergent parts of the organisation in the name of the economic. An organisational economy could start to be emergent. As Patton (1979) has said in a very different context:

> The emergence of [a practice] cannot be explained by the functions it subsequently comes to fulfil; new roles may be forced upon it, foreign to those it was introduced to bear.

---

① In his detailed study of the history of Boulton and Watts' Soho engineering factory, opened in 1796, Roll (1930, p. 250) also notes how the introduction of time sheets for workmen started to serve a number of different roles. In addition to providing a basis for ascertaining the workers' wages and entering into the determination of prices by calculating the labour costs of the engines being made, Roll commented on the ways in which the new detailed visibility of wage costs influenced the organization of work and the relationships between effort and remuneration. The data provided a starting point for making changes in the methods of production, suggesting possibilities for speeding up work and introducing further machinery. The new records also served to establish a standard or a norm for efficiency in the enterprise, enabling wages to become more related to detailed task performance. Here, as with Wedgwood, the newly established visibility of the economic itself created a dynamic for changing the organization of which it was presumed to be a reflection.

② Loft (1986b, pp. 93—94) usefully notes the interdependence between production methods and record keeping, with each facilitating the construction of the other. As she comments: "Sophisticated cost accounting systems go hand in hand with the standardization of products and production methods. The 'facts' which cost accounting systems demand can only be created with enormous difficulty where work is carried on in a disordered, anarchic way. The opposite also applies, for the operation of a complex and detailed system of organization may be virtually impossible without records. Roll (1930, p. 252) points this out, noting that many aspects of the reorganized Soho Works (of Boulton and Watt) were such as to make any check except that through written records impossible".

置于社会与组织环境中的会计研究

ACCOUNTING, ORGANISING AND THE ORGANISATION①

Turning to an organisation which already has a long history of accounting, the aim is to consider in a little more detail some of the processes through which organisational accounts change as they become intertwined with the organisation itself. By examining another case of accounting change, an illustration is provided of some of the ways in which the processes, practices and perspectives that characterise organisational life impinge on accounting. Continuing the theme introduced in the analysis of Wedgwood, consideration also is given to the ways in which accounting, in turn, impinges on the process of organising.

M was established in the early days of the present century. In the business of industrial component manufacturing, it quickly established itself as an international enterprise with manufacturing and marketing establishments in a wide variety of countries throughout the Western world. *M* grew rapidly, not least during the 1950s. Those were years of prosperity and expansion with good profits and a high return on assets employed. But this situation changed after 1960. Although product demand eased slightly, change was most evident on the supply side of the industry. In particular, the entry of Japanese manufacturers into the world market ushered in a decade of fierce competition. During the 1960s the total value of Japanese output rose by over 350% but their exports increased by almost 1,700%. Suddenly *M* was exposed to intense competition and this was greatest at the volume end of the market where, on certain individual products, the Japanese selling price was below *M*'s calculated unit cost.

A growing awareness of the dangers of Japanese competition and a dissatisfaction with the measured performance of the company caused a major re-appraisal of the company's competitive position to be undertaken. During the early 1970s a number of working parties were established to undertake a thorough investigation of the problems facing the company.

The first problem to be identified was, perhaps paradoxically, that of giving too good a service to customers. *M* had prided itself on providing for any application "the right (component), at the right price—regardless of cost". Special design departments, part of the marketing function, liaised with customers to produce compo-

---

① I acknowledge the help of John Hughes (now of the Open University) in assisting with the research on which this case study is based. The analysis also has benefited from discussions with Sten Jönsson.

nents for each and every application with little company-wide engineering and design collaboration because of the semi-autonomous nature of the organisation's constituent plants. The result was a proliferation of marginally different components produced in different plants in a number of different countries. Moreover, the decentralised strategy of organising also resulted in the same or similar products being produced in each country where there was a market for them, with a consequent duplication of tooling, set-up and other manufacturing costs for each operation and a high value of work-in-progress because of the large decentralised stocks. The problems were further exacerbated by the sheer proliferation of manufacturing plants, there often being many in the same country. During the highly profitable 1950s these problems had been of relatively little concern. Faced with a very different competitive situation, however, *M* decided to reduce considerably the number of product variants.

The perception of an external market threat thereby resulted in a detailed examination of internal manufacturing operations. At that time the batch production methods used by *M* gave a large measure of independence to the separate functions of the manufacturing process. This resulted in a great deal of operational flexibility. Rush orders could be injected easily into the system and the ramifications of machine breakdowns minimised. Such an approach was not suited to more concentrated and, consequently, higher volume production, however. The lack of inter-operation handling equipment resulted in long throughput times and high inventories. Moreover batch production of this type put a heavy burden on local production control systems, stores personnel, operators, inspectors and factory supervisors. So very active consideration was given to alternative production methods.

M decided to move, as far as possible, to production organised by means of multi-machine lines. Under this arrangement a number of similar machines are connected individually with an extensive inter-operational conveyor system. The latter provided not only transportation but also a buffer storage, enabling machine groups to work at different paces and the effects of a breakdown to be relatively contained. The capital costs of this type of plant were high, but production speeds were increased, throughput time was reduced and, as a consequence, inventory requirements were reduced also. However those advantages were gained not only at the expense of higher capital investment but also at the loss of considerable operational flexibility. The production systems would have to become more autonomous of the market, the very turbulence of which had been the initial stimulus for change.

Originally each of *M*'s plants had produced a full range of products to meet the demands of the local market. However, if production costs were to be reduced, as the international market was perceived to necessitate, it was decided that multi-product lines would have to be introduced. In turn, this meant that production runs needed to be longer if the economies of scale were to materialise. One way of doing this was to reduce the number of variants produced, but in the fiercely competitive market of the late 1960s and early 1970s this in itself was not sufficient. It was decided therefore that the manufacturing of each type of product should be concentrated in one location to maximise production volume and reduce costs.

A new production strategy gradually emerged from these examinations and discussions, and it was formally agreed in 1971. The method of implementing and achieving these aims was laborious however. The initial allocation of production represented a significant balancing problem and discussions went on for a number of years. "Weeding out" non-essential variants was also a large task as each final product variety was tested for commercial, financial and technical viability. In 1973 all variants were classified on the basis of sales value, thus identifying those which had such low sales that they were probably unprofitable. Each candidate for elimination was then examined individually. In parallel with the commercial examination, once again a technical assessment was carried out. The design, quality and materials of each were examined critically. Manufacturing and marketing considerations also entered into this assessment. Together these processes enabled M to reduce its product range from 50,000 final variants in 1972 to 20,000 in 1978. Over the same period the average annual volume per final variant rose by 300%. An additional category of product, namely "special" products, was also introduced, enabling products to be produced to customer specifications, but at extra cost. Overall, M's managements considered that the product range concentration had reduced market coverage by only 1% but that this had eliminated what had been the unprofitable sectors of the operation.

Production methods, product policies and production locations were thereby all radically changed in the name of cost. All of these strategic considerations had been infused not only by the language of cost, however, but also by the specific accounting calculations in use at M. The reduction of a *measured* notion of cost had been a primary aim. In the deliberations and policy initiatives cost had operated not only as an influential abstract category entering into the language of strategy but also as a seemingly precise outcome of a specific set of accounting procedures.

In such ways the technical practices of accounting became intertwined with the managerial functioning of M. Organisational policies came to be interdependent with the accounting representation of them. For a complex set of accounting rules defined what was and was not to be regarded as costly. Definitions of "productive" and "unproductive" cost categories influenced the changes made to specific production locations and eventually, the production of specific products. Rules by which overhead costs were to be allocated to production operations, and by what means, had a significant impact on reported cost levels. Debates over the capacity assumptions on which overhead costs were to be allocated were similarly influential in the highly detailed cost assessments, as were the technical procedures for determining how frequently standard costs were to be updated to take account of inflation and exchange rate fluctuations. Also of great importance were the procedures for accounting for operational change in M. For although the problems of the company had orginated from the perception of a changing environment, M's accounting system operated under assumptions of steady state production. The calculation and reporting of set-up and order costs and operation start costs were such that although the financial ramifications of stable production were made clearly visible, the equally significant implications of production changes were much less visible and the costs of operational flexibility and inflexibility did not enter into the accounting calculations at all. In all of these ways not only did the rhetoric of accounting come to play a significant mediating role in the policy deliberations but also the very particular physical, spatial and temporal assumptions and biases incorporated into M's formal accounting systems came to influence the relative preferences assigned to the various production strategies. The accounting system started to be not only reflective of M but also constitutive of its options and policies (Burchell *et al.*, 1985).

However the network of changes at work in M was such that accounting itself came to be subject to pressures to change. Not only had it played a significant role in mediating the relationship between managerial perceptions of a strategic need for change and the operational responses decided upon but also M's formal information systems, including those of an accounting nature, were also to be significantly changed by the different production policies that had followed the recognition of a market crisis. Under the old system of multiple local production the relationship between marketing and manufacturing had been dealt with at a local (national) level. Many of the relevant liaisons and linkages had been done informally. Although there were formal systematic flows of information, these were primarily local in nature. That was no longer adequate however. With geographically concentrated production, the marketing and manufacturing functions had been uncoupled. A new way had to be found to aggregate total forecast and actual demand for every product variant in order to plan the utilisation of capacity in each plant. What had previously been informal had now to become formal. The new production strategy had given rise to the need for a new mode of organising and radically different formal flows of information.

To deal with these problems, two new organisational structures were established. A central co-ordinating committee was set up to judge market demand and decide upon appropriate production levels in line with available capacity, inventories and strategic and operating policies. The interface between marketing and manufacturing thereby became subject to much more centralised control and new functional staff groups were set up in the head office to support this new influence structure. Also, with these rather crucial decisions requiring accurate and up-to-date information, a new management information system was established with its operating team based in a central geographical location. Utilising the forecast parameters established by the co-ordinating group, the new central information office decided upon capacity booking, factory loading, assembly scheduling and distribution instructions. To facilitate this process, feedback of actual levels of manufacturing, sales and stocks was required to be made monthly by all local establishments via M's new computer-based data transmission systems. The increasingly centralised interdependent decision making and control processes were investing in a great deal of formal information (Galbraith, 1973). M was in the process of becoming a more information intensive and information dependent organisation.

As a result of these changes, consideration also had to be given to the formal organisational structure of M. Previously the company had been structured around the national manufacturing and marketing units. As relatively selfcontained entitities, they had constituted useful business responsibility units. Performance was measured on an annual basis in traditional balance sheet and income statement terms. Longer term planning of the enterprise as a whole had been attempted but had proved a difficult and unsatisfactory endeavour. Now, however, M was a more integrated and centralised organisation. The relationships between local marketing and manufacturing had been severed. Local sales were no longer dependent on local production. Performance in total was more dependent on central decision making. With this in mind, the whole organisation started to be structured along product lines.

In the midst of such organisational changes it was recognised that the previous rudimentary controls were no longer adequate. Consideration had to be given to a more frequent, more disaggregated reporting system. Budgeting became a more iterative and time consuming process. Even when arrived at, the budget was updated by a regular series of quarterly plans. The centre now needed to be much more closely informed of local developments and revisions in local expectations. Local performance, in turn, was assessed monthly with the previous summary financial information now being replaced by an extremely detailed reporting of financial, marketing, operating and even personnel results. And, in such a newly centralised enterprise, even local performance was now conditioned by centrally mediated and much contested accounting policies for transfer prices and the allocation of costs. ①

As is shown in Fig. 1, the accounting system and its resultant problems now started to be a complex residue of marketing, production and organisational strategies. Just as accounting had mediated some of the early crucial policy decisions, now accounting was itself subject to the implications of some of its own effects.

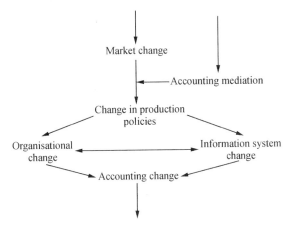

Fig. 1　Accounting implicated in organisational action.

Accounting was firmly embedded in the organisation rather than being any clearly separable part of it. The organisation was not independent of the accountings of it. Although at a point in time the practices of accounting could be identified, their functioning was intertwined with that of the organisation in both reflective and constitutive ways. Other important aspects of organisational functioning had impinged on accounting, providing pressures for it to change. In this sense accounting was a residue of past strategic choices, past decisions on models of organising and past commitments to policies for making visible, and thereby potentially governable (Miller & O'Leary, 1987), particular aspects of organisational action. All of these activities of the past had played a role in undermining the accountings of the past and creating the possibility for the accountings of today. Accounting, however, had not only been a passive phenomenon. It was not only a reflection of other aspects of organisational life but also had played a more positive constructive role in organisational functioning. Accounting had provided an operational and influential language of economic motive, its calculations had infused and influenced important policy decisions, and

---

① With increasing emphasis being placed on the control function of local performance reports, "fairness" rather than decision relevance was an important criterion for evaluating such accounting practices and changes in them. I am grateful to Sten Jönsson for bringing this point to my attention.

the visibilities it created played an important role in making real particular segmentations of the organisational arena. Accounting not only reflected the organisation as it had been but it also played a not insignificant role in positively making the organisation as it now is.

ACCOUNTING AND THE RESIDUES OF THE ORGANISATIONAL PAST

The constitutive roles of accounting provide a major focus for analysing Q, also a major manufacturing enterprise. Like M, it also had to face extreme market turbulence and change. Increasing competition, changing consumer expectations and a squeezing of profit margins also engendered in Q a sense of organisational crisis.

As an organisation, Q is even more information intensive than M. It has invested heavily in formal information and control systems, paying particular attention to those of a financial and accounting nature. The tentacles of these systems penetrate deep into the manufacturing, marketing, distribution and administrative functions of the enterprise. Detailed aspects of the organisation are made economically visible on a very regular basis. Standards, budgets and plans play a central role in the co-ordination and integration of a very large, functionally specialised and geographically dispersed organisation. Indeed it is through the formal flows of economic information that many important aspects of Q come to be known, managed and assessed. No pockets of local autonomy are consciously allowed to exist. Not only are all the parts of the vast, dispersed and varied enterprise drawn together by the information systems which provide the basis for the operational governance of Q but also the rhythms of the accounting year thereby become very influential components of the organisational construction and management of time.① The accounting eye is indeed a significant and omnipresent one.

The information economy of Q had been elaborated and refined during periods of growth and relative prosperity. Although difficulties had been encountered with this vast and expensive machinery of abstract information and administration, conditions of stable growth had rarely placed these at a premium. The abstract categories of cost and profit had been deemed to provide an adequate portrayal of the functioning of the organisation. The management of the general rather than the particular had not been seen as problematic. The resulting periodisation of governance had not created any

---

① For a further discussion of the role of accounting in the construction of conceptions of time see Hopwood (1986b).

insurmountable difficulties in the context of relative stability. The systems, for there were a vast number of only partially integrated ones, had been fine tuned and developed in relation to specific problems and presumed needs. In this way the information regime of Q had marched ever forward, gaining, in the process, an increasing measure of autonomy and further creating the basis for a detached, specialised and abstract arena of management that seemingly had less and less direct contact with the operational specifics of the enterprise.

The market crisis was to make such an information regime increasingly problematic however. With mounting uncertainty, the need for information that was not collected became ever greater. The senior management of Q started to realise that what it had been regarding as a detached and independent source of illumination—information—was in fact a direct reflection and an integral component of its system of administration and governance. What had been controlled—costs, profits, variances and volume—had given rise to an information residue. What had not been controlled, but what was now seen to be in need of control, was unreflected in the organisation's battery of information systems. The previously unmanaged—quality, detailed aspects of the functioning of the production process, employee and managerial commitment and motivation, throughput times and operational inventory holdings, technological progress, the detail of customer responsiveness—resided in the domain of the unknown. The visibilities of the present were partial, reflecting only the locus of past problems, past controls and past patterns of authority. However significant it might be, in Q the new had enormous difficulty filtering through the old. The dimensions of concern were just so different.

The organisation of the present was thereby tethered to the concerns of the past. The information systems of Q had become not only so detailed, so seemingly precise and so apparently comprehensive but also so fundamentally intertwined with the present organisation of Q that for a long time they had served to deny the legitimate existence of alternatives. Not only had their very technical quality come to be seen as so high and so all embracing that gaps had not been perceived but also the present information and control flows had become co-determinous with the enterprise itself. In an important way the accounting system of Q had become isomorphic with the organisation. Both had changed such that each was now both dependent on and reflective of the other. What had once been direct and specifically identifiable bureaucratic controls had, over time, become much more unobtrusive ones (Perrow, 1986), a central part of Q itself. Now they were implicated in the establishment of the very premises of decision making, "the control of the cognitive premises underlying action" (Perrow, 1986, p. 129), determining at a very basic level the structure of meaning and significance in the organisation.① Change is extremely difficult in such a context. It is only with great difficulty that people can start to conceive of doing anything differently. The new has few means to penetrate the consciousness established by the old.

Eventually, however, circumstances were such in Q that the radically changed environment was recognised. It slowly started to be reflected in even the traditional indicators. And although delayed, investigations prompted by this provided a basis on which some members of the organisation started to realise the significance of the changes underway.

In the context of such a perception of crisis important aspects of the organisation of Q that had been positively shaped by its regime of information systems started to be regarded as problematic. The batteries of standards, budgets and plans were seen as creating a relatively inflexible and inward looking enterprise. The phrase "paralysis by analysis" started to enter the organisational vocabulary. It was perceived that emphasis had been placed on the management of the normal rather than the irregular. The management of the abstract had created an organisation that found it difficult, if not positively traumatic, to respond to the particular. The systems of information also were recognised as having played a very crucial role in the creation of conceptions of time in Q. No only was the continual stream of organisational action periodised in a very particular way but also the regime of routine planning and reporting had resulted in a celebration of the present and the short-term. By extensive processes of budgeting and planning, the future had been brought into the present, seemingly becoming more certain, less contingent, less debatable and, possibly, less readily subject to influence in the process. After an era of emphasising the immediate in many aspects of its management, Q now found it extremely difficult to instill a more proactive conception of an influencable and manageable longer term future.

As in M, important features of organisational life had become intertwined with the functioning of an accounting system. Accounting had developed such that is was embedded in the organisational fabric, both reflecting and creating the contexts in which it operated. In Q, however, this process had gone much further. While such tendencies clearly were at work in M, in Q they had become fully realised. Although autonomous developments could and did take place in the design and functioning of

---

① As Perrow (1986) points out, with unobtrusive control, what he terms the "control of premises," organizational participants "*voluntarily* restrict the range of stimuli that will be attended to ('Those sorts of things are irrelevant', or 'What has that got to do with the matter?') and the range of alternatives that would be considered ('It would never occur to me to do that')" (Perrow, 1986, p.129; emphasis in original). Such attitudes were indeed prevalent in Q.

Q's accounting systems (and which by feeding into the functioning of the organisation, could subsequently lose their autonomy), accounting in Q had become a phenomenon that could not be regarded as being in any sense separable from the enterprise as a whole.

Past investments in a finely tuned economic visibility had radically increased the salience of the economies that could be gained from functional specialisation, geographical dispersion and a regime of administrative co-ordination. The accounting eye had become a very strategic one. The organisation had been mobilised in the name of what was known of it. Economic objectives and strategies for meeting them had been given a very precise meaning. Investments had been made in the context of a very particular economic knowledge. As a result, Q was now composed of different machines and different people with different skills located in different places, and subject to a different management regime. What is more, Q now needed its accounting systems in order to function as it did. They satisfied needs that they had played a role in creating (Ignatieff, 1984). The present structuring of the organisation presumed the existence of accounting. No longer just discrete technical procedures, the accounting systems were infused into the organisation itself.

The creation of accounting residues that, in turn, played a role in creating the organisation in which the accountings functioned had been an important part of Q's development. A visibility had become a reality. But that visibility had not always been so centrally implicated in the functioning of Q. It had been born amidst a different reality, serving different purposes than those now required of it. The accounting residues had been laid down in an organisation different from that which Q now is.

Important features of the emergent economic visibility had been created in the context of attempts to control the labour process (Clawson, 1980). A conflictful and organised work force had provided one significant base for the rise of a regime of economic calculation and administration in Q. The control of economically orientated effort had been a mobilising problem. Investments had been made in the specification of work expectations, in the linking of effort to reward and in the measurement and control of actual performance. A regime of detailed economic calculation had been created in order to render visible in a quite particular manner the functioning of the operational core of the organisation. The social control of work had provided an important incentive for Q's investment in an enhanced visibility of the economic.[1]

---

[1] Several independent and very detailed historical studies support this conclusion. Moreover these have been conducted from a number of different theoretical perspectives. However, in the name of preserving the anonymity of Q, no references are given.

Now, however, that socially constructed visibility had created an enterprise organisationally dependent on the resultant knowledge. The organisation had been reformed in the name of the knowledge of it. A managerial regime based on facts and analysis had arisen (although in a different corporate context, see Geneen, 1984). More precise articulations of objectives had been made, and these had been diffused throughout the organisation by means of the accounting calculus. New segmentations of work had been initiated in the organisation and new bases for administrative expertise forged. What had been initiated in the organisation in the name of the social came to function in the name of both the organisational and the social.

ON THE CONSIDERATION OF ACCOUNTING IN MOTION

Together the cases illustrate not only that accounting can be conceived as being in motion but also that such a perspective provides a rich insight into the organisational practice of accounting and its consequences for action. What conventionally have been seen to be the statics of the accounting craft have been seen to be in the process of changing, becoming thereby, what they were not. And such a portrayal has enabled an analysis of some of the ways in which accounting, by intersecting with other organisational processes and practices, influences the patterns of organisational visibility, significance, structure and action.

In the case of Wedgwood the emergence of a new accounting was observed. The categories and inter-relationships of an economic discourse and rhetoric (McCloskey, 1985) provided an incentive for the creation of a practical means for observing the organisation in economic terms, so making seemingly real what previously had been abstract. Although initiated as a tool for deciding upon prices and product volumes, a means thereby was created for intervening in and transforming the organisation in the name of the new economic knowledge of it. As we left our consideration of Wedgwood a basis was starting to be established upon which the accounting craft would become a more powerful means for organisational intervention and governance, able to play a more active role in the shaping of the trajectory of organisational development. Initiated to reveal what was presumed to be, the accounting eye was starting to be suggestive of organisational reform.

Such a proactive role for accounting was seen in operation in the early days of the formulation of *M*'s response to a market crisis. The otherwise abstract languages of economic motive and managerial analysis had been made into a more precise calculus for the assessment of organisational change by the accountings that had been laid down in M in times past. In this way, the quite specific properties of the accounting system played an active role in mediating the organisational response to the perceived need to change. The mobilising potential inherent in the early costings of Wedgwood was now seen in action, helping to shape in quite particular ways the marketing, production, and thereafter, the organisational, information and even accounting strategies in M. For accounting, by becoming more embedded in the organisation, not only shaped other important aspects of organisational life, but it, in turn, also was influenced by them, overtime thereby playing some role in creating the possibilities and conditions for its own transformation.

In Q the organisational embeddedness of accounting was such that it played a significant and extremely influential role in the functioning of the organisation. Although created over a long period of time and originally appealed to for reasons different from its present functioning, the accounting and other related information and control systems now created the dominant means of visibility in Q. The organisation was seen and managed through an accounting eye. The selective patterns of accounting visibility had provided a means for mobilising and changing the organisation such that it not only was dependent upon but also almost synonymous with the particular flows of information which had become intertwined with its development and current mode of functioning.

For all three organisations accounting had played some role in their transformation. The processes through which their accountings had become what they were not were starting to become, or already were, embedded in the very fabric of their functioning. Particular regimes of accounting facts had been created. An operational significance was given to economic and managerial categories and rhetoric. A seemingly precise and specific calculus had entered into organisational deliberations and debate. Accounting, in being propagated and changed, had become implicated in wider processes of organisational perception, governance and strategic mobilisation.

The consequences of such a trajectory of development were significant for all the organisations, providing, in the case of M, an important mediating influence at a time of a key strategic change, and, in Q, creating a form of organisational dependency that was to constrain and thereby, for a time, to influence the organisation's responsiveness to environmental turbulence.

Such consequences are amongst those that have provided the basis for a more widespread development of "worrying about management accounting" (Hopwood, 1985a). As was discussed earlier, there is now an increasing tendency for accounting systems to be assessed in terms of their actual as well as their intended organisational consequences. The full range of impacts that they can have on organisations is now starting to be discussed. If only because of this it is important to try to tease out and analyse in a little more detail some of the issues inherent in the cases, albeit that they have to be expressed in a tentative and partial manner at this stage in the development of our knowledge of the organisational nature of the accounting practice. For when seen in such terms, the cases are suggestive of a number of considerations which have a wider significance for the ways in which we can conceive of accounting in action and the processes of accounting elaboration and change.

Perhaps most importantly, the changes we have analysed have not reflected any simple, linear pattern of accounting development. Although abstract rhetorics of change have played a role in disturbing a prevailing status quo, no unitary mobilising force, be it an economic rationality, a social intent or a political will, has been found to be silently embedded within the shifting course of accounting's subsequent path of modification. Indeed in Wedgwood there was no easy and obvious relationship between an abstract economic category and a programme of intervention in the organisation conducted in the name of it. A diversity of quite specific issues, rationales and constraints impinged on the course of accounting change in M, together providing a means by which accounting could both shape the perception of problems and their solutions, and itself be adjusted by the shifting patterns of other organisational phenomena. In Q accounting had become so firmly embedded in both the structure and the consciousness of the organisation that it, for a time, defined what was perceived to be of economic significance. So in none of the companies were the accounts marching forward towards a conception of what they should become. No unproblematic pattern of accounting progress has been charted. The changes were specific ones, orientated to the resolution of quite particular problems and issues. Although there were most certainly doubts and uncertainties accompanying the path of accounting change, equally there was no evidence that some pre-existing accounting order was merely masked by the ignorance of the particular organisational participants we have considered. Complex, nuanced and subtle though they sometimes may have been, the processes of organisational functioning have not been shown to have hidden any abstract *a priori* path of accounting improvement.

The emergence of a particular account has been shown to be neither an unproblematic reflection of a more abstract intent nor a sudden discovery or transformation. Rather the cases have illustrated the more positive ways in which specific local origins moderated the path of accounting development and the multiple and even conflicting conditions of possibility that gave rise to particular manifestations of the accounting craft. They have pointed to the manner in which particular configurations of issues, problems and other organisational structures and practices both provided a context for and shaped the development of specific accounting changes. Some of the ways in which the particular meanings and significances attached to accounting information influenced the pattern of its transformation have been illuminated, as have the manner in which accidents, errors and deviations left their marks on the accounts that emerged. So although appeals were made to a body of accounting knowledge and technical practice, and to mobilising accounting and wider rationales, taken together the cases point to the need to see the resultant accounting changes as a combined result of both these and a multiplicity of other often minor changes in disparate parts of the organisational arena, each of which was itself engaged in for a diversity of local, tactical and conjectural reasons.

Although the process of accounting change thereby has been shown to be complex, the cases hopefully have demonstrated that such a local and contingent pattern of change is an intelligible one. An appreciation of accounting change has been shown as being able to be grounded in the circumstances in which it occurs. However, as the above discussion has tried to make clear, intelligibility is not to be confused with necessity. In none of the cases was any imperative driving a particular outcome. Nor could any be constructed on the basis of the organisational circumstances which resulted in accounting change. Rather than either assuming what accounting must be or deriving any retrospective view of the necessity of what happened, the cases demonstrate the need for an appreciation of change to be based on a more detailed awareness of the means through which accounting comes to be embedded within an organisation and the processes which provide a basis for accounting solutions to be related to other organisational problems and phenomena. They also point to the need to understand the more pro-active ways in which accounting can shift the configuration of organisational practices and processes, thereby itself providing a context for modification and change. Of equal importance, they are suggestive of the need to appreciate both the contingent and interactive nature of the circumstances surrounding those processes in any particular setting. Seen in such terms, the intelligibility which we seek to advance is shown to be dependent on the means by which we can question, interpret and interrogate the organisational functioning of the accounting craft and, thereby, on those conceptual concerns and modes of investigation and analysis which provide a basis for the appreciation of both the accounting particular and the accounting general rather than an appeal to any overarching rationale that is deemed to be implicit in either accounting practices or the circumstances that force them to change. Whilst it is recognised that organisational life involves a continuous dialogue between the possible and the actual, and that thereby conceptions of an accounting potential can play a role in mobilising accounting change, this is not to attach an obviousness, a priority or an imperative to the rhetorical claims that are associated with the accounting craft or to provide them with any privileged role in enabling accounting to become what it was not. What effects such claims have need to be seen as arising from their interaction with the other circumstances that characterise organisational life rather than an all embracing, powerfully penetrating and unproblematic logic.①

Reflecting the need to articulate a wider appreciation of accounting in action and the processes by which it changes, the analysis of the cases has been conducted in terms of a number of analytical themes. Emphasis has been placed on the particular visibilities created by accounting systems and the means by which they, in turn, shifted perceptions of organisational functioning, mediated the recognition of problems and the options available for their resolution, and infused the patterns of language, meaning and significance within the organisation. From such a stance, attention was directed to the constitutive as well as the reflective roles of accounting. For although it was recognised that a diverse array of other factors could and did impinge upon the accounting craft, at times causing it to shift its focus of attention and locus of organisational embodiment, equally the analyses were undertaken with an awareness of the more enabling properties of accounting itself. By moulding the patterns of organisational visibility, by extending the range of influence patterns within the organisation, by creating different patterns of interaction and interdependence and by enabling new forms of organisational segmentation to exist, accounting was seen as being able to play a positive role in both shifting the preconditions for organisational change and influencing its outcomes, even including the possibilities for its own transformation. Through such mutual processes of interaction, accounting was conceived as a phenomenon embedded within the organisation rather than as something that had a meaningful independent existence. The forms that it took and the influences that it had were not seen as being able to be appreciated outside of the context of the other organisational practices, functions and processes with which it became

---

① Keat & Urry (1982, pp. 245—246) make a similar point in their more general consideration of social phenomena:
   ... the profound interdependence of social entities... is important... (because) the conditions under which the causal powers of important social entities are realized consist in fact of other social entities and of the at least partial realization of their powers. This fundamental interdependence of such entities thus means that the causal powers of some entities constitute the conditions necessary for the realization of the powers of other entities. And this, of course, means that the empirical events which then come to be generated are the product of highly complex interdependent processes... Moreover, these processes are not merely to be listed so that they can be "added up"—rather they are to be *synthesized* so that their combination qualitatively modifies each constitutive entity (emphasis in original).

intertwined. Together they reflected a particular specificity of alignments and although it was sometimes possible to distinguish one organisational phenomenon influencing another, the analysis was conducted in terms of the possibility for, but not the necessity of, such influences since the mobilising factors were often so numerous, diverse, ambiguous and uncertain, and had such an equivocal *a priori* relationship to the craft of accounting, that change, be it accounting or otherwise, was seen as being something that was created rather than determined. Moreover, as organisational practices and processes over time changed together, it appeared more useful to understand the configurations of which they all formed a part since the presence of any one practice came to presuppose the existence of the others. Perhaps hardly surprisingly, such analytical themes were also sensitive to the nuances and uncertainties which moderated the trajectories of accounting change and to the ways in which the interdependent nature of the resultant organisational processes gave rise to the unintended, the unanticipated and the problematic.

The constitutive roles of accounting are worthy of particular attention, not least because they have been little appreciated or discussed.

For as we have seen, at times accounting can play a significant role in the creation of the possibilities for other organisational phenomena to become what they are not. Through its interwining with the discursive notions of accountability and responsibility, accounting can play a role in the reconstitution of organisational agents, enabling different configurations of organisational arrangements to exist. By its routinisation of information flows and the ways in which it imposes a spatialisation on time, it can change conceptions of the past, the present and the future, contributing different saliences to each which can, in turn, moderate temporal preferences and emphases, and thereby, organisational actions. Creating quite particular objectifications of the otherwise vague and abstract, and particular conceptions of economic facts, accounting also can create not only a context in which the conditions exist for other organisational practices to change but also a means by which a particular organisational visibility can compete for or be imposed upon managerial attention and, if such strategies succeed, perhaps even eventually exclude the visibility and significance of other ways of characterising the organisational terrain, as in Q. If such developments occur, the transformational potential of accounting is only enhanced, as the facts created by the craft give rise to an influential language and set of categories for conceiving and changing the organisation in economic terms. As Foucault (1972, p. 167) has noted:

> a succession of events may... become an object of discourse, be recorded, described, explained, elaborated into concepts, and provide the opportu-

nity for a theoretical choice.

So although not frequently analysed, the importance of accounting's constitutive roles should not be under-emphasised. They represent one of the significant ways in which accounting becomes embedded in the organisation of which it is a part.

Indeed accounting can become so integral a part of a configuration of organisational practices that it can create some of the possibilities that provide the basis for changing the conditions that themselves mobilise accounting change, as we saw in both M and Q. In M it mediated the selection of not unproblematic marketing and production strategies that provided the context in which the subsequent organisational changes created new information and accounting problems. And in Q, a particular regime of economic visibility laid down in the context of one set of organisational problems played its role in creating an economic awareness that transformed the organisation and created a basis for its own dependence on a much elaborated regime of accounting facts. Such illustrations point to not only the transformational potential of accounting but also some of the ways in which accounting can become a part of the factors that impinge upon it.

Central to such a view of accounting is the possibility of there being an equivocal relationship between the aims in the name of which the craft is advanced and its actual organisational consequences (also see Burchell *et al.*, 1985; Hopwood, 1983, 1986b). Not least because the generality of the accounting rhetoric can have difficulty interfacing with the detail, the complexity, the diversity and the specificity of organisational action, some of the anticipated consequences of a particular accounting intervention may not be realised (see Hopwood, 1986a). Moreover, a whole domain of the unanticipated can realise itself as accounting intersects with other organisational practices and processes, as it actively creates a new sphere of organisational visibility, objectivity and potential significance, and as, in the process of so doing, it engenders resistances to the strategies and interventions which it seeks to further.① As all the case analyses have illustrated, the consequences of accounting

---

① The observations of Hirschman (1977, p. 131) are interesting in this respect:

On the one hand, there is no doubt that human actions and social decisions tend to have consequences that were entirely unintended at the outset. But, on the other hand, these actions and decisions are often taken because they are earnestly and fully expected to have certain effects that then wholly fail to materialize. The latter phenomenon, while being the structural obverse of the former, is also likely to be one of its causes; the illusory expectations that are associated with certain social decisions at the time of adoption may keep their *real* future effects from view. Moreover, once these desired effects fail to happen and refuse to come into the world, the fact that they were originally counted on is likely to be not only forgotten but actively repressed (emphasis in original).

interventions in the organisation can disturb, disrupt and displace the organisational arena that was presumed in their formulation, thereby having the power to transform rather than merely modify the processes of organisational change.

From such a perspective accounting also can be conceived of as creating residues of organisational consequences that can change the preconditions for subsequent organisational change. It is as if organisational transformations deposit sediments which not only interact with the organisational past but also modify the possibilities for the organisational present, and its future. In this sense "the present really does contain the past which preceded it", although as Gross (1981—1982, p. 76) went on to add, "this may be unperceived". A temporal interdependency is so built into organisational life and the task of analysis, as reflected in the cases, in part becomes one of delving through the residues of organisational affairs to illuminate the patterns of pre-conditions that moderate the accounting craft.

It was with such metaphors in mind that the task of analysis was seen to be an archaeological one of carefully and cautiously sorting through the sediments of organisational history, however recent, to reconstruct the ways in which the present emerged from the past. ① However, as Foucault (1972, 1977) has come to use the terms, the mode of analysis mobilised in the present discussion has features of both a genealogy and an archaeology. An "archaeology tries to outline particular configurations" (Foucault, 1972, p. 157) in order to reveal "relations between discursive formations and non-discursive domains (institutional, political events, economic practices and processes)" (p. 162). As in the present analysis, an archaeology strives to isolate the conditions of possibility of social and organisational practices and bodies of knowledge aiming to reconstruct "a heterogeneous system of relations and effects whose contingent interlocking" (Gordon, 1980, p. 243) constitute the basis on which practice is formed, functions and has its effects. Moreover, it is the active construction of an archaeology that creates a sensitivity to the power creating potential of bodies of knowledge and organisational and social practices that come to create a conception of reality within which they function. Genealogy, on the other hand, concerns itself with ruptures and transitions whereby words, categories, practices and

---

① In fact the imagery of archaeology emerged from the initial field work in *M* and provided a basis for analysing and structuring the observations made there. At that time I was unfamiliar with Foucault's theorizing and used the metaphor in a more primitive sense. Subsequently the mobilization and structuring of the arguments in this and related articles (see, e.g. Burchell *et al.*, 1985) have been informed by an awareness of the powerful analytics proposed by Foucault (1967, 1972, 1973, 1977, 1979). However, even though it may result in a little confusion for some, the archaeological metaphor is preserved in the title out of both a sense of loyalty to the original formulation and a sense of ease with the imagery in the present context.

institutions adopt new meanings and significances as they become intertwined with new purposes and new wills, an equally important theme of the present discussion. With its emphasis on change, it is the genealogical perspective that serves to alert us to the dangers of assuming any underlying coherence, tendency or logic, such as progress, mobilising patterns of historical and organisational transformation towards some ultimate fulfilment or conclusion. As Foucault (1977, p. 146) made clear, genealogy "does not pretend to go back in time to restore an unbroken continuity that operates beyond the dispersion of forgotten things".

Although the present investigations have been both more focused and constrained than the inquiries undertaken by Foucault, they nevertheless have provided an appreciation of some of the ways in which accounting can both be transformed by and serve as a vehicle for the transformation of the wider organisation. Both a fluidity and a specificity have been introduced into our understanding of accounting in action. The significances attached to accounting have been shown in the process of their reformulation. The craft has been seen as becoming embedded in different organisational configurations and serving very different organisational functions in the process of its change. The mobilising vehicles for these changes have been seen as residing in a very diverse number of organisational processes and practices and, not least, in accounting itself.

However, at this stage in our understanding it is still important to exercise some element of interpretative caution, not least in respect of the mobilising factors that can put accounting into motion. For although the cases have provided a rich insight into at least some of the internal processes of accounting elaboration and change, together they provide less of an understanding of the means through which the external might be able to recast the internal. Tempting though it may be to suggest an analysis in terms of the mobilising potential of a perception of crisis, not least an economic crisis, some care needs to be exercised before too strong a theory is articulated on this basis. Undoubtedly crisis and economic restraint can and do generate action, not least in the accounting area (Khandwalla, 1973; Olofsson & Svalander, 1975). However, the analysis of the cases suggests that the relationship is far from being a straightforward one. In Wedgwood economic recession did provide a stimulus for change, although the relationship between an economic rhetoric of change and its implementation was not unproblematic, requiring, as it did, an intersection with operational bodies of knowledge and specific organisational practices. In M accounting mediated the response to a major market change, although it was only itself changed after marketing, production and organisational changes had created a new organisational configuration and a new set of accounting problems. And in Q, so unobtrusive and embedded within the structure and consciousness of the organisation had accounting become that initially it served to constrain change by masking the exact nature of the turbulent environment. So together the cases certainly provide no basis for any general theory of crisis driven accounting change. Indeed the mode of analysis that has been articulated should moderate our desire to state any such general view. Instead it should encourage a more precise and careful investigation of the ways in which either the perception or the actuality of external events can disturb the organisational configurations of which accounting forms a part (see Czarniawska & Hedberg, 1985). Seen in terms of the possibility to so shift the organisational terrain and the visibilities that form a part of it, a role exists for the mobilising potential, but certainly not necessity, of a whole series of intrusions into the organisation. Alongside a more nuanced view of the role of crisis (also see Brunson, 1985), we need to appreciate the ways in which new bodies of knowledge, new specialists associated with their practice, government regulatory attempts, changing theoretical and practical conceptions of organisational governance and order, and even the development of a different accounting rhetoric can provide a basis for action and change.

All too clearly there is a need for a great deal more research and a very considerable elaboration of the theoretical and analytical premises on which it might take place. Hopefully, however, the present investigation at least has served to illustrate the possibility for an analysis of accounting change that is not dependent on abstract conceptions of potential and does not impose any unifying orchestration of action. It also aims to have indicated the ways in which historical (however recent that means) analyses can give insight into accounting dynamics and, by recognising that the roles that accounting serves cannot be considered in isolation of the practices of the craft, the need for appreciations of the specific practices that constitute the craft and the organisational processes which endow them with a significance and meaning.

BIBLIOGRAPHY

American Accounting Association, Report of the Committee on Accounting History, *Accounting Review* Suppl. to Vol. 45 (1970).

Argyris, C., Organizational Learning and Management Information Systems, *Accounting, Organizations and Society* (1977), pp. 113—124.

Armstrong, P., Changing Management Control Strategies: The Role of Competition Between Accounting and other Organizational Professions, *Accounting, Organizations and Society* (1985), pp. 124—148.

Armstrong, P., The Rise of Accounting Controls in British Capitalist Enterprises, *Accounting, Organizations and Society* (in press).

置于社会与组织环境中的会计研究

Ashton, T. S., *Economic Fluctuations in England, 1700—1800* (Oxford University Press, 1959).

Baladouni, V., The Study of Accounting History, *International Journal of Accounting* (Spring 1977), pp. 53—67.

Berry, A. J., Capps, T., Cooper, D., Ferguson, P., Hopper, T. & Lower, E. A., Management Control in an Area of the N. C. B.: Rationales of Accounting Practice in a Public Enterprise, *Accounting, Organizations and Society* (1985), pp. 3—28.

Brunsson, N., *The Irrational Organization: Irrationality as a Basis for Organizational Action and Change* (John Wiley, 1985).

Burchell, S., Clubb, C., Hopwood, A. G., Hughes, J. & Nahapiet, J., The Roles of Accounting in Organizations and Society, *Accounting, Organizations and Society* (1980), pp. 5—27.

Burchell, S., Clubb, C. & Hopwood, A. G., Accounting in Its Social Context: Towards a History of Value Added in the United Kingdom, *Accounting, Organizations and Society* (1985), pp. 381—413.

Child, J., Organization Structure, Environment and Performance: The Role of Strategic Choice, *Sociology* (January 1972), pp. 1—22.

Clawson, D., *Bureaucracy and the Labour Process* (Monthly Review Press, 1980).

Cooper, D., Discussion of Towards a Political Economy of Accounting, *Accounting, Organizations and Society* (1980), pp. 161—166.

Cooper, D., A Social and Organizational View of Management Accounting, in Bromwich, M. and Hopwood, A. G. (eds), *Essays in British Accounting Research* (Pitman, 1981).

Czarniawska, B. & Hedberg, B., Control Cycles Responses to Decline, *Scandinavian Journal of Management Studies* (August 1985), pp. 19—39.

den Hertog, J. F., The Role of Information and Control Systems in the Process of Organizational Renewal—Roadblock or Road Bridge? *Accounting, Organizations and Society* (1978), pp. 29—46.

Dent, J., Organizational Research in Accounting: Perspectives, Issues and a Commentary, in Bromwich, M. and Hopwood, A. G. (eds), *Research and Current Issues in Management Accounting* (Pitman, 1986).

Di Maggio, P. J. & Powell, W. W., The Iron Cage Revisited: Institutional Isomorphism and Collective Rationality in Organizational Fields, *American Sociological Review* (April 1983), pp. 147—160.

Foucault, M., *Madness and Civilization* (Tavistock, 1967).

Foucault, M., *The Archaeology of Knowledge* (Tavistock, 1972).

Foucault, M., *The Birth of the Clinic* (Tavistock, 1973).

Foucault, M., *Language, Counter-Memory, Practice* (Basil Blackwell, 1977).

Foucault, M., *Discipline and Punish: The Birth of the Prison* (Tavistock, 1979).

Foucault, M., *History of Sexuality* Vol. 1. (Allen Lane, 1979).

Galbraith, J., *Designing Complex Organizations* (Addison-Wesley, 1973).

Geneen, H. S., The Case for Management by the Numbers, *Fortune* (October 1984), pp. 78—81.

Goold, M., Accounting and Strategy, in Bromwich, M. and Hopwood, A. G. (eds) *Research and Current Issues in Management Accounting* (Pitman, 1986).

Gordon, C., Afterword, in Foucault, M., *Power/Knowledge* (Harvester, 1980).

Gross, D., Space, Time, and Modern Culture, *Telos* (1981—1982), pp. 59—78.

Hedberg, B. & Jönsson, S., Designing Semi-Confusing Information Systems for Organizations in Changing Environments, *Accounting, Organizations and Society* (1978), pp. 47—64.

Hirschman, A., *The Passions and the Interests: Political Arguments for Capitalism before Its Triumph* (Princeton University Press, 1977).

Hobsbawm, E. & Ranger, T. (eds) *The Invention of Tradition* (Cambridge University Press, 1983).

Hopper, T., Cooper, D., Lowe, T., Capps, T. & Mouritsen, J., Management Control and Worker Resistance in the National Coal Board, in Knights, D. and Willmott, H. (eds) *Managing the Labour Process* (London: Gower, 1986).

Hopwood, A. G., Information Systems in Matrix Organizations, in Knight, K. (ed.) *Matrix Management* (Saxon House, 1977).

Hopwood, A. G., Towards an Organizational Perspective for the Study of Accounting and Information Systems, *Accounting, Organizations and Society* (1978), pp. 3—14.

Hopwood, A. G., Economic Costs and Benefits of New Forms of Work Organization, in *New Forms of Work Organizations*, Vol. 2, (International Labour Office, 1979).

Hopwood, A. G., On Trying to Study Accounting in the Contexts in Which It Operates, *Accounting, Organizations and Society* (1983), pp. 287—305.

Hopwood, A. G., Accounting and the Pursuit of Efficiency, in Hopwood, A. G. and Tomkins, C. (eds) *Issues in Public Sector Accounting* (Philip Allan, 1984a).

Hopwood, A. G., Accounting Research and Accounting Practice: The Ambiguous Relationship Between the Two, A paper presented at the Conference on New Challenges to Management Research (Leuven, 1984b).

Hopwood, A. G., The Development of "Worrying" about Management Accounting, in Clark, K. B., Hayes, R. H. and Lorenz, C. (eds) *The Uneasy Alliance: Managing the Productivity—Technology Dilemma* (Harvard Business School Press, 1985a).

Hopwood, A. G., The Tale of a Committee that Never Reported: Disagreements on Intertwining Accounting with the Social, *Accounting, Organizations and Society* (1985b), pp. 361—377.

Hopwood, A. G., Accounting and Organizational Action, A paper presented at the Annual Meeting of the American Accounting Association, New York, August 1986a.

Hopwood, A. G., Management Accounting and Organizational Action: An Introduction, in Bromwich M. and Hopwood A. G. (eds), *Research and Current Issues in Management Accounting* (Pitman, 1986b).

Horovitz, J., *Top Management Control in Europe* (Macmillan, 1980).

Hoskin, K. W. & Macve, R. H., Accounting and the Examination: A Genealogy of Disciplinary Power, *Accounting, Organizations and Society* (1986), pp. 105—136.

Ignatieff, M., Michel Foucault, *University Publishing* (Summer 1984), pp. 1—2.

Jenks, L. H., Early Phases of the Management Movement, *Administrative Science Quarterly* (1960), pp. 421—447.

Jones, H., *Accounting, Costing and Cost Estimation* (University of Wales Press, 1985).

Kaplan, R. S., Measuring Manufacturing Performance: A New Challenge for Managerial

Accounting Research, *The Accounting Review* (1983), pp. 686—705.

Kaplan, R. S., Accounting Lag: The Obsolescence of Cost Accounting Systems, in Clark, K. B., Hayes, R. H., and Lorenz, C. (eds) *The Uneasy Alliance: Managing the Productivity—Technology Dilemma* (Harvard Business School Press, 1985).

Keat, R. & Urry, J., *Social Theory as Science* 2nd edn (Routledge & Kegan Paul, 1982).

Khandwalla, P. N., Effect of Competition on the Structure of Top Management Control, *Academy of Management Journal* (1973), pp. 285—295.

Litterer, J. A., Systematic Management: Design for Organizational Recoupling in American Manufacturing Firms, *Business History Review* (1963), pp. 369—391.

Loft, A., Towards a Critical Understanding of Accounting: The Case of Cost Accounting in the U. K., 1914—1925, *Accounting, Organizations and Society* (1986a), pp. 137—169.

Loft, A., Understanding Accounting in Its Social and Historical Context: The Case of Cost Accounting in Britain, 1914—1975, Unpublished Ph. D. Thesis, University of London, 1986b.

Lowenthal, D., *The Past is a Foreign Country* (Cambridge University Press, 1985).

McCloskey, D. N., *The Rhetoric of Economics* (University of Wisconsin Press, 1985).

McKendrick, N., Josiah Wedgwood: An Eighteenth Century Entrepreneur in Salesmanship and Marketing Techniques, *Economic History Review*, 2nd. Series (1960), pp. 408—433.

McKendrick, N., Josiah Wedgwood and Factory Discipline, *The Historical Journal* (1961a), pp. 30—50.

McKendrick, N., Josiah Wedgwood: 18th Century Salesman, *Proceedings of the Wedgwood Society* (1961b), pp. 161—189.

McKendrick, N., Josiah Wedgwood and Thomas Bentley: An Inventor—Entrepreneur Partnership in the Industrial Revolution, *Transactions of the Royal Historical Society*, 5th Series (1964), pp. 1—33.

McKendrick, N., Josiah Wedgwood and Cost Accounting in the Industrial Revolution, *Journal of Economic History* (1973), pp. 45—67.

Merino, B. D. & Neimark, D. M., Disclosure, Regulation and Public Policy: A Socio-Historical Re-appraisal, *Journal of Accounting and Public Policy* (1982), pp. 33—57.

Miller, P. & O'Leary, T., Hierarchies and Ideals, Unpublished Working Paper, Department of Accounting, University of Illinois at Urbana-Champaign, 1986.

Miller, P. & O'Leary, T., Accounting and the Construction of the Governable Person, *Accounting, Organizations and Society* (1987), pp. 235—265.

Nahapiet, J., The Rhetoric and Reality of an Accounting Change: A Study of Resource Allocation. Paper presented to the First International Conference on Organizational Symbolism and Corporate Culture, University of Lund, Sweden, 1984.

Olofsson, C. & Svalander, P. A., The Medical Services Change over to a Poor Environment, Unpublished Working Paper, University of Linköping, 1975.

Otley, D. T., The Contingency Theory of Management Accounting: Achievement and Prognosis, *Accounting, Organizations and Society* (1980), pp. 413—428.

Parker, R. H., Research Needs in Accounting History, *Accounting Historians Journal* (Fall 1977), pp. 1—28.

Parker, R. H., The Study of Accounting History, in Bromwich, M. and Hopwood, A. G. (eds)

Essays in British Accounting Research (Pitman, 1981).

Patton, P., Of Power and Prisons, in Morris, M. and Patton, P., (eds) *Michel Foucault: Power, Truth, Strategy* (Sydney: Ferel Publications, 1979).

Perrow, C., Complex Organizations: A Critical Essay 3rd edn (Random House, 1986).

Pettigrew, A., Information as a Power Resource, *Sociology* (1972), pp. 187—204.

Roll, E., *An Early Experiment in Industrial Organization: Being a History of the Firm of Boulton and Watt, 1775—1805* (Longmans, 1930).

Scapens, R. W., Closing the Gap Between Theory and Practice, *Management Accounting* (January 1983), pp. 34—36.

Scapens, R. W., Management Accounting: A Survey, in Scapens, R. W., Otley, D. T. and Lister, R. J. (eds) *Management Accounting, Organizational Theory and Capital Budgeting* (Macmillan, 1984).

Schofield, R. E., Josiah Wedgwood and a Proposed Eighteenth-Century Research Organization, *Isis* (1956), pp. 16—19.

Simmonds, K., Strategic Management Accounting, in Fanning, D. (ed) *Handbook of Management Accounting* (Gower, 1983).

Thompson, G., Inflation Accounting in a Theory of Calculation, *Accounting, Organizations and Society* (forthcoming).

Tinker, A. M., Towards a Political Economy of Accounting: An Empirical Illustration of the Cambridge Controversies, *Accounting, Organizations and Society* (1980), pp. 147—160.

Tinker, A. M., Merino, B. D. & Neimark, M. D., The Normative Origins of Positive Theories: Ideology and Accounting Thought, *Accounting, Organizations and Society* (1982), pp. 167—200.

Tribe, K., *Land, Labour and Economic Discourse* (Routledge & Kegan Paul, 1978).

Wright, P., *On Living in as Old Country: The National Past in Contemporary Britain* (Verso, 1985).